About the Author

Stanley Sultan, Professor of English at Clark University, is the author of several books, including a novel, many articles on modernist writers, and short fiction.

ELIOT, JOYCE AND COMPANY

ELIOT, JOYCE
and
COMPANY

Stanley Sultan

New York   Oxford
OXFORD UNIVERSITY PRESS
1987

Oxford University Press

Oxford   New York   Toronto
Delhi   Bombay   Calcutta   Madras   Karachi
Petaling Jaya   Singapore   Hong Kong   Tokyo
Nairobi   Dar es Salaam   Cape Town
Melbourne   Auckland

and associated companies in
Beirut   Berlin   Ibadan   Nicosia

Copyright © 1987 by Stanley Sultan

Published by Oxford University Press, Inc.,
200 Madison Avenue, New York, New York 10016

Oxford is a registered trademark of Oxford University Press

Library of Congress Cataloging-in-Publication Data
Sultan, Stanley.
Eliot, Joyce and company.
Bibliography: p.   Includes index.
1. English literature—20th century—History and criticism.
2. Modernism (Literature)   3. Eliot, T. S. (Thomas Stearns),
1888–1965—Criticism and interpretation.   4. Joyce, James,
1882–1941—Criticism and interpretation.   I. Title.
PR478.M6S8   1987   820′.9′1   87-5627
ISBN 0-19-504880-6

1 3 5 7 9 8 6 4 2

Printed in the United States of America
on acid-free paper

This book is dedicated to Betty, for good reasons

Acknowledgments

Earlier versions of parts of this book appeared in *James Joyce Quarterly, Journal of Modern Literature, Southern Review,* and volumes published by Kennikat Press, Macmillan Company (London), and the presses of Clark University and the University of Delaware. I thank the editors of those publications for their hospitality.

Mrs. T. S. Eliot kindly answered the queries of a stranger. Deborah Nolen of Price, Waterhouse, Inc., helped the stranger immeasurably, by making much of his material accessible to his word processor. The assistance of two former students, Brigitte Voykowitsch's with the text, and Ingrid Adam's with the index, was unfailingly intelligent and reliable. The book has benefited from the sharp eye and sound judgment of Susan Meigs at Oxford, who edited the manuscript. And I am grateful to a number of associates at Clark University: for subventions from the Mellon Fund and the Faculty Development Fund, to the Provost Leonard Berry, Associate Provost Daeg Brenner and Research Board; for advice and help, to Lori Dembowitz of the Computer Center; for help in preparing the text, to Rene Baril, Edith Mathis, Susan Moiles, Theresa Reynolds, Helen Taylor, and Jo Warren; finally, for myriad reasons, to the staff of the Robert Hutchings Goddard Library, especially Kokab Arif, Mary Hartman, and Irene Walch.

I would be foolish as well as unjust not to recognize my debt to those students in my courses involving Eliot or Joyce, and even more to those in "Introduction to Graduate Study in English" and "Varieties of Literary Criticism," who unknowingly were my collaborators.

The final debt I wish to acknowledge is the one incurring which gave me most pleasure. Despite the cant, there is a community of scholars, who share with each other their time and knowledge. For criticism and guidance generously given when asked, I record my gratitude to the late Maurice Beebe and Richard Ellmann, and thank my colleagues and friends James Franklin Beard, Sun Hee Kim Gertz, and Bernard Kaplan at Clark, and Jules Brody, Melvin J. Friedman, Hugh Kenner, and Patrick A. McCarthy elsewhere in the community.

Contents

Introduction

This book is not quite as general as its title suggests. It explores the two authors' relations with certain antecedents, with certain contemporaries (especially each other), and with their readers. I hope it will demonstrate that if linking Eliot and Joyce seems unusual, the reason is largely historical accident. A probable cause, in addition to more obvious ones like the differences of genre and the striking contrasts in their art, is that Bloomsbury and F. R. Leavis promoted Eliot (and Lawrence), and deprecated or neglected Joyce (and Yeats); and (in due course), the British academic establishment did so for many years.

Some aspects of the company they kept (and keep) have not been considered before; others have: there is a small library of studies of each author devoted to his relations with antecedents. But most of those studies proceed from different assumptions than mine and toward a different end.

My objective is to illuminate the authors' historic mutual—to some extent joint—venture in English literature. It was part of an informal corporate enterprise. The enterprising company (in that sense of the word) included a number of their contemporaries working in all the arts, in all European countries and North and South America. During the first quarter of this century, Eliot, Joyce, and company moved the arts into the phase of Western culture now generally called Modernism.

Almost all the works of both writers belong to the new art established in the century's first quarter; but two by the American and one by the Irishman were crucial to the enterprise of establishing that art—so manifestly crucial that naming the three works almost is redundant. Appropriately, "The Love Song of J. Alfred Prufrock," *The Waste Land,* and *Ulysses* probably are the most famous English short poem, long poem, and novel written during the century.

Individually and in combination, these three historical documents/artifacts of Modernism in English literature and their relations—with antecedents, with each other, and with us, the literary culture of which they were exemplary shapers—dominate the book. Its focus on them determines which other works by the two writers it takes into account. These include a number of Eliot's essays, especially those that discuss the historical contexts of his own poetry, and fiction by

Joyce closely linked to *Ulysses*—certain stories in *Dubliners,* and *A Portrait of the Artist as a Young Man.*

Some of the chapters began as studies written and published before I became aware of the single interest behind all of them. The book has three sections; each begins with a short general chapter and is devoted to one in the diachronic sequence of three kinds of historical relation. Unable to devise more suitable titles, I have adopted from Eliot's edition of *Literary Essays of Ezra Pound* (1954; New York: New Directions, 1968), the titles of its first two sections: "The Tradition" and "Contemporaries." They more or less dictated that of the third: "The Inheritance."

If Eliot's Pound-titles suit my book, it is not on grounds of aesthetic fitness, but as applied historical method. Pound was centrally involved with the early careers of both writers, especially with their role in the institution of Modernism. And method in endeavoring to understand that singular historical development stresses conjunctions, from the fortuitous to the inevitable. My rationale is that the pattern, and the profusion, of co-incident relations of Eliot and Joyce with certain antecedents and contemporaries, constitutes historical evidence.

The chronologies of the three principal antecedent writers I implicate illustrate the method. (Of course, Dante also—to name only one other antecedent who must and shall be considered—is important for both Joyce and Eliot, as for a number of modernist writers in a number of countries—but not in this respect.) Those three writers, Baudelaire, Flaubert, and Dostoevsky, all were born the same year (1821); and the latter two had almost the same life spans (they died in 1880 and '81). Their identical birth dates may be unimportant, but their essential contemporaneity, and their temporal relationship to the generation of Eliot and Joyce, ought not to be ignored.

James, Conrad, and Yeats belong to the intervening generation and have their conjunctions with the two writers and their three works. Furthermore, of English modernists of Eliot's and Joyce's own generation—writers who, like them, began working in the first dozen years of this century and became identified subsequently as important movers into the new kind of literature—only Lawrence is excluded from the pattern of relations I adduce. Significantly, while Pound approved Lawrence's work, neither the Christian moralist nor the urbane experimentalist did so.

Later major modernist English writers, who are outside this chronology, nevertheless are implicated in the pattern. For example, Woolf and Stevens are later, historically speaking, although she both was born and died the same year as Joyce, and he was three years older than them: Woolf's first characteristically modernist novel, *Jacob's Room,* was written a decade after the early innovative work of Eliot and Joyce; Stevens was remote, and ignored even by Pound, who did not include him in his *Catholic Anthology* (1915).

Yet Woolf was a close friend of Eliot's. Her Hogarth Press published *The Waste Land.* And she had co-incident relations with *Ulysses* and its author. Her press declined to print it for Harriet Shaw Weaver's Egoist Press. Her compound of admiration, envy and depreciation of Joyce (expressed more negatively in private), informs the final essay in *The Common Reader* (1925), which has Browning's title "How It Strikes A Contemporary": it calls *Ulysses* "a memorable catastrophe—immense in daring, terrific in disaster." But when *Ulysses* was published a few months before *The Waste Land* in 1922, she had not yet developed that attitude: after completing her first two novels, she wrote an essay, "Modern Fiction" (also in *The Common Reader*), criticizing the traditional novels of "Mr. Wells, Mr. Bennett, and Mr. Galsworthy," and proposing as a model for the future "the most notable" of "several young writers" doing new work, especially his "*Ulysses,* now appearing in the *Little Review.*" She wrote the essay in April 1919, the beginning of the period of her experimental sketches published in 1921 under the title *Monday or Tuesday. Jacob's Room* appeared the next year, along with *Ulysses* and *The Waste Land.* The year following that, *Harmonium,* Stevens's first volume—dazzling in its richness and its range—was published; and as I read one of its most familiar poems, "Bantams in Pine Woods" is a covert satiric challenge by the ignored "inchling" in America's "pines" to "portly Azcan"—the then overweight expatriate "ten-foot poet" and cultural factotum "with henna hackles" who was intimately involved with both *Ulysses* and *The Waste Land.*

Some of these conjunctions of date and event, and some others thrown up by my historical method in the following pages, may be fortuitous; if so, they are merely harmonious flecks on the pattern that seems to take shape from the weaving of the rest. The historian does the presumptuous weaving and must accept responsibility for that pattern; but if the strands one selects are suited to mating and juxtaposing, there will be an intelligible design. And that design will be one more segment of the grand historical pattern now called Modernism, which has not yet receded enough to be seen as a whole.

A necessary caution is exemplified by the sequence I made above of events in—the rudimentary pattern I wove for—a three-year period of Virginia Woolf's biography as artist. Valid literary history accommodates the interaction of new developments with the received tradition. But the weaver of literary artifacts or artists into a pattern of historical relations must never forget that valid literary history also accommodates the interaction of the crucial human agent with both. By their purposeful acts, *certain* writers helped to evolve the interaction with the tradition of—or elected and helped to augment—those developments while still new, still ignored or rejected by the parade led, in Woolf's case, by "Mr. Wells, Mr. Bennett, and Mr. Galsworthy." And that contribution of the unique artist to the historical pattern simultaneously confirms the other, autonomous, dimension that consists in his or her every unique artifact.

At the other extreme from the acting artist, literary history is affected by the whole universe of human experience. To cite only nonliterary factors whose effect is direct and demonstrable: the owners of lending libraries like Charles Edward Mudie and W. H. Smith not only constrained most novels in Victorian England to a narrow morality, but established the three-volume format; and in our own time and country, the absorption of independent publishers by conglomerates with movie, television, recording and other interests, the distribution system for mass paperbacks, and even, perhaps, the ready availability of minute financial data about individual editors' activities, have combined to impede the development of new writers of fiction.

One final general point must be made. As my reiterated terms indicate, a book about *historical relations* of *artifacts* is combining two literary interests conventionally taken to be disparate if not antagonistic. Certainly, each of these two kinds of concern about literature has its own methodologies and preoccupations, and often is practiced exclusively. But it is no less certain that a truly helpful literary study usually syncretizes the two, even when its author's primary concern with one component makes the contribution of the other inconspicuous. A scholar's knowledge about contexts of literary art is most helpful when grounded in a rich intimacy with the art itself. A critic's close attention to one or more works/texts is most helpful when infused with a rich knowledge of relevent facts and circumstances. Hence, in the duels conducted in journals and reviews a few decades ago by rival champions (Literary Historian vs. Objective Critic), the horrid examples cited seldom were from the truly helpful work of the disputants themselves.

The symbiosis in this book of both kinds of literary concern has caused, at times, a conjunction of dates, writers, or events to be cited during a critical analysis, and a detail or effect of the work during a delineation of historical pattern. More frequently, involvement with one of my two concerns may make the other seem to have been forgotten; and the other will monopolize the pages in its turn. My interest being equally in the artifacts and in their relations, I have tried to make the syncretic method of truly helpful literary studies serve both ends—to use the light I can bring to each as the agent for illuminating the other.

Illumination often will disclose not answers, but questions. Both the study of literature and the study of history have evolved sufficiently by this point in our century for that to be no surprise. The conceptual basis of each of my coupled interests—the concept of the literary artifact, and that of determinable historical relations—now has been challenged. In practical terms, assumptions traditional to both my kinds of concern about literature are questioned today. One can no longer simply assume either that language embodies certain meaning, enabling an artifact, or that literary indebtedness is apodictic, a datum of history. And it is fitting that three central canonical works of the century should press such recent critical questions into sharp relief. It is even more fitting that often they indicate the answers.

THE
TRADITION

1

Trout in Milk
and Imaginary Toads
in Real Gardens

When Pooh mistakes an ambush for a gorse bush ... we know that there is
only one writer to whom we can turn: James Joyce. Now, I personally would
have been content if that difficult gentleman had never been born.... As
scholars, however, we have a duty to consider all influences objectively....
Whether ... analogue or influence ... is ... debatable, as *Ulysses* came
before *Winnie-the-Pooh* and *Finnegans Wake* after. I cannot ... propose ...
that Milne may have read Joyce; surely his imagination was ever too
pure.... But since deep similarities exist in word play, I think a reasonable
compromise would be ... *Pooh* is analogous to *Ulysses* and is an influence
upon *Finnegans Wake*.

Benjamin Thumb, "The Style of *Pooh:* Sources, Analogues, and Influences"

Among Frederick C. Crews's less genial burlesques in *The Pooh Perplex* (New
York: Dutton, 1965) is that of, in Eliot's phrase, "the seekers of sources." Most
critics and many others who attended college during the first half of the twen-
tieth century would endorse Crews's ridicule of those "seekers" for snobbery,
egregious literary judgment, and stupid historical methodology. It was a period
when teaching about literature by way of potted history and biography (also by
way of snob appeal and potted evaluation) was widespread. That teaching, and
the scholarship of the "seekers," probably share responsibility for a bias against
literary history that lingers today. Contempt for Professor Thumb is a datum of
the history of literary studies in this century.

A book about historical relations of literary artifacts, especially one that
stresses conjunctions, must consider evidence of homology and of filiation.
However, the grounds and limits of valid inference about both can be respected;
and necessary distinctions can be made. Although some of those grounds, limits,
and distinctions are obvious, I want to specify, at the outset, my understanding
of them.

3

I

Crews's clumsy Thumb not only is oblivious to the elusive nature of the three concepts designated in his subtitle; he also follows traditional practice in conceiving of *source* and *influence* as purely temporal relations: any work or writer is historically situated between sources drawn from, and influences rendered (to subsequent works or writers), in a diachronic sequence of causes and effects. However, according to this simplistic temporal conception of sources and influences, all sources *of* a work or writer under consideration are—by definition—influences *on* (influencing) it/her/him. Hence, no distinction is made, for example, between a writer's appropriating phrases or devices from, and the writer's being profoundly influenced by, an antecedent ("source") work or writer—between a historical relation the indebted writer wills and controls, and its diametric opposite.

That sort of literary history is restricted neither to satire nor to the past, unfortunately. For example, the opening section of a book published in the present decade, on "the influence of *The Waste Land* on British novels," argues the author's case in a passage reminiscent of the last sentence of my epigraph:

> The sources for post-*Waste Land* passages written by Forster, Ford, and Lawrence are questionable since similar themes appear in pre-*Waste Land* novels to some degree. However, the sheer number of characters and images compatible with Eliot's poem and the more intense effect of these in the post-*Waste Land* novels suggest that Eliot did influence these established novelists to some extent.[1]

In the next paragraph, the operative conception of influence is specified: "the issue is Eliot's presence." Not only is Eliot as influence not distinguished from Eliot as mere utilized source, but the source/influence is established by "presence." Consequently, because Richard Aldington "satirizes Eliot and parodies the poem in his novels," *The Waste Land* and its creator influenced him. Here, not appropriating at will but something even more independent—treating an antecedent work and its writer as *subjects*—is conflated with being hostage to their influence.

In the chapters on specific novelists, familiar specific grounds for hypostatizing "presence," hence source, hence influence, predominate. For example, there is similarity: in *Death of a Hero*, "Aldington creates a bleak atmosphere for a modern London which has become an urban Waste Land" (p. 11), and depicts "increasing drinking and carnality, both of which play prominent roles in *The Waste Land*" (p. 12); in *Lady Chatterley's Lover*, "The workers, like the workday crowd streaming over London Bridge in 'The Burial of the Dead,' lack hope" (p. 31), and "Like Eliot's Fisher King, Mellors experiences . . . " (p. 32). It is to designate the rude phantasms "seekers of sources" sometimes imagine "present" in—and so obtrude into—artistic creations like those novels, that my

---

1. Fred D. Crawford, *Mixing Memory and Desire: The Waste Land and British Novels* (University Park: Pennsylvania State UP, 1982), p. 2.

chapter title inverts the famous phrase from Marianne Moore's "Poetry," "imaginary gardens with real toads in them."

Imaginary toads can originate in the historian's failure to distinguish among a writer's being influenced by, appropriating from, and treating (as subject), an antecedent writer or work. But their genesis seems more often to be inadequate grounds for the primary historical inference that a causal relation really does exist ("like the ... crowd"; "like Eliot's ... " in this particular study). I shall proceed to set out my understanding of the principal distinctions, and of the principal grounds and limits of valid inference, in literary relations of homology and filiation. The persistently apt quasi-legal language, since it is not metaphorical, probably signifies a heuristic analogy.

II

Grounds for inferences about both a possible analogue and a possible antecedent seem to be of two general kinds: one kind is author's testimony, the other is manifest evidence. On the question of homology between works, except for revealing close association during their composition, neither author would seem to have any testimony to give: an author can only express an opinion. On the question of filiation from an antecedent work or author, testifying authors can be lying, or forgetting/repressing; they are not likely to be otherwise mistaken about their indebtedness. Historical judgment of the author's testimony involves her or his general reliability as a witness, possible motives for special prevarication—and the available manifest evidence. For example, Joyce can be shown to be unreliable about indebtedness, and Eliot the opposite, although possible repression by Eliot must be discussed.

The case with manifest evidence of homology or filiation seems to me much more complicated. To begin with, it never constitutes positive proof unless two writings are an original and an exact copy, or have identical elements accompanied by direct reference in one to the other. Otherwise, that they are related is not a fact but an inference: all normal evidence in the actual work of a writer, of its relations with another work, or of indebtedness of any kind to anyone or anything in the writer's experience, is circumstantial. So is external manifest evidence, such as the writer's possession—or even better, annotation—of the text of a putative influence.

In Thoreau's simile, the presence of a trout is strictly circumstantial evidence that the milk has been watered. Circumstantial evidence of a literary relation can be very convincing; but usually, of course, it is far less incontrovertible than a trout in the milk. Yet a judgment still must be made. That judgment need not be a verdict, however. If an inference of homology or filiation is not supported by reasonably close to positive evidence—and (as the vagueness of my last phrase suggests) that seems to be the usual case—the literary historian ought to specify the uncertainty. Littering a garden with the creatures of fancied relations not only misrepresents literature; it is unsound history.

Manifest evidence within the work seems to signify (circumstantially) three principal relations of *homology.* Analogues may have a common antecedent. They may be related through shared circumstances, such as a general cultural condition. And they may be simultaneous independent innovations, a confluence often symptomatic of new things happening in art.

The three principal relations of *filiation* I distinguish have been specified. A writer can be writing about a writer or work (or writers or works) referred to or drawn from, as Aldington satirized Eliot and parodied *The Waste Land,* or as in a burlesque of a literary type. A writer can appropriate from a writer or work. And a writer can be subject—that is, to some extent be hostage—to an influence.

Filiation in which the antecedents a writer draws from or refers to are themselves the writer's subject, seems essentially the same relation as quotation or reference in a profile of an individual or a review of a book. It is the latter two kinds of filiation that are the two major categories of *indebtedness:* on the one hand intentionally appropriating from, and on the other involuntarily being influenced by, an antecedent. Of the two major kinds of *appropriation* (from an antecedent) I distinguish, one invokes its source. When a writer makes a direct reference, or (more frequently) an allusion, the identity of the source, as well as the appropriated material itself, functions in the indebted work.

In the second major kind of appropriation I distinguish, the source is not invoked but suppressed, for its identity is not functional. This kind of appropriation, traditionally called *borrowing,* is a kind of higher plagiary. The fact is implicit in the criterion for judging "the way in which a poet borrows" that Eliot's 1920 essay "Philip Massinger" made famous:

> Immature poets imitate; mature poets steal; bad poets deface what they take, and good poets make it into something better, or at least something different.
> (*Selected Essays: 1917–1932,* 1932 Amer. ed. [New York: Harcourt], p. 182.)

Throughout the passage, Eliot emphasizes the writer's control over the process of appropriation. "A good poet" will choose very different poets to "steal" from; hence, the mature Webster and Tourneur do not appropriate from Shakespeare: "he is too close to them to be of use to them in this way."

As I suggest above, it seems to me in this respect that appropriation, whether invoking or suppressing the source, is significantly different from the other form of indebtedness—the condition of being influenced. That involuntary (hostage's) response is simultaneously the most important relation of a writer to an individual antecedent the serious literary historian must consider, and by far the most complex, subtle, and problematic relation. I can do no more than review briefly the two aspects of literary influence that seem most relevant to this book, and much the major part of the chapter will be devoted to my review. Eliot himself is a central figure in it; and the two aspects are the value of *identifying* influence, and its nature—specifically, the extent to which the influenced writer's response *is* involuntary.

But two additional general points must be made first. One may be among the more obvious considerations respecting filiation. In *The Art of Literary Research* (1963; rev. ed., New York: Norton, 1975), Richard D. Altick eloquently warns "the seekers of sources" that "The path of the source-student lies through the valley of echoes, the house of mirrors" (p. 102). But the danger of identifying sources (or analogues) is two-edged. The Charybdis of fanciful attributions is complemented by the monster Ignorance on its bare rock. Not only can an imaginary source be conjured, but a real one can be unrecognized: the literary historian can err by omission as well as commission. For example, the style in which the exhibitionism of Joyce's "Nausicaa," Gerty MacDowell, is narrated in the thirteenth chapter of *Ulysses*, was long considered a general burlesque of sentimental fiction; and so the point of his parody of a specific source and subject (slyly identified in the text, actually), was overlooked.[2]

My second point concerns the more general historical issue implicit in all attributions of indebtedness: causation. Was Yeats's "mature style" caused by his Abbey Theatre activity?; by his young friend Ezra Pound's influence? Are Shakespeare's "dark plays" to be attributed to his psyche?; to the box office? In *James Joyce and the Beginnings of* Ulysses (Ann Arbor: UMI, 1983), Rodney Wilson Owen argues persuasively that Stephen Dedalus's character and relevant episodes in the early part of *Ulysses* had originally been intended for the end of the *Portrait;* and he proposes two causes for what Joyce did, one psychological ("emotional") and the other practical ("the pressures of serial publication")— precisely as in Shakespeare's case (p. 51). Such historical inferences are not necessarily wrong—for either or both attributed causes may have catalyzed the process by which Joyce achieved the completed *Portrait* and conceived his new novel. But to equate artistic cause with human response is faulty historical inference deriving from a failure to distinguish response (reaction) from action. Like the rest of us, the human in the artist reacts; but the instrumental cause of the end of the *Portrait* and the beginning of *Ulysses* was a unique creative act. Freud drew this distinction between the reactions all of us experience, and the artist's special additional ability to act; it is central to our understanding of literary influence.

III

"The Problem of Influence in Literary History" is the title of the first in a sequence of forensic treatises on literary influence published during the last three decades. I call them a sequence because later ones address the arguments of, and often specifically cite, earlier ones, and because all refer to a small list of other scholars who wrote on the subject (the names of Claudio Guillén, Harry Levin, Henri Peyre, and René Wellek recur most often). The sequence comprises four essays and a book. The authors of the essays are primarily students of comparative literature; the book is by an aesthetician and considers plastic art as well as literature. Their respective positions on the value, for the study of literature, of attempting to determine influence, illustrate the grounds and limits of literary influence as traditionally conceived.

2. See Stanley Sultan, *The Argument of* Ulysses (1964; Middletown: Wesleyan UP, 1987), pp. 272–73.

Initiating the sequence, Ihab Hassan solves the "problem" by relegating influence on an author's work to the domain of biography. He proposes replacing "the vain study of sources and influences" in " the ordering and interpretation of literary events" with "the definition of the poet's type." The concept of "tradition" (as "a set of norms," not a historical period—he instances "classical" and "baroque"), would be brought to bear on the similarity between writers' work; that of "development" ("the modification of a tradition into another") would be brought to bear on causality between writers' work (would replace specifying influence on a writer): "the two concepts of Tradition and Development" may "afford a readier access to the problem of literary relationships" than "the idea of Influence."[3]

Haskell Block's treatise quotes from Wellek and Levin as examples of the "many" for whom "the concept of influence is of little or no value in Comparative Literature, and should be discarded in favor of a broader concept . . . such as the notion of tradition," then narrows its focus: "It is precisely this notion which is advanced by Ihab Hassan in terms derived primarily from T. S. Eliot's 'Tradition and the Individual Talent'." Block asserts that the concept of influence "rightly used, can provide insight into . . . works" as well as "define . . . historical relationships"; and taking as an example *Don Quixote* and the novels of Fielding, he declares simply, "I see no reason why we should define the relationship between these novels in terms of tradition when it is far more accurate to speak of influence."[4]

The next two treatises, almost contemporaneous, also are opposed to each other, though on the narrower issue of methodology. J. T. Shaw simply advocates "study of reception and popularity and . . . direct literary indebtedness including literary influence"; Anna Balakian, who cites Block approvingly, is concerned with "the need for a sharpening of the distinctions between reception of an author ["literary fortune"] or literary trend and the varieties of influence."[5] Finally, Göran Hermerén's "systematic survey of the conceptual framework used by critics and scholars when they discuss problems of influence" sets out logical and substantive conditions prodigiously: it even has a section attempting "Measurement of Influence."[6]

Not only the issues disputed, but two general points of agreement in the sequence, are edifying: each of the five scholars either derides or laments the egregious sins of "orthodox theoreticians and investigators" (Block); and even the harshest criticism of the *study* of influence articulated or cited fails to estab-

---

3. Ihab H. Hassan, "The Problem of Influence in Literary History: Notes Towards a Definition," *Journal of Aesthetics and Art Criticism,* XIV (1955), 66–76; quotations from pp. 74–76.

4. Haskell M. Block, "The Concept of Influence in Comparative Literature," *Yearbook of Comparative and General Literature,* VII (1958), 30–37, 33, 35.

5. J. T. Shaw, "Literary Indebtedness and Comparative Literary Studies," *Comparative Literature: Method & Perspective,* ed. Newton P. Stallknecht and Horst Frenz (Carbondale: Southern Illinois UP, 1961, rev. ed., 1971), pp. 84–97, p. 96; Anna Balakian, "Influence and Literary Fortune: The Equivocal Junction of Two Methods," *Yearbook of Comparative and General Literature* XI (1962), 24–31, 25.

6. Göran Hermerén, *Influence in Art and Literature* (Princeton: Princeton UP, 1975), p. xiv.

lish that influence itself is an unimportant characteristic of literature or literary history.

IV

In relating Hassan to Eliot, Block was not guessing. Of "tradition and development," "what is otherwise termed influence," Hassan's treatise declares, "Eliot's distinguished essay 'Tradition and the Individual Talent' has remained at the heart of the matter since 1919"; after quoting the essay on poets as beneficiaries and modifiers of what has gone before, Hassan tersely indicates the filiation of his second key term by "cit[ing] Eliot again, 'True originality is merely development'" (p. 75). (The source of Eliot's brief sentence is given later in this chapter, and the context in which it occurs discussed at the beginning of the next; see pp. 18 and 29–30.) Finally, the one specific instance of the study of literary influence Hassan's treatise explores is "the 'influences' of Dante, Donne, Webster [and eight others] to cite only a few" on Eliot's poetry (pp. 75–76).

Despite the general implication of his drawing on and attention to Eliot, Hassan's quotation marks around the word reaffirm that his attitude toward literary influence is not that of Eliot himself. When Eliot wrote of influence, he was not "otherwise term[ing]" tradition and development.

To the poet's declaration, in his first theoretical—and most famous—statement about literature, that a poem should result from the "extinction of personality," the separation of "the man who suffers and the mind which creates" (*Selected Essays*, pp. 7–8), the special biasses of Modernism caused enthusiastic assent. And those same biasses approved the essay's homage to tradition. Yet the approved homage in fact controverts the modernist doctrine of the autonomy of the art "object"; for it explicitly contrasts the Individual Talent's independence from "the man" and that Talent's tie to Tradition.

Eliot addressed his adoption by, in his words, the "critical movement" that included "The New Criticism" in "The Frontiers of Criticism" (1956), declaring, "I fail to see any critical movement which can be said to derive from myself" (*On Poetry and Poets* [1957; New York: Noonday-Farrar, 1961], p. 117). And in "Tradition and the Individual Talent" itself, the *autonomous* relation of the work of art to the artist—who, "creation ... accomplished," as Stephen Dedalus put it at almost the same time, is "refined out of existence," free to pare his fingernails—is contrasted by Eliot (in the paragraph from which Hassan quoted) to the *interactive* relation of the work to "the ideal order" of "the existing monuments" that constitute the universe of, "the form of European, of English literature" (p. 5). The "new work" modifies Eliot's ostensible order, "if ever so slightly"; therefore, it joins it. In addition, its creator is implicated in the relation, for the "new" poet's "meaning" and "value" involve "his relation to the dead poets and artists" (p. 4).

In subsequent general essays and studies of individual writers, culminating in the lecture near the end of his life reviewing his criticism, which he apparently had planned to expand for publication, "To Criticize the Critic" (1961), Eliot emphasized the importance of the influence of "dead poets" in a poet's relation to the past (tradition) and future (development)—the importance of influences on a poet in precisely literary history.

Eliot's commitment as a critic contrasts with that of Joyce, who never wrote about literature after the journalism of the Trieste years. Of his achievement as a critic, a study of his poetry declared recently, "He possessed the finest critical intelligence of the age"; and as this chapter was in draft, two prominent critics unsympathetic to both Eliot's criticism and the rich modernist "critical movement" the poet referred to, paid him the compliment—in reviews published one day apart in distinguished literary periodicals—of respectively designating "the heyday of academic New Criticism or Age of Eliot (circa 1945–1965)," and predicting "what the future will doubtless call the Age of Eliot."[7] Although he can be shown to be inconsistent and self-indulgent, Eliot's achievement, at the very least, is to have affected subsequent criticism more than any other major English writer of the century. But his pointing out that the "Age of Eliot" did not "derive from myself" was precision, not modesty. It was influenced only by what in his criticism and (neo-Tractarian) conservative Christian ideology could be assimilated to its perspective and concerns. Broad and diverse as these were, he himself had, from his famous first theoretical essay, a more comprehensive view of the important considerations in the study of writers and their work than was general among the modernist critics who endorsed him; for to him, literary history was a most important consideration. Furthermore, literary history was a complex interaction of new development not only with new conditions of life and with the tradition, but also with precisely the influence of "dead poets and artists."

It is because the literary historian in the poet-critic clearly distinguishes from a true influence a source ("material") from which a poet "steals" at will because it is "of use," that the principal concern of "The Frontiers of Criticism" can be to chastise "the seekers of sources" (p. 121) caricatured by Crews, for confusing poems' "material" with the poems themselves—and thereby violating one frontier of true criticism. (The other is violated by "the diversion of attention from the poetry to [the psychology or biography of] the poet," p. 125.) As instigators of the seekers' pseudo-critical "explanation of poetry by examination of its sources," he cites two *"monumental"* (sic) works, though "we may say of each: one book like this is enough": John Livingston Lowes's *The Road to Xanadu* — and *Finnegans Wake* (p. 119); and he indicts the Notes of *The Waste Land* as well.

Eliot writes that Lowes knowingly worked "beyond the frontier of literary criticism" to provide "evidence of how material is digested and transformed by the poetic genius" (p. 119). Hence Eliot distinguishes describing sources and the *process* of their "transformation" from using literary history as a vehicle for literary criticism. In discussing different qualities of achieved "transformation" *as*

7. Ronald Bush, *T. S. Eliot: A Study in Character and Style* (New York: Oxford UP, 1983), p. xii; Harold Bloom, "Mr. America," *New York Review of Books* (Nov. 22, 1984), p. 24; Jonathan Culler, "A Critic against the Christians," *Times Literary Supplement* (Nov. 23, 1984), p. 1328.

poetry by "bad" and "good" poets, in the youthful Massinger essay, he is doing true (historical) criticism.

So is he when he identifies the manifestation in poetry not of "material" coolly appropriated, but of a poet's less voluntary "relation to the dead poets." His one explicit reference to influence in the "paper" (like most of his criticism mentioned in this chapter, it was originally a lecture), concerns the poet whom he discusses most frequently on that subject. It is simultaneously both testimony and the deduction of a historical critic:

> The best of my *literary* criticism—apart from a few notorious phrases which have had a truly embarrassing success in the world—consists of essays on poets and dramatists who had influenced me. (p. 117)

He repeats this general point two sentences later; and in his next and final published work, done "To Criticize" his own criticism, he declares, "I am certain of one thing: that I have written best about writers who have influenced my own poetry" (*To Criticize the Critic* [New York: Farrar, 1965], p. 20); and repeating the point five pages later, he adds that they were "writers . . . whom I could praise wholeheartedly." (Like his conception of "the ideal order" or "form" of literature presented at the beginning of "Tradition and the Individual Talent," and his proposal in the same place that "the most individual parts of [a poet's] work may be those in which the dead poets, his ancestors, assert their immortality most vigorously," his suggestion that a critic must like a writer to write well about that writer is developed in the criticism of Northrop Frye.)

The next chapter will consider Eliot's testimony about specific influences on his poetic development embodied in "Prufrock." My purpose here is solely to characterize his attitude toward literary influence. It is expressed most clearly in the combined admiration and self-assurance with which he identifies influences on his own poetry, and in the kinds of influence he specifies.

A previous essay in which he declared that he wrote about poets out of "gratitude" for their influence is "What Dante Means to Me" (1950). It was done late enough in his life to begin with a retrospective discussion of other poets who "had a capital importance in my own development" (*To Criticize The Critic*, p. 127), and of the different sorts of influence they had. But after specifying different "poets I can say I learned . . . from" (p. 126), he devotes the essay to affirming his far less particular and more pervasive debt: to the poetry "I still, after forty years, regard . . . as the most persistent and deepest influence upon my own verse" (p. 125).

He attributes his debt to two "achievements of Dante": "The first is, that [no poet] has been a more attentive student of the *art* of poetry, or a more scrupulous, painstaking and *conscious* practitioner of the *craft*" (p. 132) (Eliot's emphasis). It influenced him "through the years of one's life" as "a moral lesson" which encompassed "a further . . . moral lesson": "the poet should be the servant of his language, rather than the master of it" (p. 133). "The second lesson [sic] of Dante . . . is the lesson of *width of emotional range*": "the poet [must] . . . capture those feelings which people can hardly even feel, because they have no words for them" (pp. 133–34). And since, as the last quoted phrase signifies,

"These two achievements of Dante are not . . . separable," "the lessons of craft, of speech and of exploration of sensibility" (pp. 134–35) are aspects of an even more general influence on his poetry.[8]

My final example of Eliot's attention to and subtle understanding of the operation of literary influence is his notorious attack on Milton in 1936 and recantation in 1947. To begin with, the two essays are essentially not about Milton's poetry, but about the influence of his poetry—principally its influence on living poets. Eliot's point in the early essay is that an influence can be negative, not just in the obvious sense that "a man may be a great artist, and yet have a bad influence" (*On Poetry and Poets,* p. 156), but also in the sense that, as Anna Balakian put it in the essay cited above, "very often the influences of authors of the same nationality and language . . . are . . . the result of reactions" (p. 29). Moreover, his supposed recantation was largely his judgment that by 1947 the state of poetry had changed.

Although in 1936 he charged that "Milton's poetry could *only* be an influence for the worse, upon any poet whatever," his actual concern is much more specific: such characteristics as its "*artificial* and *conventional*" language, in which "verbal music" dominates "sense," make it "an influence against which we still have to struggle" (pp. 157–59). In 1947, however, Milton no longer "is an unwholesome influence": "I consider him a . . . poet . . . whom poets to-day might study with profit" (p. 169). He reprints the general charge quoted above, in order to retract it respecting poets "of the past"—who themselves must bear the "responsibility" for "injudicious choice of a model"—and poets of "the remote future"—because "what can we affirm about the poetry that will be written then . . . ?" (pp. 171–72). That leaves "the immediate future," the time of developing poets. And here the "we still have to struggle" of the first essay is quietly altered, the modernists taken back in 1947 from 1936 to 1922, when *they* were "the immediate future"/"poets to-day": "the case against Milton, as it stood for poets twenty-five years ago" is the "only significant meaning of 'bad influence'" (pp. 173–74).

By mid-century, of Milton's poetry (predictably, Eliot is unrelenting on his religion and politics), only his "violence . . . to language"—the "acts of lawlessness" of his "style"—remains a harmful influence. (His style also remains "one of the marks of his greatness": *Paradise Lost* and—again Eliot cites—*Finnegans Wake* are "two books by great blind musicians, each writing a language of his own based upon English," pp. 176, 179). Milton was a negative influence "against" which—given "our tenets"—"to struggle" was necessary during the development of Modernism (p. 182). But by 1947, Milton can be a salutary influence (setting aside his own Joyce-like excess of language) on poets of "the immediate future," against certain kinds of excess in modernist tendencies.

The two Milton essays demonstrate not only both the weight Eliot gives to, and his broad understanding of, literary influence, but also his strong sense of

8. In "The Meaning of Influence," the second chapter of *Approach to the Purpose: A Study of the Poetry of T. S. Eliot* (1964; rpt. Westport, Conn.: Greenwood, 1980), G. M. Jones argues that Eliot conceived of influence as constituted by an influencing poet's work and "attitude towards the materials of his art"—and the influenced poet's own "creative mind" (pp. 25–26).

the general relation of the present to the past, a sense reflected in his objective comments on "my reaction against Milton" in "To Criticize the Critic." People favor past poets because they are "more congenial, but not necessarily of greater merit," he declares; and he was able to promote "a wider interest in" Donne and his contemporaries during the early years of Modernism, not solely because he himself "had been so deeply influenced by them" that he wrote well about them, but also because "Their poetry, and mine, were congenial to that age" (pp. 20–22).

The observation about "that age" is now a truism, of course. It also complements Eliot's idea that poets of different times find only certain of the "dead" poets—those by whom they are influenced—"congenial." But while that word can readily be used for the "age" he belonged to, and for himself as a reader/critic, to describe a poet's being influenced by "the poetry that I have found most congenial" (p. 25) seems inappropriate because of the major new development in our understanding of literary influence.

V

The indictment, in the second Milton essay, of earlier poets for their "injudicious choice of a model," seems to place the influences on poets under their control. And this attitude toward "the relation of the poet to the past" goes back to the beginning of Eliot's critical writing, where he argues that a poet must effect a "surrender of himself" to Tradition: "he can neither take the past as a lump . . . nor can he form himself wholly on . . . ," "The poet must be very conscious of . . . ," "He must be quite aware of . . . ," " He must be aware that . . . " (pp. 5–6). The substantive phrases in this passage from "Tradition and the Individual Talent" are not needed to make the point that the "extinction of personality" Eliot prescribes involves precisely judicious choice, the poet's "form[ing] himself."

This attitude is not strictly inconsistent with his view that poets need to "struggle" against negative influences, or that influence is caused by admiration; but it does not reflect, as those views do, the extent to which influence issues from the poet's real experience of—is really the result of an involuntary lived response to—past poets. The living poet's psychological reality is equally engaged by a dead poet he or she greatly admires. In "What Dante Means to Me," he declares "a really supreme poet makes poetry . . . more difficult for his successors" (p. 133).

Such a poet is so far from "congenial" as to be a source of anxiety; and the reason is a general negative influence on "his successors." During the past dozen years, anxiety has become firmly linked to specific positive influence: "influence . . . has been more of a blight than a blessing, from the Enlightenment until this moment." If that statement does not identify the critic responsible for this radical new development, the next sentence in *The Anxiety of Influence: A Theory of Poetry* (New York: Oxford UP, 1973) will: "Where it has vitalized, it has operated as misprision, as deliberate, even perverse revisionism" (p. 50). When discussing the recent sequence of treatises on literary influence, my phrase "as traditionally conceived" was intended to accommodate Harold Bloom's inspired clinamen (to borrow from his glossary) away from traditional conceptions of "the relation of ephebe or new poet to his precursors."

All our thinking about influence has been so powerfully affected by Bloom's persuasive account of its inside (and underside), one recalls with surprise that he first adumbrated it as recently as 1970, in the "Introduction" to his *Yeats* (New York: Oxford UP, 1970). The influencing artist (or artists, in a family line of original and partly "belated" "precursors"), he wrote there, is the "Covering Cherub" (a term "Blake took . . . from Ezekiel") keeping a "strong" artist out of the Eden of full self-realization. Apparently, no one of the legion of psychoanalytic critics anticipated Bloom's brilliantly sensible application, to a poet's "relation to the dead poets," of a universal relation fundamental to Freudian theory—that of a child to his or her parent-model(s).

The relation of Freud to Bloom's concept of influence involves a crucial irony, as I shall show; but he has attributed increasing importance to Freud. In more than one sense, Freud is the protagonist of his most recent theoretical book at this writing, *The Breaking of the Vessels* (Chicago: U of Chicago P, 1982), in which he declares, "Freud is . . . *the* inescapable mythologist of our age," and, "psychoanalysis itself is the culture of which it purports to be the description" (pp. 62–63). Eliot's complacent reference to influence as "choice of a model" may exaggerate his conception of it; but the "admiration" and "gratitude" which, repeatedly throughout his life, he claimed to have felt for the "congenial" writers who influenced his poetry, is totally unlike the psychic agon described by Bloom's psychoanalytics. Or is a denial of it: lying or forgetting/repressing. Did Eliot do battle in "the true wars fought under the banner of poetic influence . . . against . . . the wealth of tradition" (*Yeats,* p. 4)?

Eliot's comment on the general negative influence of "a really supreme poet" is not his only expression of a less roseate conception of "the relation of ephebe or new poet to his precursors." For example, almost two decades earlier, in a "Note on the Development of 'Taste' in Poetry" appended to the "Introduction" to the published version of his Norton Lectures, *The Use of Poetry and The Use of Criticism* (Cambridge: Harvard UP, 1933), he describes his wide reading in romantic poetry "in adolescence," which he began "at the age of fourteen or so" with "Fitzgerald's *Omar,*" then generalizes:

> At this period, the poem, or the poetry of a single poet . . . assumes complete possession for a time. . . . The frequent result is an outburst of scribbling . . . . It is not deliberate choice of a poet to mimic, but writing under a kind of daemonic possession by one poet. (pp. 25–26)

If the precursor in not the "blight" Bloom describes, he or she is much more than merely "congenial"; and the ephebe or new poet explicitly has made *no* ("injudicious" or other) "deliberate choice." However, Eliot denies the need for battle. He sees "this period" of "possession" as an early stage in a poet's development: he fixes its end, in his own case, at "about my twenty-second year," which is the year he began to write his first poetry given general publication. Bloom will have none of it.

An example of the historical conjunctions so important to my inferences in this book about the company of Eliot and Joyce, is the role of Eliot's first published theoretical essay in the debate among contemporary critics about literary influence. His essay is a more-or-less explicit context of the sequence of treatises discussed above. A single early installment of Bloom's imposing contribution to that debate, *Poetry and Repression* (New Haven: Yale UP, 1976), refers to the "noble obfuscation" of "Modern theories of mutually benign relations between tradition and individual talent, including those of T. S. Eliot and of Northrop Frye" (p. 95); but *The Breaking of the Vessels* introduces an extended discussion with the statement, "the malign influence of T. S. Eliot still lingers on, in most contemporary accounts of literary tradition" (p. 17).[9] He charges that "The famous essay of 1919 idealizes the process of literary transmission," quotes more extensively than Hassan from the passage about the poet's "relation to the dead poets and artists," and concludes that in the "idealized fiction . . . of 'a simultaneous order' that releases literary time from the burden of anxiety,"

> Eliot was deceiving us, grand rhetorician that he was. He could not have been deceiving himself. In the July 1919 issue of *The Egoist,* he had composed a brief but remarkable review ["never reprinted"], only a few weeks before writing "Tradition and the Individual Talent." (p. 18)

Bloom then reproduces the first two paragraphs of Eliot's review, "Reflections on Contemporary Poetry," which anticipate the "Note" of fourteen years later in discussing "the development of a writer." Eliot says that admiration of another writer "leads most often to imitation . . . and the awareness of our debt naturally leads us to hatred of the object imitated." He contrasts with this "a feeling of profound kinship, or rather of a peculiar personal intimacy, with another, probably a dead author," which is "a crisis"; "It is a cause of development," for "We do not imitate, we are changed . . . and we become bearers of a tradition." Bloom concludes:

> I think we can surmise that Eliot's true and always unnamed precursor was not Dante or Donne or Jules Laforgue or Baudelaire, but an uneasy composite of

---

9. His antipathy to Eliot should be noted. It extends at least from his intrepid refusal, when a freshman Instructor three decades ago, to teach poetry by Eliot specified in a course syllabus, to his statement in the August, 1977 *Esquire:* "Most overrated: T. S. Eliot, *all* of him, verse and prose. . . . His verse is (mostly) weak; his prose is wholly tendentious." Hilton Kramer quotes the whole statement in "The Triumph of Misreading," a denunciation of Bloom's poetics in *The New York Times Book Review* (Aug. 21, 1977), pp. 3, 28, that emphasizes Bloom's derogative dismissal of Eliot. Ironically, less obduracy might have enabled Kramer to observe that Bloom's poetics encourages our attributing the dismissal not to a disinterested appraisal of Eliot's achievement, but to his own "deliberate, even perverse revisionism." That Bloom has long been waging "true war" against a precursor is suggested by his invoking, while this is being written, Eliot's notorious 1928 self-labelling—with "Anglo-Catholic" suitably adapted—in a context that has nothing to do with Eliot. Near the beginning of "Inescapable Poe," (*New York Review of Books* [Oct. 11, 1984], pp. 23–26, 35–37), he writes that Poe "abominated Emerson," who "(like Whitman, like Lincoln) was not a Christian, not a royalist, not a classicist" (p. 24). Eliot is not even mentioned until Bloom quotes from the essay "From Poe to Valéry" (1948) in his next to last sentence.

Tennyson and Whitman, with Whitman being the main figure. The language of
kinship and crisis was discarded by Eliot because it placed the principal empha-
sis upon . . . the fantasias and defenses of a poet's personality. (pp. 18–21)

Setting aside that Eliot dates the writing of "the famous essay" two years
earlier (1917) than its appearance in the September *Egoist,* is Bloom's "surmise"
correct? Was Eliot "deceiving us" in that and the subsequent reprinted critical
essays that discussed literary influence? Was what Bloom calls Eliot's "'official'
view of the relations between tradition and the individual talent" (p. 19), his
assertion that (in the words of the essay), the effective artist separates "the man
who suffers" from "the mind which creates," in "a continual extinction of per-
sonality"—that the effective poet to some extent does "form himself"—a con-
scious misrepresentation by Eliot of his true experience of influence?

Bloom describes *The Anxiety of Influence* as a "meditation on the melan-
choly of the creative mind's desperate insistence upon priority" (p. 13). But in
his judgment, while a "strong" artist overcomes each successive influence, Eliot
was deceptive rather than forthrightly desperate. His "surmise" is that Dante,
Donne, Laforgue and Baudelaire were conjurations to hide the truth—"with
Whitman being the main figure."

T. S. Eliot and the Poetics of Literary History is the unwieldy but precisely
descriptive title of a noteworthy book on Eliot published the year after *The
Breaking of the Vessels* (1983). Its author is strongly influenced by the poetics
Bloom sees informing "the relation of ephebe or new poet to his precursors" in
literary history. Of his mentor's attitude toward Eliot, Gregory Jay declares that
"What brings Bloom to a boil," is "Eliot's movement away from a 'Romantic'
belief in the poetic subject's achievement of sublime immortality" through "the
[poet's] transumption [a kind of controlled reassimilation] . . . of the precursor's
figures."[10]

Jay's "deliberate . . . revisionism" consists in respect for the achievement
and motives of a "haunted seeker of new horizons" (p. 250). Unlike his precur-
sor, Jay sympathetically probes Eliot's (surmised) "revisionary repression
directed at his own nature, as well as at the nature of the Romantics," and "con-
struction of authorizing foreign traditions to legitimate his break with America"
(pp. 27, 16–17).

Not a rhetorician's deception, but a strong poet's anxiety caused Eliot to
"simultaneously set out to exorcise nature, America, and Romanticism, retro-
spectively giving to them negative interpretations that were evidently not his
first ones" (p. 27): hence, "Eliot's conversion to Anglo-Catholicism"; and his

---

10. Gregory S. Jay, *T. S. Eliot and the Poetics of Literary History* (Baton Rouge: Louisiana State
UP, 1983), p. 69. Although Jay differs with, and cites critiques of, Bloom's poetic, his general relation
to it can be illustrated by his characterization of "Prufrock" as "continu[ing] the genre Bloom calls
the 'crisis ode.' The achievement of the poem, however, comes in the aporia between this grammat-
ical enunciation of belatedness [i.e., "the poet's failed quest for the Romantic sublime"] and the rhe-
torical manipulation . . ." (p. 94). It is interesting that Eliot used the currently popular "aporia" three
decades ago, in the second paragraph of "The Frontiers of Criticism."

"pantheon" of "critics, poets, and saints," whose function for "the individual talent" is "to transfigure the pandemonium of feelings in his American nature" (p. 21).

The language of crisis, of "the true wars fought . . . against . . . the wealth of tradition," is unmistakable, as is the hovering presence of Eliot's early essay— seen as initiating not deception but exorcism. Jay's sympathetic treatment of Eliot as ephebe does not, however, resolve the aporia: Eliot's professed conception of the working of literary influence is directly controverted by the new poetics of literary history with, apparently, support from the poet's own testimony in unguarded moments.

Does the influenced poet "form himself" on guidance taken from a congenial dead poet, as Eliot usually claims—or war against the blight of a precursor, as Bloom insists? Is either alternative exclusively valid—or are these contrary and ostensibly total theories of literary influence in fact complementary, and so partial? Whether or not they can be reconciled, they must be confronted, with each other. And the confrontation must be full enough to do justice to both. A suitable beginning is the evidence for Bloom's surmise about Eliot's own, secret, Covering Cherub.

VI

"A Pact," Pound's apostrophe in *Lustra* (1916) explicitly to Walt Whitman—"I have detested you long enough"—proposing "to make friends" with "a pigheaded father," formally ended a negotiation he had begun years before. A few months after taking up residence in London, while Eliot was still an undergraduate and he in his early twenties, Pound proclaimed what Bloom would claim about his future friend. "What I Feel About Walt Whitman," a brief essay dated February 1, 1909 and written with his eccentric spelling, begins, "From this side of the Atlantic I am for the first time able to read Whitman . . . . " Although its title eerily anticipates that of Eliot's essay on Dante, Pound plainly does not feel simple admiration for a congenial dead poet. And his ambivalence not only is greater than it would become in "A Pact" (first published in 1913); it also is too specific and too charged to be explained as the general negative influence of, in Balakian's phrase, "authors of the same nationality and language":

> I honor him for he prophesied me while I can only recognize him as a forebear of whom I ought to be proud.

Whitman is Pound's forebear/precursor precisely as American and romantic:

> His crudity is an exceding great stench, but it *is* America. . . . He *does* "chant the crucial stage" and he is the "voice triumphant." He is disgusting.

Finally, to mock—not merely to question, as I did above—the attitude toward influence implied by the word Eliot would use more than half a century later, Pound used "congenial" ironically, in a confession that would confirm Bloom's surmise if Pound were Eliot:

> Personaly I might be very glad to conceal my relationship to my spiritual father and to brag about my more congenial ancestry—Dante, Shakespeare, Theocritus, Villon, but the descent is a bit difficult to establish.[11]

But the young Pound is not Eliot, who when mature reviewed a biography of Whitman with both cool praise and calm criticism of its subject (as well as of the second poet in Bloom's "uneasy composite"). This review, entitled "Whitman and Tennyson" and published at the end of 1926, also was—like most—never reprinted. And the *nature* and *tone* of Eliot's remarks in it belie any suggestion of lifelong struggle against secret precursors.

Although "When Whitman speaks of the lilacs or of the mocking-bird" he reveals a greater "tone" and "vision," and both poets are "masters," Eliot mildly (and calmly) reproves both for romanticizing:

> both Tennyson and Whitman made satisfaction almost magnificent. . . . It is not the best aspect of their verse . . . . But Whitman succeeds in making America as it was, just as Tennyson made England as it was, into something grand and significant. You cannot quite say that either was deceived, and you cannot at all say that either was insincere . . . . They had the faculty . . . of transmuting the real into an ideal. . . . But this, and [Whitman's] "frankness" about sex . . . sprang from what may be called either "idealisation" or a faculty for make-believe, according as we are disposed.

In addition, although Whitman was "a 'man with a message,' . . . that message was sometimes badly mutilated in transmission."[12]

These comments, both the praise and the blame, reveal none of the psychomachia surmised by Bloom and plainly expressed by Pound. Furthermore, while not incontrovertible, they are reasonable things to say about the two poets. And when, to praise Pound by contrast less than two years later, Eliot criticizes Whitman harshly, it is an expression of his concern as a poet for the poet's craft, which he attributed to Dante's influence. In an introduction to a *Selected Poems* by his friend (London: Faber & Gwyer, 1928), he declares:

> Pound's originality is genuine in that his versification is a *logical* development of his English predecessors. Whitman's originality is both genuine and spurious.

11. Pound's brief essay is printed in *A Century of Whitman Criticism,* ed. Edwin Haviland Miller (Bloomington: Indiana UP, 1969); quotations are from pp. 125 and 126. "Whitman," in *A B C of Reading* (1934), retracts much of his early enthusiasm. Then in Cantos 80 and 82 (*The Pisan Cantos,* 1948), he again treats Whitman as his forebear. For an account of his attitudes to Whitman focussed on his poetry, see Hugh Witemeyer, "Clothing the American Adam: Pound's Tailoring of Walt Whitman," *Ezra Pound Among the Poets,* ed. George Bornstein (Chicago: U of Chicago P, 1985), pp. 81–105.

12. "Whitman and Tennyson," review of Emory Holloway, *Whitman: An Interpretation in Narrative,* in *The Nation & The Atheneum,* XL (Dec. 18, 1926), 426.

Genuine in being a logical development of the prose of "predecessors":

> It is spurious in so far as Whitman wrote in a way that asserted that his great prose was a new form of verse. (And I am ignoring in this connexion the large part of clap-trap in Whitman's content.) (p. xi; rev. ed., 1948, p. 10).

Had Eliot arbitrarily yoked Whitman into an introduction to Pound's poetry, he might have given support to Bloom's surmise. But the historical critic was "speaking of origins" for "several types of verse that have developed in English," "for instance, my own type of verse, that of Pound, and that of the disciples of Whitman"; and he made the now-conventional identification of Browning and Yeats as "the first strong influences upon Pound." Furthermore, he was "certain—it is indeed obvious—that Pound owes nothing to Whitman" (pp. viii–ix).

However, Pound's own youthful testimony in his Whitman essay belies Eliot's conventional modernist inference about his predecessors/forebears/precursors, as much by its (to put it mildly) less restrained idiom as by its substance. "It is a great thing, reading a man to know . . . 'His message is my message . . .' ," Pound writes; and, respecting precisely versification:

> As for Whitman, I read him (in many parts) with acute pain, but when I write of certain things I find myself using his rythms.

On the other hand, the essay also belies any surmise of anxiety over Whitman's influence. First of all, Pound readily acknowledges his less "congenial" but actual "spiritual father." Secondly, his psychomachia of ambivalence is scarcely expressed before it is resolved: he declares, "And yet if a man has written lines like Whitman's to the 'Sunset breeze' one has to love him" (p. 126), and pronounces a judgment that could not be more contrary to Eliot's if it were calculated:

> Like Dante he wrote in the "vulgar tongue," in a new metric. The first great man to write in the language of his people. (p. 127)

As the manner and matter of Pound's testimony (and his subsequent poem) discredit Eliot's inference that Whitman did not influence Pound, so the manner and matter of Eliot's comments on Whitman discredit Bloom's contrary surmise about Eliot: it is no denial of "the amply-recognized Eliot-Whitman connection" (Jay, p. 168), to distinguish *familiarity* from evidence of influence. Eliot may have *inferred* wrongly from what he knew of Pound rather than from his friend's poetry; and Bloom seems to have *surmised* wrongly out of a poetic of "revisionary repression" of the truth. In the passage (quoted from above) in which Eliot is "speaking of origins" of "types of verse," he writes, "I did not read Whitman until much later in life [than his early twenties], and had to conquer an aversion to his form, as well as to much of his matter, in order to do so" (pp. viii–ix). If he is lying, he is committing not only a considerable deception but, since the context is an introduction to the work of another poet, a wholly gratuitous one. Furthermore, a full quarter-century later, in "Walt Whitman and Modern

Poetry," a talk he gave in 1944 to Allied servicemen in London, Eliot himself made my point:

> I never read Whitman properly until I was of an age where I could no longer be influenced by him.[13]

In a psychoanalytic context, the subject's denial can be confirmation, and few toads really are imaginary. But to my mind, that the Eliot who wrote as he did about Whitman concealed or repressed anxiety over Whitman's influence on him is a poorer surmise than is Eliot's dismissing Whitman's influence on Pound a poor inference. On the other hand, Pound's freedom from anxiety need not reflect against Bloom's theory of influence: it can be attributed to Whitman's not being a powerful influence on him, or even to his not being himself a truly strong poet. In other words, the evidence in the specific case of Whitman affirms neither Eliot's nor Bloom's representation of the way influence works. And the basic problem—whether it works as benefit derived or anxious agon—remains. One possible approach to solving it is to distinguish between the real domain of an *inference,* and the ideal one of a *surmise.*

VII

Noting that it was "never republished," Jay quotes most of the initial two paragraphs of Eliot's (in Bloom's phrase) "remarkable review," quoted in full the year before by Bloom, in which Eliot contrasts a young poet's "imitation" and consequent "hatred" of an admired writer, with the "kinship" with "probably a dead author" that "is a cause of development." However, Jay does not emphasize the seeming contradiction of "Eliot's idealized fiction . . . of 'a simultaneous order'" with no "burden of anxiety" that Bloom calls deceptive, first expounded in the oft-quoted passage in "Tradition and the Individual Talent" and reiterated. Jay emphasizes the paragraphs' conclusion. "We do not imitate, we are changed," Eliot concludes: the ephebe becomes a fully-fledged "person." And Jay observes:

> The love affair with the prior poet is an act of self-figuration, troping or meta-morphosing the newcomer "from a bundle of second-hand sentiments into a person." In the mirror that is the beloved precursor, the speculative new poet imagines himself. (pp. 73–74)

Although his interjection in the same place, that Eliot's "never republished . . . disturbing account" appeared "six months after the death of his father," reflects Jay's poetics of literary history, the two paragraphs do contain both the "erotic" and the "familial" metaphors he notes. But do those metaphors of love

---

13. Transcribed by Donald Gallup in "Mr. Eliot at the Churchill Club," *Southern Review* 21 (1985), 969–73, 970. He also recanted his earlier judgment: "Whitman's verse . . . is perfect, although at first it looks far from it. This singularity is very great and makes Whitman unique in the whole history of literature"; and, "superficially . . . very much like Tennyson," Whitman "is a greater poet" (971).

and descent concern only a "desire for identity" or, as Eliot asserts, experienced *real* identity? Is the "new poet imagin[ing]"? In other words, is Eliot's assertion that the young poet is "changed," made "a person," quoted by Jay only to be troped or metamorphosed?

In fact, in "Philip Massinger," published the year after the review, Eliot made his famous declaration that it is specifically "immature poets" who imitate; and the initial paragraphs of the review concern a poet's "development" precisely *out of* the immature "hatred" (for the admired and imitated older writer) Bloom considers significant, and *into* the artistic "person" whose real existence Jay's ideal formulation denies.

Jay's refusal to grant Eliot authority over what he says happens to the young poet—*even as testimony about himself*—is, like Bloom's refusal to believe Eliot, of a piece with the refusal to accept Eliot's proposal that a poet can have a measure of control over the working of literary influence. For theirs is a poetics of involuntary struggle—of action only as reaction. It cannot accommodate Eliot's conception of influence as response-and-action, in which a poet gratefully extracts benefit from a precursor ("probably a dead") poet.

The question whether influence works solely as reaction, or as response leading to purposive action, is part of a larger question that also implicates causation in art; Eliot's familiar early answer to it has been cited more than once. His declaration was:

> The mind of the poet . . . may partly or exclusively operate upon the experience of the man himself; but the more perfect the artist, the more completely separate in him will be the man who suffers and the mind which creates . . . . (*Selected Essays*, pp. 7–8)

In *Eliot's Early Years* (New York: Oxford UP, 1977), Lyndall Gordon criticizes "the dogmatic 'Tradition and the Individual Talent,' with its theory of impersonality" for "obscuring the personal nature of Eliot's poetry" (p. 166). And her chapter "Beyond Philosophy" establishes how starkly personal is much of his early poetry. In his more recent book, Ronald Bush asserts the importance of "Eliot's psyche" in his poetry, quoting Randall Jarrell's characterization of him as "the victim and helpless beneficiary of his own inexorable compulsions [and] obsessions" and as—more specifically to the point here—"From a psychoanalytical point of view . . . the most interesting poet of [the] century" (p. x). (Jarrell has "your century"—"the future" is addressing "us" in 1962.)

The recent books of Gordon, Jay, and Bush have expounded the daemon of a suffering and driven man in the poet eloquently. But Eliot's early (and persisting) distinction of man and mind has not thereby been discredited. Bush honors that distinction when he declares "the major poems . . . *mime* [my emphasis] the central configurations of their author's psyche" (*T. S. Eliot*, p. xi). Hence, for example, while Gordon's biography, on which he draws, suggests connecting the title character of "La Figlia Che Piange" with Emily Hale (pp. 55–57), his discussion of the poem never mentions that extrinsic connection (pp. 11–14). Eliot did not publish the starkly personal (inadequately "separated" or "mimed") early poems mentioned above; he pointedly emphasized, in the singular title he gave the volume comprising those he did publish, *Prufrock and Other Observations* (1917), the distinction stated in his essay the same year; even the pronouns in his statement carefully distinguish "man who" and "mind which"; and—to fix the relevance of this general issue to my subject, the working of influence—his unreprinted review begins "It is not true that the development of a writer is a function of his development as a man" even though (he says reasonably) "there is a close analogy between the sort of experience which develops" each.

This is not to deny the value of surmises that the new poetics of literary history has provided. For example, to take the most concrete of the triad of influences that Bloom identified as sources of anxiety for Eliot (Nature, Romanticism, and America), I surmise that the surmise of both Jay and Bloom that Eliot was anxious about America's influence on him has considerable validity. But is the disturbing influence that of precursors—Whitman and, as Jay proposes, Emerson—or is it more likely the respective influences of his mother and his father, and the influence of Harvard? In little more than half a year he acted decisively against all three: his precipitate and catastrophic marriage to Vivienne Haigh-Wood occurred in the summer of 1915; and the next March, in Gordon's words, "he put all thought of America and academic prospects behind him" (p. 85). It is generally accepted that his mere return to Cambridge that spring for the *pro forma* defense of his thesis on F. H. Bradley would have initiated a career as "teacher in the philosophy department" (Gordon, p. 65) at the prestigious university with which his family was associated; although he did not intend his marital unhappiness, he declined material security and social standing in favor of drudgery and uncertainty.

But America/family/Harvard are not precursor poets. And if it can be objected that praising the fiction of Fitzgerald, Dos Passos, and Hemingway in his review of the Whitman biography, and sending a fan letter to the stranger who wrote *The Great Gatsby,* involved no threat to Eliot's identity as a poet, his doing these things also indicates an active interest in American literature. Moreover, in that mid-life period he began to write and speak freely about America and his family (see Gordon, p. 166). Finally, the subjects and settings of his early poems are almost always American, and those of his later ones frequently so, when they can be given any distinct national identity. He closely resembles Joyce, who when young preferred privation on the continent to living in Dublin (and chose foreign precursors for his art), but who throughout his life made Dubliners and Dublin his only subjects and setting. Jay has the psyche of the man Eliot anxiously motivating the "construction of authorizing foreign traditions to legitimate his break with America." But Stephen Dedalus controverts that new poetics in *Ulysses* when he says of the artist Shakespeare's unfortunate marriage, "A man of genius makes no mistakes. His errors are volitional and are the portals of discovery" (190).[14] Was the exile in which Eliot and Joyce achieved art

14. Numbers in parentheses are references to pages in the "corrected and reset" edition of *Ulysses* (New York: Random House, 1961); in both substantives and accidentals, quotations conform to the "Critical and Synoptic Edition," ed. Hans Walter Gabler, Wolfhard Steppe, and Claus Melchior

anxious avoidance, or cunning choice? We know that both men's impulsive marriages were "the portals of discovery" for the artists. The issue is no other than, once again, the issue in the contrary representations of the working of influence as a writer's "war" with the precursor, and "form[ing] himself." It is possible that—like the attributable causes of artistic creation—the contraries of influence as anxious reaction and as grateful response are reconciled at a higher level of integration; but as with acts in life, impulsive or deliberate, respecting both the superficially deferential young American and the superficially arrogant young Irishman, Eliot's acting artist in the man cannot be simply identified with Bloom's reacting man in the artist.

I repeat that to make this distinction is not to deny the value of the new poetics of literary history, which has richly informed and directed our understanding of the relations between poets. It is rather to invoke the elder Eliot's frontier between true historical criticism and what he called "the diversion of attention from the poetry to the poet." But Bloom reproaches Eliot for disregarding "the fantasies and defenses of a poet's personality": the new poetics of involuntary struggle—of action only as reaction—disdains Eliot's distinction as artificial. It is a distinction crucial to the contrary representation of the working of literary influence Eliot proffered throughout his criticism. That is, Eliot's conception of influence as response and active derivation of benefit is inseparable from his insistence in later life that surmises about the man in the artist are across one frontier of criticism, while inferences about the artist in the man are within the critical domain. Eliot's conception attributes to the artist in the man the capacity for action respecting predecessors, as well as the experience of reaction to precursors.

In his "Introduction," Jay observes that Eliot uses "kinship metaphors in regard to poetic genesis . . . with monotonous regularity" (p. 4); and he later specifies, "Throughout his career, Eliot uses genealogical metaphors to describe . . . the working of influence" (p. 25). Pound wrote of "loving" Whitman; and even setting aside the "feeling . . . of a peculiar personal intimacy, with another . . . author," a "passion" like "personal intimacies in life," Eliot described in the unreprinted review, he later wrote on the subject of those two paragraphs (in his "Note on the Development of 'Taste' in Poetry") that the influencing poet "assumes complete possession," "daemonic possession," over the (undeveloped) adolescent one, "much as in our youthful experiences of love" (pp. 25–26). To Jay, these tropes are not unexceptional but "homoerotic," expressing a "love affair with the prior poet" (p. 74). A corresponding significance is attributed to kinship metaphors by a poetics emphasizing the "family romance" (Bloom, after Freud) of ephebe and "beloved precursor." The attribution is made even though family relations would almost inevitably suggest metaphors for describing historical relations; for that reason, the *absence* of such metaphors

---

(New York: Garland, 1984), unless otherwise specified. A rough conversion to the trade edition of that text (Random House, 1986) can be achieved by adding 2 to a page reference, then subtracting according to the following formula: 18/100 to p. 400 + 25/100 to p. 600 + 8/100 after p. 600.

might indicate to the psychoanalytically-oriented a mechanism of anxious avoidance or more anxious denial.

An instance of Eliot's use of a kinship metaphor illustrates neatly the different consequences of surmising the reaction of the man in the artist out of an ideal formulation, and inferring action by the artist in the man from real experience. And it suggests that Eliot's view of influence as response and active derivation of benefit is neither a deception nor a delusion—at least with respect to influences on his own poetry. Regarding the role of the ostensibly false precursor Jules Laforgue in his early development, which will be discussed in the next chapter, Eliot writes in "What Dante Means to Me" that Laforgue's similar temperament made him "like an admired elder brother." It might be surmised that his simile of a kinship relation largely free from anxiety is deception; but in this instance, the whole emphasis of the new poetics on the relations of the men in the poets is a peripheral one. Eliot explicitly subordinates his response to Laforgue's temperament to the influence on his poetry of the poet in that admired brother: Laforgue's "form of expression" provided him with a "clue" to "the poetic possibilities of my own idiom of speech" (*To Criticize the Critic*, p. 126). This is not the place to consider the validity of Eliot's specific attribution of influence to Laforgue, or even that of his assertion that the historical relation is one not of imitation but of true influence, enabling the development of something that was "my own." My intention is to establish the peripheral importance for Eliot's poetry of the declared influence of a similar temperament on Eliot the man, as compared to the *consequence* of Eliot's "recognition of a temperament akin to one's own": the influence on Eliot the poet. And that latter attributed influence—of the "form of expression" Laforgue gave, *in his poetry,* to his temperament—is in the domain of criticism; for it concerns the relations of the influenced poet in the man.

Furthermore, the validity Eliot's testimony may have for historical criticism of his poetry, like the validity of a third party's attribution of influence on the poet in any woman or man, is a matter of inference from the poetry, not surmise out of an ideal model. When Jay traces Eliot's "spiritual autobiography" to "John Winthrop, Cotton Mather, Jonathan Edwards, Emerson, and Hawthorne," in preference to "the assumed parentage of Donne or Lancelot Andrewes" through which Eliot ostensibly "imagines his own identity"/ "imagines himself" (pp. 21, 74), Jay's surmise about his "autobiography" and imaginings is as good as mine. But that *biographical* surmise is not the same thing as an inference about the precursors of the *artist*. Eliot the poet could have "assumed" the parentage of Donne and Andrewes in the tangible sense wholly unintended by Jay—"form[ed] himself" as their offspring. Also, "foreign traditions" may indeed "legitimate" their influence on him—by manifesting themselves in his poetry. My point is obvious: what is true about the man in the artist may have to be surmised; what is true about the artist in the man can be inferred from his art.

The truth revealed by inference is more often the possibility than the certainty of influence. Furthermore, Laforgue's similar temperament was instrumental in the influence his poetry may have had on Eliot's poetry. Still, only the latter influence is in the domain of historical criticism. Although Bloom more often brilliantly infers the presence of influence from a poet's real art than surmises it out of his own ideal model, the new poetics of literary history does not honor Eliot's distinction between biography and criticism.

That poetics of anxious reaction precludes active choice by the influenced poet, insisted on in Eliot's conception. It has been pointed out that his conception of the influenced poet actively "form[ing] himself"—as a poet making poetry—is inseparable from his distinction between biography and criticism. Correspondingly, the new poetics of anxious (involuntary) reaction, which disdains his distinction as artificial, denies—even while it heroizes strong poets who prevail over the influence of their precursors—that the strong new poet's accomplishment combines an act of judgment with her or his response to a precursor, to "form himself," achieve "development," and so make art.

By stressing the pressure of psychic states common to all humans, and so designating artists' choices as strictly reactive, determined solely by the motives of behavior, the new poetics of literary history excludes precisely what is unique to artists—the ability to exercise choice (Eliot's term) in achieving new art. Ironically, in doing so the new poetics controverts the distinction Freud drew a few months before Eliot wrote "Tradition and the Individual Talent," in his "Introductory Lectures to Psychoanalysis," between "one [who] is a true artist," and other humans with equally unfulfilled needs. The artist "has more at his disposal" *("verfügt er über mehr")* than we do. Freud's distinction is much like the one Eliot was about to make, between "the man who suffers and the mind which creates": Freud attributes to the artist the ability to elimate the strictly personal and the proscribed from "his phantasy" by a "mysterious power of shaping"; he treats the artist as able "to accomplish" *("leisten")* her or his art by deliberately choosing to do so—he treats art made as action taken, something distinct from merely expressing our common psychic states.[15]

Yet if Eliot's conception of the working of literary influence is not refuted by Bloom's, neither is the reverse true. Eliot acknowledges that he did not seek out beforehand, as influences on his poetry, the poets who "inspired" him. Whatever choice he exercised followed his experience of, and involuntary response to, those poets' art. And he is too shrewd to deny equally involuntary, and even unconscious, elements in the process of self-formation out of the new poet's response to the congenial admired predecessor(s). For his part, Bloom acknowledges that the artist engages in such a process of self-formation: the strong poet has precisely that ability to "form himself"—however anxiously and involuntarily—in successful struggle with the oppressive admired precursors(s).

The differences between the response of the "man" and subsequent action of the poet in Eliot's theory, and the reaction—"the fantasias and defenses"—of an undifferentiated "poet's personality" in Bloom's, remain; and they are considerable. But to the extent that Eliot's general testimony about himself is authentic—and the new poetics has denounced but failed to discredit it—his

15. The passage is at the end of the twenty-third lecture. See, e.g., Sigmund Freud, *A General Introduction to Psychoanalysis,* rev. ed. (1924; rpt. Garden City: Doubleday-Permabooks, 1953), pp. 384–85. The lecture was delivered in the winter of 1916–17; see p. 10.

account of the way influence worked in him is authentic. And that Bloom's shrewd revisionary account of the way influence works also is authentic, is corroborated even by Eliot's own infrequent contrary testimony.

The truth probably is that in any given case, one theory is more effective than the other for understanding the relations of influence in literary history. The crucial determinant may be the temperament of the new artist, or some specific characteristic of the art of the predecessor/precursor, or any one—or more—of a number of other possibilities. For example, Bloom's study of Eliot's near-contemporary was the occasion of his original adumbration of his poetics of influence. One can accept that Yeats attempted what Blake achieved (with the influence of Milton): a transumption of Milton/Blake/Shelley/Browning. But cannot also—for example—Wordsworth's poeticized philosophy, his masterly passages of poetry that discourse about the psychology and even the metaphysics of experience, be shown to be a true influence on Yeats's equivalent "high talk"? Not a source of imitation, for Yeats does not imitate it, but a cause of development, in Eliot's full sense? Yet Bloom says Yeats "always tended to dislike and ignore" Wordsworth (*Yeats*, p. 88); and he seems to be absolutely right.

However useful it is for increasing our understanding of Yeats's response to precursors, and his consequent place in literary history, Bloom's theory of influence—short of a surmise about defensive deception—cannot account for an influence on Yeats (for which he may not have been grateful—of which he may not even have been aware), that can reasonably be inferred from his art. Eliot's theory would have no difficulty with Yeats's ignoring Wordsworth, and yet having "form[ed] himself" with the "clue" provided by Wordsworth's poetical discourse.

My point is that although the two theories are contrary, their common elements suggest that both are aspects of a more comprehensive conception of the nature of literary influence; and so, it may be possible to reconcile them on that higher level of integration. What such a more comprehensive theory might be, I do not know. In the second paragraph of his "Introduction" to *Yeats*, Bloom declares, "Poetic influence is a labyrinth that our criticism scarcely begins to explore" (p. 4); it appears to be so still.

Here would be an ideal stopping-place for this detailed but inconclusive confrontation of Eliot and Bloom, and so a proper terminal point of my review of the grounds and limits of valid inference in the most important relation in literary history. However, what immediately follows Bloom's declaration at the beginning of his first statement about that relation crystallizes the issues more effectively than any summation could do. He continues, "Borges, the scholar of labyrinths, has given us the first principle for the investigation of poetic influence," and he quotes four sentences from James Irby's close translation of a brief essay by Borges having in its title a word Bloom himself favors, "Kafka and His Precursors" ("Kafka y Sus Precursores," from *Otras Inquisiciones*, 1960). In the four quoted sentences respectively, Borges declares: that word is "indispensable" for critics and connotes no "rivalry"; "every writer *creates* his own precursors"; "His work modifies our conception of the past, as it will modify the future"; and the "identity or plurality" of precursors is "unimportant."

Bloom says his "theory of poetic influence . . . swerves sharply from Borges" but "accepts the poet's *creation* of his precursors as a starting point." Bloom's swerve includes redefining the concept referred to in italics by both: in the "wars"against "the wealth of tradition," the poet "creates" his precursors not by identifying and adopting them, as Borges (and Eliot) says, but in a wholly different sense from Borges's: "by necessarily misinterpreting them" (p. 5). And his swerve is completed by his totally rejecting "the aesthetic idealism" of Borges's benign conception of "the relation of ephebe or new poet to his precursors," "noble as [it] is."

Bloom calls Borges's account of a new writer's relation to past writers noble idealism, yet accuses Eliot of deception for the "idealized fiction" of his very same account (Bloom specifies the passage) of a poet's "relation to the dead poets and artists" in the essay that Hassan said three decades ago "has remained at the heart of the matter since 1919." Furthermore, not only is it clear from the four sentences Bloom quotes, as from the whole last paragraph of "Kafka and His Precursors," that Borges is adopting Eliot's "congenial" and ostensibly deceptive view: Borges announces the fact. The third sentence of the quoted passage, which deals with the relation of the new writer's work to the past and future, has a footnote Bloom does not mention; and it cites precisely the same seminal passage for critics (of all persuasions, as has been shown) discussing literary influence in recent decades—the passage in which, as Northrop Frye put it in *The Critical Path* (Bloomington: Indiana UP, 1971), "T. S. Eliot had already spoken of tradition as a creative and informing power on the poet specifically as a craftsman" (p. 23).[16]

16. Borges's footnote, "See T. S. Eliot, *Points of View* (1941), pp. 25–26," refers to pages containing the passage in a selection of Eliot's critical essays published by Faber in England.

2

Tradition and the
Individual Talent in "Prufrock"

"The best known English poem since the Rubaiyat" it was called in 1959 and probably both was so and is.[1] Certainly, no other poem is more likely to be included in a collection of poetry of our century; and two generations of teachers have introduced it to secondary-school seniors and college freshmen. Long before 1959, "The Love Song of J. Alfred Prufrock" had achieved special canonical status.

One cause of its status was high regard for the poem itself. But I believe another was historical, and that the vantage afforded by the quarter-century since 1959 reveals this particular one of Eliot's early poems to be a most eloquent cultural artifact—both as harbinger of Modernism and as paleomodernist specimen. I also believe its special status persists; its pertinence to the present debate in criticism will be addressed in the last section of the book. But my concern here is Eliot's created harbinger and specimen as an event in literary history.

Perhaps even more than most history, that of literature can never be positive; at best, it is a persuasive—informed and sensible—account of the past. And attempting to formulate the significant circumstances of a single literary event like the advent of "Prufrock" is only relatively less daunting than attempting a more general history. Since the evidence of its principal historical relation—filiation—is circumstantial, all Eliot's appropriations for the poem, and all influences on it, must be inferred. (The influences I infer comport with his conception, not with the new poetics of literary history.) In addition to appropriations from and influences of the past, the advent of "Prufrock" involves its context—its creator's circumstances—and its immediate cause—its creator's act, as distinct from his response (reaction) to earlier art and to his experience of reality.

Yet the act of the young Eliot's individual talent occurred, as Taine put it, in a particular milieu, and at a "moment" when English poetry was ready for something new. In an address and essay of his late years, "American Literature

1. Hugh Kenner, *The Invisible Poet: T. S. Eliot* (1959; rpt. New York: Harbinger-Harcourt, 1969), p. 3.

and the American Language" (1953), the man looks back on both milieu and moment:

> From time to time there occurs some revolution, or sudden mutation of form and content in literature. Then, some way of writing . . . is found by a few people . . . no longer to respond to contemporary modes of thought, feeling and speech. A new kind of writing appears . . . ; we hear that the tradition has been flouted, and that chaos has come. After a time it appears that the new way of writing is not destructive but re-creative. It is not that we have repudiated the past . . . but . . . that in the light of what is new we see the past in a new pattern. (*To Criticize The Critic*, p. 57)

And two paragraphs later, the poet characterizes the precise revolutionary situation during his youth:

> In the first decade of the century the situation was unusual. I cannot think of a single living poet, in either England or America, then at the height of his powers, whose work was capable of pointing the way to a young poet conscious of the desire for a new idiom. . . . What the poets of the nineties ["all, with one exception, dead"] had bequeathed to us . . . was the assurance that there was something to be learned from the French poets of the Symbolist Movement . . . . (p. 58)

The previous chapter discussed Eliot's testimony/assertion that literary influence consists in a "new" writer's "forming himself" on guidance taken from "congenial" previous writers. In treating influence as a benign historical relation of the past (Tradition) with the evolving future (Development), he was applying what seems to me one of his fundamental beliefs: that the instrumental generative process in literary history is a dialectic of *reciprocal* interactions between the old and the truly new. Each of the passages just quoted articulates one half of the complex relation of prospective/retrospective interactions he conceives. One interaction in the complementary pair is that "the new way of writing is . . . re-creative"; its equally generative reciprocal is that "a young poet conscious of the desire for a new idiom" needs predecessor poets "pointing the way."

By his own account in 1953, no living poet's work "was capable of pointing the way" to what was to be the young Eliot's own distinctive accomplishment in "a new idiom"; instead, a "relation with the dead poets and artists" provided what needed "to be learned" for the "revolution, or sudden mutation of form and content" realized in "Prufrock." Its reciprocal in the interactions between his own new development and the tradition, Eliot describes a quarter-century earlier, in his introduction to Pound's 1928 *Selected Poems*.

Preparing to praise his friend's "originality"—superior to Whitman's—as "*logical* (sic) development," he distinguishes "poets who develop technique, those who imitate technique, and those who invent technique," then becomes more general:

> When I say 'invent,' I should use inverted commas . . . because it is impossible . . . . The poem which is absolutely original is absolutely bad; it . . . [has] no relation to the world to which it appeals.
> Originality, in other words, is by no means a simple idea in the criticism of

poetry. True originality is merely development; and if it is right development it may appear in the end so *inevitable* that we almost come to the point of view of denying all 'original' virtue to the poet. He simply did the next thing. (pp. x–xi)

"Originality is merely"—he says, using his word for growth toward self-realization by an individual poet—"development." He is punning; for as well as development *of* literature, he continues to mean here development *in* a new poet.

A new (original) poet develops in response to certain of "the dead poets and artists" who created the "existing order," the "form . . . of literature," in the words of the passage in "Tradition and the Individual Talent" repeatedly cited by students of literary influence; and development in the "order" of literature itself is described in the same passage: "the past [is] altered by the present as much as the present is directed by the past"—"in the light of what is new we see the past in a new pattern," as Eliot put it nearly four decades later, in 1953. The two senses of "development" designate the dyad I have described, of reciprocal generative complements in a single process in literary history. It is in the context of this reciprocally prospective and retrospective historical dialectic that new (original) poetry "may appear . . . *inevitable*," the poet "simply [doing] the next thing."

Eliot's understanding of originality as two complementary senses of development in poetry is characteristically both shrewd and historical. And it indicates (as it endorses) my purpose: to adduce the principal antecedents of and influences on "Prufrock"; to describe its "moment"; and to weave this historical pattern without making a singular creation appear "simply . . . the next thing" and its advent, to use his italicized word, inevitable; for that would be foolish history.

The first poem in every volume of his poems that it appeared in, and his first to receive general publication, "Prufrock" also is almost the first poem he wrote "that he wished to preserve."[2] By his own apparently accurate account: it "was conceived some time in 1910" (actually in February, while he was still an undergraduate); he took "several fragments which were ultimately embodied in the poem" with him from Harvard to the Sorbonne "in the autumn of that year"; and it was finished (during a visit to Munich, actually) in "the summer of 1911."[3] Hence, Eliot had written "Prufrock" three full years before he met Pound and was introduced to "Les Imagistes" and Pound's campaign to "get Milton off the back of English poetry." At a time when Yeats had just completed the first general revision of his "high romantic" early poetry, a really remarkable event occurred. A repressed young man who outwardly was not merely conventional but quintessentially stuffy, proved to be an "invisible" (Conrad Aiken and Hugh Kenner) poet of—in his word—revolution. That American graduate stu-

---

2. "Conversation Galante," the first two "Preludes" and "Portrait of a Lady" antedate its completion. See, e.g., *Invisible Poet*, pp. 33, 35; and Grover Smith, *T. S. Eliot's Poetry and Plays* (Chicago: U of Chicago P, 1961), p. 9. The quoted phrase is from the flyleaf of *Collected Poems: 1909–1962* (New York: Harcourt, 1963).

3. John C. Pope, "Prufrock and Raskolnikov Again: A Letter from Eliot," *American Literature* 18 (1947), 319–21, 319. For general confirmation of Eliot's dating see, e.g., the chronology facing p. 17 in A. D. Moody, *Thomas Stearns Eliot: Poet* (Cambridge: Cambridge UP, 1979).

dent barely into his twenties *developed* an unprecedented (and not often equalled since) panoply of modernist qualities. "Prufrock" would be a harbinger of Modernism if it did no more than render consciousness directly in language. But it also is wholly constituted by mental process: it has a formal strategy that identifies its subject with the expression of its subject. It relies fundamentally on allusion (Eliot was to call this "the mythical method" when praising *Ulysses*). It carries to an extreme complexity and flexibility of tone, and heterogeneity of materials. And it is characterized by discontinuity of discourse subtly invested with coherence/formal integrity (through radically idiolectic strategies of contrast, recurrence, juxtaposition), and by no less distinctly modernist cadences, setting, and theme. In Pound's words and emphasis, in the famous series of letters prodding the reluctant Harriet Monroe to print in *Poetry* a poem apparently too "modern" even for her, the twenty-two-year-old T. S. Eliot had "modernized himself on his own."

Eliot's reference to "several fragments . . . ultimately embodied" suggests that, unlike contemporaneous poems such as "Portrait of a Lady," and just like *The Waste Land* a decade later, "Prufrock" as we know it emerged out of a different and not very clear initial conception; poems so strikingly new when each appeared were new to their creator also. But while the poem that was to become central in Modernism was retrieved from Pound's collaboration and modulated into *The Waste Land* only in its final stages, Eliot made the early "modern" artifact Pound unearthed and wisely championed entirely "on his own."[4] To call his achievement remarkable is not to exaggerate, but to judge historically.

Before Pound's eventual success with Monroe, Eliot and the few fellow-poets who knew and liked "Prufrock" had failed to place it. Harold Monro not only rejected it for *Poetry and Drama* but, according to Conrad Aiken, thought it "bordered on 'insanity'." Pound could safely predict that his friend's "individual and unusual" poem would "at once differentiate him from everyone else, in the public mind";[5] but public reaction to it is less significant historically than the resistance of these and other editors of that era, some of whom are now renowned for their eagerness to promote new poetry, including other poems by the young Eliot. Perhaps the primacy he always accorded "Prufrock" in his volumes was more than pride of place—was a declaration about the historical status signified by the resistance to it of such editors, as well.

If it was, his quiet declaration that "Prufrock" began something really new ("From time to time there occurs some revolution, or sudden mutation . . . ") is congruent not only with his description of originality, but also with his lifelong

---

4. For an account of Eliot's fashioning *The Waste Land* out of the drafts, see pp. 143–54.

5. Letter to Harriet Monroe, dated December 1, 1916. *The Letters of Ezra Pound: 1907–1941*, ed. D. D. Paige (New York: Harcourt, 1950), p. 66. The previous quotation is from a letter to her dated September 30, 1914 and printed on p. 40. Monro changed his mind when he read "Prufrock" again in *Poetry*; see Ellen Williams, *Harriet Monroe and the Poetry Renaissance: The First Ten Years of Poetry, 1912–22* (Urbana: U of Illinois P, 1977), p. 127. The testimony of Aiken is from "King Bolo and Others," *T. S. Eliot: A Symposium . . .*, ed. Richard March and Tambimuttu (1949; Freeport, NY: Books for Libraries P, 1968), p. 22.

careful attributions of debt to "the dead poets and artists"; for the attributions do not express ostentatious modesty any more than the declaration is boasting. "Tradition and the Individual Talent" says of "the new" that "its fitting in is a test of its value"; and the historical relations of "Prufrock" seem to confirm that. To have achieved the harbinger and archetype of Modernism "on his own" was not to have created that "sudden mutation" *ex nihilo:* "True originality is . . . development."

The most general of those historical relations should be mentioned first. The young Eliot's radically innovative poem exemplifies the then new art's undeniable filiation (though the degree is much debated) from Romanticism. Such romantic imagery as "sea-girls wreathed with seaweed" is exploited in the poem, not adopted; and its affinity with the romantic quest poem is an ironic one. Yet, its link to the romantic motif of the melancholy of inadequacy that has caused failed aspiration, is direct.[6] Furthermore, it exemplifies the modernists' perpetuation of a central romantic commitment from the time of Novalis. Strindberg and Yeats, Proust and Kafka, Joyce and Pound—and the mature Eliot—all had as their principal subject the psychic experience of the writer.

In *Eliot's Early Years,* Gordon calls "Prufrock" one of his "less obviously autobiographical" early poems (p. 45). Her distinction is relative: she herself proposes autobiographical elements for almost two pages. The connection between the consciousness and situation of Prufrock and the young poet's own is indicated by Eliot's revelation to his friend Richard Aldington a decade later that abulia was "a lifelong affliction." Most of his friends who knew him when young later described him as "Prufrockian," and he himself apparently "once referred casually" to Prufrock, in a lecture, as a young man, and called him "partly" autobiographical during a late (1962) interview.[7] The later poem after Edward Lear beginning "How unpleasant to meet Mr. Eliot!," whose conversation is restricted to "If and Perhaps and But," may be playful self-caricature, but it cannot be totally alien to his perception of himself.

If the romantic elements in "Prufrock" are as relevant to its inchoate Modernism as are those that comment on romantic imagery and attitudes, its principal more remote ancestors also are relevant. The medieval poet who provided

6. For instance, in ch. XIX of Shelley's novel, Frankenstein's creature says:

For a moment my soul was elevated from its debasing and miserable fears . . . . For an instant I dared to shake off my chains and look around me with a free and lofty spirit, but the iron had eaten into my flesh and I sank again, trembling and hopeless, into my miserable self. (Mary W. Shelley, *Frankenstein* [London: Dent, 1963], p. 171)

Other instances are Werther, Heathcliff, Julien Sorel, Peer Gynt, even to an extent Stephen Dedalus. In *T. S. Eliot and the Poetics of Literary History,* Jay argues that the motif developed only gradually, by way of Browning, out of "the Greater Romantic Lyric" (pp. 94–99); but his purview is limited to poetry. Its late appearance in poetry also is principally associated with dramatic speakers (characters) replacing lyric ones.

7. The statement to Aldington is in a letter quoted in T. S. Eliot, *The Waste Land: A Facsimile . . . ,* ed. Valerie Eliot (New York: Harcourt, 1971), p. xxii. See also: Elisabeth Schneider, *T. S. Eliot: The Pattern in the Carpet* (Berkeley: U of California P, 1975), pp. 27–28, 31–32; *Invisible Poet,* p. 40; and n. 30 to "Ghostly Selves" (pp. 241–42) in Bush, *T. S. Eliot,* respectively.

its epigraph, important to modernist writers from Joyce to Akhmatova, is by Eliot's testimony more important to him than any other. And the affinity modernist English poets felt for the renaissance dramatic and lyric poetry he identified as models was partly his own doing. All this is familiar. So is the kinship of the dramatic-monologue portraits by Tennyson and Browning, which (possibly excepting Browning's ironic ones) is more obvious than close. However, direct links to other near-contemporaries have little relevant historical significance: Eliot's early poems are full of traces of poets ranging from Vergil to Swinburne.

Echoes of and (in Eliot's sense) thefts from "Prufrock's" predecessor as the "best known English poem" (which "almost overwhelmed" him when "fourteen or so"), have been proposed.[8] Other elements traceable to the *Rubaiyat*, its translator, and his biographer in the "English Men of Letters" series (A. C. Benson), long recognized in "Gerontion," have been expounded recently.[9] With some justice—but there are attendant problems (see p. 255)—critics have related the ending of the poem to Arnold's "The Forsaken Merman," and details of it to Stevenson's "Crabbed Age and Youth"; with less it is proclaimed that Eliot took his title from Kipling (presumably from "The Love Song of Har Dyal").[10] At the Sorbonne, Eliot read Dostoevsky's three major novels (Pope, 319), finding him (it is significant) congenial; and "resemblances" to *Crime and Punishment* exist (see p. 74). These detections of the young poet's use of his reading, when valid, show Eliot anticipating the aleatory method that would become so prominent in modernist art. But the sources themselves did not "point the way" to the young revolutionary's "individual and unusual" poem.

Much more indicative of "something . . . learned" are traces of two of Conrad's stories, "Heart of Darkness" and "The Return," and of Baudelaire's *Les Fleurs du Mal*.[11] We know that "Heart of Darkness" had affected Eliot sufficiently that a decade later he turned to it for the epigraph for "The Hollow Men" and (originally) *The Waste Land;* significantly, it has had a status in this century (including in classrooms) similar to that of "Prufrock." And "from Baudelaire," Eliot wrote in 1950, in "What Dante Means to Me":

> I learned first, a precedent for the poetical possibilities, never developed by any poet writing in my own language, of the more sordid aspects of the modern metropolis, of the possibility of fusion between the sordidly realistic and the phantasmagoric . . . that the sort of material that I had . . . experience that an

---

8. Leonard Unger, *Eliot's Compound Ghost: Influence and Confluence* (University Park: Pennsylvania State UP, 1981), pp. 29–30. For one attribution to the *Rubaiyat*, the Marvellian "To have squeezed the universe into a ball," Schneider proposes instead a passage in Arthur Symons's *The Symbolist Movement in Literature* (p. 13n). For Eliot's statement about the *Rubaiyat*, see the previous chapter, p. 14.

9. See Schneider, p. 46; and *Eliot's Compound Ghost*, pp. 22, 23, 27–28.

10. See Moody, p. 36; Darrel Abel, "R. L. S. and 'Prufrock'," *Notes and Queries* 198 (1953), 37–38; and T. S. Matthews, *Great Tom: Notes Towards the Definition of T. S. Eliot* (New York: Harper, 1973), p. 36. Kipling's poem is in "Beyond the Pale," a story in *Plain Tales from the Hills.*

11. Regarding Conrad, see B. C. Southam, *A Guide to the Selected Poems of T. S. Eliot,* 3rd ed. (London: Faber, 1977), p. 102; and *Eliot's Compound Ghost,* pp. 65–66, 108. Regarding Baudelaire, see, e.g., Schneider, pp. 12–13; and Moody, pp. 29–30.

adolescent had had . . . in an industrial city in America, could be . . . the source
of new poetry . . . . [12]

The words "possibilities" and of course "developed" are important, for he was
familiar with recent treatments of "sordid aspects of the modern metropolis" by
W. E. Henley, John Davidson, and James Thomson.[13] The historical context of
"Prufrock" includes their generally grim urban poetry; but it was by way of Bau-
delaire he realized "possibilities" to "develop." The young Eliot learned "from
him, as from Laforgue" that he could make "new poetry" about a world of one-
night cheap hotels, soot, and sewers—and have a vision of mermaids occur in
his poem. Equally important, Baudelaire and, on subsequent evidence, Conrad
(but not Laforgue or the minor British poets of the time) showed him it was
possible to make moving and profound art about what was to become a major
modernist preoccupation: the impress of urban industrial civilization on the
human spirit.

The *"Spleen et Ideal"* section of the *Fleurs du Mal* has a sequence of four
poems (LXXVIII-LXXXI) entitled *"Spleen."* Despite the near archaism of the
word in English, Eliot published a poem with that title in *The Harvard Advocate*
in January of his senior year, one month before he began "Prufrock." In it the
ideal of "Sunday faces," "conscious graces" and "Evening, lights, and tea" is
splenetically subverted by "cats in the alley" and a personified Life who is
"bald," "fastidious and bland," and "Punctilious of tie and suit."

Laforgue also is behind the undergraduate poem; and Baudelaire had not yet
been digested, for the spleen recalls Laforgue's stance of ironic condescension to
the futility of life.[14] A satiric mask of romantic *weltschmerz,* Laforgue's flippant
forbearance is very different from the *"acedia,* arising from the unsuccessful
struggle towards the spiritual life" Eliot described in "Baudelaire" (*Selected
Essays,* p. 339). Hence (to use Eliot's words), the influence of Laforgue's "tem-
perament" is more direct than on "Prufrock," for which it provided a crucial
"clue" to development: Eliot's rapid movement from "Spleen" to the "sudden
mutation . . . in literature" of his "individual and unusual" poem, is from a
more impersonal version (the difference is significant) of Laforgue's romantic
irony, to a poem in which the sort of spiritual crisis "universal in modern life"
("Baudelaire," p. 341) that Baudelaire's poetry *expressed,* is rendered *dramati-
cally* (again the difference is significant).

In "Heart of Darkness," the "horror" realized by Kurtz, accomplished prod-
uct of Western culture and technology, seems to me prophetic: "Exterminate all
the brutes!" was his "exposition of a method" that within a few decades, thanks

12. *To Criticize The Critic,* p. 126. His statement eleven years later, in the title essay, that "the
modern poet who influenced me was not Baudelaire but Jules Laforque," is in the context of his
observation that a great poet "can hardly influence, he can only be imitated" (p. 18). See also Moody,
pp. 4–5.
13. See Schneider, pp. 10–13; and Herbert Howarth, *Notes on Some Figures Behind T. S. Eliot*
(Boston: Houghton, 1964), pp. 106–7.
14. See, e.g., Moody, p. 20; and Leonard Unger, *T. S. Eliot: Moments and Patterns* (Minneapolis:
U of Minnesota P, 1966), pp. 10–11.

to the efficiency made possible by the industrial technology our civilization had achieved, was applied successfully to millions of designated brutes, including children. In any case, Conrad's story, published the year before the twentieth century began, portrays the moral monster a highly civilized individual becomes by indulging self-aggrandizing impulses, not a highly civilized individual's isolation and futility. But the impress of urban industrial civilization on the human spirit, central to "Prufrock," is equally central to "Heart of Darkness." The similar special status of the two works in our century has been mentioned. The historical similarity between them also includes the evolution of each. Conrad's "An Outpost of Progress" (1897) is related proleptically to "Heart of Darkness" almost exactly as "Spleen" is to "Prufrock." In both cases, the writer moved decisively from a thin if timely work to one of a totally different artistic order, a new creation that achieved great richness and power, and that did so by breaking new ground; yet in both cases, the centrally important early modernist work was essentially a realization of the earlier one's potentialities.

Despite Baudelaire's example of serious spiritual engagement with urban life, his less illustrious compatriot seems more instrumental in the evolution of the poet of "Prufrock" out of the poet of "Spleen." It was as the designated influence on Eliot's early poetry that most English-speaking readers first heard of Jules Laforgue (and Tristan Corbière). But this history is of a particular, archetypally modernist, poem; and Laforgue does seem to be one of its two chief agents. The other, almost equally familiar as generalized Influence on Early Eliot, seems to be Henry James.

In Hugh Kenner's imposing *The Pound Era* (Berkeley: U of California P, 1971), with its account "of how our epoch was extricated from the *fin de siècle*" (p. xi), the opening paragraphs describe an elderly Henry James *"en promenade"* in London and his emblematic encounter with the eponym of the book and its "era." Following this protasis the chapter presents James as the forebear whose

great sensibility brought in a generation.
     * * *
But for that sensibility "Prufrock" is unthinkable .... (pp. 15–16)

By "sensibility" Kenner seems to mean James's "attunement with the invisible," his ceremoniousness, and above all his commitment to precisely rendering an experience in every nuance of its complexity. In one of two pieces in a special James issue of *The Little Review* in August 1918, Eliot praises him for his ability to render experience directly, using a famous statement that is often quoted out of context. James had achieved "mastery over, ... escape from, Ideas"; "instead of thinking with our feelings ... we corrupt our feelings with ideas." The statement "He had a mind so fine that no idea could violate it" was made in this context; hence, the judgment with which Eliot concludes the paragraph: "He is the most intelligent man of his generation." In the other piece, he praises James for sharing with Hawthorne a concern for (in James's quoted phrase) "the deeper psychology" of characters; and, writing during the time that modernist fiction's great concern for precisely that had just begun to be expressed, he declared that "in comparison with" those two novelists "almost all others may be accused of either superficiality or aridity."[15] Lyndall Gordon cites two subsequent occasions when he affirmed James's influence on him (pp. 46n, 49).

One of Harriet Monroe's complaints to Pound about "Prufrock" was that it was "too much like Henry James"; and a number of critics have identified James as a direct influence on that specific poem, most of them citing characters in James's work as models.[16] But whatever a reticent young Eliot may have owed for J. Alfred to romantically reticent or ineffectual James characters, the relevant—historically significant—influence concerns not a type of character, but an exemplary "sensibility," which was manifested in a way of making art with characters. James's commitment to the precise rendering of experience and to "the deeper psychology" resulted in a fiction described in his own criticism, a fiction in which a subject's experience of reality is itself the reality portrayed, as though, in the words of Eliot's doctoral dissertation on Bradley, reality "exists only as it is found in the experiences of finite centres."[17] As a result, the work becomes a hermetic ("dramatic") object embodying the "reality" of its experiencing subject. Browning, for example, portrayed character—by relating the subject's reflections or discourse. But James portrayed *consciousness*—by relating the subject's experience. And then Eliot in "Prufrock" (and certain subsequent modernist novels) *presented* consciousness—by relating as verbalization a record of the subject's ("finite centre's") enacted experience. Today all this is familiar ("it may appear . . . *inevitable*"); but for the twenty-two-year-old student in 1910 James's fiction seems to have been a bridge. Eliot's subsequent interest in Bradley indicates the likely depth of his response to James's way of making art.

The other bridge seems to have been a poetic *oeuvre* Eliot believed himself to be the first person in the United States to own (Howarth, p. 105). And while the fiction of James, apparently even more positively than the poetry of Baudelaire, bore him to his subject, and to high purpose, Laforgue's poetry enabled his "development" of manner and method. Howarth writes:

> But even Baudelaire had not aroused him to the intuition of a form and a voice in which he could make poetry of his own knowledge of the city . . . . Then Laforgue came to him, revealing form, voice, stance. (p. 107)

15. Quoted from Edmund Wilson, ed., *The Shock of Recognition* (New York: Farrar, 1975), vol. II, pp. 856–57, 861.

16. See, e.g., George Fraser, *Essays on Twentieth Century Poets* (Totowa, NJ: Rowan, 1977), p. 105; *The Pound Era*, p. 16; F. O. Mathiessen, *The Achievement of T. S. Eliot*, 3rd ed. (1958; rpt. New York: Galaxy-Oxford UP, 1959), p. 70; Moody, pp. 30, 37; *Eliot's Poetry and Plays*, p. 15; William York Tindall, *Forces in Modern British Literature: 1885–1956* (1947; rpt. New York: Vintage, 1956), p. 278; *Moments and Patterns*, p. 12; *Eliot's Compound Ghost*, p. 9. For Monroe's remark, see Stanley K. Coffman, *Imagism: A Chapter for the History of Modern Poetry* (Norman: U of Oklahoma P, 1951), p. 43.

17. Quoted from J. Hillis Miller, *Poets of Reality: Six Twentieth-Century Writers* (1965; rpt. New York: Atheneum, 1969), p. 134. Miller discusses Eliot's early poetry, including "Prufrock," as "more or less contemporary" with his dissertation, although he began graduate study in philosophy after "Prufrock" (as well as other poems) was written, and "there is no evidence" that he had "been acquainted with Bradley's work" when he wrote it (*Eliot's Compound Ghost*, p. 11). For a more persuasive attribution of intellectual indebtedness to Henri Bergson, see Piers Gray, *T. S. Eliot's Intellectual and Poetic Development: 1909–1922* (Sussex: Harvester, 1982), pp. 52–84 *passim*.

And Gordon proposes that after securing the *Oeuvres complètes* in 1909, he

> began to pour out new poems. From Laforgue, Eliot learnt ... to confess through the defeatist persona his own despair and, at the same time, to shield himself by playing voices against one another .... He learnt, too ... to dramatize his most serious ideas as irrational, even ridiculous, emotions. (p. 29)

The first book in English devoted to the French poetry that influenced such modernists as Yeats, Stevens, Pound, and the Imagists was Arthur Symons's *The Symbolist Movement in Literature,* written with Yeats's close collaboration and dedicated to him. The undergraduate poet read it; and Eliot wrote in middle age, "But for having read his book I should not, in the year 1908, have heard of Laforgue.... "[18] In his "Introduction" to the 1928 volume of Pound's *Selected Poems,* he made the familiar declaration, "the form in which I began to write, in 1908 or 1909, was directly drawn from the study of Laforgue together with the later Elizabethan drama" (p. viii).

The Laforgue connection was promptly established by two important early studies of Eliot's poetry, Wilson's in *Axel's Castle* (1931) and Leavis's in *New Bearings in English Poetry* (1932). Leavis quoted Eliot's declaration, and both critics drew the connection between "Conversation Galante" and one of Laforgue's *Complaintes,* which was quoted in Symons's half-dozen pages.

For one who did not live quite to his twenty-seventh birthday, Laforgue left a respectable corpus of imaginative prose writings, criticism, and idiosyncratic poetry. Laforgue's urban imagery has been mentioned; and in his aleatory way, Eliot mined the poetry for "Prufrock."[19] It is generally agreed that Laforgue's characteristic tone, also mentioned, which different critics have described as "cosmic detachment," "gentlemanly despair" and "bittersweet dandyism," affected all Eliot's early poetry. Eliot's recognition of "a temperament akin to one's own" in Laforgue, "like an admired elder brother," was mentioned in the previous chapter. In discussions that illuminate the hoary subject of Laforgue's influence, three recent critics make the important corrective point implied in his simile, and consonant with his view of originality as development: in A. D. Moody's words, "The effect of his reading Laforgue was that he was galvanized into being himself."[20]

The previous chapter also proposed that Eliot's response to Laforgue's fraternal temperament is not his point in the passage. Instead, he subordinates his response to his interest in what he considers the "form of expression" corresponding to Laforgue's temperament: the French poet's combination of elegance and slanginess. Laforgue's "form of expression," he writes, "gives a clue to the discovery of one's own form," to "the poetic possibilities of my own idiom of speech" (*To Criticize the Critic,* p. 126). And that it was not the boulevardier's

18. Quoted from *The Criterion* IX (Jan., 1930) in *Eliot's Compound Ghost,* p. 97. The statement occurs in a review of *Baudelaire and the Symbolists* by Peter Quennell.

19. See, e.g., the pair of "declamations" by *"Le Monsieur"* and *"La Dame"* in *Le Concile fée-rique,"* and *"Solo de Lune"*; see also Howarth, p. 196.

20. Moody, p. 18. Schneider writes, "the mask that Laforgue had devised fitted Eliot nearly enough to point the way to his own" (p. 13). Gordon writes that he "transformed [Laforgue's] state of mind into something cooler, more relentless, that came from himself" (p. 30).

stance but the artist's "form"—not manner but method—that was of primary importance, is indicated by his statement thirty years before, in "The Metaphysical Poets" (1921), that Laforgue and Corbière "are nearer to the 'school of Donne' than any modern English poet," because all were "trying to find the verbal equivalent for states of mind and feeling" in a civilization of "great variety and complexity": "The poet must become more and more comprehensive, more allusive, more indirect, in order to force, to dislocate if necessary, language into his meaning" (*Selected Essays,* pp. 248-49).

The idea is as familiar to us, near the end of the century, as that of the hermetic work whose subject expresses itself. But "Prufrock" was created when the century had scarcely begun; the "states of mind and feeling" it comprises have a uniquely wide range among Eliot's early poems; and—the significant point— we know so from its diction. Laforgue's poetry provided the young Eliot with the "clue" for evolving a language of his own which would be equal to the task, adumbrated for him by James's fiction, of precisely rendering in all its complexity an experiencing consciousness.

In the quoted acknowledgment of debt to Laforgue in his introduction to the Pound volume, Eliot uses the word "form" differently from "form of expression": he derived "the form in which I began to write" not from a "clue to" diction ("idiom of speech"), but from "the study of" the "versification" of "Laforgue together with the later Elizabethan drama." Laforgue increasingly employed heavy rhyme in his poetry, often to ironic effect (as Eliot did in "Prufrock" far more than in his other early poems), and combined varied line-lengths and meters with Alexandrines. "The *vers libre* of Jules Laforgue," who was "certainly the most important technical innovator" in French poetry, Eliot wrote, "stretches, contracts, and distorts the traditional French measure as later Elizabethan and Jacobean poetry stretches, contracts, and distorts the blank verse measure." The discussion of invention and originality quoted from earlier begins three paragraphs later. A "technical innovator" does not, he declares, "invent technique ... because [in the phrase he uses in defining "true originality"] it is impossible" (p. x). But as with his functional diction in "Prufrock," so with his elastic versification in it, Eliot did not merely "imitate technique" developed by the innovators he cites: his debt to Laforgue and the English tradition (the "school of Donne" and the "later Elizabethan drama") is for providing the "clue" his own authentic "originality" used precisely to "develop technique."

Eliot insists that in poetry the true innovator never invents; instead, he or she "forces" and "stretches," "dislocates" and "distorts" what has been given into something new. But if what has been given is itself new, as James and Laforgue, for example, were new in his youth, then newness might be compounded—even, metaphorically, squared. Hence, the right individual talent could be devoted to tradition and vigorously decry "the poem which is absolutely original"; could not only be grateful for, but seek out, "congenial" influences to provide "clues" ("point the way"); and yet could actually "develop" what proved to be the harbinger of a wholly new English poetry. That is what the young T. S. Eliot seems to have done.

Finally, Laforgue provided the clue for—pointed the way to—the narrative strategy Eliot developed to achieve his neo-Jamesian objective of rendering directly an experiencing consciousness. And the historical conjunction involved is especially significant of "Prufrock's" place in the history of Modernism in English literature.

When *Ulysses* appeared in 1922, its most accessible part proved to be its most sensational: Molly Bloom's concluding chapter. The new narrative strategy of representing consciousness as language had been introduced to readers of avant-garde literature by the published earlier chapters of *Ulysses* and the first novels of Dorothy Richardson. Molly's stream-of-consciousness, uninterrupted inner ("interior") monologue, helped fix that strategy as the most distinctive innovation of modernist fiction. Ignoring Richardson and feasible antecedents in earlier English novelists, Joyce attributed the invention of *monologue intér-ieur,* as his friend Valery Larbaud named the new narrative strategy, to a novel by the still-living late nineteenth-century French writer Edouard Dujardin, and thereby made the old man famous and appreciative ("James Joyce, *maitre glo-rieux . . . qui a dit au mort . . . Relève-toi Lazare*"); the story is relatively familiar.[21]

But the *monologue intérieur* is more complex. Symons wrote, "It is an art of the nerves, this art of Laforgue"; Karl Robert Eduard von Hartmann's *The Philosophy of the Unconscious (Philosophie des Unbewussten)* "became a veritable bible to him"; and Laforgue's friend Gustav Kahn drew attention to his attempts to reproduce thought, especially in *Dernier Vers.*[22] These attempts usually take the form of sudden apostrophe or emotional interjection, as in the popular *"Solo de Lune."* But however qualified, Laforgue's endeavor to supplant discourse with the direct verbal representation of a mental state, is apparent. In his comprehensive essay on "Eliot and Ninteenth-century French Poetry," Francis Scarfe writes,

> Laforgue invented a new kind of dramatic monologue, usually known as the interior or internal monologue . . .

and then affirms Eliots (and others') literary indebtedness, and the historical conjunction:

> From Laforgue, his close friend, Edouard Dujardin, without acknowledgement, developed the technique of his short novel *Les Lauriers sont coupés.* This technique was taken up by Valery Larbaud and James Joyce . . . . Eliot, long before them, had taken the form directly from Laforgue himself . . . .[23]

Laforgue is not mentioned in a book on the "technique" Dujardin published after his resurrection, although its *index des écrivains cité* covers six pages.[24] However, the bulk of Laforgue's poetry had been written and published (in three

21. See, e.g., Richard Ellmann, *James Joyce,* rev. ed. (New York: Oxford UP, 1982), p. 520n.

22. Symons, p. 60; *Selected Writings of Jules Laforgue* (New York: Grove, 1956), pp. 6, 84; see also p. 21.

23. In *Eliot in Perspective: A Symposium,* ed. Graham Martin (New York: Humanities, 1970), pp. 45–61, p. 53.

24. Edouard Dujardin, *Le Monoloque Intérieur, son apparation, ses origines, sa place dans l' oeuvre de James Joyce* (Paris: Messein, 1931). "[I]l a été ébauché dans les Lauriers sont coupés et réalisé dans Ulysse" (p. 73).

volumes) when he died the year *Les Lauriers sont coupés* was published (1887); and the two friends read and discussed each other's work. Apparently if Dujardin "developed the technique," it was with Laforgue "pointing the way." And Eliot "had taken . . . from Laforgue" only a few years before Joyce did (if he did) from Dujardin, a "form" his originality metamorphosed in "Prufrock." Other of his early poems, "Portrait of a Lady" and "Rhapsody on a Windy Night" especially, have a Laforgian-Jamesian focus on the speaker's consciousness; but only "Prufrock" is a direct enactment of mental process, constituted by the verbal representation of the phenomenon itself—denominated by Henry's brother William James the stream—of consciousness.[25]

"Prufrock" inaugurates the focus and the narrative technique that were to become so prominent in modernist English literature. In fact, it anticipates the most sensational and famous instance of the use of that technique. Their joint use of it constitutes one of the relations of Eliot and Joyce, the subject of this book: the last chapter of *Ulysses* is, precisely like "Prufrock," (1) an uninterrupted verbal representation ("stream") of consciousness that is simultaneously (2) a soliloquy, expressing (3) a conflict between alternative attitudes the outcome of which is (4) fundamental to the character's destiny.

To attribute the origin of Molly Bloom's soliloquy to "Prufrock" would be specious—imagining a toad in Joyce's luxuriant garden—anyway; but the present historical concern is much broader than the attribution of sources. And evidence of the role of "Prufrock" in the advent of a new kind of literature abounds. Taking Molly's soliloquy as reference, and looking backward, "Prufrock" has a special relation both to a story Molly's creator wrote in 1905, and to the earlier portrayal of psychological bifurcation by various writers of the *fin-de-siècle,* more than once by both Wilde and Conrad. Eliot was to call the portrayal in Laforgue's poetry "a *dédoublement* of the personality."[26]

In "A Painful Case" Joyce presented, in a dreary urban setting, an emotionally blocked middle-class man, radically isolated as a consequence, aware of his predicament and suffering in it, who nevertheless himself has frustrated an opportunity for rescue. Joyce was twenty-three, Eliot's age when he finished "Prufrock," six years later.

Implicit in the literary motif of doubleness is psychomachia; and its pertinence to the spirit of that time was exemplified in William Sharp's creation of Fiona Macleod, and in the preoccupation with masks of Sharp's friend Yeats. In *Aurélia,* Gérard de Nerval wrote *"Une idée terrible me vint: 'L'homme est double,' me dis-je."* Among other writers of the time, Laforgue himself, in the phrase *"Mon Moi" ("Dimanches");* Nietzsche, *"Ich bin ein doppelgänger" (Ecce Homo,* I, 3); and Rimbaud, *"Je est un autre,"* express psychomachia—a psychological situation, expressed by writers with whom Eliot recognized an affinity, at the very center of "Prufrock."

25. Discussing the "continuous nature" of "consciousness" in "Chapter IX. The Stream of Thought" (1: 224–90) in *The Principles of Psychology,* 2 vols. (1890; New York: Holt, 1902), James proposes, in italics, *"In talking of it hereafter, let us call it the stream of thought, of consciousness, or of subjective life"* (p. 239).

26. T. S. Eliot, "A Commentary," *Criterion* XII (1933), 470; quoted in Gray, p. 68. The portrayal in "Prufrock" is discussed in the last section of the book; see pp. 242–45.

Like the final chapter of *Ulysses,* these examples of cultural and literary relation are elements in the historical situation of "Prufrock," further establishing the role it played as harbinger of, and archetypal "development" of the received tradition into, a new poetry—the role which helps explain its special canonical status in the literature that has dominated most of this century.

Leavis's declaration in 1932 that it "represents a complete break with the nineteenth-century tradition, and a new start" is a symptom of its historical role, as is G. S. Fraser's in 1948 that "As the Russians all came out of Gogol's *Overcoat,* we might say that we all came out of Prufrock's drawingroom. Nearly every important innovation in the English verse of the last thirty years is implicit in this poem."[27]

But Fraser's allowing the declaration to stand in a book published in 1977 is historical confirmation more than symptom. In the alembic of "Prufrock" Eliot combined the ingredients bequeathed him with others he found about him, and distilled what he had to hand into something new and intoxicating.

27. F. R. Leavis, *New Bearings in English Poetry* (1932; Ann Arbor: U of Michigan P, 1960 [1964]), p. 75; "A Language by Itself," *Symposium,* p. 175, and Fraser, p. 106. The essay and statement also appear in Fraser's *Vision and Rhetoric* (London: Faber, 1959).

3

An Old-Irish Ghost in *Ulysses*

One of the most dramatic contrasts between Eliot and Joyce was their relative candor about relations with predecessors/precursors. The previous chapter mentioned Joyce's questionable attribution of the origin of the inner monologue to Edouard Dujardin. In the next chapter, I infer major relations he never intimated, of *Ulysses* and an antecedent, equally famous novel not normally associated with it: fundamental characteristics it seems to share uniquely with *Crime and Punishment.* This chapter concerns a minor ghost in *Ulysses,* an apparition raised subsequently—although subtly—by the author himself.

Joyce raises the Old-Irish ghost in *Finnegans Wake* I. The trial of "Festy King" in its fourth section concludes with the familiar charge that Shem is a sham ("Shun the Punman!"), having plagiarized the crucial letter in evidence— as some Irish critics said of the bulk of Joyce's own most recent work, *Ulysses*— from Irish sources, accompanied by a catalogue of the sources. "From dark Rosa Lane a sigh and a weep," it begins (James Clarence Mangan's familiar translation of the Irish lyric begins "O, my Dark Rosaleen / Do not sigh, do not weep!"); and it proceeds through references to Seumas O'Sullivan and a minor poet, A. M. Sullivan ("I am the Sullivan"), Maeve (Mab) and her "fairy forts" ("Mebbe fair efforts"), Charles Lever and Samuel Lover (the given names are reversed and punned on, not the surnames), and other Irish subjects and writers, to conclude with a group of men with similar-sounding names who have generally eluded identification: "from Pat Mullen, Tom Mallon, Dan Meldon, Don Maldon a slickstick picnic made in Moate by Muldoons. The solid man saved by his sillied woman."[1]

The phrase "the solid man," however, does identify William Muldoon (1852-1933), inventor of the medicine ball, trainer of John L. Sullivan, and organizer of the New York Police Athletic Association, an American wrestler and physical culturist of Irish descent who was so called in his later years (Edward Van Every, *Muldoon, the Solid Man of Sport* [New York: Stokes, 1929]). Consequently, "Muldoons" would seem to be plural; and if that is so, Mullen, Mal-

---

1. The passage in on pp. 93–94 of *Finnegans Wake* (London: Faber, 1949).

lon, *et al.,* to be the elusive "Muldoons" referred to. Furthermore, Joyce's allusion to "the solid man" is not out of place following the group of names: those names are, like "Muldoon" itself, modern variants of the name of an ancient hero, "Maelduin"—instances of "Maelduin-again." However unlikely may be any debt to Seumas O'Sullivan or Charles Lever, Joyce seems to be attesting subtly in this passage that the early Irish story of a truly solid man has a significant relation to the action and protagonist of *Ulysses.*

I

Three specimens remain extant of the *"Imram"* or "voluntary sea expedition" story, one of the chief types of ancient Irish literature, also known in other orally-based literatures. (As with so much from the Old Irish, the surviving texts are Middle-Irish.) The well-known medieval "Voyage of Saint Brendan the Navigator" is thought to be partly derived from one of these ancient "Voyages," which also seems to be the most familiar to Irishmen and English-speaking people generally of the past century, "The Voyage of (the Curragh of) Maelduin" (Mael Duin).[2] Its relative familiarity apparently originates in the inclusion of an English prose version, "The Voyage of Maildun," in the Irish Folklorist Patrick Weston Joyce's *Old Celtic Romances,* first published in 1879. The next year Tennyson published in his new volume, *Ballads and Poems,* "The Voyage of Maeldune," a poem based on P. W. Joyce's piece, although it is much briefer, more lush, and more bloody than its source.[3] Evidence of its familiarity to Irish writers ranges from the young Yeats's recommendation of *Old Celtic Romances* in print in 1895 and his use of a spelling similar to P. W. Joyce's (Maeldun) in *The Celtic Twilight* (1893) to one of Louis MacNeice's last works, "The Mad Islands" (1962), a modernized radio play of the Voyage of "Muldoon, who has a quest."[4] In an introduction, MacNeice refers to things "Tennyson did in his 'Voyage of Maeldune,'" which he wrote in 1881 [sic] after reading P. W. Joyce's *Old Celtic Romances,* where the story was first published in English" (p. 8).

Old Celtic Romances had gone through a series of three "revised and enlarged" editions with a total of four printings by the time another Joyce began

2. See, e.g., Myles Dillon, *Early Irish Literature* (Chicago: U of Chicago P, 1948), pp. 124, 125. The other two extant *Imrama,* presumably of an original seven, are those of "Snedgus" and "Lochan" (or "The Sons of O'Corra"). The "Voyage of Bran" is really an "Adventure" *(Echtrae),* or visit to the other world.

3. See, e.g., *The Poetic and Dramatic Works of Alfred Lord Tennyson,* ed. W. J. Rolfe (Boston: Houghton, 1898), pp. 479–80; and *Old Celtic Romances,* 2nd and 3rd eds., p. xiii. (For information about editions of *Old Celtic Romances,* see n. 5 below.)

4. In a letter printed in *The Daily Express* (Dublin), Yeats listed *Old Celtic Romances* among thirty "Irish books ["my neighbors"] . . . should read"; he and the folklorist had corresponded as early as 1889. See, e.g., *The Letters of W. B. Yeats,* ed. Allan Wade (New York: Macmillan, 1955), pp. 96, 100, 246-47. For "Maeldun," see, e.g., the beginning of "The Friends of the People of Faery," W. B. Yeats, *Mythologies* (1959; New York: Macmillan-Collier, 1969), p. 117. The radio play is printed in Louis MacNeice, *The Mad Islands and The Administrator* (London: Faber, 1964).

work on *Ulysses* in 1914, for the period was that during which the Irish cultural revival and nationalist literary movement dominated Jame Joyce's native country.[5] There is more precise evidence suggesting that he knew the folklorist's "Maildun": had he ignored it initially, he most likely would have read Tennyson's poem when a young man, and that could have led him to it; in 1909 he advised a correspondent searching for the text of a traditional Irish song to get in touch with "my namesake, Dr. P. W. Joyce"; another letter reveals that he owned at least one of P. W. Joyce's books;[6] he alluded to a second book in "Gas from a Burner"; and it was the opinion of a fellow-writer and lifelong friend who shared the cultural environment of his youth, Padraic Colum, that he almost certainly would have read the English version of the *Imram* by his "namesake."[7]

Although shortly after the publication of *Ulysses* Joyce wrote about Irish with some authority in a letter to Valery Larbaud, his command of the language was not good enough, according to Colum, to have coped with the Middle-Irish texts of "Maelduin";[8] and it cannot be said definitely that he was familiar with P. W. Joyce's "Maildun." However, grounds for inferring the indebtedness of *Ulysses* to the eighth- or ninth-century narrative exist: (1) the passage in *Finnegans Wake* establishes that he at least knew *of* an Irish work about a "Muldoon" when writing it; (2) the evidence presented above makes his familiarity with "Maildun" very likely; (3) after "Maildun," other versions and accounts of the Maelduin *Imram* were published in books about folklore and Irish legend (including a translation by Lady Gregory in her popular *Book of Saints and Wonders*); and finally, (4) given the references elsewhere in *Finnegans Wake* to his previous works and to hostile criticism of them, and his penchant for subtly disguised autobiographical revelation ("Shem is as short for Shemus as Jem is joky for Jacob"), certain significant similarities between elements of the *Imram* and elements of *Ulysses* suggest strongly that the passage in *Finnegans Wake* is an acknowledgment of his indebtness to it.

The fact of significant similarities is (inevitably) circumstantial evidence of a relation between "Maelduin" and *Ulysses,* but evidence as tangible as is a trout in milk. If the truth is that Joyce did not know the *Imram* in any form, the relation is only that of a striking analogue. But there are good reasons for believing that an eighth- or ninth-century Irish spirit walks the pages of his novel.

5. The second edition, of 1894, had a version of the *Imram* of Lochan added; the third, of 1898, 1907, and 1914 (subsequently, also 1920), a version of the Deirdre story added to that. All were published in London, some in Dublin and New York as well. A new edition was published in Dublin by Talbot in 1961 and New York by Devin-Adair in 1962.

6. *Letters of James Joyce,* I, ed. Stuart Gilbert (New York: Viking, 1957), p. 66, and III, ed. Richard Ellmann (New York: Viking, 1966), p. 343.

7. The poet and playwright also wrote about Joyce, chiefly in his memoir with Mary M. Colum, *Our Friend James Joyce* (London: Gollancz, 1959). Colum's observation, and that about Joyce's command of Irish, were made in response to questions during a conversation in 1967; he died in January 1972.

8. The letter is dated July 28, 1924; *Letters* I: 217–18. See also *James Joyce,* pp. 61 and 655, for Joyce's limited knowledge of Irish.

II

Although the use to which Joyce puts *The Odyssey* in *Ulysses* is immeasurably more extensive, he does overtly exploit another classic story of a returned wanderer. The story of Sinbad contributes only incidentally, until he uses it to indicate what Leopold Bloom has accomplished in his wanderings. The one plainly named figure among those with whom the novel says Bloom "has travelled," just before it turns to Molly, is the first in the catalogue, "Sinbad the Sailor." In the subsequent few words Bloom is said, with a late-Victorian phrase signifying something impossible, to have returned with a "Sinbad the Sailor roc's . . . egg"; whereupon, as though to signify he has achieved that very return to one's wife after long absence which a few pages before he had regarded as "impossible," his final chapter ends with the roc's egg in their marriage bed, in the form of the large dot (737).

Maelduin's voyage takes him to thirty-one islands, on each of which he and his crew see or experience "marvels" that have analogues in the other *Imrama* and in such similar stories as that of Jason and the Argonauts; so analogues in both the story of Sinbad and *The Odyssey* should be no surprise. However, it is at least interesting that the sole analogue to "Maelduin" the Sinbad story contains is the roc. And it is either sheer accident, or significant for *Ulysses,* that in contrast to occasional analogues with Maelduin's experiences in the ancient narratives of voyagers other than Sinbad, the kinship between the Irish poem (its extant form is actually both prose and verse) and Homer's is strikingly close.

In both, the basic action of "wanderings" leads to the righting of a wrong done to the hero's family. As does *The Odyssey,* "The Voyage of Maelduin" opens with a young man (Maelduin himself) who is impelled to undertake a quest out of devotion to a father whom he does not know. Odysseus fails to achieve a rapid journey home from Troy because, with the very people of Ithaca in sight, his crew disobey Eumaeus's injunction against untying the bag of winds he has given them, and the released winds blow the ships far away. Maelduin's search for his father's murderer is thwarted in a very similar way: through the fault of three of his companions. When he sets out, his three foster brothers oblige him to "violate" the instructions given him by a druid; after only two days, his curragh approaches an island; he overhears a man on the shore boast of his father's murder many years before, and his quest seems over—when "the wind arose," and a storm sends him on his wanderings (pp. 117-18).[9]

Maelduin's "adventures" themselves involve boulders being hurled at their escaping curragh by a giant monster who had hoped to eat its occupants, and similar bombardments on three other occasions by a monster, a giant man, and a giant woman; encountering Laestrygonian-like voracious animals which eat at each other; landing on islands like that of the lotus-eaters, which members of the crew are unwilling to leave, and an island of intoxicating fruit, reminiscent of the sirens as well as of the lotus-eaters; a prophecy that all but one man will

9. Page references for the *Imram* are to the three editions 1879–1920 of *Old Celtic Romances.*

return home safe (the inverse of the prophecy of Tiresias in *The Odyssey*); the underworld (under the sea); a Scylla-like ravenous sea monster; and a woman who—as though combining Circe and Calypso—has magical powers, develops a special interest in Maelduin, entertains him and his crew in her palace for a year, promises them eternal youth and "for ever a life of ease and pleasure" (p. 153), and is refused because of their longing to return home.

These similarities with *The Odyssey* suggest why the author of *Ulysses* would have had an interest in "The Voyage of Maelduin"; but they need not signify any special relation between it and his novel. Such a relation is indicated more positively by elements which the two Irish works have in common, and do not share with *The Odyssey*.

Some of those elements are worth mentioning only as part of the complex. For example: a horserace is vital to the action of *Ulysses,* and a horserace occurs in "Maelduin"; and, at one point in both novel and poem a small repast appeases hunger for a long period. Of a bit more interest are two specific formal similarities between novel and poem. The first concerns the eighteen undesignated chapters of *Ulysses.* Unlike all extant texts of early Irish tales, including all others of "Maelduin," the oldest text of the poem, in the eleventh-century manuscript "The Book of the Dun Cow," is divided into (thirty-five) untitled sections, a fact P. W. Joyce notes in his preface to *Old Celtic Romances.*[10] The second is that, unlike *The Odyssey,* and precisely like Joyce's use of *The Odyssey* 198in *Ulysses,* "Maelduin" allots to each "adventure," no matter how brief, a separate section.

A more important similarity is the names of the poem's and novel's heroes. Odysseus's first calling himself *"'outis'"*—"no one"—then boastfully identifying himself to the cyclops (who promptly reveals he is Poseidon's son), is crucial to the action of Homer's poem. *'Outis* is the first part of a pun on Odysseus's name (*'outis-Zeus);* and his denying the divine part of himself is significant for Bloom's very different conduct with the cyclopean "citizen" in *Ulysses.* But whereas Odysseus's name is totally unlike Bloom's, the Germanic name "Leopold" means "bold for the people," and the Irish "Maelduin" means "chief of the fort."

It is one profound similarity, however, that suggests strongly the indebtedness Joyce may have been declaring obliquely in *Finnegans Wake.* Perhaps the single most striking contrast between Homer's Achaean hero and his modern Dubliner is the conduct of each when he returns to his defiled home: Bloom will make no move against Boylan himself. He hates violence; and he knows that he was not innocently wronged by Boylan, as Odysseus was by the suitors. For Molly consented readily, and ultimately, he himself was to blame: he sees himself as "the matrimonial violator" (733). The home of the man who murdered Maelduin's father is only two days from Ireland along a known route. And so, when he finally arrives back at that neighboring island, Maelduin regards himself as having "returned" from his "wanderings." Like Antinous and his fellow-

---

10. Page viii in the editions of 1879–1920; it was omitted from the recent edition. The sections of the poem are numbered in the margin.

suitors in *The Odyssey,* Maelduin's enemy is feasting among his company. And Maelduin does not take revenge.

While *The Odyssey* is characteristic of primitive heroic poetry in its violence and bloodshed, "The Voyage of Maelduin," similar to *The Odyssey* in so many respects, is an unusual work for a heroic culture (even a Christianized one). Almost every man in Maelduin's company (of sixty in most versions) returns home safely; a final holocaust—for reasons, and in circumstances, so much like those of *The Odyssey* as to almost certainly invoke the contrast—is avoided; and above all, the hero does not wreak vengeance on the man who grievously wronged his family. A critic contrasts Joyce in *Ulysses* "to almost all writers who have contrived such parallels," because he

> picked not the countinuing doom of the house of Atreus or the horrors which follow for generation upon generation in the line of Thebes but the one [Greek] myth which strikingly ends in resolved human happiness—the journeyings of the wanderer who . . . reaches his home and recovers his wife.[11]

Joyce may have further affirmed a civility, which the seventh chapter discusses more extensively, by subtly implicating a "myth" of his own people that was remarkably like *The Odyssey,* except for one conspicuous fact: it was far more congenial to his pacific nature than just about any other heroic story, *The Odyssey* included. Toward the end of his quest, Maelduin meets an old penitent who tells him that it will be over soon, but then enjoins him against taking revenge "in any way" on the man who killed his father, saying:

> As God has delivered you from the many dangers you have passed through, though you were very guilty . . . ; so you forgive your enemy the crime he committed against you. (p. 171)

And in the affinity of this with Joyce's treatment of Bloom, especially of Bloom's return to his defiled home, one can detect the ghostly apparition, among those with whom Bloom had "travelled" on his odyssey, of the man who eschews revenge to announce, with relief, "It is I, Mailduin, returned safely from all my wanderings" (p. 176).

In *James Joyce and the Making of* Ulysses (London: Grayson, 1934), Frank Budgen reports Joyce calling Bloom "a complete man—a good man" (p. 18). That like Maelduin and Odysseus he also is a "solid" man seems to be declared in the revelatory passage from *Finnegans Wake.*

William Muldoon had and was divorced from two wives, and so scarcely was "saved" by either. Maelduin has *no* "woman." And Penelope cannot in any sense be called "sillied," being neither silly, nor sullied, nor made the object of Odysseus's silliness. On the other hand, the end of Bloom's story seems to be that he becomes a "solid man" (recovers his full manhood) and returns, whereupon the sullied wife toward whom he had acted in such a monumentally silly way deliberates, and reaches the decision which is his salvation. Who but "Leopold" can be the particular variant of "Muldoon" whom Shem ostensibly pro-

11. Anon., "Which Man, in Which Novel," *Times Literary Supplement* (May 11, 1967), p. 400.

duced by plagiary—"The solid man saved by his sillied woman" whom Joyce identifies?

So far reasonable inference takes one, although in the form of a (rhetorical) question. The chief question remains still: the ancient Irish ghost continues to stalk the pages of *Ulysses*. The described similarities do not constitute positive evidence that the *Imram* truly influenced—any more as congenial predecessor than as threatening precursor—Joyce's modernist novel. But what is the historical relation of the two works? Did Joyce indeed draw from the story of Maelduin, which so strikingly mediates between that of Homer's Odysseus and that of his Dublin protagonist, when he was writing *Ulysses*? Alternatively, did he become familiar with it very shortly thereafter, recognize its relevance, and for that less valid reason conclude the catalogue of Shem's plagiaries as he did when composing the passage in *Finnegans Wake*? The latter case would make "The Voyage of Maelduin" an Old Irish analogue to *Ulysses* in certain formal and substantive respects. According to Shem's accusers, it has the more instrumental relation of a true source. The evidence remains (inevitably) circumstantial. Even the testimony is facetious—and is not explicitly the author's. But to be facetious is to be jocose—and Shem is as short for Shemus as Jem is joky for Jacob.

4

Dostoevsky, Joyce, and God

In good Aristotelian fashion, the *dénouement* of James's *The Ambassadors* follows directly from a *peripeteia*-accompanied-by-*anagnorisis* when its plot is at the point of greatest complication. These occur in a linked sequence of three chapters, immediately after Lambert Strether has finally decided, and acted—at the likely price of his own future security and possible happiness—to support Chad Newsome's inclination toward Madame de Vionnet. The first of the linked three, Chapter XXX, presents Strether taking a day of respite in the country. The chapter ends abruptly; and XXXI begins (with the words "what he saw": *anagnorisis*) when he comes upon the couple—who pretend that they too are down only for the day. The "sequel" (James's word) to that blatant coincidence develops directly. In XXXII Madame de Vionnet asks Strether to call, and he learns whom he must really try to protect, who is the spider in the relationship and who the fly.

The crucial element in this tight sequence of *anagnorisis* and *peripeteia*, and so in a sense the crux of the whole plot of the novel James's "Preface" designates "quite the best, 'all around,' of all my productions," is the catalytic incident for which James created the central chapter of the three by an abrupt interruption— that apparently fortuitous meeting in the country I have called a blatant coincidence. Joyce's relation to Dostoevsky (and God) derives above all from coincidences no less blatant in—and no less crucial to (cruxes of) the plots of—two works no less distinguished: *Crime and Punishment* and *Ulysses*.

I

That a significant relation exists between Joyce and, of all earlier writers, Dostoevsky, may seem unlikely. Anglo-Saxon criticism of Dostoevsky's fiction conventionally characterizes it as powerful, intense, driven, etc., above all as almost evangelically religious—and as having the artistic deficiencies in form and finish considered appropriate to its distinctive qualities. So regarded, it could not seem more unlike the fiction of Modernism's consummate craftsman-artist/Irish *eiron*, in his turn conventionally considered skeptical of all belief—and above all too elusive ever to be caught asserting any. However, the patronizing conventional view of Dostoevsky's craftsmanship is not shared by most central European or Soviet critics.[1] Nor was it shared—recently published evidence suggests—by James Joyce.[2]

At about the time Joyce completed *Ulysses*, the partial publication of which had already brought him acclaim in modernist literary circles, his son Giorgio pronounced *Crime and Punishment* the greatest novel ever written. It was a queer title, Joyce responded to the neat thrust of filial rebellion, for a book that contained neither crime nor punishment.[3] If "contained neither" is a rhetorical exaggeration, and literally it would be inaccurate, this was perceptive criticism of a novel then new to English-language readers.

But its dismissive tone has seemed to confirm the absence of affinity between the two writers; and for half a century no strong evidence or testimony existed to contradict it.[4] Then in 1974, an Irish intimate of Joyce's named Arthur Power published an account of their friendship in Paris during the 1920s which quotes observations by Joyce on literature and writers which are more extensive than any previously available. Although the time that had elapsed warrants skepticism, above all about specific words and phrases attributed to Joyce, in the foreword the prominent Joyce scholar who edited *Conversations With James Joyce* expresses complete confidence in Power's report.

The friendship began while *Ulysses* was in press, and Arthur Power quotes Joyce arguing the superiority of "modern" to both "classical" and "romantic" literature; praising not only writers one would expect like Yeats, but Proust and Gide and—contrary to other evidence—Eliot; discussing very knowledgeably (throughout almost all of Chapter VI) Pushkin, Turgenev, Tolstoy, Chekhov, and Dostoevsky; and declaring that Dostoevsky "is the man more than any other who has created modern prose, and intensified it to its present-day pitch." He is "great," Power reports Joyce as saying, has "genius," and "many people" consider *The Brothers Karamazov* "one of the greatest novels ever written. Certainly it made a deep impression on me." (As so often with sons, the spur of

1. See Edward W. Wasiolek, "On the Structure of *Crime and Punishment*," *PMLA* 74 (1959), 131–36, 131–32; a negative variant is in his preface to *Dostoevsky: the Major Fiction* (Cambridge, MA: MIT P, 1964). The first chapter of Mikhail Bakhtin's classic *Problems of Dostoevsky's Poetics*, tr. R. W. Rotsel (n. p., [Ann Arbor, MI]: Ardis, 1973), is a discussion of contemporary German and Soviet criticism. (It was first published in 1929, as *Problems of Dostoevsky's Art: Problemy tvorchestva Dostoevskogo*.) The patronizing view also has not been shared by certain American critics, among them George Gibian, Michael Holquist, the late Ernest J. Simmons, and Wasiolek himself.

2. Joyce's familiarity with that craftsmanship was limited to Constance Garnett's then new translations. My own familiarity with *Crime and Punishment* is limited to her translation and two more recent ones: I cannot read Russian. But my limitation causes my experience of *Crime and Punishment* to correspond to Joyce's.

3. Reported by Samuel Beckett; see *James Joyce*, p. 485 and p. 787 n.5.

4. Joyce took Garnett's translation of *The Idiot* with him when he moved from Trieste to Zurich; he bought her translation of *Crime and Punishment* between its publication in 1916 and 1920 (i.e., while he was working on *Ulysses*). See "Appendix: Joyce's Library in 1920," in Richard Ellmann, *The Consciousness of Joyce* (New York: Oxford UP, 1977). Along with most other important books of the time, it was alluded to in *Finnegans Wake* (e.g., pp. 235, 489). Budgen's book reports that Joyce compared Dostoevsky unfavorably to Rousseau (p. 184).

Giorgio's rebellion seems to have been the anxiety of influence.) In another place, Power quotes Joyce linking Dostoevsky with one of his heroes: "the best authors of any period have always been the prophets: the Tolstoys, the Dostoevskis, the Ibsens—those who brought something new into literature."[5]

In his preface Power says each of the "talks I had with Joyce" is "reconstruct[ed] . . . from notes taken . . . after spending an evening with him" (p. 9). Even if his late report is only approximate, it still suggests that the association of *Crime and Punishment* and *Ulysses* may not be preposterous. Yet is it sound? Great novels impose themselves permanently on one's imagination and memory; and imagination and memory will suggest similarities between great novels that one has only imagined, or created by misremembrance. In both philosophy and artistic practice the two writers differed widely. Joyce was a former socialist and a secular libertarian, while Dostoevsky was a theocratic pan-Slav who doubted humankind's capacity for freedom. (It is because they so eloquently express that doubt, perhaps, that the *Notes from Underground* and Ivan Karamazov's "Grand Inquisitor" parable have so affected Western readers in this century.) Religion, a central concern in Dostoevsky's work, was not so in Joyce's; and Dostoevsky treated it more profoundly as well as more respectfully than did Joyce. His portrayal of reality is essentially pathetic; the mature Joyce's, comic. Finally, the difference in their artistic practice could not be greater: Dostoevsky repeated himself obsessively in novel after novel, while Joyce may have been more concerned about avoiding doing so than about anything else.

The discrepancies between the work of the eastern Orthodox evangelist and that of the western humanist artificer born after he died are numerous, and obvious. Nevertheless, with *Crime and Punishment* and *Ulysses* they built successive edifices—each in his own way—on the same ground and largely with the same materials.

Both novels are specifically renditions of the modern city: maps have been printed in critical studies of them; and in both, most of the action occurs either in the streets (usually at specified locations) or just off them, in places of refreshment or entertainment, public buildings, shops, bookstalls. Joyce's boast that the Dublin of 1904 could be rebuilt from the text of *Ulysses* was not empty; for example, dozens of landmarks, including seven public monuments in less than four pages (92–95), are identified as the Dignam funeral procession passes them in the sixth chapter. In addition to the topography, the novels portray in detail the daily life, citizenry, and social fabric of the capital cities of distinct and impoverished nations at the opposite ends of Europe—apparently its two most impoverished nations, in fact.

Notable as they are, it is not in these general similarities that the significant relation between the two novels consists, but in a truly unique complex of particular ones. Both present the stories of young male intellectuals at crises of utter desperation in their lives; furthermore, the psychological/spiritual predicaments of these young men are almost identical, have almost identical causes, and even-

5. Arthur Power, *Conversations with James Joyce,* ed. Clive Hart (London: Millington, 1974), pp. 58–60, 53. For the time and circumstances of their meeting, see pp. 28–32.

tually resolve very much the same way. Both novels confront their chief characters—Leopold Bloom as well as Rodion Raskolnikov and Stephen Dedalus—with fundamental, vital, choices, formulated in identical binary terms of acceptance and resistance, submission and self-assertion. Finally, in both novels these characters (and others) must make the vital choice—decide whether to submit or struggle—in one or the other of identical alternative kinds of situation: the alterable circumstances created by other humans, and the inalterable conditions of existence imposed by—the attribution is made in both—God.

Even more striking than the congruent concerns of the two novels are the similar formulations they use to embody those concerns in character and action. Not only their respective troubled young men, but also representative secondary characters, are similar and used to serve similar purposes. At crucial points in both, the action portrays coincidences plotted to serve the same ends; and in both, those coincidences themselves become an important subject.

Drinking in the maternity hospital in *Ulysses*, Stephen is badly frightened by a thunderstorm because God could punish him by such a "crack of doom" (395). To the end of his life, Joyce spurned the Church into which he was baptized, and every other. But a secularist need not be an atheist; and the fear which he had, also to the end of his life, that lightning would strike *him*, suggests a belief—given Stephen's reason for a similar fear—that such a co-incidence would not be an accident. And "brings us by a commodius vicus of recirculation back to" the coincidences crucial to the plots of *Crime and Punishment* and *Ulysses*.

They are important because of what they signify. When I first published *The Argument of* Ulysses two decades ago, reviews treated its delineation of religious statement in *Ulysses* sometimes gently, but always firmly, as akin to a social lapse caused by deficient breeding.[6] Now, the (quaint?) prejudice about what James Joyce would and would not affirm in his novel has a powerful ally in the popular critical view that nowhere among its ambiguities and self-subvertings does *Ulysses* affirm at all—that it never signifies simply. Critical fashions aside, instances of plural and contradictory signification do abound in *Ulysses*; and some exist in *Crime and Punishment*. Hence, it is possible to argue that ambivalence toward God, in the minds of Dostoevsky and Joyce (especially the notoriously-lapsed Irish Catholic's) has caused what the crucial coincidences signify to be subverted by elements—in *Ulysses* at least, if not in both novels-as-texts—whose contrary signification can be deconstructed. The following pages are intended to show that this argument would be more subtle than sound.

A sounder argument against the significance I attribute to coincidences in the action of *Ulysses* would challenge my designating it a novel. The study of Joyce's notebooks, drafts and proofsheets that commenced more than two decades ago has established beyond reasonable doubt the fundamental changes *Ulysses* underwent during composition: as he worked, Joyce increasingly syncretized, with an initial narrative not too different from his earlier fiction, a poly-

---

6. See, e.g., the reviews in *Times Literary Supplement* (May 23, 1968), p. 526; and *Hudson Review* 21 (1968), 382–83. In *Argument*, see esp. pp. 60–62, 165–75, 216–17, 257–60, 280–84, 299–301, 333–55, 373–82, 387–93, 452–58.

phonic verbal composition, to make *Ulysses* the special compound it is, of "symbolic structure" (alternative terms used recently are image/patterns/language/symbol) and "human drama" (the complementary terms are, respectively, drama/story/character/story). Those changes are discussed more fully in the last section of the book (pp. 262–63), as is the tendency of earlier critics to belittle one of the two elements of the compound, and to write of *Ulysses* as either a novel with ornamental complications, or a "poem" (as some called it) with a trivial action (pp. 264–68). Today critics avoid that myopia by "enjoy[ing] the drama of the alternatives," with its wealth of plural and contradictory signification.[7]

However, a vital part of Joyce's ostensible novel-as-symbol seems to me exempt from the enjoyable drama. Again in the last section, I discuss in its theoretical context the grounds of exemption (pp. 271–72). *What* is exempt is the sequence of events—actions, speeches and thoughts—Joyce caused to occur. *Ulysses* embodies a metalanguage of fiction that can never be equivocated by an author, only—at considerable risk to his creation—trivialized. Its metalanguage is that sequence of things Joyce chose to make the language of *Ulysses* (explicitly if eloquently) represent as distinctly *happening* in it. His drama of alternatives has been enjoyed at the neglect of the eloquent metalanguage of events that transcends alternative effects of his language, and that constitutes no less than the significant action of a novel. Among the most articulate of those events are the coincidences he devised and made crucial to his plot.

A persistent tradition—ranging from certain Attic plays based on Hellenic legends of *anangkē* and *nemesis*, through certain novels by Hardy, to Faulkner's *Absalom, Absalom*—comprises fictions of catastrophe in which blatant coincidence has a significance that is equivocal and/or is controverted by other elements, such as the operation of free choice. But a second tradition involving blatant coincidence, at least as old as the stories of Joseph and Moses, comprises fictions of success and happiness; and in it, desirable blatant coincidence is presented implicitly but without equivocation as a mimesis, not of lucky accident in life, but of more or less deserved cosmic benevolence. That implied transcendental explanation of often outrageous fortuities in a plot is fundamental to Romance, and (presumably reinforced by the Leibnizian doctrine satirized in *Candide*) to many of the fictions of the European Enlightenment.

The crucial plot coincidences of that second tradition are so overtly and unequivocally the manifestation of a benevolent Providence as to have caused pointed rejoinders—metaphysical counterstatements precisely by way of plot—by writers from Sade (as in the end of *Justine*) to, again, Hardy. I believe, and shall try to establish, that the situation is no more equivocal in *Crime and Pun-*

---

7. The phrase is Arnold Goldman's in *The Joyce Paradox: Form and Freedom in His Fiction* (London: Routledge, 1966), p. 78. The pioneer study of Joyce's process of composition was A. Walton Litz's *The Art of James Joyce: Method and Design in* Ulysses *and* Finnegans Wake (London: Oxford UP, 1961). A recent similar study, Michael Groden's Ulysses *in Progress* (Princeton: Princeton UP, 1977), also discusses "unilateral interpretations" of the novel as either "human drama" or "symbolic structure" (pp. 17–21). The other terms for its two elements come from the books cited and from Hugh Kenner, *Joyce's Voices* (Berkeley: U of California P, 1978). See, e.g., p. 41.

ishment and *Ulysses* than it is in the beginning of *The Tempest* or the end of *Tom Jones.*

The metalanguage of distinctly represented events cannot be subverted—equivocated—by other elements of a story; and without contradiction, it can be kept from taking the story to closure. Unlike most of Dostoevsky's other novels, but like Stephen's story in *Ulysses*, at its end *Crime and Punishment* is both inconclusive and essentially affirmative. This hopeful outcome is achieved in the two novels by plot coincidences that signify the agency of a benevolent Providence—by represented events that can be explained even in *Ulysses*, even with the most ingenious hermeneutic agility, in no other way.

II

Sade and Hardy achieved their counterstatements about Providence by plotting their novels to make, out of the *significance* which fictions of the second tradition implicitly give to desirable blatant coincidences, an explicit subject. The coincidences in *Crime and Punishment* and *Ulysses* are both blatant and crucial because they too are subjects: their significance is not only unequivocal, it is insisted upon. Both novels use coincidence to signify explicitly the traditionally implied benevolence of Providence that Sade and Hardy explicitly controvert.

The situation with the crucial coincidence in *The Ambassadors* is precisely opposite, and so illuminating. In the twenty-thousand word "Project of Novel" he wrote before beginning it (the reader's report for Harper and Brothers concluded "I do not advise acceptance. We ought to do better"), James describes the coincidence he projected:

> Strether . . . has taken the train to one of the suburbs of Paris quite at random . . . . Suddenly . . . in a suburban village by the river . . . he comes upon Mme de Vionnet and Chad together . . . presented somehow in a light that . . . represents them as positively and indubitably intimate with the last intimacy . . . .[8]

James expounds in detail the reactions and conduct of Strether and the couple, and the profound effect the "encounter" (the only term he uses, once, and with no qualifying epithet) will have on Strether; he does not remark on its coincidental nature.

The treatment of it in the novel is, of course, richer. Strether likens the countryside he is visiting to a "painting" and then, recalling James's own famous distinction between "picture" and "scene" ("the representational" and "the scenic") in fiction, thinks of the situation in Paris from which he is trying to escape temporarily as his "drama." Eventually, he feels himself totally in the "painting" ("his tension was really relaxed"), and just before Chapter XXX ends and the coincidence occurs, he "though hungry felt at peace."

However, the "encounter" is foreshadowed from the beginning of the chapter. Strether had determined to travel at least an hour from Paris, and after

8. *The Notebooks of Henry James,* ed. F. O. Mathiessen and Kenneth B. Murdock (New York: Braziller, 1955), p. 409. The reader's "memorandum" is printed on p. 372.

eighty minutes "he found himself getting out as securely as if to keep an appointment." He has the persistent feeling that the "painting" is really "a scene and a stage." In his thoughts, he remains "engaged with others and in midstream of his drama." Finally, he anticipates that the dinner he arranges for at the inn, which he is to share with a man and woman who have gone rowing, will be "a comfortable climax."

The encounter is foreshadowed, but apparently just for effect. Nothing either before or after Madame de Vionnet and Newsome row into Strether's presence specifies that the crucial, blatant coincidence is more than an accident. Strether leaves the train because it "pulled up just at the right spot": the prospect from the train reminds him of the "Lambinet" landscape behind his "painting" trope. He can scarcely expect fully to escape from his mental preoccupation with his Paris "drama"; consequently, his Paris "scene" imposes on the bucolic "painting." Finally, James's casual irony at the expense of Strether (and the reader) in "a comfortable climax" suggests that the coincidence is doing no important thematic work. When in Chapter XXXIV Maria Gostrey mentions the "extraordinary meeting in the country," Strether pronounces it "an accident . . . amazing enough. But still, but still—!" And the novel does not contradict him: James has done precisely as his "project" said he would do. The blatant coincidence of the meeting by the river seems to be nothing more than the most radical consequence for *The Ambassadors* of "the major propriety" James declared in his preface, of "keeping it all within my hero's compass": Strether "properly" has to experience—to apprehend himself—the nature of the relationship between Madame de Vionnet and Newsome; for him to come upon the couple *in delicto* was not James's style; hence, there is an accidental meeting in revealing circumstances. James's blatant coincidence may accomplish a great deal, but the fact that it is a coincidence signifies nothing.

Here precisely is its illuminating difference from the blatant coincidences in *Crime and Punishment* and *Ulysses*. Indeed, the plots of both novels present not single coincidences but *sets* of them. In life, the statistical probability that a set of related coincidences are just accidents diminishes exponentially as their number increases. This fact is one means both novels use to insist on their coincidences.

III

The set of events in *Crime and Punishment* both crucial to the plot and significant as coincidences relates to Haymarket Square in St. Petersburg; the set in *Ulysses* concerns the dream Stephen recalls having had the night before the novel begins.

Stephen's story is the religious one in *Ulysses*. Bloom's corresponding dream, significant because the novel associates it coincidentally with Stephen's, is not instrumental in his story. The instrumental coincidences in Bloom's story, those exploiting the Gold Cup race actually run at Ascot on June 16, 1904, would pass as tight plotting in another novel. Furthermore, Joyce does not present those coincidences as divine instruments of Bloom's destiny. Bloom's predicament is wholly of this world and in his hands: if he is to return to his Ithaca, he must be, *mutatis mutandis,* the hero who does so by his own acts.

The predicaments of the overreacher Raskolnikov and the cosmic rebel Stephen are opposite to Bloom's, for both need do nothing, only change their attitudes toward God; and divine agency explicitly leads them to do so. Indeed, the coincidences in Stephen's story are blatant partly to serve as revelation—to reveal to him what they signify.

Stephen needs that revelation because he hates as well as fears God: God is "ghoul," "hyena," "corpse chewer," executioner *("dio boia").* Another epithet, "Nobodaddy," one of the words Joyce has Stephen take from the Rossetti Manuscript (appropriately, Stephen reads Blake), occurs in the second stanza of the poem beginning "Let the Brothels of Paris be opened": "Then old Nobodaddy aloft / Farted & belched & coughd / And said I love hanging & drawing & quartering / Every bit as well as war & slaughtering." Raskolnikov is more restrained, but agrees with him. Both characters are given atheist foils—Svidrigaylov and Malachi Mulligan—to help distinguish atheism from their authentic antitheism.

Raskolnikov and Stephen try to defy a God Whom they fully acknowledge, but denounce as cruel and oppressive. Raskolnikov commits murder; but his transgression (the Russian word in the title has a religious as well as a legal meaning[9]) is against God. This is shown clearly in the process of his movement to confession and the form of his penance. By spurning his loot, he reveals early that his motive was not robbery. What it was has been much debated. He may have desired to prove his freedom from the "slave morality" of obedience to God, as he finally says, or may even have endeavored by a desperate act against his fellow humans—God's creatures—to end his alienation from God and them. Whatever his motive, he shares, along with Stephen's defiance of God, Stephen's desperate frustration.

And in similar predicaments, Raskolnikov and Stephen express them in similar ways. Despite their youth, Raskolnikov has published an article in a leading journal, and Stephen has composed an impressive *tour de force* purporting to be biographical criticism of Shakespeare's works. Both novels devote space to the substance of these intellectual accomplishments: the police examiner Porfiry questions Raskolnikov about his opus during their first meeting; Stephen expounds his in the National Library to a group of Dublin *literati,* including the editor he hopes will buy and print it. And both novels do so for the same reason: to characterize. Raskolnikov's exposition of the freedom of the "extraordinary individual" from all moral law including God's commandments ("the ancient law," p. 249), and Stephen's "theory" that "being no more a son, [Shakespeare] was and felt himself . . . the father of his own grandfather" (208)—that God is indeed Nobodaddy—are disguised expressions of the similar and similarly obsessive endeavor of each to deny God's sovereignty over him.

9. For the meanings of the word and of some characters' names, see the Norton Critical Edition *Crime and Punishment,* ed. George Gibian, tr. Jessie Coulson (New York: Norton, 1964), p. 528. Page references are to that edition.

The young men's hostility toward and unsuccessful defiance of God cause anger, frustration, ineffectuality; but their hostility and defiance do not alone account for the spiritual (psychological, in secular terms) predicament which activates the story of each. For in the novels they are not just generally but acutely troubled: their stories are of mortal crisis. The additional element complicating things for the defiant young antitheists is an apparently contradictory guilt, felt by Stephen about his dead mother, while his hostility and defiance are directed to the Father he challenges with hollow bravado (242, 395). Furthermore, the young men's guilt is made redemptive in both novels, for the same reason: it is the appropriate expression of their healthy impulses, which are in conflict with their intellectual attitude. (Porfiry speaks of "a heart troubled by theories," p. 437.) This etiology is declared by the narrator in *Crime and Punishment* (p. 521) and revealed when Stephen's apparition of his mother precipitates the climax of his story (579-83).

Raskolnikov's guilt is generated by his double murder, Stephen's, by his having refused to pray to the "hangman God" for his dying mother, whom he loved. These guilty acts motivate their similar mortal crises. But in both cases, the specific catalytic acts themselves are of secondary importance (hence Joyce's sarcasm to Giorgio regarding the title of *Crime and Punishment*). Raskolnikov's and Stephen's stories are about their predicaments, compounded of the guilt each feels and his willed defiance of God. For the willed defiance prompts each to *intellectually* distort his (redemptive) *feelings* of guilt: Raskolnikov's contempt for his "weakness" (pp. 402–4) and Stephen's polarizing his mother and Father.

IV

Believing in but unwilling to submit to God; wracked by guilt as a consequence of their deeds of rebellion; above all, oppressed by their awareness that the deeds were futile and by their sense of helpless subjection, Raskolnikov and Stephen are in equally desperate situations. The very nature of their similar predicaments signifies that they consider God to be a principal actor in their stories. Their creators cause God to be so by the sets of blatant coincidences. Dostoevsky even boldly brings up in his novel what he and Joyce are doing.

He makes it part of Raskolnikov's story. The young man's name contains the Russian word for schism *(raskol)*—designating the struggle in his character between the intellectual assertion of will or self that causes his transgression, and the emotional impulse to reverence that activates his guilt. While in the humanistic *Ulysses*, self-assertion and submission are alternative modes of conduct equally appropriate for the alternative situations of its two principal characters, Dostoevsky's Christian Orthodox novel involves only one principal character. For it presents a single (orthodox) view of those modes of conduct as respectively the ways to damnation and salvation.

Crime and Punishment anticipates *Ulysses* in distinguishing between submission to mere circumstances, which both novels deplore, and submission to the conditions of life ordained by God, which both advocate. But while the distinction is central to the stories of Bloom and Stephen, Dostoevsky portrays it using minor characters, and only as a clarifying detail in a pattern frequently found in his characterization. The pattern, noted by critics attentive to his artistry, is an elaborately delineated binary opposition throughout *Crime and Punishment*, between precisely Raskolnikov's contending attitudes: the assertion of will opposing the impulse to reverence and—consequently—to fellow-feeling *(caritas)*. The richness of Dostoevsky's delineation, some elements of which have escaped notice, will be taken up below. Relevant here are the characters in the novel who are seen to represent Raskolnikov's opposed attitudes, Svidrigaylov and Sonya.

Svidrigaylov is the model of Raskolnikov's (and Stephen's) aspiration. He insists on control and on living out of his will; and he ends a suicide. Dostoevsky carefully makes him enjoy performing acts of kindness: like Mulligan a cynic and total nihilist, he is not evil like Mulligan; for to have him so would partly blunt his representative function. Sonya, a recipient of his kindness, has a name that is as meaningful as Raskolnikov's. It is the diminutive of Sofya, a word that in the Orthodox church signifies not our Western sense of wisdom, but awareness of the sacredness of the created world, a quality of reverent *gnosis* characterized by Henry Gifford, in a review of a biography of Aleksandr Blok in the *Times Literary Supplement*, as "creation's response to the Creator" (March 14, 1980, 283).

Sonya, perhaps the most ascetic and spiritually virginal character in literature, plies the trade of prostitute by which she provides for her father's second family, in Haymarket Square. Raskolnikov coincidentally overhears that his intended victim will be alone the following night, and commits himself to the murder, in the same place. When he submits to expiation, it is to the "crossroad" at the center of the crowded Haymarket Square that Sonya sends him, to kiss the ground and confess to his fellow creatures of God his transgression against two of them and their Creator. And at a critical point between transgression against and submission to God, the point of his final resistance, he coincidentally comes upon Svidrigaylov there.

Haymarket Square is the place where the embodiment of reverence and consequently *caritas* mortifies her body for others, and the embodiment of egoism follows his almost precisely antithetical "occupation," "debauchery" (p. 451). Correspondingly, it is the place where Raskolnikov resolves to commit his transgression of murder, where he finds himself when making his final defiant assertion of his will against God's way, and where he begins to atone for murder.

Sonya sends him to Haymarket Square. But both of his earlier experiences in this place, itself made so coincidentally important, occur there coincidentally. And it is then that Dostoevsky boldly brings up the significance of coincidence in Raskolnikov's story.

One of the elegances of *Crime and Punishment* is the pattern it sets up linking Sonya and the formidable Porfiry, who never meet. They function as comforter and accuser, although when Porfiry finally makes his direct accusation, he shows that the agent of justice also is merciful. Raskolnikov's movement from transgression to submission has three distinct stages: he meets with each of them three times in the course of it, always going from a confrontation with Porfiry to the solace of Sonya.

He confesses to Sonya on his second visit, but rejects her entreaty to take himself to the cross-roads at Haymarket Square. Immediately after his final meeting with Porfiry, who in departing wishes him "happy new beginnings!" (p. 443), his will asserts itself and prevents his completing the process of submission to God in a projected third visit as he resists finally yielding to the better part of him, Sonya's way. And he specifies for himself the alternative to that devout way Dostoevsky embodies in the novel:

> He must choose between her way and his own. Especially at this moment he was in no condition to see her. No, would it not be better to try Svidrigaylov, and find out what he meant? And he could not help acknowledging to himself that for a long time he really had felt a kind of need of Svidrigaylov for some reason. (p. 444)

Raskolnikov chooses to visit Svidrigaylov—who, that evening, following the visit, is to tell Sonya Raskolnikov's choices, his way and hers:

> Rodion Romanovich has two ways open to him: a bullet through the brain, or Siberia. (p. 480)[10]

After "Nightmares all night long!"—for like Stephen, Bloom and Raskolnikov, Svidrigaylov has significant dreams—the embodiment of ego shoots himself in "his right temple" (pp. 490–91).

But during the afternoon Raskolnikov, at his critical juncture "between her way and his own," goes to call on Svidrigaylov, the embodiment of his willful way. He never completes his visit, and would have been disappointed if he had:

> . . . he stopped in the middle of the street and looked round: where was he, and which way had he come? He found himself . . . thirty or forty yards from the Haymarket, which he had just crossed. . . . He was about to go back, at a loss to understand why he had turned into Obukhovsky Prospect, when . . . he suddenly caught sight of Svidrigaylov himself, sitting at a tea-table. . . . This produced a strange, almost terrifying impression on him. (pp. 445–46)

This blatant coincidence is no Jamesian "encounter" made necessary by the exigencies of a particular narrative point of view. Dostoevsky could simply have had Svidrigaylov at home. The fact is so evident, that his departure from elementary good plotting draws attention to the gratuitous coincidence, confirming its significance for the novel. The last sentence quoted indicates that Raskolnikov considers the coincidence significant. When he joins Svidrigaylov in the tavern, the latter dismisses his prostitute companion, and the two men discuss it:

> "I was going to your place to look for you," began Raskolnikov, "but why did I suddenly turn into the Obukhovsky Prospect just now from the Haymarket? I never come this way. I always turn right from the Haymarket. And this is not the way to your place. But I turned along here, and here you are! Strange!"

10. The Garnett translation of the two passages is essentially the same; for the phrase "a kind of need of Svidrigaylov," it has "that he must see him." See the Harper edition (New York: Harper, 1951), pp. 470 and 507. There are no important differences between the two translations of the novel in the wording of any passage I quote.

"Why don't you say straight out it's a miracle?"

"Because it may be only coincidence."

"Oh, all you people are the same!" laughed Svidrigaylov. "Even if you believe a miracle has occurred, you won't admit it." (p. 447)

No agent of faith, Svidrigaylov soon says he had told Raskolnikov twice he could be found at that tavern. Raskolnikov cannot recall having been told; and in the novel, he has not been. Svidrigaylov then discloses to Raskolnikov (and the reader) his life of rational skepticism and self-assertive hedonism, and complains of its sterility. They part; Svidrigaylov is followed to his suicide the next morning; and when Raskolnikov again appears in the novel, the next evening—"after an inward strife prolonged for almost twenty-four hours" (p. 492)—he takes leave of his mother and sister and makes the third visit to Sonya, to submit himself to God.

As this second Haymarket occurrence in the novel which is a crucial plot coincidence seems to lead to his beginning its expiation, the first one, Raskolnikov's overhearing in Part One that the pawnbroker was to be alone the following evening, leads to the transgression itself. That coincidence also follows directly a contrary resolution by Raskolnikov. Furthermore, the author is almost equally explicit about its significance.

Raskolnikov wakes from his dream of the peasant killing his horse with a crowbar, and resolves not to carry out the murder; "and his heart was light and tranquil. 'Lord!' he prayed [!], 'show me the way, that I may renounce this accursed . . . [sic] fantasy of mine!'"(p. 57). He crosses over the Neva, "free now. . . from the temptation"—and his prayer seemingly is answered with renewed temptation:

When, later, he recalled this time . . . he was always struck with superstitious awe by one circumstance which . . . seemed to him afterwards to have determined his fate. He could never understand or explain to himself why . . . he went out of his way to cross the Haymarket instead of returning home by the quickest and most direct route. The detour was not a great deal farther, but it was obviously quite unnecessary. . . . But why . . . did such an important and fateful encounter for him take place in the Haymarket (through which he had no reason to go) just at this time, just at this moment of his life, when his mood and the circumstances were exactly those in which the meeting could have so fateful and decisive an influence on his destiny? It was almost as if fate had laid an ambush for him. (pp. 57–58)

Many times during the novel, Raskolnikov excuses himself using the complaint that "fate had laid an ambush for him." Dostoevsky does not promote this comfortable rationalization—Raskolnikov makes his own choices—but he does blatantly have "fate," the hand of God, create "circumstances." The two blatant coincidental occurrences that are linked respectively to the beginning and end of Raskolnikov's transgression, also are the result of wholly unexplanable detours through Haymarket Square. Coincidentally, that place is associated with his story in the other ways mentioned (as well as in a number of minor ones). And Dostoevsky implants in his novel an elaborate discussion of the significance of each of the two blatant coincidences, on the second occasion introducing the operative word: "Why don't you say straight out it's a miracle?"

The coincidences in the elaborate Haymarket pattern are joined by a number of others related specifically to the murder, "special coincidences" (p. 60) such as Raskolnikov's "stroke of luck" (p. 69) in coming upon another axe when he cannot get to the one he'd planned to use (which Dostoevsky simply could have made accessible to him); and his overhearing in a tavern, immediately after his initial visit to the pawnbroker, a stranger expound to another a rational justification for killing her. This previous action is presented as a flashback. It begins on the second page following the passage just quoted; and the point made there is repeated:

> Raskolnikov was deeply disturbed. . . . But why must he listen at this particular moment to . . . those particular ideas when there had just been born in his own brain *exactly the same ideas*? And why, at the very moment when he was carrying away from the old woman's flat the germ of his idea, should he chance upon a conversation about that same old woman? . . . This always seemed to him a strange coincidence . . . as if there was something fateful and foreordained about it. (p. 63)

My thesis seems evident. An author who incorporates a system of coincidences in a fiction—some crucial to the plot, some more easily avoided than created—and who provides repeated commentary on their significance, is saying "straight out it's a miracle." Raskolnikov's transgression generates his guilt; his guilt makes his predicament manifest to him; and his acute suffering causes his movement to confession, then submission to God, then gradually less grudging expiation in Siberia until eventually his story concludes with the "happy new beginnings" of Porfiry's (literal) valediction—with, in the phrase repeated throughout the epilogue, "a new life." The transgression is the necessary initial step in the process. Raskolnikov believes God may have "ambushed" him into contemplating the step; Dostoevsky went to considerable lengths to inform the reader that this has been the case—and for every subsequent step of the way as well.

V

Raskolnikov suspects very early that the God he defies is taking a hand in his destiny; eventually, Stephen comes to recognize the same fact. It is a fact in *Ulysses* because of the metalanguage of events. The set of coincidences Joyce fashioned and made crucial to Stephen's story signifies it.

The context of Stephen's story is provided in his creator's portrait of the young man when a bit younger. In the last chapter of the *Portrait*, Stephen declares to his friend Davin his refusal to submit to the conditions Ireland imposes on its people, "nets flung at ["the soul"] to hold it back from flight": "I shall try to fly by those nets" (corrected text [New York: Viking, 1964], p. 203). Later in the same chapter, he observes from the steps of the National Library portico the flight of unfamiliar birds, takes it for an "augury," decides "Then he was to go away," and receives confirmation "from his heart" (pp. 224–26). As the beginning of his story in *Ulysses* confirms, he misreads the "augury" (the birds "came back"); the young idealist has distorted reality once again. His brief stay on the continent having been ended by his mother's terminal illness, he is immobilized in Ireland. He can no longer deny his predicament and cannot cope with it. His epithet for himself, "lapwing," another borrowing from the Rossetti Manuscript, alludes to the reason why; the Blake quatrain begins: "O lapwing, thou fliest around the heath / Nor seest the net that is spread beneath." That real, abiding net is identified in his last conversation in the *Portrait*, by his closest friend, Cranly. He has resolved to depart ("fly") so that his soul can "express itself in unfettered freedom" (p. 246). But Cranly elicits from him the confession that, although he (using Lucifer's phrase) "will not serve" (p. 239) "the God of the Roman Catholics," God is "a malevolent reality" (p. 243): he carries the "net" of his faith with him. Knowing that, Cranly presciently mocks his bold declaration (p. 247); and after less than a page, the action gives way to Stephen's journal entries, whose testimony of confident expectation ends Joyce's portrait of the artist as a distinctly young man.

Near the end of the third chapter of *Ulysses*, just four pages before Bloom is introduced, Stephen, sitting on a rock on Sandymount strand and at the end of his rope, or in another idiom, very close to breakdown, struggles to remember a dream he had the night before:

> After he woke me up last night same dream or was it? Wait. Open hallway. Street of harlots. Remember. Haroun al Raschid. I am almosting it. That man led me, spoke. I was not afraid. The melon he had he held against my face. . . . In. Come. Red carpet spread. You will see who. (47)

"He" is Haines, Mulligan's English visitor. And his "raving . . . about a black panther" in a nightmare, of which Stephen complains to Mulligan in the conversation that begins the novel (4), seems to have interrupted Stephen's dream. A few minutes later the third chapter ends. Stephen picks his nose, turns to see if he is being watched, and sees "a threemaster, her sails brailed up on the crosstrees" (51). Budgen reports that when he pointed out sails were bent on *yards* not *crosstrees*, Joyce replied "There's no sort of criticism I more value than that. But the word 'crosstrees' is essential" (p. 57).

Stephen next remembers the dream just after he has expressed his denial of God's sovereignty over him in the National Library, vocally in the guise of his lecture about Shakespeare, and silently in a parody of the Apostles' Creed using "crosstree" for Christ's cross (197). The chapter is the ninth of the eighteen in *Ulysses*, and with its end both the day's quotidian nature for Bloom and Stephen, and the novel's conventional narrative—what Joyce called "the initial style" (*Letters* I: 129)—also end. Joyce wrote "End of First Part of *Ulysses*" at this point in the fair copy (Rosenbach manuscript); and in an important sense, it marks a division of the novel into two parts. In the company of "mine enemy" (197) Mulligan, Stephen leaves his audience; and on the portico he recalls, "Here I watched the birds for augury" (217). But there are no birds; he resigns himself to his plight ("Cease to strive"); and Joyce ends the chapter and the first part of *Ulysses*.

But moments before its end, Stephen is physically separated from his "enemy" by "A man [who] passed out between them," and thinks briefly of achieving his departure. In the *Portrait*, naive optimism causes him to misread the birds; here, despair causes him to ignore an augury of the escape from his predicament he so much craves and needs. The opposition of Bloom and Mulligan articulated at this point in the novel, as characters representing the fateful alternatives for Stephen, recalls that of Sonya and Svidrigaylov.

Bloom and Stephen come on each other—coincidentally—an unusual number of times for a single day in a city of a quarter-million people. In earlier chapters, Bloom has seen Stephen (returning from his reflections on the beach) during the funeral procession (88); and they have seen each other when Stephen is in the company of the men from the newspaper office, shortly after the men gossip in Stephen's presence about Bloom and "Madam Bloom . . . . Dublin's prime favourite" (135). The involvement of the two develops with each coincidental occurrence. After the next one (when Bloom is invited to join the medical students and Stephen drinking in the maternity hospital, and he naively tries to allay Stephen's fear of the lightning storm), Bloom follows Stephen into the Dublin brothel district Joyce renames nighttown, to minister to him until his story ends.

In the present chapter, Bloom has called out one of the librarians listening to Stephen, and Mulligan has moved their involvement closer by speaking about him to Stephen. "He knows you. He knows your old fellow," Mulligan says (201). Eventually, the novels shows this to be an instance of Joyce's irony, for Bloom never discovers his affiliation with Stephen's Old Fellow.

Joyce uses allusion, symbolic pattern, and ventriloquist statement throughout *Ulysses* to associate Bloom with Elijah and Christ. His obvious differences from them are modulated by similarities in his character and actions that make comparison possible—mainly to indicate the similarity most instrumental in the novel: his messianic function for Stephen. Typically, and delightfully, he is unaware of it. As so often in *Ulysses*, Joyce's irony works not to subvert meaning but to enrich its circumstances.

Having gradually approached their first encounter, Bloom and Stephen experience it at the end of this chapter. And when Bloom goes "between" Stephen and Mulligan, the novel reads:

> The portico.
> Here I watched the birds for augury. . . . Last night I flew. Easily flew. Men wondered. Street of harlots after. A creamfruit melon he held to me. In. You will see. (217)

At the place where he once sought an omen of achieving the "flight" he craves, at the point in *Ulysses* where both its quotidian events and its conventional narrative are about to end, Stephen is confronted by Bloom and recalls that his dream of invitation also is a dream of liberation: "I flew. Easily flew."

But liberation is not at hand. His recollection inverts the proper sequence of his "flight" and ("after") its promised agent: he continues to think in terms of escape, not deliverance—of self-assertion rather than of grace. Correspondingly, his reference to "wondering" spectators recalls a characteristic human interest detail in Ovid's account of Daedalus's and Icarus's flight ("*pisces,* / *aut pastor ... arator* / *vidit et obstipuit,*" *Metamorphoses* VIII, 217–19). Hence, his old metaphor for escape from oppression, become recollected dream-symbol, not only bridges the *Portrait* and *Ulysses*; it also invokes his family name and his past youth: Stephen shares the disobedience of his father, and the failure to come to terms with reality, that destroyed Icarus.

Although Bloom's appearance causes Stephen to think of departure, and to recall (defectively) the valuable aspect of his dream, his perspective on their encounter is less privileged than that of the reader; and he promptly resigns himself to his plight. The event functions solely as Joyce's exposition—both of the craved omen, and of Stephen's failure to recognize it. Likewise, although "crosstrees" may appear to be only Stephen's word, and his referring to the crucifixion "on crosstree" (197) only his pun, the three-masted ship with (three) "crosstrees," in a place where it can "watch" Stephen when he first recalls the dream, was placed there by the author, is Joyce's exposition. And so the (incorrect) literal meaning of "crosstrees" belongs to Stephen, but his punning use of it in the parody of the Apostles' Creed is anticipated (in the Calvary allusion) by the complex executive consciousness that presides over narrators and characters in *Ulysses*, discussed in the last section (pp. 276–77). Stephen's dream of deliverance, "crosstrees," and Bloom the intercessor, are connected as the chapter ends: the black panther of the nightmare that the first action of the novel introduces, and that interrupted Stephen's dream, is traditionally an emblem of Christ; and immediately after Stephen's recollection of the dream Joyce has Bloom, dressed in black, lead Stephen (and Mulligan) away, with the "step of a pard" (218).

As "crosstrees" is not exclusively Stephen's, neither is the reference to a "pard." It has been argued that in a novel which takes place so largely in each protagonist's consciousness, patterns of association have no special status, convey no meaning *of* the novel: that the function of "pard" is limited to characterization of Stephen. But to argue so requires ignoring the carefully prepared for, and orchestrated, *conjunction*—complete with panther connection—between Stephen's meeting with Bloom and his recollection of the content and import of his dream of liberation: the metalanguage of events effectively forestalls any "drama of the alternatives" here. And that coincidence of events is shown to be no accident later, when Bloom is identified as the "he" of the dream, and the dream comes true.

In fulfilling the dream, Bloom effects Stephen's deliverance not by the shabby offer of his "melon" at home (his "spreading" the "red carpet" to Molly), but by his literal—although secular—ministry. Bloom's unknowing demonstration that he is the man who was promised, and Stephen's eventual realization that Bloom was indeed sent to help, not to oppress—that the feared and hated "malevolent reality" is benevolent—are what deliver Stephen and end his story.

The disobedient, self-deluding son Icarus of the *Portrait* becomes in *Ulysses* the faithful and obedient son Telemachus.

Dostoevsky has Raskolnikov think and talk about coincidences to draw attention to that plot element in his novel, and to insist on what it imports. So Joyce, with the same purpose respecting the import of Stephen's dream, provides a coincidental complement. He gives Bloom a dream that is unrelated to Stephen's story, yet corresponds to his dream in time, in setting and imagery, and in substance; and he has Bloom recall it where Stephen first recalls his. When Bloom masturbates in response to Gerty MacDowell's exhibitionism, in a direct and eloquent negation of the desired return to Molly which is at the center of his own story, Bloom is leaning against a rock on Sandymount strand. And he then recalls his dream of the night before—as Stephen has done, in two parts. The first almost exactly duplicates phrases in Stephen's first recollection: "Come in. All is prepared. I dreamt. What?" (370). As Stephen's second recollection reveals his dream to be a dream of liberation, Bloom's second identifies his, correspondingly, as a dream of return: "Dreamt last night? . . . She had red slippers on. Turkish. Wore the breeches. Suppose she does? Would I like her in pyjamas?" (381).

Bloom's causing Stephen's dream to come true either is meaningless chance, or it is what Stephen eventually takes it to be: the fulfillment of a prophesy. Were it chance, Joyce would have been developing an elaborate system of related elements in his novel in order to undermine Stephen's story pointlessly. And the victim of his cruel and cynical mockery of his own creature would have been, reflexively, the novel embodying that character's story. At the climax of Stephen's story, in the parlor of Bella Cohen's brothel on a "street of harlots," the set of crucial plot coincidences related to his dream makes explicit that God is, as in *Crime and Punishment*, active in *Ulysses*.

The event of Stephen's striking the parlor chandelier with his walking stick, in a symbolic attack on—the ultimate transgression against—God, is the most dramatic in the novel; but it does not equal in intensity the psychological events that cause it (or Bloom's climactic psychological experiences, which occur just before). To recount the action briefly: drunk, Stephen dances frenziedly to the player piano; he imagines that his beloved mother has come as the emissary of the hated Father, calling on him to "Repent!" and warning of "the fire of hell!"; he responds "The ghoul! Hyena!" and "The corpsechewer!" (581), and shouting the name of Siegfried's sword, enacts his own *Götterdämmerung* against the light above (he does little damage to the delicate chandelier, actually); he rushes out, speaks to an Irish prostitute in the company of two British soldiers, and is knocked unconscious by one of them. For his part, the formerly submissive Bloom, who has already begun protecting Stephen's final wages from his profligacy, rejects the excessive demands of the overbearing madam but pays for the lamp damage, tries to prevent the altercation in the street, protects Stephen from arrest, and ministers to him. Bloom's new and requisite assertiveness reflects the climactic (psychological) events in his story in *Ulysses*; the things he does are part of the climax and resolution of Stephen's story.

At the climax of his story, Stephen apprehends that the mother of his guilty love and the Father of his enmity are one; and he responds by rejecting not his view of the "corpsechewer," but his evangelizing mother. As Raskolnikov persists for so long in regarding his redeeming impulse to accept God's way as "weakness," Stephen persists in regarding his as jeopardizing the "freedom" of his "spirit." And as Raskolnikov mistakenly attributes to "the devil" (p. 69) the "stroke of luck" by which he finds the axe, Stephen mistakenly identifies the deliverer he dreamed of as "Beelzebub" (571).

It is at this point in the novel that Joyce integrates the set of plot coincidences involving Stephen's dream and Bloom with the principal element of Stephen's story, his predicament of mother and Father. As Dostoevsky does, he uses a triadic pattern. The first time Stephen remembers his dream is when he sees the three "crosstrees" at the end of the group of three chapters devoted to him with which *Ulysses* begins. The second time is when Bloom briefly separates him from his "enemy" at the end of the first part of the novel. The third time occurs in the parlor on the "street of harlots" specified in the dream, moments before he begins his frenzied dancing:

> Mark me. I dreamt of a watermelon.
>
> . . . .
>
> (*extends his arms*) It was here. Street of harlots. . . . Beelzebub showed me her, a fubsy widow. Where's the red carpet spread? (571)

In a delightful example of ironic juxtaposition Bloom, solicitous, says "*(approaching Stephen)* Look"; but unlike Bloom himself, Stephen (characteristically) understands the relevance of Bloom's exclamation: his very next fantasy is of the Ascot Gold Cup race won by the "dark horse" (572-73) whose winning, he heard at the end of the preceding chapter (426), Bloom had prophesied; and he explicitly identifies God's agent at the end of the chapter, when Bloom rouses him after the fight ("Who? Black panther vampire," 608). Stephen defiantly rejects both Bloom's "Look" in unwitting direct response to his question—with the words "No, I flew. My foes beneath me. . . . Free!," and its immediate reiteration ("I say, look")—with "Break my spirit, will he?" (572).

Stephen recognizes that Bloom was sent by God; but, his "heart troubled by theories," he cannot accept an emissary of the "corpsechewer" as his deliverer. When Mr Deasy speaks of "the manifestation of God" in the second chapter, Stephen defines God as "A shout in the street!" (34); and in this chapter, he identifies the singing of the soldiers and girl outside as "Our friend, noise in the street!" (574). Presumably, on being roused by Bloom he apprehends that he struck at God, and God promptly knocked him unconscious. This formulation could be Stephen's alone, the coincidence of events in parlor and street having been created by Joyce to permit Stephen to make it, created for the sake of characterization, not statement.

However, Stephen does not just recall a witticism, strike a chandelier, and provoke a random tough he himself has designated the manifestation of God; the sequence of coincidental events Joyce devised is more elaborate. As coincidences assist Raskolnikov in his transgression, begin the process, so the singing in the street *is what causes Stephen to begin dancing* (574–75): *precisely* "the manifestation of God" as Stephen defines God initiates the process leading to Stephen's climactic experience of his beloved mother's evangelism for the Father and responsive act of outraged rebellion against Him—and to the consequence. Moreover, the connection between God; the cycle begun and ended by the soldiers in the street, which contains the climax of Stephen's story; Bloom; and Stephen's dream, is announced beforehand. When Bloom enters the brothel, "(*Outside the gramophone begins to blare* The Holy City," [a contemporary hymn]), and it distracts Stephen, who says "Damn that fellow's noise in the street"; then while the others chat, *"(Stephen turns and sees Bloom)"* (504–6). Some lines of the hymn are given, but not the first two: "Last night as I lay asleeping, / There came a dream so fair." Once again, the coincidence of events Joyce created is an articulate metalanguage.

As Raskolnikov submits grudgingly to God's dominion at first, so does Stephen. Impassively, he allows the "black panther vampire," God's emissary, to accompany and minister to him in the next (sixteenth) chapter, which begins III, the "nostos." The complex working out of that next-to-last phase of Stephen's story is discussed in the last section (pp. 281–85), in the context of the narrative style of the chapter. But the elements of it can be delineated here.

In Book XVI of the *Odyssey*, Athene calls Odysseus out of the hut of his swineherd Eumaeus, instructs him to reveal his identity to Telemachus, and improves his appearance to help his son recognize him; correspondingly, Bloom unconsciously reveals his provenance across the table in the cabmen's shelter. However, Stephen already identifies Bloom with God. His unnecessary revelation prepares for—and defines—the revelation less than ten pages later that is necessary to the resolution of Stephen's story: God the Father's revelation of His true nature to His (troubled and defiant) son. It is for that second revelation the allusion to the Eumaeus episode in the *Odyssey* functions.

Both incidents are quite brief. In the first one, silly, secular, *kindly* Bloom has been reproaching Stephen for provoking the fight with the soldiers; of course, he is totally unaware of its significance. Newly able—after his climactic trauma in nighttown—to speak freely about his Jewishness, he tells of his altercation with the anti-semitic chauvinist during the afternoon. He told the citizen "his God, I mean Christ, was a jew too . . . like me" he says and, as he subsequently becomes aware, goes on to misrepresent what happened. Then his eyes (on the next page, Stephen notices them repeatedly, and Bloom becomes "the person who owned them pro. tem.") are emphasized:

> That was one for him. A soft answer turns away wrath. . . . Am I not right?
> He turned a long you are wrong gaze on Stephen . . . . (643)

Thereupon, "their two or four eyes conversing," Stephen quotes his "noncommittal" phrases from the Vulgate (*Romans* 9.5) signifying that "Christus" (the Messiah-Deliverer) could appear as "Bloom . . . or after all any other, *secundum carnem*." Stephen's attitude to the freethinker-Messiah's ministry is less hostile; nevertheless, he promptly rejects once for all the food and drink Bloom has been urging on him.

It is possible to be simplistic about the significance of that proffered snack, and of the cup of cocoa—solid combined with liquid, "Epps's massproduct"—Stephen drinks in the next chapter: it is possible to regard both snack and cocoa solemnly as symbolic of the Eucharist. An alternative is to recognize that both are implicated in a complex sequence of events in the novel, and that their contexts validate granting them a playfully intimated analogical significance. Thus: in an apposite earlier passage in which Bloom urges the roll and coffee on Stephen, "Our name was changed too, he added, pushing the socalled roll across" (623); on another occasion, he refers to the "bun" as "disguised" (634); and when Stephen rejects the snack once for all, the narrator says he "shoved aside his mug of coffee or whatever you like to call it" (645). The roll and coffee are Eucharistic wafer and wine neither literally nor symbolically. They could not effect Holy Communion if Stephen partook of them—and "Epps's massproduct" does not do so. Instead, both snack and cocoa adumbrate the significance of what is happening in the events themselves of the novel, by effecting *an analogy with* the receiving of Communion (hence, the playful references to them).

Less hostile but still defiant of God after Bloom's unnecessary revelation, Stephen changes after God's subsequent, necessary one. His crucial change occurs when Bloom, in his initial (shabby) effort to pry Molly away from Blazes Boylan, shows Stephen the photograph of the "Madam Bloom" gossiped about in Stephen's presence. By having "showed me her, a fubsy [grass] widow" (571), he has—as Stephen put it in his first recollection of his dream—"held against my face" Molly, "The melon he had" (47) at home. And so, unknowingly (of course), the compassionate and vulnerable Bloom has revealed that God's emissary is simultaneously the deliverer Stephen dreamed of. The coincidence with Stephen's three recollections of his dream of, respectively, three-masted schooner, first full encounter with Bloom, and intercession by Bloom, now falls into place for him: it is not "Beelzebub" but God's agent whom the dream portrayed. The God Stephen rejected as cruel announced His ministration in a dream and has provided it promptly the next day.

During the unnecessary first revelation, Bloom quotes Scripture: "A soft answer turns away wrath" (*Proverbs* 15.1). But as he acknowledges privately, his soft answer had not succeeded in turning away the citizen's wrath. Stephen's unwitting deliverer, who does not even believe in the God Who sent him, also delivers, unwittingly, a message from God. Stephen's fulfilled dream of delivery is God's soft answer to his wrath; and God's soft answer, revealed to him across the table by Bloom, "turns away" his wrath at God. The situation recalls the lesson of His goodness with which God answers the equally self-jeopardizing wrath toward Him of the prophet Jonah. When Stephen is frightened by the storm in the hospital, the reader is informed—in the idiom (significantly) of *Pilgrim's Progress*—that Stephen would find "Holiness" only through "Grace" (395). He recognizes the fulfillment of his dream to be that grace. What else can it signify?

Hence, he allows Bloom to take him home for his first nourishment in days. Bloom says "Lean on me," and takes his arm; and "—Yes, Stephen said uncertainly because he thought he felt a strange kind of flesh of a different man" (660).

On the way, he does something totally inconsistent with the bitter, sardonic, troubled young man of most of the novel: he sings, beginning with "variations . . . on" Sweelinck's (keyboard) accompaniment to a Protestant hymn, "*Mein junges Leben hat ein End,*" which—recalling "a new life" for Raskolnikov at the end of his story—is mistranslated "Youth here has End" (663).

The end of the sixteenth chapter indicates a significant change in Stephen's condition, and so a positive resolution of his story in *Ulysses*. The catechistic narrative of the next chapter, during which his story is concluded, is treacherous in certain respects. The absurd inclusiveness of the catechetical respondent is compounded by antic shifts from a style of scientism and pedantic precision, to one of tropes and romantic phrasing; and it is subverted by errors, even of arithmetic. The nature and function of the catechism are discussed in the last section (pp. 286–89). But that the respondent is an unreliable authority is no hindrance here, for his/its simple narrating—reporting as a witness—is subverted in no way. Once again, there is a metalanguage of events: the things that happen during the chapter tell their story. Stephen accepts the proffered nourishment, "Epps's mass-product." The "cocoa having been consumed," he immediately chants his variant of the anti-semitic "Hugh of Lincoln" (690). Bloom is disturbed, understandably. But the reader need not be: "the victim predestined" recalls Stephen's likening himself to Christ and Caesar in the preceding chapter (615, 635); Bloom is called "victim predestined" by the narrator; finally, Stephen's "commentary" on his song describes his dream and Bloom's fulfillment of its promise (692). Then, minutes before Stephen walks out of the novel, he makes an "exodus" from the Blooms' kitchen into their garden. Bloom places a lighted candle in the doorway, while he puts his "Diaconal Hat" on his head and "intones" to himself the Vulgate version of the Passover psalm of deliverance (698).

A number of critics have discussed the close analogue Joyce created here to Dante's emerging with Vergil from Hell in *Purgatorio* I, and to his witnessing the chanting of the same psalm by the newly redeemed souls in II.[11] One recent critic has elucidated the analogy further. In the important Easter Vigil on Holy Saturday, the paschal candle identified with Christ, and used to sanctify the next year's baptismal water, is lit not by a full priest, but but a *deacon*; simultaneously, all the lights of the church, extinguished at the Tenebrae service on Holy Thursday, are turned on.[12] And "when they, first the host, then the guest [in his deacon's hat], emerged" from the kitchen door, a "spectacle confronted them": "The heaventree of stars" (698). Baptism (initiation/dedication) and redemption (deliverance) are elaborately invoked, in a reversal of Stephen's futile attempt in nighttown to destroy the light of God.

---

11. See, e.g., William York Tindall, *A Reader's Guide to James Joyce* (New York: Noonday, 1959), pp. 225–26; Mary T. Reynolds, "Joyce's Planetary Music: His Debt to Dante," *Sewanee Review,* 76 (1968), 450–77, 456–58; A. Walton Litz, "Ithaca," *James Joyce's* Ulysses: *Critical Essays,* ed. Clive Hart and David Hayman (Berkeley: U of California P, 1974), pp. 385–405, 399–400; and *Argument,* pp. 391–92.

12. Robert Adams Day, "Deacon Dedalus: The Text of the *Exultet* and Its Implications for *Ulysses,*" *The Seventh of Joyce,* ed. Bernard Benstock (Bloomington: Indiana UP, 1982), pp. 157–66.

It is not possible to demonstrate briefly that the outcome of Stephen's story is unequivocally as I am representing it; but nothing in the novel controverts or subverts his understanding of what has happened to him on the day of *Ulysses*: he had a dream of deliverance; the dream—coincidentally—has been fulfilled; and the fulfillment itself effects the deliverance. It releases him from his conviction that the manifest provenance of dream-and-fulfillment, the abiding "reality" of existence, is "malevolent"; and therefore, it releases him from the predicament that is destroying him.

As is Raskolnikov's, his story is psychological: he too is rescued by a change of attitude. But the events leading the mature Joyce's young man to the change of attitude that ends his youth, no less than the object of his changed attitude, define Stephen's psychological story as precisely—unequivocally—spiritual. The very first words spoken in *Ulysses* are the first words spoken in the *introit* to the Catholic Mass, "*Introibo ad altare Dei*" (3). The irony that Mulligan speaks them could signify merely an incidental attack on Roman Catholicism. But although Joyce firmly rejected all formal religions, the words have a specific meaning; and the evidence is that his irony is both more high-spirited and more elegant. The evidence is that he appoints the atheist to announce what Stephen will do in the course of the novel.

VI.

To this point, I have shown how the story of Stephen in *Ulysses*, and the plotting strategy Joyce employs to involve God instrumentally in its outcome, are similar to the story and plotting strategy of *Crime and Punishment*. Augmenting those striking similarities between the two novels is the texture of artistic working that establishes the mid-nineteenth-century Russian evangelist's reciprocal affinity with the modernist Irish artificer. "[T]he man more than any other who has created modern prose" developed in his novel a cluster of related patterns to illuminate its action and the psychomachia of the tag-named Raskolnikov that causes it: the contention between his natural impulses and his totally contrary intellectual attitude. Although he uses them extensively, Dostoevsky does not limit himself to opposed pairs of representative characters. Other essentially binary oppositions constellate with the opposed pairs of characters to achieve a coherent entity of symbolic exposition.

Sonya and Svidrigaylov as embodiments of Raskolnikov's alternative "ways," and the carefully balanced opposed instrumental roles, in his movement to expiation, of Porfiry the accuser and Sonya the comforter, are two such binary patterns. Others illustrate Dostoevsky's (and Joyce's) distinction between submission to mere circumstances, and devout submission to God's imperatives.

The distinction is represented by the opposition of Sonya and her spineless father Marmeladov, whose name contains the word for jam or jelly. And it is elucidated by two additional relationships: that of both father and daughter to the seduced drunk girl whose introduction to the novel is placed between theirs; and the opposition of Marmeladov and Svidrigaylov. Dostoevsky specifies the three alternative ways of relating to God and God's reality—ways of living in the world—that he propounds by explicitly contrasting, as reciprocal foils, each of the three characters representative of those ways—Sonya, Marmeladov, Svidrigaylov—separately with each of the other two.

Raskolnikov's persistent alternating between his decent impulses and the assertion of ego is fully represented in the incident with the drunk girl. He confronts the well-dressed man who is about to victimize her a second time; gives twenty kopecks he finds in his pocket to the policeman to take her home; experiences "an instant revulsion of feeling," and tells the policeman to "Let him amuse himself " ("what is it to me?"); then projects her future of degradation and early death—with gradually renewed concern (pp. 47–48).

In her prostitution, Sonya is not a victim but a martyr—one who bears witness to Christ's sacrifice. The girl will become a prostitute too; but she is being victimized by mere circumstances, which she fails to resist. Like the girl, Sonya's "drunkard . . . weakling . . . infamous" (p. 21) father fails to resist circumstances, and is destroyed by them. With the girl introduced to the novel between them as vehicle, father is contrasted to daughter. Sonya's sacrifice, her volitional act of submission, out of love, to what the world will do, with the strength to act provided by (her devotion to) God, presents a contrast to the girl's and Marmeladov's self-destructive—and therefore sinful—failure to act. Totally abject, Marmeladov also is contrasted to Svidrigaylov's total assertion of ego, his insistence on absolute control. Hence: Svidrigaylov shoots himself in the head; and Marmeladov is run over lying drunk in the street. Marmeladov's transitory presence in the novel distinguishes Sonya's devout right action in the world from mere failure to resist it—the baneful excess which is the contrary of Svidrigaylov's. Through him, Dostoevsky deftly achieves thematic comprehensiveness.

Not only its consequences, but the drunkenness itself, of Marmeladov (and the ruined girl), functions in the binary opposition to Svidrigaylov: it contrasts directly with Svidrigaylov's suicidal "madness." Their drunkenness is a trope for surrender of the God-given capacity to preserve their (sacred) life in the world. The substantive basis of the trope—that drink does inhibit reason and the sense of self—enables Dostoevsky to build on his opposed types of total self-assertion and total self-abdication, another binary opposition.

Marmeladov is a transitory character because his submission to mere circumstances is no more a problem for Raskolnikov than Bloom's is for Stephen. And Svidrigaylov, who *is* the type of Raskolnikov's benighted tendency, cannot drink: "one glass lasts me all the evening, and even then I get a [!] headache" (p. 450). (Razumihin, Raskolnikov's healthy foil, "could indulge in endless drinking bouts, or refrain . . . altogether," p. 49.)

On certain occasions, Raskolnikov drinks a glass of beer—and it has a "healing" (p. 122) effect on the homicidal "monomania" (p. 26) he evolved by intellection and the assertion of ego. The first occasion is placed in the opening pages of the novel, following his visit to the pawnbroker with his father's watch. He is revolted by his intention of murdering her:

> But words and exclamations were not a sufficient outlet for his agitation. . . .
> He looked round and saw that he was standing outside a public house . . . . He

had never set foot in such a place before, but now his head was swimming and
his throat was parched. He felt a need for cold beer . . . . He . . . drank his first
glass thirstily. He began to feel better at once, and his thoughts grew clearer.
(p. 7)

As the word "thoughts" suggests, he is undergoing the familiar reversion to his
benighted tendency. His being "agitated," he promptly decides, "was simply
physical weakness":

But in spite of the scorn . . . his outlook had grown cheerful, as if he had been
suddenly freed from a terrible burden, and he cast friendly glances at the other
people in the room. (pp. 7–8)

He recognizes "something morbid in his sudden recovery of spirits," for true
recovery will require the long process that is the novel; but it is here and now
that he meets Marmeladov; and his subsequent compassion for Marmeladov
takes him to Sonya. The plotting is reminiscent of Stephen's seeing the three-
masted schooner just after his first recollection of his dream, in the early pages
of his story.

The narrator emphasizes that Raskolnikov's friendly attitude toward others
in the tavern is linked directly to his sense of freedom from a "terrible burden":
"Raskolnikov . . . as we have said, had lately avoided all social contacts, but now
he felt drawn to people. . . . he took pleasure in this visit to the public house"
(p. 8); and he becomes "interested from the first glance" (p. 9) in Marmeladov.

The tavern is precisely a *public* house. And the principal expression in the
novel—aside from his guilt—of Raskolnikov's redemptive natural impulses, is
his "friendly attitude toward" "other people," his fellow-feeling with fellow-
members of the human community (God's creatures): his compassion for the
drunk girl, Marmeladov, Sonya and her family, his sister Dounia. Dostoevsky
not only erects, on the binary opposition of Marmeladov and Svidrigaylov, an
opposition between drink and Raskolnikov's benighted thought, he also ampli-
fies his pattern, and ties it to the fundamental schism in his protagonist. He does
so by associating appropriate opposing locales with the egoism of Raskolnikov's
"theories" and with the *caritas* of his "heart"—respectively, his room and public
places: the tavern; the boulevard where he comes on the girl; the crowded street
where Marmeladov has been run over; the Marmeladovs' congested tenement;
and, ultimately, the teeming crossroads at Haymarket Square where he begins
his expiation with public confession.

Raskolnikov's room is "a tiny little cubby-hole of a place," with "yellowish
dusty wall-paper" (p. 25). To establish the pattern, Dostoevsky gives Sonya's
room "yellowish, dirty" wallpaper (p. 303) and the room Svidrigaylov takes the
night before his suicide wallpaper that is "dirty and faded . . . although its orig-
inal color (yellow) could still be guessed at" (p. 484). But he makes Svidrigay-
lov's room, like Raskolnikov's, "cramped and stuffy," "a tiny hutch of a place,"
and Sonya's "a large room . . . rather like a barn," almost infinite in size, in fact:
"one corner . . . seemed to run off into obscurity, and when the light was poor
the whole of it could not even be seen properly." Consistently, while Sonya
speaks repeatedly of God's mercy to the truly repentant, and Marmeladov imag-

ines heaven as the place "where they grieve over mankind . . . but they do not reproach" even "swine" like himself (pp. 20–21), Svidrigaylov confirms his relationship to both opposites—and the significance with which Dostoevsky is investing rooms—by imagining "eternity" as "one little room . . . black with soot, with spiders in every corner." And to Raskolnikov's objection, "But surely, surely, you can imagine something juster and more comforting than that!," he replies, "Juster? For all we know, that may be just; . . . I would certainly make it like that" (pp. 277–78).

Hence: in the passage in which Raskolnikov's room is first described, the reader is told, "He had resolutely withdrawn from all human contacts, like a tortoise retreating into its shell" (p. 25); his mother observes, "What a dreadful room you have, Rodya, just like a coffin," to which he responds, "if you knew what a strange idea you have just expressed, mama!" (p. 222); and after confessing to Sonya, on his second visit, he says, "I lurked in a corner like a spider. You've been in my wretched little hole . . . . Oh, how I hated that hole. But all the same I would not leave it. I deliberately stayed in it!" (p. 400). And quite early, twice within a few pages, Dostoevsky makes the connection between Raskolnikov's room and his benighted tendency more or less explicit: after Raskolnikov has read his mother's letter, "his face . . . wet with tears," "At last it began to seem close and stuffy in the shabby little room" (p. 37); and as Raskolnikov resists his murder plan just before his dream of the bludgeoned horse, "the idea of going home seemed suddenly unbearable: it was there, in that dreadful little cupboard of a place that the thought of *it* had been maturing in his mind for more than a month" (p. 50).

The binary opposition Dostoevsky established in *Crime and Punishment* between Sonya and Porfiry elaborates the process of Raskolnikov's expiation. The oppositions of Svidrigaylov and Marmeladov, and (with the ruined girl as a vehicle) of Sonya and Marmeladov, expound Dostoevsky's distinction between proper submission to God's dominion, and the deplorable submission to mere circumstances. Finally, he augments his long-recognized embodiment of Raskolnikov's two conflicting tendencies in the opposition of Sonya and Svidrigaylov, by the use to which he puts other elements of *Crime and Punishment*, symbolically, in binary sets. All are woven together to illuminate the central subject of the novel, and one element of each set joins readily with the corresponding element of each of the others: the connection of ego/thought-room-Svidrigaylov is neither forced nor far-fetched; nor is the opposed set.

Selecting details from a rich work of art always threatens to misrepresent its use of them as crude. These patterns are embedded deftly in a novel of more than five hundred pages. And they are only a selection. Dostoevsky's use of water, color and insect imagery, and dreams, to cite four patterns serious critics have discussed, is mentioned only in passing—and other kinds of artistic working not at all. Even were it possible to delineate the myriad elements of his conscious, controlled artistry in *Crime and Punishment*, my purpose is solely to demonstrate its presence, to establish a neglected dimension of the relation between this doctrinaire, didactic novel and *Ulysses*. The cluster of illuminating patterns confirms what is indicated by the sure hand with which its creator not

only employs coincidence in *Crime and Punishment*, but expounds the signifi-
cance of what he has employed.

VII

Although in many respects they are very dissimilar novels, the similarities
between *Crime and Punishment* and *Ulysses* seem to be both striking and radi-
cal. What is their actual historical relation? My very demonstration that their
authors wrote on the same ground, and largely with the same materials, may
have disqualified my qualifying phrase, "each in his own way."

Joyce added the new English translation of *Crime and Punishment* to his
library while *Ulysses* was in progress; and that fact, his observation to his son
Giorgio about it, his admiration for Dostoevsky's work reported by Arthur
Power, all indicate he had read it. If so: respecting the radical similarities
between those otherwise dissimilar novels that are more singular than is rich
artistic working, how much was Joyce's way his own? The evidence of that par-
ticular alien presence in *Ulysses* is less positive than is a trout in milk, but it
seems more substantial than the ghost of "The Voyage of Maelduin."

Specifically, the three principal singular similarities—Joyce's use of blatant
coincidence to represent divine intervention; like the elaborate portrayal of St.
Petersburg, his more elaborate portrayal of his own country's capital city; and
his whole delineation of his characters' predicaments, the choices available to
them, and the human condition dictating those choices—suggest his *indebted-
ness* to *Crime and Punishment*. If *Ulysses* is indebted, is the relation of all three
similarities that higher plagiary called *borrowing*? Or does Joyce's declared
admiration for Dostoevsky bespeak in one case or more the power, in fact, of
influence? An influence on the consummate modernist English novel, of not
Flaubert or Ibsen but Dostoevsky, is contrary to received opinion. But no less
contrary are the similarities, singular and otherwise, between it and the Russian
evangelist's doctrinaire *Crime and Punishment*.

In his later years, Faulkner spoke openly of precisely Dostovesky as having
"influenced me a lot."[13] So did the more pertinent American writer. The second
chapter mentioned Eliot's having read Dostoevsky's major novels while study-
ing at the Sorbonne and writing "Prufrock." In the same letter (March 8, 1946,
to John Pope), he commented on the recipient's detailed exposition of "resem-
blances" of characterization, imagery and phrasing between *Crime and Punish-
ment* and "Prufrock," "as if Dostoevski had provided a quarry for the building
of just this fantastically dissimilar poem."[14] Eliot's comment was, "I think you
have established very conclusively the essentials of your case" (Pope, 319). Pope

13. Quoted in Edward Wasiolek, "Dostoevsky and *Sanctuary*," *MLN* 74 (1959), 114–17, 114
n.1.
14. John C. Pope, "Prufrock and Raskolnikov," *American Literature* 17 (1945), 213–30, 219,
222–23. A confusion of chronology led Pope to make close comparisons with the Garnett translation
of *Crime and Punishment;* as Eliot's letter printed in the sequel to this essay pointed out, he read the
novel in French.

raises the general question of kind of indebtedness (of precise historical relation) at the beginning of his final paragraph, by inferring "the sympathy that unites Dostoevski and Eliot, these almost antipodal representatives of the modern spirit in literature" (229); Eliot's felt "sympathy," and the relation that the particular "modern spirit" of Eliot, Joyce, and their contemporaries has to his response to Dostoevsky, will be considered in the next chapter (pp. 106–7).[15]

Joyce acknowledged no influence or other debt to Dostoevsky. Furthermore, he apparently never mentioned *Crime and Punishment* to Arthur Power, even while praising Dostoevsky on a number of occasions. The next section discusses Eliot's declining to mention *Ulysses*, despite its manifest influence on *The Waste Land*, in the elaborate Notes (pp. 171–74). However, Eliot's policy is one of the indications that the Notes are functional, not documentary; and he spoke and wrote freely about his poem's profound debt to Joyce's novel. Whether or not *Ulysses* owes an equally profound debt to Dostoevsky's novel is a simple question of literary history; and I cannot answer it satisfactorily. But the question itself seems unsatisfactory. The reason may be because it is extremely simple.

The similarities between the two novels relate principally to the story of Stephen's predicament, its consequences, and its context; and in those respects (among others), Stephen Dedalus is undoubtedly—however complicatedly—an autobiographical character. Therefore, those similarities with the story of Raskolnikov must be precisely and strictly similarities, nothing more. *Crime and Punishment* may have influenced Joyce's formulation of what specifically he would show his character as having to do, and/or why—or it may not: Joyce himself may already, in life, have done as Stephen must do, and understood why. Turning from the character to the plotting of his story: Joyce may owe his strategy for representing divine intervention in Stephen's life to *Crime and Punishment*—or again he may not. Setting aside his own (despite his disclaimer) great ingenuity, there exist both the ancient tradition of benevolent crucial coincidences in fictions, and its parodic detractors. Regarding the third singular similarity—the elaborate description of the cities—that the modern metropolis is a highly appropriate subject probably was evident to the author of *Dubliners*, as it already had been to various nineteenth-century novelists; and the detailed portrayal of Dublin was consonant with his elaborate realism in the novel.

The alternative possibility, that the relation with *Crime and Punishment* is a case of higher plagiary, invokes the general problem that borrowing (for Joyce does not steal from it—"make different") diminishes the indebted work as derivative, a judgment that could scarcely be more irrelevant than it is to *Ulysses*.

When Stephen finishes his long discourse on Shakespeare, one of his auditors complains, "You have brought us all this way to show us a French triangle" (213). Stephen's apologue has had more consequence, and so has mine. The great movement for newness of Joyce, Eliot, certain contemporaries in all the arts, and their disciples, now seems to be history. What Modernism was in lit-

15. Ronald Bush discusses Eliot's response to and comments on Dostoevsky in *T. S. Eliot;* see, e.g., pp. 51–52, 57, 172, 253 (n.29).

erature is a problem as engrossing to serious critics as it is important; the next section begins with an attempt to address directly the relations of Eliot and Joyce to it; and Dostoevsky seems to be a seminal figure. Respecting the specific relation of *Crime and Punishment* to *Ulysses*, more significant for literary history than the question of direct specific influence is the fact of confluence, whatever the cause: even if Dostoevsky had not actually "point[ed] the way," both writers were—and Joyce recognized the fact—blazing segments of the same trail. In other words, however much indebtedness may be involved has less historical importance than the similarities themselves between the Irishman's great modernist novel and the great novel by the nineteenth-century Russian writer who, Power reports Joyce as having said, "brought something new into literature": "It was his explosive power which shattered the Victorian novel" (pp. 53, 58).

These similarities between the two novels illuminate neglected elements of Modernism in literature, and so broaden our understanding of it. For example, more major modernist writers than is generally acknowledged make metaphysical assertions or questions an important subject of their work. Those whose work is like *Ulysses* in this respect include—aside from the eventual Christian playwright and poet Eliot—the Joyce of *Finnegans Wake*, Yeats, Kafka, Pirandello, Faulkner, the later Strindberg and Shaw, in a sense even Stevens and Lawrence.

Almost all these modernists also make social and moral assertions in their work. And so, contrary to the popular critical doctrine mentioned early in the chapter, that *Ulysses* affirms nothing—that all the meanings and attitudes embodied in it are ironically equivocal—does Joyce in *Ulysses*. For example, as in *Crime and Punishment*, so in *Ulysses*, the atheist foil to the troubled young protagonist is portrayed as extravagantly licentious. Ironic meaning can no more be found behind Joyce's conjunction of materialism and depravity in Mulligan than in his depiction of divine intervention in human affairs.

Indeed, his abundant and famous irony in *Ulysses* usually functions not to subvert or simply equivocate *meaning*, but in a larger context to assert meaning. And the instances of his irony mentioned above, in which Mulligan and Bloom are oblivious of the true meanings of their words and acts, exemplify Joyce's characteristic mode of ironic equivocation. Whatever the gradation of tone, from high-spirited fun to sharp reproof, his irony usually contributes—satirically—to metaphysical, moral, or social assertion. Ultimately, if *Ulysses* the "symbolic structure" gratifies by its ingenuity, and "the drama of the [two] alternatives" gratifies by its richness, the "human drama" does so by the attitudes that it unequivocally asserts: compassion for human troubles, amusement at human foibles, convictions about the human condition.

But more illuminating about Modernism, because more fundamental, is Joyce's attitude toward Dostoevsky—the qualities he chose to praise, the affinity he felt—as reported in *Conversations With James Joyce*, which now should have substantial (if not precise literal) credibility. It is in his attitude, if anywhere, that influence—in Eliot's sense—operated. Dostoevsky seems to have provided a "clue" that helped the "new writer" to "become himself" and achieve a "revolution, or sudden mutation of form and content in literature."

I shall now address more precisely, and individually, the two issues devolving from what has been shown about the relations of Dostoevsky, Joyce, and God: Joyce's general practice of making unequivocal assertions in the abundant ironic equivocation in *Ulysses*, and a fundamental affinity between Joyce and Dostoevsky.

Bloom's Jewishness is an important element in the novel, and so an ideal instance of Joyce's use of ironic equivocation. His mockery seems to me simultaneously benevolent toward Bloom and the vehicle of an unequivocal social and moral assertion.

The latter issue is more complicated. According to Power, Joyce situated Dostoevsky's "modernity" not in the quasi-modernist patterns of images and symbols in his fiction, nor in other aspects of his novel-making craft manifestly similar to Joyce's own, but in a linked pair of very different qualities of his art: its concern with "modern psychology" (p. 78); and its "explosive power"—"for he was always enamoured of violence, which makes him so modern" (p. 59). Hence, "the motives he employed in his work, violence and desire, are the very breath of literature" (p. 58). Joyce's specifying that Dostoevsky's art is "modern" because of its concern with psychology, is instructive about himself and about Modernism. His citing "violence and desire," not so much expands as contravenes the modernist myth about the cerebral Irish *eiron*.

VIII. Point of Jew in *Ulysses*

"'Is he a jew or a gentile or a holy Roman or a swaddler or what the hell is he?' says Ned" Lambert to his companions in Barney Kiernan's pub (337). In this novel filled with questions about paternity, Bloom seems to be beyond question—in himself, to the rest of Dublin and, functionally, for Stephen—the Jewish son of his Jewish father. Yet his account to Stephen of his declaration to the citizen, quoted above, "I . . . told him his God, I mean Christ, was a jew too . . . like me" continues, "though in reality I'm not" (643).

Critical debate of the question "Is Bloom a Jew—or not?" has been characterized by answers not merely definite but emphatic, and has increased in the present decade. For example, within months of each other, an essay in a journal asserted "Leopold Bloom is not Jewish," and a volume of papers drawn from the 1979 International James Joyce Symposium was published with a section devoted to three essays asserting the opposite.[16] Ned Lambert's question is heuristic for readers. Behind Bloom's patent equivocation about whether or not he is Jewish lies Joyce's apparent equivocation. Why does Joyce—like the Irish (and the Jews) in a popular joke—answer a question with a question?

It is a fictional character, not a real person, whose ethnic identity is dubious; and Bloom's creator took steps to put it in question. Consequently, the proper

16. Erwin R. Steinberg, "James Joyce and the Critics Notwithstanding, Leopold Bloom Is Not Jewish," *Journal of Modern Literature* 9 (1981/82), 27–49; and Edmund L. Epstein, "Joyce and Judaism" (pp. 221–24), Morton P. Levitt, "The Humanity of Bloom, The Jewishness of Joyce" (pp. 225–28), and Marilyn Reizbaum, "The Jewish Connection, Cont'd" (pp. 229–37), *Seventh of Joyce*.

critical question is not the simple one first asked by Ned Lambert and recently given emphatic contrary answers; the proper question is that germane to the literary work portraying the character: What is the point (function) of Joyce's equivocation? When the question in the joke is put to him, the answer the Irishman gives is "Do we?," the Jew, "Why not?"; but neither casual response will do for art. In fact, Joyce's satiric equivocating about Bloom's ethnicity, simultaneously both Horatian toward Bloom and Juvenalian toward the fellow Dubliners who constitute Bloom's society, is an important aspect of his portrayal of—in the snide euphemism of Joe Hynes, who is both indebted to Bloom and his most politically "progressive" fellow Dubliner—"the prudent member" (297).

Despite the ambiguity Joyce created, Stephen and Molly as well as Bloom's fellow Dubliners consider him different in that respect from them, and he does too. (His Jewishness comes up again and again in his inner monologue, and extensively in his fantasies in nighttown.) The respondent in the catechism chapter designates him "a jew" (691). To the 1979 Symposium, the late Gerschom Sholem quoted David Ben-Gurion as having declared, "Well, the rabbis might not say that Bloom was a Jew, but *I* do" (Epstein, p. 221).

Nevertheless, the rabbis have considerable evidence. Bloom regards Judaic "beliefs and practices" as no more "rational" than "other" ones (724). His knowledge of Judaism apparently extends little beyond the first four letters of the Hebrew alphabet, exactly one dozen common Judaic terms ("Hagadah, Tephilim, Kosher, Yom Kippur ... "), the six-word "*Shema*," snatches from the *Song of Songs*, and the "first distych" of "*Hatikvah*" (487, 544, 688, 689). His father became a Protestant before his birth (716). He himself not only was born and baptized a Protestant and later baptized a Catholic (682), but had a non-Jewish mother (the parent who determines Jewishness), and is not even circumcised (373).

The extent of Joyce's equivocation is indicated by the parentage he provided Bloom's *mother*: her father, "Julius Higgins (born Karoly)," may have been a Jew; but once again, the mother in the case (Fanny Hegarty) was not (682). Plainly, Joyce was not obliged to furnish their evidence to the rabbis by inventing such an array of details subverting Bloom's Jewishness. Certain historical events form a context for understanding why he did so.

As a consequence of immigration, the Jewish population of Ireland increased more than tenfold in the thirty years before the day of *Ulysses*. And from early in that year, 1904, until shortly before Joyce emigrated to the Continent in the autumn, there was a dramatic outbreak of anti-Semitism in Ireland, including an organized boycott of Jewish businesses in Limerick.[17] Distinguished figures like Michael Davitt attacked the anti-semitic campaign in print, and eventually succeeded in discouraging it; but not before such manifestations as an exchange of letters in Standish O'Grady's *All Ireland Review* about the stoning of a rabbi in Limerick a few weeks before Bloomsday ("They are killing the place with

17. Marvin Magalaner, "The Anti-Semitic Limerick Incidents and Joyce's 'Bloomsday'," *PMLA* 68 (1953), 1219–23, 1222.

extortion"). About the status of Jews in Ireland at the time of *Ulysses*, Edward Raphael Lipsett, a journalist who was a contemporary Dublin Jew, wrote in the London *Jewish Chronicle* of 21 December 1906, "You cannot get one native to remember that a Jew may be an Irishman. . . . the position of Jews in Ireland is peculiarly peculiar."[18]

The reason for Joyce's equivocating about Bloom's ethnicity is neither that "cosmic irony" once popularly attributed to him, nor the now-popular indeterminacy of meaning. It is artistic method. His equivocation is both faithful *mimesis* and satire; and it enables unequivocal assertion. He has created, and placed among anti-semitic fellow Dubliners, a character who "in reality" both is and is not a Jew. Bloom's "reality" corresponds precisely to reality for most of the small percentage of individuals in modern western society who are not wholly Gentile from birth to death. Certainly, a born Jew who is religious is a Jew, and a Muslim Israeli is not a Jew. But—setting aside part-Jews for simplicity's sake—what of a convert to Judaism, or a born Jew who has become an Episcopalian? Neither nationality nor religious belief defines a Jew; furthermore, after millennia of individual and group conversions to Judaism, genealogy is not definitive; and given Danish Jews, Abyssinian Jews, and Chinese Jews, culture is not. Hence, on the simplest mimetic level, the condition Joyce created for Bloom is a serious artist's response to the problem of an adequate definition of Jewishness in our civilization.

But the principal function in *Ulysses* of Bloom's equivocal condition is not mimetic; the *mimesis* serves a satiric—an assertive—end. And a good deal more than benevolent mockery of the freethinker-Messiah is asserted. For Joyce's characterization engenders an obvious question: if Bloom's ethnicity is so ambiguous that he both is and is not a Jew, how important is the issue? The answer *Ulysses* provides is that whether Bloom is or is not a Jew has precisely the importance given it by those who make the question important—at Bloom's expense. He himself says he is Irish, for the sound reason that "I was born here" (331); and (much like the real Irish journalist Lipsett), Irish is all he wishes to be, at least consciously. But the anti-Semites surrounding him have created and sustain, in his social reality and consequently in his own mind as well, a difference from themselves that has no positive value for him—whose only value is their pleasure in the gratuitous cruelty of their prejudice. The mode of Joyce's portrayal of a Jew who "in reality [is] not" is benevolent mockery of Bloom; but his more telling point is a satiric indictment of Bloom's society.

Contraries in most respects, the oafish improvident Nationalist citizen, and snobbish prudent Unionist Mr Deasy, are made to share a single bigotry, and with equal viciousness. But excepting these parodies of patriotism and wisdom, the mature Dubliners tend to be only casually cruel, not actively malignant; for example, they usually suppress in Bloom's presence the anti-Semitism they articulate freely throughout the novel in conversation about him and about

---

18. Quotations from Magalaner, 1220; and Louis Hyman, *The Jews of Ireland from Earliest Times to the Year 1910* (London/Jerusalem: Jewish Historical Society of England and Israel Universities P, 1972), p. 176.

Jews. Furthermore, Stephen's contemporaries are relatively free of the prejudice (as were Joyce's own friends, apparently—with the notorious exception of Oliver Gogarty).[19] Perhaps because his real fellow Dubliners also were not vicious, Joyce augmented the indictment in *Ulysses* with a reproach apparently directed privately to them. His means was one of the many details in the novel rooted in Dublin actuality—but one that, while widely known, was known only locally.

The novel shows Bloom being Jew-baited as soon as he is in company—that of the funeral-goers in the sixth chapter ("—Are we all here now? . . . Come along, Bloom," 87). The baiting occurs when Martin Cunningham, having pointed out the lawyer and money-lender Reuben J. Dodd—one more of the novel's deplorable fathers—walking by their carriage, comments "We have all been there," then excepts Bloom. Bloom tries to ingratiate himself by telling of Dodd's reward of a florin to the boatman who frustrated his son's recent attempted suicide in the Liffey; and "got a pole and finished him out," Cunningham says, having first "thwarted" Bloom's effort "rudely" (94). Later, in Barney Kiernan's, mention of Dodd during discussion of a Jewish swindler directly precedes the citizen's "—Those are nice things . . . coming over here to Ireland filling the country with bugs" (323). The citizen disregards that the swindler's victim also is a Jew, and seems to think Dodd one as well. If so, Joyce has portrayed a stupid bigot's back-formation, from the money-lender's business and Old Testament first name.

The actual Reuben J. Dodd's son (and namesake), at the time of the Liffey incident also a solicitor, had been Joyce's classmate at Belvedere College. And as the Dodds were Catholics, so is there no evidence that their fictional counterparts are anything else; furthermore, both Bloom and his associates—unlike the citizen—seem fully aware of the fact.[20] Jack Power's "—Of the tribe of Reuben" (93) in the funeral carriage would be superfluous if Dodd were a Jew (it remains a slur on Bloom in any case); and Bloom's later private "Now he's really what they call a dirty jew" about Dodd (183) would lose the bitter irony of "really" and "they call."[21] For Joyce to have changed the actual Catholic money-

19. In *James Joyce and the Beginnings of* Ulysses (Ann Arbor: UMI Research P, 1983), Rodney Wilson Owen points out that five days after commenting critically in a letter to Stanislaus on the first of three anti-semitic articles by Gogarty ("Ugly England," in *Sinn Fein*), Joyce mentioned his 1906 *ur-Ulysses,* the projected *Dubliners* story "Ulysses," about the rumored Jew and cuckold, Mr. Hunter; and Owen suggests a connection. See pp. 4–5 and 9–10.

20. The Dodds' religion has been documented a number of times, most recently in Bruce Bradley, S. J., *James Joyce's Schooldays* (New York: St. Martins, 1982), pp. 102, 108. Chapter XXII of *The Jews of Ireland,* "Some Aspects of the Jewish Backgrounds of *Ulysses*" (pp. 167–92), presents the results of a prodigious tracing of the actual origins of Jews in the novel, including converts and descendants of converts; and the Dodds are not mentioned there, because "Dodd, in fact, was an Irish Catholic and not a Jew, as Bloom and all his companions in the funeral cortege knew quite well" (p. 164).

21. For the Gentile identity of the character in *Ulysses,* see, e.g., two articles in the *James Joyce Quarterly*: Robert Boyle, S. J., "A Note on Reuben J. Dodd as 'a dirty jew'," 3 (Fall, 1965), 64–66; and Patrick A. McCarthy, "The Case of Reuben J. Dodd," 21 (Winter, 1984), 169–75. In "Hades," pp. 91–114 in Hart and Hayman, Robert Martin Adams cites Bloom's remark as evidence that Joyce changed Dodd's religion (p. 97 and n.7). I mistakenly took Dodd to be Jewish in *Argument* (pp. 99, 239, 244).

lender into a Jew would have been a gratuitous anti-semitic act on his part, while his character's retaining Dodd's religious identity plainly advances his indictment of anti-Semitism.

The private reproach to his fellow Dubliners is effected by his inclusion in *Ulysses* of the Liffey incident. *Why* did he include it? It actually occurred near the end of 1911, seven and a half years after June 16, 1904. Such an extreme violation of historicity in a novel most of whose public events were announced or reported in the Dublin newspapers of June 16 and 17, 1904, is an earnest of the significance he attached to it.

Most of the details in the *Ulysses* version are accurate; but the young lawyer did not necessarily attempt suicide—he may have been trying to miss the boat his father had been putting him on; he was truly drowning; and he was not fished out with a pole by a boatman—a dockworker jumped into the Liffey and saved him; the lawyer was taken to a hospital, but not the working man, who became seriously ill as a consequence, leaving his family without support; and when he sent his wife to the elder Dodd soliciting help, she received a bit more than a florin (a half-crown). Finally, Joyce suppressed in *Ulysses* one additional detail. It would have been so pointedly ironic if incorporated that the effect would have been crude. Yet the creative pressure it exerted can be imagined, and may even explain his use of the anachronistic Liffey incident, which occurred only a few years before he wrote his version into the Jew-baiting in the sixth chapter. His use of it would have had a special bite for readers in Dublin, because they were likely to know the actual circumstances of Reuben Jr.'s rescue: the brave dockworker who saved the life of the miserly Catholic money-lender's son in 1911, and suffered considerably as a consequence, was named Moses Goldin.[22]

Irony abounds in *Ulysses*. Characteristically, it has a larger function: not subverting, but augmenting, what the novel asserts about its life and ours. In this example, the irony genially mocks the confusion of Bloom, the Jew who "in reality" is not. But Joyce's creation of a protagonist who is not Jewish enough for the rabbis has a sharper ironic function—a satiric attack on bigotry, accomplished by portraying the protagonist as simultaneously more than enough of a Jew for the anti-Semites Bloom lives and works among. His Irish Catholic who is "really what they call a dirty jew," linking his fictional Dodd directly to the two overt anti-semitic offenses to Bloom, augments his satiric attack. And by way of Dodd's historical original and the actual Liffey incident, he privately reproaches his fellow Dubliners.

So often the object of his benevolent mockery, Bloom is here also the instrument for his scathing satire. His sincerity is suggested by the evidence that the projected story "Ulysses" was to portray the Jew Hunter at a funeral and in a pub afterward, the two settings of the anti-Semitism (and of the Dodd business) in the novel.[23] Joyce's equivocation about Bloom's ethnicity embodies in *Ulysses*

22. See *James Joyce*, pp. 38–39, especially the newspaper account printed there of the attempted suicide and its aftermath. See also Adams, "Hades," where a "possible" irony is suggested—impossible, if the character Dodd were Jewish.

23. "It seems that the story centered on a Jewish cuckold's trip to Glasnevin Cemetery and the rejection, in a pub after the funeral, of his claims for Irish citizenship" (Owen, p. 3; see also p. 8 and n.36 on pp. 126–27).

his unequivocal contempt for bigotry, and indignation respecting its exactions. The novel's assertion of contempt and indignation contrasts splendidly not only with Pound's eventual horrible anti-Semitism, but also with that (though less extreme) of the other members of Pound's modernist quadrumvirate, Eliot and Wyndham Lewis. In "James Joyce and the Vortex of History," chapter 6 of his *Vortex: Pound, Eliot, and Lewis* (Ithaca: Cornell UP, 1979), Timothy Materer delineates a number of causes for the mutual disaffection of Joyce and the other three "men of 1914" after the triumph of *Ulysses* and *The Waste Land*. But it is no surprise.

IX. Dostoevskian Joyce

No less than does the plotted pattern of coincidences, the characteristic irony in *Ulysses* asserts its author's beliefs and values. Still, the tolerant humanist Irishman does his asserting by a witty indirection both characteristic for him, and very different from—essentially contrary to—the intolerant Orthodox Russian's hortatory expositions and blatant satire. Joyce's whole artistic manner makes incongruous, and so suspect, the merits Power reports he specified—such as "explosive power" ("which shattered the Victorian novel"), and "the motives [of] violence and desire"—as grounds for proclaiming Dostoevsky "the man more than any other who has created modern prose, and intensified it to its present-day pitch."

If one asks where in *Ulysses* is the "modern . . . pitch" of intensity to warrant Joyce's designating Dostoevsky his precursor in "modernity," an answer immediately suggests itself: in the "violence and desire" of Bloom's and Stephen's respective climactic experiences in nighttown. That instance seems as isolated as it is obvious; but the general implication threaded through Joyce's purported phrases reveals it to be, in actuality, a key.

The "violence and desire" of nighttown are essentially mental action. Even Stephen's striking at the chandelier and confronting the British soldiers are presented as his "acting out" mental states. When Joyce designated "violence and desire" to be not *emotions*, or *expressions*, but *motives*—mental action—he specified how, in his judgment, Dostoevsky achieved "explosive power" to create and intensify "modern prose": by portraying "motives." And it is precisely the emphasis on "modern psychology" found in Dostoevsky's work, Joyce's perception of which caused him to identify Dostoevsky as the chief precursor of modernist "prose" writers, that characterizes his own nighttown chapter. In it, physical events are essentially subordinate to psychological ones. This is not only attested to by the paucity of physical action during its nearly two hundred pages, but also directly expressed in its quasi-dramatic format, an elegantly appropriate embodiment of the events that dominate it—the sequences of Bloom's and Stephen's instantaneous fantasies. For the few physical events in the chapter, that format might seem a cumbersome vehicle—if it simply presented them mimetically. In fact, it does not present but *re*presents events, both physical and psychological: it effects Joyce's expressive metamorphosing

("Circe") of them.[24] The exaggerated setting at the very beginning (429–30), for example, establishes the assertive expression of his psyche (as executive consciousness) metamorphosing physical events; and such incongruities as the elegant Latin in the represented psyche of Bloom (482), who has been shown to believe the Catholic legend I.N.R.I. means "iron nails ran in" (81), establish his expressive metamorphosing of psychological events.

Mostly psychological events are expressively represented in the nighttown chapter; but it is not more fully committed to psychology than most of *Ulysses*. Only one of the eighteen chapters in the novel, that in which Bloom contends with the citizen in Barney Kiernan's, involves little psychological portrayal: the nameless narrator reveals himself, but that is incidental to his acerbic gospel of Bloom preaching "—Love .... I mean the opposite of hatred" (333) and the citizen attempting to "crucify" the "bloody jewman" (342). Of the remainder, the tenth, Joyce's *"entr'acte"* analogous to the non-episode in the *Odyssey* of the wandering rocks, and three others, are partly psychological portrayal; those three present Bloom's thoughts on the strand (after his encounter with Gerty Mac-Dowell), in the hospital, and in the cab shelter. And thirteen chapters, numbering more than three-fourths of the pages in the novel, primarily portray the principal characters' mental events—concluding with Molly's Prufrock-like consciousness-debate.

Throughout his novel, Joyce the early modernist emphasizes the inner lives of its principal characters. Furthermore, the locus of inner life is the *arena* of action: the significant action of *Ulysses* is exclusively psychological. For the novel portrays situations crucial to the destinies of three Dubliners; and the resolution of the situation confronting each of them requires no more—though demonstrably no less—than a change of attitude. Joyce's commitment to "modern psychology" made inevitable not only the subject and placement, but also the very existence, of Molly's final chapter.

He seems to have perceived his commitment, fundamental for his own modernist novel, to be fundamental for modernist literature in general. Power reports him saying about himself and the truly "modern" writers contemporary with him:

> We prefer to search in the corners for what has been hidden; and moods, atmospheres and intimate relationships are the modern writers' theme. (pp. 52–53)
> You ... should realize that a new way of thinking and writing has been started .... Previously, writers were interested in externals ...; but the modern theme is the subterranean forces, those hidden tides which govern everything .... (p. 54)

He condemns Power's preference for "classical writers,"

> who show you a pleasant exterior but ignore the inner construction, the pathological and psychological body which our behaviour and thought depend on. (p. 56)
> It ["the classical style"] can deal with facts very well, but when it has to deal with motives, the secret currents of life which govern everything, it has not the

24. Ms. Brigitte Voykowitsch, a graduate student, pointed this out to me.

orchestra, for life is a complicated problem. It . . . no longer satisfies the modern
mind . . . . (p. 74)

Our object is to create a new fusion between the exterior world and our contem-
porary selves, and also to enlarge our vocabulary of the subconscious as Proust
["no one has taken modern psychology so far"] has done. (pp. 74, 78)

And, citing Eliot with approval as an example, he declares:

the modern writer is far more interested in the potential than in the actual—in
the unexplored and hallucinatory even—than in the well-trodden romantic or
classical world. (p. 75)

Joyce was not alone in this conception of modernist writing. Woolf also
articulated it. In her 1919 essay in *The Common Reader* (1925; Harmond-
sworth: Penguin, 1938), "Modern Fiction," she singles out "*Ulysses,* now
appearing in the *Little Review*," in a paragraph:

seek[ing] to define the quality which distinguishes the work of several young
writers, among whom Mr. James Joyce is the most notable, from that of their
predecessors. They attempt to come closer to life . . . . (p. 149)

The next sentence, specifying "what interests and moves them" because "closer
to life," is her famous injunction:

Let us record the atoms as they fall upon the mind in the order in which they
fall, let us trace the pattern, however disconnected and incoherent in appear-
ance, which each sight or incident scores upon the consciousness.

Her citation of *Ulysses* follows; and then she "hazards" a "theory" about "Mr.
Joyce's intention":

Mr. Joyce is spiritual; he is concerned at all costs to reveal the flickerings of that
innermost flame which flashes its messages through the brain . . . . (p. 150)

Dostoevsky made the substance of his work not just the manifestations, as
some novelists had done for centuries, but the actual events of his characters'
psychological reality. That like him—and James and Conrad after him—"mod-
ern writers" of fiction were doing so as well, is no revelation; for it was apparent
to readers almost from the beginning. But that familiar fact alone does not define
the relation of Dostoevsky's psychological practice to *Ulysses* and Modernism.
More definitive of its relation is the extent to which his practice exemplified
Joyce's (and Woolf's, and the poet Eliot's) *conception* of the "modernity" like-
minded "young writers" were opposing to the contemporary epigones of "the
Victorian novel" ("Mr. Wells, Mr. Bennett, and Mr. Galsworthy" were Woolf's
roster). One thing Joyce's exemplary modernist novel exemplifies is an art fun-
damentally committed to portraying "the subterranean forces, those hidden
tides which govern everything." Correspondingly, his reported general concep-
tion of "modern" writing gives pride of place to a commitment by his fellow
modernists that was fundamental to the art of the Russian who died before he
and most of them were born: the commitment to portraying the events of psy-
chological reality.

The second aspect of Dostoevsky's antecedent relation to Joyce that also is psychological, is the place in Joyce's art of his own "desire." And if in this Dostoevsky did not point the way, or directly encourage by his precedent, the affinity of his precedent remains. When Joyce associates the characteristically modernist emphasis on psychology not with detached analysis, but with "explosive power," "violence and desire," he himself does violence to our conception of Modernism—constructive violence. For the association resolves in his identifying, as the fundamental characteristic of all literature which "satisfies the modern mind," one not often mentioned by critics of his and his contemporaries' fiction, poetry, and drama. In one place the self-conscious arch-modernist, committed to "a new way of thinking and writing," is quoted by Power as saying flatly, "The object of any work of art is the transference of emotion" (p. 98); and in another, "the object of a work of art is not to relate facts but to convey an emotion" (p. 106). Joyce directs one to recognize the extent to which accomplished modernist poems are memorable not chiefly for their virtuosity as well wrought urns, but because of (for example) the compassion/pain embodied, true, but also "convey[ed]" ("transfer[red]") in "Prufrock," or the paternal love and concern in "A Prayer for My Daughter," or the celebratory stoicism in "Sunday Morning."

Consistently, he is reported saying of *Ulysses*:

> Emotion has dictated the course and detail of my book . . . . In the intellectual method you plan everything beforehand. . . . But the emotionally creative writer . . . creates a significant image in the only significant world, the world of our emotions. . . . (p. 95)

No novelist seems to have *planned* more than Joyce, with his elaborate schemata of the "episodes of *Ulysses*" and his colored pencils; but the crucial word in his description of "the intellectual method" is not "plan" (or the synonym he may have used instead), but "beforehand." He drew up and distributed two elaborate schemata (if not more) that contradict each other in details; hence, at least one would appear to have been devised not "beforehand," but after the fact, for publicity purposes. We now know that both were, essentially.[25] And we know something more important: we now have irrefutable positive evidence that Joyce spurned "the intellectual method." The very creation of *Ulysses* was not the work of a god-like artificer conceiving his handiwork "beforehand" with calculation, and executing it with calm control, but the work of an "emotionally creative writer," in the fullest sense of his own phrase.

The evidence involves two related points already made. One is that during

---

25. They were prepared in late 1920 and 1921; less than three weeks before he sent Carlo Linati the first "sort of summary—key—skeleton—scheme" (Ital. *schema*), as his letter is translated (*Letters* I:146), he sent John Quinn a "scheme" of the eighteen chapters in three parts, that simply listed the Homeric tags (I:145). He gave the second elaborate schema to publicists for the completed book (Valery Larbaud, Herbert Gorman, and, eventually, Stuart Gilbert), changing it and suppressing portions in the process. See, e.g., Monika Fludernik, "*Ulysses* and Joyce's Change of Artistic Aims: External and Internal Evidence," *James Joyce Quarterly* 23 (1986), 173–88 *passim;* also, Hugh Kenner, *Ulysses* (London: Allen, 1980), pp. 3, 23.

composition, a relatively orthodox narrative of events underwent fundamental alteration: Joyce compounded that "human drama" increasingly with an "alternative" element of "symbolic structure"/stylistic "arrangement." The other is that when the "First Part" of *Ulysses* ends with the meeting between Bloom and Stephen, not only the quotidian nature of the day for them, but also and simultaneously the novel's uniform narrative mode, comes to an end—so that the changes in its story initiated by the beginning of its second part exactly coincide with the advent of its "alternative" formal element. Thus, the next chapter, which Joyce called "an *Entr'acte*" (*Letters* I: 149), separates familiar from new modes, as well as events.

"You will scarcely recognise parts of *Ulysses*, I have worked so much on them," Joyce wrote to Valery Larbaud when it was nearing completion (*Letters* III: 49). That he "recast" and especially "amplified" (*Letters* I: 172) his novel even while it was in press has long been known. But continual elaboration—through as many as twelve different drafts and sets of proof (Groden, p. 3)—was not just his way of working. He was integrating the new art his "method" created, weaving the increasingly prominent "alternative" element of *Ulysses* into its early chapters.

When he released those early chapters years before for periodical publication, he had presumed they were finished. In fact, his late recasting and amplifying of them was only the most overt manifestation of totally unplanned departures the "emotionally creative writer" made from his original conception of his novel. Notebooks, drafts, and proofsheets confirm that, in Groden's words, "he markedly altered many of his artistic goals while writing *Ulysses*" (p. 18).

The evidence of Joyce's altered goals is discussed in the last section (pp. 262–63). His departures from his original conception included two major new creative initiatives.

The first begins with the *"Entr'acte,"* and is expressed principally in the different narrating voices and parodies of styles from the twelfth chapter, in which Bloom confronts his cyclops, through the fourteenth, with its sequence of English prose styles. With the nighttown chapter, Joyce initiated the second and more dramatic major departure, changing the narrative mode radically chapter by chapter to the end of the novel; simultaneously, he did most of the elaboration that made the earlier chapters "scarcely recognis[able]"—and, in its final stages, exasperated the French printer.

Most important here, those initiatives truly were creative—Joyce did not "plan . . . beforehand" either major departure. The drafts of the "cyclops" and nighttown chapters show him actually *evolving* his new narrative modes; in each case, in Groden's words, "He began the episode without a clear idea of the technique he would use . . . " (p. 115). He did not conceive and then implement ingenious new techniques. Instead, the "emotionally creative writer" had *felt*—twice—that his book needed to change, and had created anew in obedience to his feeling. Joyce the cerebral artificer of modernist myth never existed. Wit and artistic ingenuity (as well as colored pencils) he employed generously in his achievement of *Ulysses*; but in doing so, he was submitting those "intellectual" resources to the "constant emotional promptings" by which "A book . . . as one writes . . . will form itself": "in my opinion the modern writer must be an adventurer above all" (Power, p. 95).

Joyce's relation to Dostoevsky extends beyond the striking similarities of plotting and characterization in *Crime and Punishment* and *Ulysses*, and the rich play of image and symbol characteristic of modernist fiction in Dostoevsky's novel, to a sincere asserting of doctrines and values in both. And these elements of the relation enlarge the common view of the nature of *Ulysses* and of Modernism. Finally, Dostoevsky anticipated what seems to have been a fundamental commitment of artistic purpose which the author of *Ulysses* shared with Eliot and other modernist writers. The evidence confirms that, in two senses, "Emotion has dictated the course and detail of my book."

In the sense that the course and detail of *Ulysses* were dictated by its characters' emotions, Dostoevsky seems to have a relation to Joyce corresponding to the role for the poet of "Prufrock" of the older American, already expatriate in London, who was committed to portraying consciousness ("the deeper psychology" in James's own phrase) in his fiction. This cannot be known with the certainty a trout in milk makes the presence of water known, for Dostoevsky's fiction, and *Ulysses*, differ in psychological emphasis from Joyce's earlier fiction only in degree. But if Dostoevsky was not instrumental in this respect, directly "pointing the way" for the making of *Ulysses*, there is strong evidence that Joyce recognized a precursor along a way, followed by modernists like him and Woolf and Eliot, that he had come upon himself.

In the sense that the emotion that dictated to him was Joyce's own, the correspondence of Dostoevsky's role for him is to the role for Eliot of both major influences on "Prufrock." James had provided a model, in Eliot's own phrase, "of thinking with our feelings"; and Laforgue, a model not only of introjecting one's own "stat[e] of mind and feeling" into one's work, but also of evolving radical new means for doing so. And here, although the evidence is still, as it inevitably must be, circumstantial, the evolution of *Ulysses* in progress—an evolution that began after Joyce first encountered the "explosive power" of Dostoevsky in his newly translated novels—provides more solid evidence that Dostoevsky helped Joyce "become himself" and achieve a "revolution or sudden mutation of form and content in literature."

CONTEMPORARIES

5

"Our Modern Experiment"

The phrase is Pound's, used the year *Ulysses* and *The Waste Land* appeared, 1922. The aging Eliot, declaring "us" successful in his 1953 retrospective account, specified the historical conditions of "some revolution, or sudden mutation . . . in literature" like theirs:

> Then . . . writing . . . is found by a few people . . . no longer to respond to contemporary modes of thought, feeling and speech. A new kind of writing appears . . . . (*To Criticize The Critic,* p. 57)

These excerpts from the passage are quoted again because in them he describes "A new kind of writing" as *consequent* to new "thought, feeling and speech." If certain changes in ideas and concerns, in sensibility, and in attitude toward discourse, motivated Pound, Eliot, and others ("a few people") to undertake their "experiment," then Modernism in literature was not strictly the "experiment" itself, but also the "contemporary modes" generating it.

In the guise of providing causality, his statement actually is simplifying the causes of the "sudden mutation" into Modernism. Most directly, his (habitual) focus on the relations of art and its creators ignores the context—the historical conditions—of the "modes of thought . . . ." In *The Struggle of the Modern* (Berkeley: U of California P, 1963), Stephen Spender defines the art of his modernist predecessors as "that in which the artist reflects awareness of an unprecedented modern situation in its form and idiom" (p. 71). The "form and idiom" of "a new kind of writing" derived from "modes of thought, feeling and speech" which in turn derived from "awareness ["by a few people"] of an unprecedented modern situation." Conceiving the attitude and art strictly in terms of "aesthetic" or "stylistic" experiment is superficial; the point has pertinence below.

It is all reasonable, and still simplistic. For its historical purview is limited to immediate conditions, as Eliot's own painstaking articulation of the dialectic of Tradition and Development in literary history makes plain. And its geographical purview excludes the prior manifestations of Modernism in the Germanic countries, beginning with *Men of the Modern Breakthrough* (1883), by the Danish critic Georg Brandes—for whom "Joyce had a lifelong admiration."[1] Yet development does, and in 1953 Eliot asserted that during his youth a revolutionary development did, occur. By then, few believed otherwise.

I. Contexts

That a cultural hegemony can undergo sudden change, anyone who has lived through the revolution in public mores in industrialized Western countries during the last two decades will not doubt. A movement can undermine a period, supplanting it with another because—as I understand the two terms—unlike a *school,* or group of artists who evolve and follow a special fashion that does not violate the character of a period, a *movement* is a consensus of artists—and their allies—who work, some of them independently and even in isolation, some without conscious intention, to effect a fundamental change in the established conception of their particular genre of art, and conception of reality insofar as that genre engages reality.

One of the major historical myths of our culture has the form of an extended trope keyed to a martial metaphor of the Paris art "world": in the first decades of this century, an *avant-garde* of consecrated and intrepid crusader-artists besieged a complacent citadel of cultural mediocrity; it fell to them; and it promptly was occupied and instaurated by their young recruits. The passage of time seems to confirm the rough validity of that historical myth, at least for English literature.

It seems to increase understanding of the avant-gardist writers' crusade as well. Innovations in "way of writing" were apprehended earliest: myriad formal audacities, including the structural use of myths and earlier works; authorial concealment, idiolectic effects, and other strategies for creating an "autonomous object" or "heterocosm"; parsimony; complex tone and texture. Gradually, the etiology of such innovations—the motivating new "thought, feeling and speech" cited by Eliot—is being recognized. The modernists' commitment to authenticity, and to acknowledging the non-rational, issued in an emphasis on portraying consciousness, for example; and that emphasis was instrumental in both the modernists' circumvention of the intervening narrator and the evolution of audacious forms of objective presentation—instrumental as well in such complexities as syntactical discontinuity and associative patterns of images and motifs.

But historical understanding is not won easily. Explicit statements of the (ostensibly modernist) principle of parsimony, for example, and the concept that function must determine form, go back at least to Keats's "On The Sonnet," which insists that "Misers of sound and syllable" eliminate "dead leaves in the bay-wreath crown" and that "Sandals ... fit the naked foot of poesy." And despite their proclaimed hostility to Romanticism, the modernists' preoccupa-

---

1. *Det moderne Gjennembruds Maend.* For the relations of Germanic and English Modernism, see Malcolm Bradbury and James McFarlane, "The Name and Nature of Modernism," *Modernism,* ed. Bradbury and McFarlane (1976; Harmondsworth: Penguin, 1978), pp. 19–55, pp. 36–50. The quotation is from *James Joyce,* p. 230n; see also Owen, p. 103.

tions also made reflexive connections with essential doctrines of the earlier revolution, such as the generative image and symbol, the imperative of innovation, the status to be accorded the artist's psychic experience. These (and other) affinities ignored by modernist theoreticians themselves, beginning with Pound and T. E. Hulme, have caused a debate in recent decades about the extent to which *The Creative Experiment,* as C. M. Bowra entitled his classic account of a modernist revolution in Western literature (1949), is really nothing more than *(mutatis mutandis)* a developed Romanticism, as Edmund Wilson actually had implied two decades earlier, while Modernism was still ascendant, when he characterized it in *Axel's Castle* (1931) as *symboliste.* In the decades following Bowra, what Wilson implied has been asserted, first in John Bayley's *The Romantic Survival* and Frank Kermode's *Romantic Image* (both 1957), then by others, repeatedly by George Bornstein and Harold Bloom through the 1970s. This historical revisionism now is challenged by two new books on Modernism. The first argues for "the counter-Romanticism of Modernism"; the other that it is both perpetuation and revolution.[2]

It would be folly to attempt here to resolve the debate about Romanticism and Modernism. My concern is specifically with the place, in the movement that succeeded in supplanting a prior artistic period with the dominant period of our century, of the authors of "Prufrock," *Ulysses,* and *The Waste Land.* Still, my understanding of the relations of Romanticism and Modernism must be declared, to avoid the hovering presence of so fundamental an open question.

I think it reasonable, if reductive, to attribute a radically generative priority to Romanticism, conceived as one of two broad romantic movements, more or less simultaneous, only tenuously linked, that originated a full century before Modernism. They were movements of dissent from prevailing tendencies in an increasingly urban, mercantile, industrialized, mechanized and organized civilization. The other romantic movement, antecedent to Socialism, was essentially political, opposed the social and economic hegemony, and concerned the plebeian majority. Romanticism, the romantic movement antecedent to Modernism, was essentially cultural, opposed the spiritual and artistic hegemony, and concerned the privileged (educated, partly leisured) minority. Socialism evolved rapidly (Owen was born the year after Wordsworth, Fourier as well as Coleridge the next year), Modernism only after long incubation.

The rejection by cultural Romantics of the prevailing epistemology and metaphysics, values and social priorities, dictated a new art. But the art that revolutionary counter-culture created, especially the literature, did little more than initiate the developments its doctrines implied. This is because while the prevailing culture changed (partly in response to both romantic movements of

2. Ricardo J. Quinones, *Mapping Literary Modernism: Time and Development* (Princeton: Princeton UP, 1985), esp. pp. 23, 31–32, 120–36, 187–91; C, K. Stead, *Pound, Yeats, Eliot and the Modernist Movement* (New Brunswick: Rutgers UP, 1986). Stead proposes that while Romanticism was perpetuated in Imagism, "What Eliot and Pound added" to "invent Modernism" was aggregating images "without logical or narrative continuity" (p. 39; see also pp. 75–77). The phrase quoted from Quinones is on p. 120. For a critical review of major earlier contributions to the debate, see Monroe K. Spears, *Dionysus and the City: Modernism in Twentieth-century Poetry* (New York: Oxford UP, 1970), pp. 15–20. The whole first chapter, "The Modern and the Past," is a learned and enlightening discussion of Modernism as a historical concept.

dissent), it did persist. As political revolutions in North America, France, and elsewhere deliquesced after an initial acute success—as their social and economic doctrines became assimilated to the political hegemony they had altered, but not displaced—so romantic literature became assimilated to the cultural hegemony it had altered. The romantic political dissent was perpetuated—by the germinal socialist movement; the cultural dissent was not. It was the modernist writers who truly realized the potentialities of the artistic doctrines of Romanticism; hence, doctrinal affinities such as those mentioned above.

The latter part of the nineteenth century—the interval following the assimilation of (cultural) Romanticism to proprieties for literature imposed by the established society and preceding the advent of Modernism—was the period of incubation for the new revolutionary movement. The incubator was attacks on specific proprieties. To Tennyson's (Trollope's, etc.) proper "idealisation," in Eliot's words, of "England as it was," Hardy, for example (in France, Flaubert, in Scandinavia, Ibsen) opposed truth-telling; and Joyce would pay homage to the two Continental writers for that reason as well as for their commitment to craft. To the moralistic propriety, Pater (the *symbolistes,* Wilde) opposed the principle of aesthetic primacy. They and other writers, committed to emotional intensity; or to conveying the complexity of reality and/or the relativity of perception; or to portraying consciousness ("the deeper psychology"); or to sensuality (eroticism, decadence); or to one or another combination of these, challenged the established literary proprieties during that interval. In the old speaker's octameters of the title poem of *Locksley Hall Sixty Years After, Etc.,* published the year after Pound's birth and two years before Eliot's (1886), Her Majesty's Laureate accused "Authors" of corrupting "the budding rose of boyhood" and "maiden fancies" with "the drainage of your sewer" and "the troughs of Zolaism"; and his indignant sarcasm enjoined them, "Rip your brothers' vices open, strip your own foul passions bare; / Down with Reticence, down with Reverence—forward—naked—let them stare."

Tennyson's indignation documents both the proprieties to which romantic literature eventually had been assimilated, and the responsive challenges to them. A generation later the Modernists integrated, in their equally self-conscious successor to the original romantic cultural movement of dissent, all the intervening attacks on those literary proprieties. The pressure for new forms this new international movement exerted—some of which already (by Flaubert and James, Mallarmé and Laforgue, Ibsen and Strindberg) had been adumbrated, to "point the way"—was difficult to resist, as the generation of Conrad, Yeats, Pirandello and Valéry discovered; but even if orthodox conventions of poetry, fiction, and drama had not been inadequate to new "thought, feeling and speech," the likes of Eliot and Joyce were no respecters of literary conventions.

They did respect their tradition. A focus on its relations with Romanticism disregards other contributors to Modernism. One was the earlier heritage of Western culture, including the hegemony originating in the Renaissance that the Romantics challenged. The common belief that "the Modernist artist (and Joyce is said to be the prime villain in this) has cut us off from our history" ("its discontinuity from earlier tradition . . . is now viewed as its major defect") ignores the facts. To take only the author cited—and set aside the obvious refutation in

Eliot's case— "*Ulysses* [as one critic recently put it] concedes priority on every page, beginning with its title."[3] The writers of the modernist movement related both to the Romantics, and to the Romantics' contrary predecessors; the writers also both assaulted conventions, and assimilated tradition. In both cases they were—I propose below—not being inconsistent, but expressing aspects of the essence of Modernism in English literature.

Another contributor to Modernism which a focus on its relations with Romanticism disregards was the prevailing latter-nineteenth-century culture itself, the attacks on whose established proprieties had "pointed the way." An example of the positive contribution of that culture is its elucidation of the evolution, historical relations, and semantic richness, of languages. *The Pound Era* traces a line: from early inquiries into "continuities of meaning" (p. 104) in words; through Emerson; through Richard Chenevix Trench (notable poet and philologist, and Anglican Archbishop of Dublin during Yeats's first nineteen years), whom Kenner quotes declaring, "Many a single word . . . is itself a concentrated poem, having stores of poetical thought and imagery laid up in it" (p. 103); through the (Oxford) *New English Dictionary on Historical Principles,* which "was originally suggested and its characteristics indicated by Trench in 1857" (*DNB,* XIX, 1120); through Ernest Fenollosa; to Pound. Pound brought the creator of the Noh-inspired *Four Plays for Dancers* into direct relation with it, of course; chance or (Joyce would have assumed) fate, did so for the creator of *Ulysses* and *Finnegans Wake:* the model for Haines in *Ulysses* was Trench's grandson, Samuel Chenevix Trench (Richard Samuel Dermot, 1881–1909), who had awakened Joyce and Oliver Gogarty in their Martello tower during his nightmare of a black panther.

Limited to the place of Eliot and Joyce in the new movement, my focus on Modernism also excludes broad social considerations. In *The Cultural Contradictions Of Capitalism* (New York: Basic, 1976), Daniel Bell writes illuminatingly of "modernity, the thread that has run through Western civilization since the sixteenth century":

> The Western ideal was the autonomous man . . . .
> . . . In the economy, there arises the bourgeois entrepreneur. . . . In the culture, we have the rise of the independent artist . . . .
> The impulse driving both the entrepreneur and the artist is a restlessness to search out the new, to rework nature, and to refashion consciousness. (p. 16)

And he begins his sub-chapter "Enter Modernism":

> We come to an extraordinary sociological puzzle. A single cultural temper . . . has persisted for more than a century and a quarter . . . . The most inclusive term for this cultural temper ["this sentiment that, antedating even Marxism, has been attacking bourgeois society"] is *modernism:* the self-willed effort of a

---

3. The first quotations are from Morton P. Levitt, "The Modernist Age: The Age of James Joyce," *Light Rays: James Joyce and Modernism,* ed. Heyward Ehrlich (New York: New Horizon, 1984), pp. 136–37; the other is from Philip M. Weinstein, *The Semantics of Desire: Changing Models of Identity from Dickens to Joyce* (Princeton: Princeton UP, 1984), p. 279. Weinstein's point about Joyce is made by a number of critics, and discussed at length by Jeffrey M. Perl in *The Tradition of Return: The Implicit History of Modern Literature* (Princeton: Princeton UP, 1984).

style and sensibility to remain in the forefront of "advancing consciousness."
(p. 46)

But Bell's sensitive social generalizations here are exceptional. On Modernism, the fancy boosterism of his associate Irving Kristol's *Reflections of A Neoconservative* (New York: Basic, 1983) entertainingly resembles the traditional (neo-Aristotelian) Marxists' judgment. Their culprit is egoism (see pp. 199–203); his is religiosity. He dismisses the modernist rejection of established culture as the expression of "utopian romanticism" (p. 39), as—ironically—"spilt religion," in the phrase the modernist Hulme used to define Romanticism. Kristol's conceiving ("simply") two possible elements—in the pronouncement, "modernism in the arts can best be understood as a quasi-religious rebellion against bourgeois sobriety rather than simply as a series of aesthetic innovations" (p. 35)—indicates the current state of most broad social analysis. Hence, in "Beyond Modernism, Beyond Self" (*Art, Politics and Will: Essays in Honor of Lionel Trilling,* ed. Quentin Anderson *et al.* [New York: Basic, 1977], pp. 213–53), which "continues and enlarges with literary evidence" (p. 213n) the "argument" presented in his book, Bell characterizes Modernism monistically as "subversive of all restraints," and proposes that "in the world of drugs, rock music, and oral sexuality, one sees a culmination of modernist intentions" (pp. 231–32). The first and third instances of "a culmination" can be set aside as historically unsound (to do more would be, as Bell is, saying more about oneself than about either). And literary Modernism was no more generative of rock music than it was of junk food or any other aspect of our culture its subtle, demanding, *articulate* art projected. It is here that appreciating its relation to its "unprecedented modern situation" (in Spender's phrase) is pertinent. Eliot wrote in "Ulysses, Order, and Myth" of "material which you must simply accept." Bradbury and McFarlane wisely aver that "Modernism is not art's freedom but art's necessity"; it "responds to the scenario of our chaos" (*Modernism,* p. 27). And Quinones, that the modernists "were committed to depicting the changing truths of their time and their experience . . ." (p. 252). Bell's monism constitutes—simply—blaming the messenger.

My focus disregards not only social considerations, but also the psychological sources of modernist "thought, feelings and speech." Distinguished critics (including Wilson, R. P. Blackmur, and Trilling) long ago shrewdly characterized Modernism as a response to an alienating environment, the loss of faith, the irrational in us; supporting evidence in "Prufrock" and *Ulysses* for all three attributions already has been presented. But I can make no other sort of contribution to understanding those sources, even in the psyches of Eliot and Joyce. My concern is solely the historical role of the authors of "Prufrock," *Ulysses* and *The Waste Land* as members of the advanced guard that invested the citadel.

II. Make It New

Quinones begins *Mapping Literary Modernism* with the confident declaration that "Modernism . . . has entered into history" (p. 3). Nevertheless, it may be best to proceed no further before acknowledging that my casual use from the first page—that all recent use—of the defining term begs two questions. A historical question it begs is the validity of the myth: whether or not there did in fact exist a distinct (finite) movement and period (now part of literary history) with its own set of doctrines and practices, to warrant the suffix of *Modernism*. A theoretical one is whether or not there is any justification for appropriating the body of the term, capitalizing it, and so to some extent compromising its former usefulness as a common epithet of simple temporal signification, all in order to create an awkward neologism. Of readers who recognize the period and accept the term as fully as I do, I ask indulgence: this section will discuss the latter, theoretical, question; the next section will consider the historical one. My addressing both would not have been excessive circumspection very few years ago; and certain readers may not consider it so yet, for one or the other.

The term is awkward, and seems overworked recently, in part because it is awkward; but it is not new. It actually was used pejoratively by Swift in a letter to Pope (23 July 1737) to designate the doctrines and practices of one side in the "Ancients and Moderns" dispute. Two years after *Ulysses* and *The Waste Land* appeared, John Crowe Ransom used it to ask a question—"And yet what is Modernism?" (*The Fugitive*, February 1924)—whose short form, with the verb in the past tense, has been the title of at least two essays in the past quarter-century. In 1927, Laura Riding (Jackson) and Robert Graves published *A Survey of Modernist Poetry*. The "Prefatory Note" to Janko Lavrin's study of various twentieth-century European writers, *Aspects of Modernism*, published in 1935, began by calling the term "hackneyed"; it was by no means so, but can be found in other criticism of the same and the next decade, to designate precisely the characteristic doctrines and practices of a movement and period to which "Prufrock," *Ulysses* and *The Waste Land* belonged.

The currency of both the concept and that name grew gradually until, during the 1970s, its present broad acceptance became established. The Autumn 1971 issue of *New Literary History* was devoted to "Modernism and Postmodernism," and so not only declared as fact the finite and historical nature of the former, but called attention to the apparent lack of a name for the new movement it asserted had begun; and by then more and more individuals were using the term in their criticism with a firm denotation. Nevertheless, *Modernism* remained unacceptable usage in the early 1970s, to judge from two related kinds of evidence: none of eight then-current glossaries of literary terms consulted listed it; and it occurred rarely if at all in university course titles (for example, my department did not permit use of either the word or its adjective).

Then, within half a decade, a minor historical change manifested itself. During the later 1970s new editions of three of the eight glossaries were published, and all listed *Modernism* or *The Modernist Period;* and the usage became otherwise institutionalized. As confirmation, Methuen's "Critical Idiom" series was augmented by Peter Faulkner's *Modernism* in 1977. Faulkner noted that other names (*Vortex, Imagism*) had been proposed for the movement and period (p. ix); this one seems to have taken.

The acceptance is not universal yet, despite the intervening years. Resistance to innovation in literary history—to a new formulation about art and culture that upsets the received dogma, and even to a seemingly new coinage—is expected, inevitably transitory, and unimportant. But thoughtful critics as well have rejected categorically both the name *Modernism* and the very conception of a delineable period. They have not been merely resisting innovation; and to ignore their judgment would be both discourteous and irresponsible.

The question of the name itself is not trivial because reality is organized as it is perceived, in cultural history no less than in other things: the shape and even the actual existence of a finite literary period is defined by the central characterization of it, which is manifest in its name. If indeed awkward, the coinage "Modernism" out of the root epithet is no more so than "Romanticism" and distinctly less so than "Neo-Classicism" (or "Postmodernism"). More grounds exist for objecting to the use of the root itself; and the fact that the familiar phrase "the modern tradition" gives an impression of absurdity reveals those grounds. One manifest cause of the impression is that the epithet denotes an immediate relation to the present. Yet the manifest cause is not a sufficient one: strictly speaking, a fully developed tradition can be of very recent origin, hence modern. Nor is the suggested anachronism sufficient grounds for objection (although with the passage of time it becomes increasingly more so): a term signifying recency can be employed for the historical period proximate to ourselves.

The seeming absurdity has another cause, however, more subtle and much more important. In addition to the primary sense of "modern," which is wholly relative to the present time of its user and so is ahistorical, the epithet has a sense that is *anti*historical: the sense of *modernity,* of newness as a quality challenging the past—challenging precisely tradition. It is usually in that sense artists throughout history have called their work "modern."

That sense of the epithet "modern" provides the perspective whereby "modernist" joins "romantic" and "classical" as designations of universal or normative, not historically-delimited or descriptive, qualities. The analogy Eliot and others have drawn between the literature and culture of the early twentieth century, and those of the early seventeenth, may be said to be between a romantic and a renaissance modernism. Such a statement may be made and will be understood because to some extent "modernism" names a normative concept, wholly outside historical limits.

However, whereas the other two normative concepts are compatible with periods in literary history (indeed were derived from appropriate periods), the concept of modernity is, as has been pointed out above, antihistorical—explicitly antagonistic to historical continuity. And that is why calling a finite period "Modernism" has been judged by some not merely a verbally inept expedient unfortunately become current, but gross error.

One must grant that the epithet "modern" does not lend itself readily to historical use; however, to grant that is not to concede the general case against Modernism as a finite movement and period to which the name is given quite properly.[4]

4. For a historical discussion of variants of "modern" (and of antecedent "new" in Britain) for literature of this period, see "The Name and Nature of Modernism," *Modernism,* pp. 21–22, 37–40. Quinones provides a brief bibliography of other historical accounts (p. 259 n.1).

This negative case is put most eloquently perhaps, and its implications are explored most fully, by the late Paul de Man, in his book of "Essays in the Rhetoric of Contemporary Criticism," *Blindness and Insight* (New York: Oxford UP, 1971). Both the extent to which de Man's broadly ranging book is specifically concerned with the historical concept Modernism, and his attitude toward that concept, are revealed in the fact that his opening and closing pages discredit two popular and contradictory critical "mystifications," as he justly calls them, about its essential quality. One designates as the essential quality of Modernism, the artists' having turned from their individual consciousnesses toward reality; and the other "mystification" designates the exact reverse. But these deserved rebukes are little more than the setting for his argument: that Modernism is an untenable concept because a paradoxical one.

De Man presents his thesis in the essay before the last, "Literary History and Literary Modernity." He articulates: the "radical impulse that stands behind all genuine modernity," as distinguished from both "the contemporaneous" and mere "passing fashion" (p. 147); the necessity for that radical impulse in an artist; and the antagonistic but complex relation between the modernizing impulse and the artist's heritage (between originality—Development—and Tradition). Then de Man advances to his argument proper: "the challenge to the methods or the possibility of literary history" (p. 144) inherent in the antihistorical nature of the concept modernity. And he refines his argument by describing the contradiction between modernity and history as, more than that, a significant paradox. It is a paradoxical proposition that "modernity becomes a principle of origination and turns at once into a generative power that is itself historical" (p. 150). In the final essay, "Lyric and Modernity," he relates to this untenable paradox a historical fallacy: the second "mystification" he rebukes, that of characterizing Modernism as a turning (by artists, in history) from reality. In art "mimesis and allegory" are—like "history" and "modernity"—neither sequential nor dialectical but (in a paradox that is true) simultaneous; and "The worst mystification is to believe that one can move"—trace history—from "mimesis" to "allegory" (pp. 185–86).

These extractions from de Man's subtle and reflective discussion of Modernism do not attempt to represent it, but are limited instead to its exposition of the basic objection thoughtful critics make to the use of the name and to the conception of a finite period. My defense of both name and conception can be demonstrated in a slight perversion of his untenable paradox. For, however antihistorical may be the concept modernity, it is no paradox but precisely literary history if, during some time period, *a doctrine of artistic commitment to* "modernity becomes a principle of origination and turns at once into a generative power that is itself historical." To place before de Man's paradox those italicized words, is to shift the ground of judgment from the intrinsic *logical* and *rhetorical* validity of the historical concept and name "Modernism," to its proper locus.

The proper locus of judgment is not the intrinsic validity of Modernism, but precisely its *legitimacy*—which is to say, its accuracy—as historical description. For describing appropriate historical circumstances, *despite* the contradiction in calling a finite period "Modernism," the concept and name are appropriate. When those circumstances have occurred, the historical reality makes the question of internal validity irrelevant: the contradiction is not in one's logic, but in the reality. If "Modernism" is precisely descriptive of the essential doctrines, intentions, and unconscious assumptions of the artists whose work constitutes the movement and period—if what the name specifies is the historical reality of an -ism of modernity—such objections are not warranted.

That is precisely the case. The epithet "modern" provides a name in literary history despite internal contradiction, because the concept involved is not one of a *principle* (modernity) paradoxically obliged to contradict itself when placed in history; instead, it is a strict *historical* concept. It designates a *movement* and *period* of the past in which artists were committed to that principle. Consequently, the theoretical question is not begged but irrelevant.[5]

The historical question is relevant perforce, and is complex. Whether or not "our modern experiment" created a distinct (finite) period, it existed beyond doubt; and the suffix of its name is no less appropriate than the root, for *-ism* signifies commitment to a doctrine and program. Both the doctrine and the program of the movement are nicely encapsulated in the imperative Pound used as the title of a collection of his essays: *Make It New* (1934). Of one of the Chinese emperors, Canto LIII has:

> Tching prayed on the mountain and
>   wrote MAKE IT NEW
> on his bath tub
>   Day by day make it new
>
> . . . .

Down the right side of the passage are printed the Chinese character for the imperative, twice, enclosing the character for "day," twice. According to *The Pound Era,* the sequence of four characters is the proper form of the "maxim" (make it new / day / by day / make it new); Kenner quotes both the passage and the gloss on the character in Pound's Chinese dictionary, which includes, "Fresh, new; to renovate; to improve or renew the state of " (p. 448).

The "it" for the "Guide to Kulchur" seems to be not only one's work, but also the Tradition: "renovate" (Pound's word), "remake what we have been

---

5. Quinones's "Conclusion: Purviews and Purposes" (esp. pp. 252–53) deals effectively with the practical complement to de Man's theoretical argument: that historical "Modernism is . . . a congealment . . . of an impulse of *modernité* that must always be . . . changing" (p. 246). In "The Poverty of Modernism" (*The Innocent Eye on Modern Literature & the Arts* [New York: Farrar, 1984], pp. 329–41), Roger Shattuck makes a related charge. "Modernism is not [he writes] a meaningful category of literary history or art history"—"not a period . . . not a proper school or movement . . . serves no heuristic purpose . . . suggests no stylistic practice"—because it "embodies a disabling contradiction": its "only general characteristic . . . is the celebration of individual experience," and that is "not repeatable" (p. 338). But as this book is being readied for the printer he qualifies his sweeping rejection, declaring in "Catching Up with the Avant-garde" (*New York Review of Books,* December 18, 1986, pp. 66–74), "I believe the term modernism might usefully be applied for the period 1900–1930" to "English, Irish and American literature [the concern of this discussion] and art" (p. 70).

given." The -ism is one of modernity not just as innovation but also as *reno-vation*. And since originating and renewing are correlates, Pound agrees with Eliot that "True originality is merely development." Hence, the text of an unti-tled lecture Eliot gave in Dublin on January 24, 1936, simultaneously echoes Pound and reiterates his concept by declaring, "The perpetual task of poetry is to *make all things new*. Not necessarily to make new things."[6] No more than that of Eliot or Joyce, is Pound's modernist doctrine one of "discontinuity from earlier tradition."

The -ism is a doctrine that enjoins originating as renewing, renewing as orig-inating. Its special fitness for the historical phenomenon it designates is sufficient reason why the name "Modernism" persisted and has gained currency, when it failed to do so during the debates of the Ancients and the Moderns in France and England around the turn of the eighteenth century, or at any other time.

To speak reductively of "Prufrock," *Ulysses* and *The Waste Land* as mod-ernist is not to define them, but to specify their historical association. Our aware-ness of certain doctrines, intentions, and unconscious assumptions of their time tells us the ways *Gulliver's Travels* is neo-classical and Byron's *Don Juan* is romantic; and we would be informed about each work by their opposite histor-ical circumstances if their dates of composition were reversed—would be directed to romantic characteristics in *Gulliver's Travels* and classical ones in *Don Juan*. We would be more informed about those particular works than about most others of the time of each if their dates were reversed, but only relatively more informed.

Lawrence was more of a modernist *artist* in certain exquisite stories and in his versification than in his novels, whose modernism is principally new atti-tudes, and explicit treatment of certain subjects. All works of art are only partly characterized by their respective periods, even when the periods are most appro-priately named, because the names designate doctrines, intentions, and uncon-scious assumptions; and so, at most the names designate characteristics of works and tendencies in works that are related to those things, rather than the totality of any work of art. Good art never matches its manifestoes.

Clearly, our conceptualizing of a period is not adequately definitive to be an encompassing category for any individual work. The inadequacy does not war-rant questioning whether the modernist movement prevailed and dominated lit-erature in English for a time; nevertheless, that sort of question is endemic in the whole endeavor of literary history.

The endeavor remains valid and profoundly necessary. When more than the recital of facts, history is generalization. To generalize is to be reductive, but it is not consequently to lie; to generalize about the past can be instead to mythol-ogize. Literary periods are myths, persuasive accounts of reality that are neither demonstrable fact nor demonstrable fiction, and valuable to us so long as we are their masters, not their slaves.

6. T. S. Eliot, "Tradition and the Practice of Poetry, with an Introduction and Afterword by A. Walton Litz," *Southern Review* 21 (1985), 873–88, 876.

III. What Was Modernism?

The myth of the victorious modernist siege, and the period it brought into being, seems from our vantage as persuasive as any. The sense in which a historical question is begged, is the implied assertion in *Modernism* that a movement established a distinct most recent (finite) period in the history of our culture.

Some who have helped promulgate both the historical myth of Modernism, and the name, reject any hypostatizing of an integral period. There are three principal alternative formulations: (1) that what we call Modernism had two stages—was in effect two periods created by the same artists; (2) that there has been no finitude—no discrete period as such; and (3) that the (a single) period is characterized by irreconcilable contrary tendencies. All three contribute to historical understanding.

In 1967, Frank Kermode postulated "two phases of modernism, our own and that of fifty years ago," a tradition-oriented strain "affirming a relation of complementarity with the past" and, with "between them, a continuity of crisis," a successor "anti-traditional" phase; eleven years later—in an essay whose title he took from Levin, and this section took from them—Robert Martin Adams concurred, although reserving judgment on whether or not "our own" latter "phase" had ended in the interim.[7] Where critics like Kermode and Adams distinguish two finite periods of Modernism, Harold Rosenberg sees none. For him there has been rather the defeat of history by modernity in a transcendence of periods during the past century. In *The Tradition of the New* (New York: McGraw, 1959), he writes of "an art whose history, regardless of the credos of its practitioners, has consisted of leaps from vanguard to vanguard . . ." (p. 11).

Literary movements can have unforeseen consequences. And literary periods—to the extent that those myths constructed by our historical imaginations exist, and are not merely noumenal formulations—do not end and begin with the closing and opening of a curtain, as anyone who has tried to trace the "true beginning" of a period knows. Keeping these postulates in mind, I propose that although the historical conception expounded by Rosenberg provides a valuable insight, it, as the once-prevailing conventional wisdom did, essentially avoids the issue. The conception of Modernism as having had two phases contrasts with the third conception of it, as one period comprising opposed elements. For they designate what are in essence the same two tendencies as, respectively, primarily sequential phases and primarily simultaneous elements.

As good a brief characterization of those contraries as any is the title of Monroe K. Spears's study of modernist poetry, *Dionysus and The City*. Spears's "Apollonian" (Kermode's "traditional") tendency was controlled or intellectual or classical or realist or formalist or animus or yang. Spears's "Dionysiac" (Kermode's "anti-traditional") contrary was unrestrained or sensual or romantic or

---

7. Frank Kermode, "The Modern Apocalypse," in *The Sense of an Ending: Studies in the Theory of Fiction* (New York: Oxford UP, 1967), pp. 93–124; the quotations are on pp. 103, 112, and 122. Robert Martin Adams, "What Was Modernism?," *Hudson Review*, 31 (1978), 19–33. See also "Modernisms" (ch. 1, "The Modern"), in Kermode's *Continuities* (London: Routledge, 1968). For a discussion of Kermode's conception of Modernism, see Spears, pp. 204–14.

egoist or aleatory or yin. One could continue to collocate epithets for both tendencies.[8]

If attempting here to resolve the debate about Romanticism and Modernism would be folly, attempting any definitive assertion about Modernism as a whole would be arrogant folly. *An Annotated Critical Bibliography of Modernism* by Alistair Davies (Sussex: Harvester, 1982), published while interest continues to accelerate, has a general section that lists (through 1981) more than two hundred "major" books and essays in English about literary Modernism, and is incomplete.

Books published every year since the bibliography attest to the complexity and elusiveness of the subject. They are not just more recent blind persons' accounts of the elephant, but new contributions to an accretive devolution of understanding, helpful to me as I hope this discussion of the relations of Joyce and Eliot to literary Modernism will be in its turn. In 1983, *Modernism Reconsidered* (ed. Robert Kiely [Cambridge: Harvard UP]) appeared, with a number of general essays, one of which, by Ronald Bush, I draw on extensively. Two books published the next year are Douwe W. Fokkema's *Literary History, Modernism and Postmodernism* (Amsterdam: Benjamins, 1984), and Michael H. Levenson's *A Genealogy of Modernism: A study of English literary doctrine 1908–1922* (Cambridge: Cambridge UP, 1984). Levenson's title specifies both his historical formulation and his emphasis: he "follows the thread of concepts . . . the constituent ideas of English modernism" (p. viii); a chapter discussing a modernist poem is included because "*The Waste Land* . . . stands as itself a doctrinal act . . . a critical gesture" (p. 168). Fokkema's chief concern is *Rezeptionsgeschichte,* history as informed by what Balakian called "literary fortune": the relation of western European (especially Dutch) "texts" each to the historical evolution of a particular "group code or sociocode" (p. 11), "system of compositional and thematic conventions which governs [its] production and reception"—in sequence "the replacement of Romanticism by Realism, of Realism by Symbolism and Modernism, and of Modernism by Postmodernism" (p. 5)—with emphasis on the "main conventions" and "particular themes" of Modernism (p. 12). The two most recent books (1985 and 1986) have been cited already. The title of *Mapping Literary Modernism* designates a more precise cartography, a neater specificity, than I can accept; but its concern with modernist values and sensibility, and its emphasis on thematic elements in modernist literature, complements nicely Levenson's study of modernist critical doctrines ("constituent ideas"). Stead's book, presumably the latest as this goes to press, complements both. It proceeds by close comparative analysis of individual poems, to argue the poetic achievement of Pound, as against specifically ("modern") Yeats and to a smaller extent (fellow "Modernist") Eliot: "Yeats's enslavement to fixed forms and modes meant that in Pound's eyes . . . he could not 'make it new' . . . (p. 32); "enslavement" registers Stead's bias.

8. For example, in "Toward a Redefinition of Modernism," *Boundary 2,* 2 (1974), 539–56, William A. Johansen writes, "A Contemporary reader . . . finds . . . in Modern writers . . . polarized alternatives of order or disorder, knowledge or experience, Aristotle or Longinus, Classicism or Romanticism, art or life, speech or silence . . ." (p. 544).

The conclusions as well as the approaches of the books described sketchily above differ, and differ with mine. But there are important points of agreement; and these could signify devolved understanding. Relevant here is that most subscribe to one or another of the three antecedent conceptions of Modernism—that it had two stages; that there was no finite period; and that it had two irreconcilable contrary tendencies—formulations I have said contribute in different ways to understanding What, for the authors of "Prufrock," *Ulysses* and *The Waste Land,* It Was.

On January 29, 1927, while Joyce was working on *Finnegans Wake* and Eliot was about to begin *Ash Wednesday,* the literary historian of the two published a review in *The Nation & Athenaeum.* It was principally about *The Future of Futurism,* a short book by his friend John Rodker, a regular contributor to the *Egoist* who had proposed publishing *Ulysses* and was involved in the reprinting (1922) of the first edition by the Egoist Press (*James Joyce,* pp. 490, 505–6n). The younger modernist's

> thought is apparently influenced by Mr. Wyndham Lewis and T. E. Hulme (which we are glad to find), and his syntax seems to be influenced, attractively, by Mr. Joyce's third manner.

But Eliot takes issue with Rodker's prognosis for Modernism:

> Mr. Rodker seems to think, in short, that the future of literature lies in two directions: in the line of "Blake, Mallarmé, Roussel, and the development of all those qualities we have called mental agility," and the other the line of "the sublimity of the bowels as in Tchekhov and Dostoevsky." Or, to put it crudely (if I understand him correctly), the direction of abstraction ("pure poetry"), and on the other hand the investigation of the subconscious. Now Mr. Rodker seems to me to have made only one mistake . . . and that is to identify the general future with *his* present.

Eliot's own prognosis, which alludes to another book under review, Gertrude Stein's *Composition as Explanation,* makes plain that if he gave the review its title, "Charleston, Hey! Hey!," he was expressing not lightheartedness but indignation:

> What warrant is there for believing that our sensibility will become more "complex" and refined? . . . I am inclined to wonder . . . whether complication of syntax always implies complexity of thought or sensibility, whether the thought and sensibility of the future may not become more simple and indeed more crude than that of the present . . . ; whether the omens are not with Miss Stein and the author of "I'm gona Charleston Back to Charleston". . . . If this is of the future, then the future is, as it very likely is, of the barbarians. (595)

Eliot's reference to Joyce's "third manner" reflects his ambiguous attitude toward *Finnegans Wake,* mentioned earlier (pp. 10 and 12); its relevance to *Ulysses* will be considered shortly. The lengthy excerpts reveal that Eliot implicitly accepts Rodker's delineation of two "lines" corresponding to the "Apollonian" and "Dionysiac" contraries; and, judging from the italicized "*his* present" and gloomy prognosis, that he believed in January 1927 that a literature characterized by the two contraries was a thing of the past. In other words, Eliot's own conception of Modernism back in 1927 combined the first and third historical formulations of recent critics: Modernism originally had two contrary elements; and, during the decade that began with *Ulysses* and *The Waste Land,* it was evolving into a second (potentially a "barbaric") phase. The historical reality seems more complicated still; but there is a good deal of evidence for the validity, within its limits, of his conceptual model.

In "Beyle and Balzac," a review of the second volume of George Saintsbury's *A History of the French Novel, to the Close of the Nineteenth Century* published in *The Atheneum* of May 30, 1919, a half-year before he first mentioned having *The Waste Land* "in mind" (*Facsimile,* pp. xvii–xviii), Eliot contests Saintsbury's preferring the latter novelist and pairing with him one of Eliot's own two exemplars ("Monks of fiction"—"recluses dedicated to perfection"—A. Alvarez has called them) of artistic commitment: "Arnold and Pater" (1930) invokes "the devotion of Flaubert or Henry James" (*Selected Essays,* p. 357). Against Saintsbury's pairing *Balzac* with Flaubert, Eliot writes:

> There is something that ["Stendhal and Flaubert"] have in common, which is deeper than style and is the cause of style; shared, too, with Turgenev, to a less extent with Hardy, Conrad, Hawthorne, James, hardly at all with our Victorian novelists.

The last phrase recalls Woolf's "Mr. Wells, Mr. Bennett, and Mr. Galsworthy" in "Modern Fiction," written the previous month, and Joyce's remarks to Power a few years later on the superiority of "modern" to "Victorian" fiction. The common virtue of Stendhal and Flaubert that is the cause of style is revealed by two statements in juxtaposition:

> In the great artist imagination is a very different faculty from Balzac's: it becomes a fine and delicate tool for an operation on the sensible world. (392)

> But the patient analysis of human motives and emotions, and human misconceptions about motives and emotions, is the work of the greatest novelists. (393)

Eliot's ideal novel, during the time that he was to designate in 1927 (and I propose was) the original phase of Modernism, has the object ("an operation on the sensible world") and method ("something ... deeper than style [that] is the cause of style") of the "modern" novel described by Woolf and (according to Power) Joyce, the novel in which "several young writers, of whom Mr. James Joyce is the most notable ... attempt to come closer to life."

And although Eliot does not explicitly state in this 1919 review any more than in his 1927 one that the "lines" were combined in the original Modernism, he *does* imply in this review that his ideal novel combines them, as Joyce was combining them at the time in *Ulysses.* Eliot's ideal novel in 1919 syncretizes (Apollonian) qualities such as *mimesis* and craft, with (Dionysiac) qualities such as innovation and "promptings," into "a new way of writing"—enacted "human motives and emotions" ("the atoms as they fall upon the mind"; "motives ["violence and desire"], the secret currents of life").

Joyce's syncretism in *Ulysses* of "intellectual" resources and "constant emotional promptings" received attention in the first section of this book; Eliot's in his poetry during the first phase of Modernism will be taken up here. Aspects of both contraries are present in all good literature, of course; the point has been made (good art never matches its manifestoes). But Joyce and Eliot during those years exemplify what seems a conscious endeavor of the modernists generally: to explore (new) ways of both fully embodying traditional/formal/representational values, and fully rendering radical/phenomenological/expressive pressures, in their art.

In *Yeats At His Last* (Dublin: Dolmen, 1975), I discussed the poet's articulation of a model for art: a Yeatsian antinomial consort of "calculation"/"intellect" and "character"/"sexual instinct" (pp. 7–19). Stevens's famous "rage for order . . . /The maker's rage to order words" expresses the same syncretism of articulation and impulse, complexity and energy. Although proper individual attention to these and other major modernist English writers is beyond my scope, I propose that, during the original phase of Modernism, lyric poetry as well as fiction and narrative poetry was characterized, not merely by the concurrence of the ostensibly irreconcilable contrary "lines," but by their synergetic combination—that in fact the modernists' successful syncretism of the contraries was the radical source of the newness that distinguished their art. That is probably a major reason why critics find a valid general description of modernist poetry and fiction so elusive.

Eliot does not fail to bring into "Beyle and Balzac" Joyce's "man more than any other who has created modern prose" by "his explosive power which shattered the Victorian novel":

> If you examine some of Dostoevsky's most successful, most imaginative "flights," you find them to be projections, continuations, of the actual, the observed: . . . Dostoevsky's point of departure is always a human brain in a human environment, and the "aura" is simply the continuation of the quotidian experience of the brain into seldom explored extremities of torture. (392)

In admiring both Flaubert and Dostoevsky, Joyce need not have made them polarized epitomes of the "line" (as Eliot put it in 1927) of "abstraction" or craft and that of "explosive power": Eliot proposes that Flaubert and Dostoevsky share a commitment to performing "an operation on the sensible world" of "motives and emotions" that is "the cause of style"; they share, as I tried to show in my discussion of *Crime and Punishment,* a commitment to craft as well. And as I point out there (pp. 74-75), like the author of *Ulysses,* the author of *The Waste Land*—who read Dostoevsky's major novels in French during the year he wrote "Prufrock"—has a significant relation to the writer whose "point of departure is always a human brain in a human environment."[9]

The other monk of fiction, James, had been more influential on him "initially," Eliot declared in an interview in 1924 (Gordon, p. 46n). But in a "Lon-

---

9. In "Beyond Modernism," Bell instances Dostoevsky, Schopenhauer, and Nietzsche as leading to the modernist emphasis on the will and "derogation of the cognitive" (p. 227); Quinones emphasizes Nietzsche, in a sympathetic and discriminating treatment. I find more evidence for Dostoevsky's relation to the modernist *art* of both Eliot and Joyce, although Eliot at least almost certainly read both Schopenhauer and Nietzsche—probably first as a young philosopher.

don Letter" on "The Novel" dated "August, 1922" in the September number of *The Dial* (LXXIII, 329–31: *The Waste Land* appeared two numbers later, in the middle of October), he wrote of "tapping the atmosphere of unknown terror and mystery in which our life is passed" (330), and observed:

> My own view is that Dostoevsky had the gift, a sign of genius in itself, for uti- lizing his weaknesses; ... a fundamental weakness can, given the ability to face it and study it[, be] the entrance to a genuine and personal universe. (331)

"Modern/Postmodern," Ronald Bush's 1983 essay, is "intended as a bridge" between *T. S. Eliot* and a book in progress on "the passing of modernism"; in it, he recalls "the force of Eliot's psychological situation" when he was writing *The Waste Land,* and proposes that Eliot utilized *his* weakness, with Dostoevsky "pointing the way": the poem "drew heavily on a study of Dostoevsky for its nightmarish intensity even as it orchestrated its fantasies with the craft of *la poésie pure.*"[10]

The last phrase recalls Eliot's review of Rodker's book, to which the subtitle of "Modern/Postmodern" alludes; and the "orchestration" Bush attributes to *The Waste Land* is precisely a combining of the two "lines." He infers that by 1927 Eliot had understood the "new kind of writing" of the original phase of Modernism to be a fiction and poetry characterized by that syncretism:

> According to his way of thinking, the two streams of Rodker's vision had once been united.... Henry James ... was followed, as the [1936] "Milton" essay points out, by James Joyce, at least by Joyce "in his early work, and ... in [the first] part of *Ulysses* [sic]." We need only complete Eliot's thought to add that ... Joyce was ... typical of the modernist movement. It is the very essence of the high modernism of the early twenties that the currents Rodker associated with Dostoevsky and Mallarmé were somehow made to reinforce one another. Thus the representative modernist masterpieces (the *Cantos, The Tower, Ulys- ses, Women in Love, To the Lighthouse*) yoke together elements of symbolist music and psychological exploration. There is, however, no better example than *The Waste Land,* which drew heavily on a study of Dostoevsky for.... (p. 193)

As I do, Bush concurs with the literary history Eliot proffered when he cou- pled the two "lines" with the emphatic "*his* present" in the Rodker review: that such a "high modernism of the early twenties" existed; and that before 1927 it had ended. Bush's assumption, "complet[ing] Eliot's thought," that in addition Eliot conceived Modernism's original phase to have been characterized by a suc- cessful syncretism of the contraries, reinforces my inference above. It is not proven, but the "Beyle and Balzac" review of 1919 and the *Dial* "London Let- ter" of 1922 strongly support it; furthermore, they indicate that Eliot actually had that acute historical insight at the time of *Ulysses* and *The Waste Land.*[11]

10. Ronald Bush, "Modern/Postmodern: Eliot, Perse, Mallarmé, and the Future of the Barbar- ians," *Modernism Reconsidered,* pp. 191–214, pp. 199, 193. See also *T. S. Eliot,* pp. 51–52, 71, 72.

11. Bradbury and McFarlane subscribe to its validity: they "suppose" an "appallingly explosive fusion" of "intellect and emotion," "Apollo" and "Dionysus" (p. 48); see also, McFarlane's "The Mind of Modernism," pp. 71–93 in *Modernism.* Quinones seems to have something related to it in mind in his fourth chapter, "The Modernist Sensibility," an exposition of the Modernists' "divided consciousness"; see also p. 17.

Bush's own conception of the original phase is different from mine (and apparently Eliot's), only in his precise specifying of its syncretized contraries, and in his generalizing the role of one of his specifics in *Eliot's* subsequent development—"symbolist music" *("la poésie pure")*—to the later history of Modernism as a whole.

His history of the later evolution of Modernism informs "Modern/Postmodern," and is articulated in the preface to *T. S. Eliot:*

> Like the modernist movement as a whole, his early work nurtured two conflicting forces. . . . Then in Eliot as in his contemporaries the bond between the forces snapped, and the international style of 1922 became a thing of the past.
>
> The inclinations I am referring to are . . . a poetry, so to speak, of pure music. And, opposing that, a disposition . . . toward fidelity to the subtlest expressions of the innermost self . . . . For a brief moment in the late teens and early twenties, these forces reinforced one another . . . in the masterpieces of high modernism . . . . In *The Waste Land* or *Ulysses,* an ornate pattern of myth and music coexists with the most radical kind of emotional sincerity. But by the time of the *Four Quartets* or *Finnegans Wake,* the modernists' understanding of sincerity (and of the self) had been transfigured. (pp. ix–x)

This passage is neatly complemented by one in "Modern/Postmodern":

> Having been driven to explore the Romantic conception of sincerity to its absolute, not only Eliot but Yeats, Lawrence, Woolf, and Joyce finally . . . grew weary of exploring the intensities of the individual psyche. In *Last Poems, The Plumed Serpent, Between the Acts,* and *Finnegans Wake,* they reduced the importance of dramatic voice, immersed themselves in history and myth, and delighted in complex musical organizations . . . . (p. 200)

One reason I have quoted at length from Bush's beguiling model of two phases of Modernism is my partial agreement with it[12]; the other is his catalogues of exemplary works in the respective phases, which provide specific foci for examining it. The model is that indicated by Eliot in the Rodker review of 1927. I not only agree with its general conception of the original phase; I accept Bush's description of the two phases—as an account specifically of *Eliot's* art in the original phase of Modernism and evolution out of that phase. Bush's erudite critical biography shows persuasively that the specific individual aspects of the two contraries he generalizes for the modernists—"pure poetry" and "fidelity to the subtlest expressions of the innermost self"—are the central respective aspects of them for Eliot.

Eliot combined "the currents Rodker associated with Dostoevsky and Mallarmé" (as Bush puts it) during the original phase of Modernism, and then aban-

12. Again, other recent studies provide reinforcement. By specifying that his inclusive dates, 1908–1922, are "boundary stones" (p. viii) in the *genesis* of Modernism in English literature, Levenson implicitly delineates the first of the two phases. Stead has a first "stage" ("1900–25") dominated by experiment, and a second ("1925–50"), in which the poets turned to "public issues, particularly politics and economics" (p. 4). Quinones "charts" four phases in his diachronic "map"; but his first two correspond chronologically to the first phase of Levenson, Stead, Bush, and me, and the other two to our second phase. It should be noted that the first of Kermode's "two phases of modernism" conflates the two, since in 1967 he referred to "our own" phase.

doned the former one. On November 15, 1922, precisely midway between its periodical and book publication, he wrote to Richard Aldington, "As for *The Waste Land,* that is a thing of the past so far as I am concerned and I am now feeling toward a new form and style" (*Facsimile,* p. xxv). Bush reports that he told Arnold Bennett the same thing two years later (p. 81), by which time he was working on "The Hollow Men." Bush proposes as the "most important" reason why Eliot abruptly abandoned his variant of early Modernism's syncretism that, "consciously or unconsciously, he decided that he could not, would not . . . write a poetry that continually sensitized his own internal fragmentation and brought him unbearable anxiety" (p. 73).

Eliot's movement to his second phase of "pure poetry"—his abandoning the "current" of "Dostoevsky" for exclusive commitment to that of "Mallarmé"—involved the discovery of precisely Mallarmé as "congenial" influence. Bush traces his evolution, through *The Hollow Men* and *Ash Wednesday*—poems embodying "not our feelings, but the pattern which we may make of our feelings"—to his neo-*symboliste* fulfillment in *Four Quartets*—a cycle of poems that explicitly aspires to the condition of music. The quoted phrase is from Eliot's introduction (1924) to a translated poem by a newly revaluated poet, "Le Serpent" by Paul Valéry. In "Modern/Postmodern," Bush writes that Mallarmé "was at first too daunting a master," and Eliot began with "the great man's followers" (p. 203); but by 1933, in an unpublished lecture given at Johns Hopkins, "defending a kind of figuration that had found little place in his early verse, Eliot advises that it is a mistake to suppose that a simile or a metaphor always has to be visible to the imagination." And Eliot's lecture takes up a sonnet of Mallarmé's that contributed to "Burnt Norton," *"M'introduire dans ton histoire,"* with special attention to lines such as "Tonnere et rubis aux moyeux" (p. 210). It should be noted that, accompanying his reversion to *symboliste* "pure poetry" with Mallarmé "pointing the way," Eliot reverted, beginning with *Ash Wednesday,* to an older tradition, and a singular one for a modernist: Christian meditative lyric and homiletic drama.

Eliot's evolution out of the original phase of Modernism is exceptional, however. "Fidelity to the subtlest expressions of the innermost self" is a first principle of expressionist art. And that all the modernist writers shared this "Dionysiac" element—even to the extent that many wrote largely about their own psychic reality—has been pointed out. Yet the enactment of a *character's* consciousness was a *mimetic* ("Apollonian") emphasis of modernist narrative that Eliot *conflated with* this informing principle of fidelity to one's "innermost self." He turned a modernist mirror into a lamp: he enacted his *own* consciousness in much of the poetry he wrote during the original phase of Modernism—most pertinent here, in both "Prufrock" and *The Waste Land.* Hence, most of the other major English creators of "our modern experiment" were not moved as he was—by psychic pain—to abandon their particular variants of the "Dionysiac" element of the original syncretism as he so abruptly abandoned his.

If one asks, Why then did they do so?, the answer is, Most did not. The reason the original phase ended is that some did abandon the original syncretic "revolution, or sudden mutation . . . in literature." In its later phase, Modernism differed from its original phase not because a different hegemony replaced the original one—as the first historical formulation mentioned above, and Eliot, Bush, and others propose—but because the original hegemony was replaced by none. Among the writers Bush mentions, Eliot evolved as he did; Joyce and Pound evolved in a uniquely modernist way; and Yeats, Woolf, and Lawrence essentially persisted in their original syncretisms.

For example, "the importance of dramatic voice" is even greater in *Last Poems* than in *The Tower*. Hence, the repeated imperative "Swear" in the first section of "Under Ben Bulben" makes the poem with which Yeats began the volume a dramatic monologue; and its last section exploits its allusion to the dramatic voice of King Hamlet in the cellarage by announcing that the poem is spoken from beyond the grave ("Under bare Ben Bulben's head / In Drumcliff churchyard Yeats is laid"). *The Waste Land* and *Four Quartets,* most of *Ulysses* and *Finnegans Wake,* the first *Cantos* and the last, are not readily identifiable as by the same writer. But, despite the fact that Yeats, Woolf, and Lawrence (to his early death) evolved—both exfoliated and actively innovated—as serious artists do, Bush's examples for all three (*The Tower* and *Last Poems, To the Lighthouse* and *Between the Acts, Women in Love* and *The Plumed Serpent*) have the familiar continuity of works by the same writer. In *Between the Acts* there is greater emphasis on the play of language, and in *The Plumed Serpent* on myth; but both emphases were apparent during the original phase of Modernism in, for example, *Ulysses* and *The Waste Land.*

The persistence in English literature of that original phase can be demonstrated in other ways. Generalizing Eliot's case, "Modern/Postmodern" declares that "by 1927 the 'investigation of the subconscious' was no longer a proper subject for serious literature" (p. 201); but (setting aside the complicated situation in *Finnegans Wake*), the narrative works he cites controvert this. Although its concerns go well beyond the rendering of individual consciousness, *Between the Acts* does not neglect to "record the atoms as they fall upon the mind" of each principal character. And in *The Plumed Serpent,* Kate's is the controlling point of view for the good reason that the central plot element is not the sensational neo-primitive religious society perpetrated by Ramon and Cipriano, but Kate's evolving mental experience of them and it. To mention only one prominent example of this persisting central concern of modernist narrative, Faulkner, a writer too young for the original phase, two years after Eliot's pronouncement published *The Sound and the Fury,* whose first part enacts Benjy Compson's consciousness (and presents his special dramatic voice). Although there are other exceptions as well as Eliot, Joyce, and Pound (such as William Carlos Williams and the Objectivists), most original modernist writers persisted in, and recruits adopted, the original "revolution." Stevens's syncretism of rage and order in "The Idea of Order at Key West" dates from 1934. And Yeats articulated his corresponding poetic in "Under Ben Bulben" and "The Statues" during the last year of his life.

That the original phase of Modernism in English literature remained viable, helps to explain its later adoption by two practitioners of the most closely related art. Sean O'Casey and Eugene O'Neill were born during the same decade as

Joyce, Woolf, Pound, Lawrence, and Eliot. By the turn of the century, the departure from realism into modernist dramaturgy had been made possible by new electric technology such as the spotlight and the revolving stage, and had been strikingly achieved by Strindberg's *Ett Drömspel* (1901). George Bernard Shaw employed that dramaturgy in parts of *Man and Superman* in 1903, and within a decade Yeats (with assistance from Fenollosa through Pound) was evolving his verse dialogue and austere staging into a fully modernist drama. Nevertheless, O'Neill and O'Casey did not write their first plays employing modernist (*expressionist* in the taxonomy of "theatre" history) dramaturgy—*The Great God Brown* (1925) and *The Silver Tassie* (1928)—until after the hegemony of the original phase of Modernism had ended.

Remaining to be accounted for is—of the six modernists cited—the evolution of Joyce and Pound. I believe that their later development is illuminated by the suffix of "Modernism," by Pound's imperative, "Make It New," and by the second historical formulation—involving "leaps from vanguard to vanguard" in Harold Rosenberg's phrase—mentioned above. It is a uniquely modernist development because Joyce and Pound turned the means of the revolution in art into its end. Neither the generation of Conrad and Yeats, nor Joyce's and Pound's contemporaries, including Eliot, shared their emphasis on innovation for its own sake. The -ism of modernness, which had been a response to new historical conditions (including "modes of thought, feeling and speech")—the response of "a few people" to the felt need for a revolutionary Development—they made, I believe, a categorical imperative of their writing. Their evolution is uniquely modernist because of their strict conception of modernness in art, a conception they seem to have shared (significantly) with both Igor Stravinsky (born the same year as Joyce) and Pablo Picasso (born the year before). According to that strict conception of modernness, the new, once accomplished, enters the tradition—with the consequence that renovation and innovation must be accomplished anew.

One can make most historical sense of Joyce's radical innovation in *Finnegans Wake* by seeing it as expressing the same impulse that motivated his two major stylistic departures in *Ulysses:* a categorical imperative to make new art. The radical evolution of the *Cantos* can best be explained the same way. During the second phase of Modernism, Joyce and Pound seem to have acted as though the pronoun in "Make It New" refers *neither* to what one has inherited, *nor* to what one is undertaking to make, but instead to what one *has just made*. One's own once-new work, by its very existence, becomes part of the tradition that one *must* depart from. In a history of twentieth-century music published shortly before Stravinsky's death, speculations about future developments were made contingent on (as I recall the clause) "what the old man may do next." Critics speculate about what Joyce might have done next—and would have speculated so about Pound, had he finished the *Cantos*. This is because Joyce and Pound evolved, from their place in the "experiment" or "revolution" finite in time of the original phase of Modernism, to a dedicated experiment*alism*—to a "continuing revolution."

The first of the three formulations seems to have been correct in distinguishing two phases of Modernism; but they were not respectively "traditional" and "anti-traditional." The change that brought about a second phase of Modernism was not to a new hegemony, but to the supplanting of hegemony by three alternatives. Most writers evolved preserving the syncretism of "Apollonian" and "Dionysiac" elements that characterized the original "revolution." Some abandoned its innovations for an austere art of crafted nuance, as—with the distinguished exception of *Murder in the Cathedral*—Eliot did. And some made innovation itself a categorical imperative, as did Joyce and Pound.

Furthermore, the reason for postulating a single historical entity—with two phases, whose second evolved in three divergent ways—is the persistence of fundamental attributes of Modernism; for example, the second phase, like the first, is precisely tradition-oriented in all its three strains. It is to the function of the tradition in their modernist poetic, that a recent book on the subject attributes the reactionary politics of the chief poet in the persisting strain, and the poet in each of the other two.[13] Hence, no less than are *Ulysses* and *The Waste Land*, both cited examples of continuing innovation—*Finnegans Wake* and the later *Cantos*—are steeped from their very titles in their authors' literary and historical heritage. In 1963 (in *The Struggle of the Modern*) Spender wrote, "The confrontation of the past with [the] present seems to me ... the fundamental aim of modernism" (p. 80). And in the second "What Was Modernism?," Adams emphasized "the deliberate cultivation of the past" (p. 20) and declared eloquently, "modernism gives us a sense of an entire cultural heritage being ploughed up and turned over" (p. 28).

Measures of the divergence that characterizes the second phase of Modernism are Yeats's troubled remarks about his friend's *Cantos* in "A Packet for Ezra Pound" and—even more—Pound's persistent criticism of "all the circumambient peripherization" (*James Joyce*, p. 584) that was *Finnegans Wake* in progress. Early harbingers of divergence were Eliot's strictures against Pound's poetry and criticism beginning in 1919, recounted by Levenson (pp. 213–16), and Pound's negative initial comment on Joyce's first stylistic departure, following the "first part of *Ulysses*," that "a new style per chapter" was unnecessary (*Pound/Joyce*, p. 157). The parameters of divergence are nicely illustrated by Eliot's evolving attitude toward Joyce's divergently evolving art. The enumeration in his phrase "Mr. Joyce's third manner," in the Rodker review, conveys a shade of irony. His statement in the first Milton essay that "the later part of *Ulysses* shows a turning [toward] phantasmagoria" does not seem to me as reproving as it does to Bush; Eliot attributes that development, and the limitation he perceives in *Work in Progress* (emphasis on "an auditory imagination"), in part to Joyce's increasing blindness (*On Poetry and Poets*, p. 162). Then, after two more decades, the evolution of gentle irony in 1927, to palliation in 1936,

13. In *Yeats, Eliot, Pound and the Politics of Poetry: Richest to the Richest* (Pittsburgh: U of Pittsburgh P, 1982), Cairns Craig writes: "The thread that ties the modernists together in their poetic is ... the concept of a poem that 'borrows its beauty' [Yeats] from the memories our minds have stored, or that have been stored in the transpersonal memory of the tradition" (p. 64); and, "Yeats, Eliot and Pound were driven to politics in order to maintain the institutions and the patterns of society which preserved and promulgated the kinds of memory on which their poetry relied." (p. 71.)

issues in the pointed equivocation about *Finnegans Wake* of "The Frontiers of Criticism" (1956): it is *"monumental"*; "every student of poetry" should read "at least some pages of " it; and "one book like this is enough" (p. 119).

A dramatic index of Eliot's departure from the hegemony of the original phase of Modernism during the few years between *The Waste Land* and his reference to "Mr. Joyce's third manner," is that before his poem became "a thing of the past so far as I am concerned," he felt the awed admiration for *Ulysses* that will be discussed in the next chapter; and specifically of "the later part of *Ulysses*," he wrote to "the man from New York," John Quinn, while he was working on *The Waste Land*, "the latter part of *Ulysses* . . . is truly magnificent" (*Facsimile*, p. xx).

However increasingly Eliot's poetry diverged, during the second phase of Modernism, from the "permanent revolution" exemplified by Joyce and Pound, he was too good a critic and historian to regard them as having joined the "barbarians" he foresaw. Not only the traditional component in their later work, but also, for example, their commitment to craft, and their concern for achieving embodied form, explain his continued—if increasingly qualified—respect for their art. Whether or not Pound's moving lament in Canto CXVI, "I cannot make it cohere," expresses a transitory judgment, it expresses an abiding value.

Nevertheless, Eliot's strictures in "Milton I" about the possible baneful *influence* of "the later style of Joyce," which "may prove to be . . . a blind alley for the development of the language" (p. 162), indicate concern that his former close associates may be "pointing the way" to barbarism. Of the two sequential, individually homogeneous, phases of Modernism it postulates, *The Sense of an Ending* says, "one reconstructs, the other abolishes, one decreates and the other destroys the indispensable and relevant past" (p. 123). Any attempt at a historical sketch is obliged to propose not only the beginning of the movement become period of "Prufrock," *Ulysses,* and *The Waste Land*, but also—though that is even more foolhardy—its end; and my proposal is that Kermode's two phases of Modernism are, instead, that movement become period and its successor movement. "Our own" phase of Modernism that Kermode postulated in 1967 seems, two decades later, not a second form of a modernist hegemony, but the advent in Modernism of new Development: the "Future of the Barbarians" as the subtitle of Bush's essay, "Modern/Postmodern," renders Eliot's gloomy prognosis of 1927. The new movement comprises those writers of recent decades who have been engaged in "our own" time's "modern experiment."[14]

In "Toward a Redefinition of Modernism," Johansen writes:

The new sensibility . . . is another symptom of our compulsion to be new: postmodernism, out-moderning the moderns.

The contemporary strategies of antimyth, antimetaphor, being against interpretation, and postmodernism . . . all define themselves by rejecting earlier

---

14. Fokkema devotes the third and final part of *Modernism and Postmodernism* to a careful survey of significant differences between the modernist and postmodernist "codes," although he avers "I . . . will never be able to prove that the discontinuity is more important than the continuity" (p. 38).

modes of thought, especially modes peculiar to the Moderns of the early twen-
tieth century. (543)

The writers of recent decades referred to are no more generally read than were
the modernists during their original phase. And one consequence of the history
of Modernism is that most critics today, aware of earlier critics' derision of
many great modernist works when they began to appear, including both *Ulysses*
and *The Waste Land,* hesitate to judge the current movement. But its clumsy
name may not be tentative: the name embodies Johansen's point, that these con-
temporary writers "define themselves" by their rejection of Modernism.

Like all reductive generalizations about history, this trims away part of real-
ity. Their theoretical and polemical writings invoke their Instructors: Joyce and
Kafka; Williams, Stevens, Dickinson, Whitman, Blake—and above all, Pound.
Nevertheless, theirs is a self-conscious, systematic negation of Modernism in
general. Three relevant conclusions may be drawn. The first is that their explicit
negation is a tacit tribute to its importance for them. The second is that their
tribute is evidence of its achievement. The third is that their negating it, by
asserting explicitly a successor -ism, signifies a turn of history. Modernist writers
continue to publish, as "Victorian" writers did in the original phase of Modern-
ism; but the hegemony has been ended by a new movement.

That the writing in question departs fundamentally from Modernism can be
indicated briefly, for the purposes of this sketch, by pointing to precisely its
"post-" as "anti-" program of abolishing instead of reconstructing, destroying
instead of decreating, the heritage of tradition. *The Struggle of the Modern* spec-
ifies that "we owe the great achievements of modern art" to the syncretism of
"the individual imagination" and "an eighteenth-century, almost classical crit-
ical awareness and artistic self-consciousness" (p. 23). In *Afterjoyce: Studies in
Fiction After* Ulysses (New York: Oxford UP, 1977), Robert Martin Adams
writes of the modernists' "revaluation of classical antiquity," that "modernism
might perhaps be described as a second wave of neo-classicism under the stim-
ulus of the Cambridge anthropologists" (pp. 194–95). And Eliot's fear, in the
Rodker review, "whether the thought and sensibility of the future may not
become more simple and indeed more crude than that of the present," was fear
of a barbaric suppression of the modernists' Apollonian exercise of intelligence,
development of standards, cultivation of taste.

The first "What Was Modernism?" was a lecture by Harry Levin that in 1960
adopted Arnold Toynbee's phrase, "the Post-Modern Period"; in 1965 Levin
wrote, for its inclusion in his *Refractions: Essays in Comparative Literature*
(New York: Oxford UP, 1966), a preface distinguishing "that anti-intellectual
undercurrent which, as it comes to the surface, I would prefer to call post-mod-
ern" (p. 271). In his successor essay of that title, Adams glosses Levin's point
about the "post-modern" development of the "Dionysiac" component of Mod-
ernism; he writes, "For all that it included a broad streak of anti-intellectualism,
modernism was in many respects a learned, a clerkly phenomenon" (p. 26). The
point made by Spender, Adams, Eliot, and Levin can be illustrated by the
polemical and theoretical writings of the most anti-intellectual and anti-tradi-

tional modernist, Lawrence: obliged by the inevitable contradiction to do so, the romantic epistemologist and metaphysician could preach against intellect and reason with erudition and articulate rigor.

By 1960, when Levin put Modernism in the past, almost all the major modernist writers in English were dead or had ceased to write. During that decade, writers who began as modernists, such as Robert Lowell and John Barth, turned in the new direction. A third relevant historical development has been a new challenge to the former hegemony of objective criticism, by a criticism that corresponds to new developments in poetry and fiction. Whereas the criticism generated by Modernism emphasized intellect and craft, articulating an autonomous heterocosm ("The artist, like the God of the creation . . . within or behind or beyond or above his handiwork . . . paring his fingernails" having "separate[d] . . . the man who suffers and the mind which creates"), new criticism, like new writing, has stressed indeterminacy and individual experience. The fourth, and most substantive, kind of historical evidence of a new movement's asserting itself during that decade, is the nature of the new developments in writing.

Some clearly are related to the Modernism all have consciously opposed. Solipsistic fiction about writers of fiction, and poetry about ephemera of the poets' experience, has modernist parents and romantic grandparents. It is true that indeterminacy, aleatoriness, minimalism, illusionism, oppose the modernist emphases on intellect, craft, and formal integrity, "repudiating the artist's role of God over his own creation," as Adams puts it in his "What Was Modernism?" (30); however, all can be found in certain modernist writers.

What is perhaps the key differentiating characteristic of "Postmodernism" can be specified by way of Kermode's distinction between reconstructing/decreating, and abolishing/destroying, the tradition. The new writing of the last quarter-century has repudiated not only the doctrines and values of Modernism, and the "Apollonian" defining qualities of modernist writing mentioned, but all prior writing—in direct contrast to Modernism's involvement with the past. The result is that the vital connection on which the modernist reconstruction/decreation of traditional metrics, form, and narrative depended—the continuity within which it worked against (in both senses) past achievement—has been ruptured. For example: when modernist formal audacity and controlled non-metrical verse evolved—under the principle "make it new" and the impetus of modernist poets like Williams and the later Pound—into open form and the anti-metric of the utterance-line (named by Charles Olson "composition by field" and "projective verse" as early as 1950); and when audacious narrative strategies evolved into cut-and-fold and "joky nihilism" (Adams); evolution became entropy. The new -ism is like a technique for jumping that rejects the firm footing needed to do it effectively. Whether or not, as seems to be the case in the 1980s, developments new in the '60s and waxing in the '70s have crested, they have not after a quarter-century prevailed; the successor movement helps to confirm the truly radical revolution and abiding achievement, in English literature, of Modernism. That period may be dead, but it does not seem to have been successfully buried.

IV. Pound's Decade

The preceding sketch of the history of Modernism is warranted by its pertinence to the relations of "Prufrock," *Ulysses,* and *The Waste Land.* One can postulate an original and a succeeding phase of the same historical phenomenon not only because the same writers were involved in both. One also can postulate a single Modernism because most of those writers and their recruits continued to practice its art of syncretism. And finally, one can do so because the chief writers who developed in exceptional ways in the second phase, Eliot, Joyce, and Pound, were respectively two central figures and a prime mover in the movement that established itself during the original phase. The relation of those central figures to that prime mover is a crucial element in the relation of their works to Modernism.

The popular conception of Pound is as a poet unfortunately distracted (in both senses of the word) by economics, then led by that obsession with gold and usury to notorious politics. The reactionary politics of modernist English writers was a consensus only negatively: as reversion (reaction back) from an evolving liberal social democracy. Their actual beliefs ranged from Eliot's neo-Tractarian Toryism, the gentrified English anticipation of America's Christian Right he shared with Belloc, Chesterton, C. S. Lewis, and others; through Yeats's combination of Old-Tory doctrine and a leader cult proclivity *he* shared with the ostensible rational-socialist Shaw; through Lawrence's doctrines of natural power and inferiority, favored by the Nazis; to Pound's and his friend Wyndham Lewis's fascism. Their (to me, at least) deplorable politics is understandable: they promoted *radical change* in art and culture; they did so *to preserve, by renewing,* the heritage of a civilization they believed had valued and sponsored high art; their commitment to craft was to *discipline;* and their commitment to authenticity and the creative imagination was recognition of *exceptional individuals.* But few Continental Modernists shared that politics (Pirandello and Céline recall Yeats and Pound); and writers from Joyce the democratic sceptic, to Brecht the Communist creator of new "production," demonstrate eloquently that it was not inevitable in Modernism. Pound's was the most egregious case— even Lewis recanted his book that prematurely praised Hitler.

His political history makes the thought seem bizarre at first; but Pound's economics may well derive from an aesthetically based socialism in the tradition of the early William Morris and of Oscar Wilde. He related the "Douglas Theorem" to his own concerns and values by conceiving that the power of the bankers over monetary policy is power over fiscal policy, hence over economic life— which extends the influence of the owners/administrators of capital to every aspect of a civilization. C. H. Douglas himself, an engineer by profession, had similarly broad concerns, as well as quasi-socialist values. For example, in both serial and book publication, his title for the initial statement of his doctrines (which points out that the original meaning of "wealth" was "well-being"), is *Economic Democracy* (1920). And, although he seems to confuse democracy and liberty, his hostility to the capitalist-sponsored money market—if I understand him correctly—is based on a vitalist variant of the concept of surplus value.[15] The surplus value accrues not to the productive entrepreneur, but to the bankers.

In a tribute to "the greatest living poet writing in ... English" as he approached his eightieth birthday, Hugh MacDiarmid, who was a Communist, defends Douglas (a friend) and Pound on the "Money Question."[16] He endorses Douglas's doctrine that "the property conception of credit" (Pound's *usura*) "effects a continual and increasing indebtedness of the community to the banks"; and he declares, "The values to be safeguarded in the Douglas Commonwealth are Liberty, Leisure and Culture."[17]

Whatever its status as economic theory, Douglas's thought has clear relevance for the values and concerns of both MacDiarmid and Pound. It is the ground on which apparently irrelevant ideas of Pound's coalesce in the ethos of a culturally rich and socialist civilization: value is created by the work of people, and the work of true artists creates the greatest value, beauty; in the art of poetry, rhetoric corresponds to usury in society—it evades work and spuriously breeds a debased product—while the image (by the later *Cantos,* also the very words heard or read) is the honest coinage of reality. Pound wrote to Louis Zukofsky, "My poetry and my econ are NOT separate or opposed. Essential unity."[18]

For one zealous to have civilization fulfill itself in both beauty and justice ("with usura the line grows thick"), right action involves the militant refinement of taste as well as of statecraft; and during his earlier years the assayer's son who would develop an obsession with gold was both a remarkable appraiser of precious literary metal and a militant partisan of those who worked it. The eponym

15. Where they coexist, liberty and democracy are reciprocally dependent; but they are distinct. Hence, Ireland is an authentic democracy which has legislated certain sharply restricted individual liberties; and, members of the propertied class in dictatorships in which individuals control the wealth, or of the ruling caste in dictatorships in which the state controls it, usually have greater liberty of action than citizens in most democracies.

16. Another note on politics seems in order. One of the political conventions of our ostensibly apolitical Anglo-American literary criticism, is to declare that accomplished writers like the Scot MacDiarmid/Grieve and the Irishman O'Casey, because accomplished, were too artistic and too intelligent *really* to be Communists—they only unintelligently thought they were. During most of the modernist period, a knowledgeable writer with a grievance against British imperialism could deplore Stalin, and yet both help to preserve into the future the state-capitalist dictatorship Lenin had set up in traditionally autocratic Russia, and wish that his own country would be persuaded to adopt a traditionally liberal native equivalent. Critics do not patronize the reactionary modernists for their generally more unsavory politics.

17. Hugh MacDiarmid, "The Return of the Long Poem," *Ezra Pound—perspectives: essays in honor of his eightieth birthday,* ed. Noel Stock (Chicago: Regnery, 1965), pp. 90–108, pp. 90, 104, 106. For a discussion of Douglas's ideas as relevant to Pound, see *Pound Era,* pp. 301–17.

18. Lewis Hyde, *The Gift: Imagination and the Erotic Life of Property* (New York: Random House, 1983), p. 230. Hyde writes that "Pound sought a 'money system' that might replicate, or at least support, the form of value that emanates from creative life"; later, he quotes Pound's comment on the purchaser of a rare book, "Interest on 20,000 bucks wd. keep a live writer for life. Wot these bastards lack is a little intelligence" (pp. 233, 242).

Hyde analyzes the evolution of Pound's poetry/politics as "a will to power born of a frustrated compassion" (p. 241)—out of an initial syncretism (he considers it an unstable tension) of "Eleusinian (or Dionysian) ... fecundity" and "Confucian ... order" (p. 217). He achieves sympathy for Pound without extenuation.

Kenner gave Modernism in the title of *The Pound Era* is not parochialism but justice, which is to say, good history. The year before (1970), Spears wrote in *Dionysus and the City,* "It is misleading to call Pound the father of modernism. . . . But Pound is undeniably the catalyst of literary modernism, the impresario and promoter of it as a conscious movement" (p. 105). Others may have a better claim to the eponym on grounds of achievement, and even of influence: *Afterjoyce* lists—in addition to the familiar Eliot—Joyce, Kafka and Picasso (p. 194). But achievement and influence are weak grounds for characterizing a rich period by the name of a single artist.

Pound's more substantial claim is his generative role as historical actor. If, like that of Morris's Marxism, the slow emergence to critical awareness of Shaw's generative role in the development of the British Socialist movement reflects, in part, the political bias of our literary culture, it also partly reflects scepticism about the instrumental power of historical actors in intellectual and cultural affairs. With the passing of time, more and more evidence accumulates of the young Ezra Pound's instrumentality as a compound of revolutionary leader and midwife of the modernist movement.

For his role he may have been indebted to a master who had recently proven that in the arts a human mover can make things happen. He became intimately associated with Yeats before the end of the first decade of the century; and by that time Yeats, undeterred by his predecessors' failure, had created a self-conscious national English literature in Ireland: reviewing books of Anglo-Irish writers; producing a constant stream of newspaper and magazine articles that exhorted Irish writers to use certain material and to work in certain ways, and Irish readers to buy, read, and recommend certain writers; printing lists of the best Irish books; persuading publishers to put out works on Ireland or by Irishmen; organizing literary societies and two theatrical groups, the second of which made history in its own right; starting special periodicals; prodding Irish intellectuals to do books of translation from the Irish and of Irish folklore, Irish history, Irish social studies; encouraging and attempting to promote the careers of Irish writers. Yeats began that activity at about the time Joyce began his schooling; yet before his college years were over, Joyce could treat a fully Irish literature and drama in English, in a piece like "The Day of the Rabblement," as cultural fact. Yeats was not alone, of course; and it is a historical irony that despite the advent, as a direct result of the movement, of Synge and a number of lesser figures, he was also its chief embellishment; but most people who have written on the subject agree that an Irish literature in English as self-conscious as American literature exists, and that it would not have come about when it did—if at all—without his efforts.

Sometimes in concert with Yeats (when each was not busy working on the other to reform him in his own image), and with Eliot and others as well, but uniquely committed, Pound set himself to the same sort of work—on behalf of the kind of literature (and music, painting, sculpture, art theory) he was determined to move forward. He arranged for publication, sought out writers, attached himself to and helped start periodicals, wrote manifestoes, organized splinter movements, raised money for writers, advised and taught, preached and exhorted.

An essay on Pound that Eliot published in *Poetry* in 1946 addresses his friend's "influence on men and on events at a turning point in literature":

> I have been writing . . . of a particular period, that between 1910 and 1922
> . . . . This is the period . . . in which he exercised a vital influence upon English and American poetry, although this influence has been largely felt by a younger generation, many of whom never knew him personally, and some of whom may be unaware of the extent of the influence upon them. . . . Pound did not create the poets: but he created a situation in which, for the first time, there was a "modern movement in poetry". . . .[19]

Pound's arrest and confinement may explain Eliot's having written "Ezra Pound"; they may even explain his emphasizing in it Pound's contribution to specifically American literature, and asserting that "the future of American letters was what concerned him most" (p. 18). But Pound's predicament does not explain (away) Eliot's judgment that he was the instrumental historical actor in the modernist movement, at least for the genre relevant to *Poetry*. Considerable evidence of Eliot's acumen as a literary historian has already been given.

An important aspect of the historical action by which Pound "created a situation" was his identifying (discovering), tutoring, and promoting unknown modernist writers. Although in his Rome Radio broadcasts he had castigated Archibald MacLeish at length for serving "a gang of criminals" ("Roosevelt, Lehman, Baruch, Morgenthau"—"Roosevelt and his Jews or the Jews and THEIR Mr. Roosevelt"), MacLeish conducted the effort that in 1958 terminated both his hospitalization and the criminal charges against him.[20] In that effort, MacLeish enlisted three of the four most eminent living American writers: Eliot, Frost and Hemingway.[21] Pound had helped initiate the careers of all three.

In his introduction to *Ezra Pound: perspectives,* Noel Stock points out that Pound was instrumental in the publishing of Hemingway's first book, *In Our Time* (Paris, 1924), and quotes its author's declaration that (explicitly) not Gertrude Stein, but Pound, had taught him "more about how to write and how not

19. "Ezra Pound," *Poetry* LXVIII (Sept. 1946); reprinted in various volumes of essays on Pound. I quote from *Ezra Pound: A Collection of Critical Essays,* ed. Walter Sutton (Englewood Cliffs: Prentice, 1963), pp. 17–25, pp. 19–20.

20. See, e.g., William H. Pritchard, *Frost: A Literary Life Reconsidered* (New York: Oxford UP, 1984), p. 250; and *Pound Era,* p. 535. Pound's phrases are quoted from a broadcast devoted to MacLeish made on April 23, 1942; on July 2, he called MacLeish "my most obtuse opponent, or my most enthusiastic opponent"; and he mentioned MacLeish in three more broadcasts, to February 19, 1943. The quoted phrases are from *Ezra Pound Speaking: Radio Speeches of World War II,* ed. Leonard W. Doob (Westport, CN: Greenwood, 1978), pp. 104–5, 189. The version of the April 1942 speech in Charles Norman, *Ezra Pound* (New York: Macmillan, 1960), pp. 391–93, differs in details.

21. Frost, who was the most "Rotarian"—as he himself sometimes put it—of the three and a friend of Sherman Adams, then "Assistant to the President," had the audience with Eisenhower, and signed the letter to the court (drafted by MacLeish), which named Eliot and Hemingway as endorsers. It is printed in Norman, p. 454, and Lawrance Thompson and R. H. Winnick, *Frost: The Later Years 1938–1963* (New York: Holt, 1976), p. 257.

to write" than anyone (pp. ix–x). His 1932 "Note" about the influence of Pound's "work," printed in Stock's volume, indicates both his sense of Pound's role in Modernism, and his personal experience of Pound's (as well as another friend's) influence:

> Any poet born [since 1890] who can honestly say that he has not been influenced by or learned greatly from the work of Ezra Pound deserves to be pitied rather than rebuked. It is as if a prose writer born in that time should not have learned from or been influenced by James Joyce or that a traveler should pass through . . . a sandstorm and not have felt the sand and the wind. (p. 151)

In the same way, a tribute to Pound's generosity in the posthumous *A Moveable Feast* (1964; New York: Bantam, 1965) indicates both his personal experience and Pound's activity as modernist mover:

> Ezra was the most generous writer I have ever known and the most disinterested. He helped poets, painters, sculptors and prose writers that he believed in . . . . He worried about everyone . . . . (p. 110)[22]

Frost had been less grateful. He took his family to England at the end of August, 1912, a move that for a poet with "small victories . . . was surely not expedient nor obvious good sense, even though it worked out magnificently well" (Pritchard, p. 4). It did so largely because of Pound. At the opening of Harold Monro's Poetry Bookshop in January 1913, Frost met F. S. Flint. Flint strongly urged him to meet Pound, and arranged a terse invitation. According to Frost, he waited more than a month before calling on Pound; informed Pound that *A Boy's Will* probably was bound and about to be sent to reviewers; was taken to his publisher's, where Pound secured a copy; was made to sit while Pound read in it; and then was sent home, so Pound could get to work reviewing it. "And I never touched it."[23]

Pound promptly announced to Harriet Monroe's assistant, "Have just discovered another Amur'kn. VURRY Amur'k'n, with, I think, the seeds of grace," and promised the review, which was in draft; the review followed, with a covering letter to Monroe promising "some of [Frost's] work" (Pound, *Letters*, pp. 14, 16). *A Boy's Will* was published in April; Pound sent his review to *Poetry* in March, and it appeared in the May number; he also reviewed Frost's first volume for British readers, in the *New Freewoman* (to begin the coming year as the *Egoist*). The next month, he was continuing "to boom him and get his name stuck about" (Yeats was impressed, and Pound arranged a meeting); and he

22. Hyde provides "anecdotes" of Pound's generosity on pp. 231–33, 239–40; two men who knew him during the 1930s both have emphasized this quality in conversation with me. Samuel Putnam, *Paris Was Our Mistress: Memoirs of a Lost & Found Generation* (New York: Viking, 1947), reports Hemingway as "patronizing" about Pound's influence (p. 128). Putnam characterizes Pound (p. 142) as "politically" a "cracker-barrel philosopher"—"(a metaphor . . . of which he himself was fond)."

23. Lawrance Thompson, *Robert Frost: The Early Years 1874–1915* (New York: Holt, 1966), pp. 407–11 passim; and Pritchard, pp. 11, 16–17. Pritchard's *Life Reconsidered* is skeptical about Frost's account.

called a new poem "better than anything in" *A Boy's Will:* it was "The Death of the Hired Man ["Farm Hand"]" (*Letters,* pp. 20–21).

The relationship was short-lived. The emergent poet was almost forty and testily self-protective; the modernist mover was overbearing and twenty-five. Incorporating Frost into his larger agenda, Pound both used Frost's earlier scant success in order to chastise American editors, and called the poetry "simple" and "homely" in order to emphasize its "sincerity"—thereby helping to initiate the familiar patronizing of the Vermont yeoman-poet. Frost was respectively worried and annoyed.[24] As an example of his consequent "campaign of disparagement" of "this man who had actually done more than anyone else to make Frost's literary start in London successful," Lawrance Thompson quotes from a letter Frost wrote in July; the first clause of an indignant sentence begins with a phrase that makes the relevant point, "The fact that he discovered me gives him the right . . ." (p. 421). In 1935, the year before privately expressing his resentment of "the Pound-Eliot-Richards gang in Eliot House" at Harvard (Pritchard, p. 202), he wrote publicly about Pound himself, "The first poet I ever sat down with to talk about poetry was Ezra Pound. It was in London in 1913" (Thompson, p. 589). And he was turning forty—and undiscovered. Past eighty in the same city, in 1957, he made a historical observation to Eliot that is more broadly pertinent:

> You and I shot off at different tangents from almost the same pin wheel. We had America in common and we had Ezra in common . . . . (Thompson and Winnick, p. 257)

It is not possible here to document every case of Pound's instrumental role in the careers of modernist artists; and new evidence of it continues to turn up, anyway. Also, such activities cannot be isolated from other aspects of his historical action, such as his promotion of modernist literary periodicals and presses.

For example, a three-page letter in 1918 to a new correspondent who had sent him some poems from America, a letter closely packed with questions, judgments, general advice, and proposed revisions, and which ends "Does your stuff 'appear' in America?," asks if she has a book in print—"And, if not, can I get one into print for you?" (Pound, *Letters,* pp. 141–44). (Marianne Moore's answer, printed in *Pound—Perspectives* [pp.116–20], contains biography, gratitude, responses to specific suggestions for revisions, and the sentence "I do not appear." Past thirty, she had succeeded in placing poems only in Alfred Kreymborg's *Others,* the *Egoist,* and *Poetry.*) In a brief letter to Harriet Shaw Weaver dated the next day (December 17, 1918), Pound made a proposal he had made two years before to an American publisher, on behalf of Joyce's *Portrait.*[25] He

24. For Frost's concern that Pound would prejudice American editors against his work, see Thompson, pp. 412, 440, 472–73; Pritchard, pp. 70–74, 109. For his annoyance, see Thompson, pp. 419–21, and Pritchard, pp. 69–70.

25. He had prevailed on John Marshall to substitute the *Portrait* for his own collection of articles, *This Generation;* see Noel Stock, *The Life of Ezra Pound* (New York: Pantheon, 1970), p. 192. According to Jane Lidderdale and Mary Nicholson, *Dear Miss Weaver: Harriet Shaw Weaver 1876–1961* (New York: Viking, 1970), Marshall in fact declined to print it before he left publishing (p. 124).

proposed that Weaver not print a short book of his own, because "I should much rather" the money be spent on one "by some new poet. I believe I have one in sight" (*Letters,* p. 144); and her Egoist Press published (in 1921, without the poet's knowledge) the first book by another Pound protégé who became a major modernist figure. But it is no less impossible to distinguish his aid to a young poet, from his promotion of the publishing of new writers by the likes of the *Egoist* and its press, than it is to distinguish—as his motive for sacrificing his own book to Moore's (or Joyce's)—simple kindness, from historical purpose. It also is not necessary to do so to both establish the nature, and indicate the extent, of his public activity as prime mover of Modernism. His private activity can only be imagined: a letter from Eliot of February 2, 1915, for example, asks "please tell me who Kandinsky is" (Stock, p. 111); Pound had written about Kandinsky in A. R. Orage's *The New Age.*

In addition to that indefatigable activity, his arrogant self-assurance, shrewd promotional ability, kindness, and abnegation, Pound endowed the movement with a remarkable talent, already exemplified: the ability to distinguish modernist promise and achievement. His judgment was far more unerring than Yeats's with Irish writers. Probably only Edward Garnett and Horace Liveright can be compared with him; and Garnett rejected the *Portrait* (*James Joyce,* p. 403).

As early as March 1914, when Lawrence was the obscure author of two early novels, *Sons and Lovers,* and his first volume of poems (which Pound reviewed favorably in *Poetry* two months after he reviewed *A Boy's Will*) and Joyce was almost totally unknown, Pound wrote to Amy Lowell, "I think Lawrence and Joyce are the two strongest prose writers among les jeunes, and all the [older writers] are about played out" (Pound, *Letters,* p. 34). The following February, he wrote H. L. Mencken that "The prose writer I am really interested in is James Joyce" and described Edgar Lee Masters (with strong reservations) and Eliot as "the most hopeful American poets" (*Letters,* p. 51). The same month, in an article in *The New Age,* he wrote:

> So far as I know there are only two writers of prose fiction of my decade [!] whom anyone takes in earnest. I mean Mr. Joyce and Mr. D. H. Lawrence. . . .
> I have never envied Mr. Lawrence, though I have often enjoyed him. . . .
> Mr. Joyce writes the sort of prose I should like to write were I a prose writer.[26]

Pound's extreme selectivity in these examples probably can be attributed to the modernist mover's special purpose: a review of Frost's *North of Boston* declaring his book "a contribution to American literature" had appeared in *Poetry* two months before he wrote to Mencken; and he was actively promoting Williams and H. D. to other editors. His special purpose also explains his hyperbole. The new writers hyperbolized—Lawrence, Joyce, Eliot, Frost—exemplify his judgment.

By 1915 he had enlisted the support not only of Weaver, but also of the other outstanding patron of Modernism, John Quinn. A plan to start an American

26. Quoted from *Pound/Joyce: The Letters of Ezra Pound to James Joyce, with Pound's Essays on Joyce,* ed. Forrest Read (New York: New Directions, 1967), p. 32.

magazine Quinn would raise money for and Pound would edit evolved, by 1917, into an arrangement to take over a section of the *Little Review,* beginning with the May issue. The first year saw work by Eliot, Yeats, and other modernists, in addition to a great deal by Pound and Lewis; and it ended with the first chapters of *Ulysses*—to be read there by Woolf.

During negotiations, Pound wrote to one of the co-editors, Margaret Anderson, "I want a place where I and T. S. Eliot can appear once a month . . . and where Joyce can appear when he likes, and where Wyndham Lewis can appear if he comes back from the war" (*Letters,* pp. 106–7). Lawrence had published another volume of poems and *The Prussian Officer,* with its many richly crafted stories; but he is not denominated one of the central figures of the modernist movement in English literature. Using the same phrase he had used in pairing Lawrence and Joyce at the midpoint of the decade—with its revealing coupled words, whether the pronoun be genitive, dative, or both—Pound replaced Lawrence with Lewis at the decade's end, declaring in "Wyndham Lewis" (1920), "The English prose fiction of my decade is the work of this pair of authors" (*Literary Essays,* p. 424). Pound's own decade would seem to have begun about the beginning of 1913, and ended with the publication of *The Waste Land* in the closing months of 1922. Some today would accept his quadrumvirate; most would accept all but Lewis, and add few others active during those years that established the first phase of Modernism; no one would quarrel with his naming of Joyce and Eliot.

The prime mover of Modernism, who prodigiously assisted and promoted major modernist writers, ministered to those two central ones in both ways more than to any other. Furthermore, not only did he assist Joyce and Eliot—financially, practically, and critically—most, and promote them most: his assistance and promotion were instrumental in, and may well have been crucial to, the careers of both. This is the supremely pertinent fact about Pound's place in the relations of "Prufrock," *Ulysses,* and *The Waste Land* to Modernism.

Thus, he used his revealing phrase more selectively still in a promotional piece on the *Portrait* in the August 1917 issue of the *Little Review,* averring "Joyce is the best prose writer of my decade" (4, p. 7); and even-handedly, he published in *Poetry* the same month a reivew of *Prufrock and Other Observations* that declared, "The reader will find nothing better" than "Mr. Eliot's work" in "French, English or American since the death of Jules Laforgue," and "will be extremely fortunate if he finds much half as good" (*Literary Essays,* p. 418). With both books that anticipate the central modernist achievements their authors were to publish in five years—both of them modernist landmarks in their own right—the reviewer and publicist played a far more crucial role, as well.

Forrest Read's *Pound/Joyce* is essentially a 300-page documentary record of the one's ministry to the career and canon (with doubts about *Finnegans Wake*) of the other. Its initial document is a letter dated 15 December 1913 that begins, "Dear Sir: Mr Yeats has been speaking to me of your writing" (p. 17). When he received it, Joyce was nearing the end of his thirty-second year; and he had published, in addition to the slender volume *Chamber Music,* a few stories and poems, reviews and articles, mostly in Dublin and Trieste newspapers. Although he did not know it at the time, a letter that had arrived less than three weeks earlier, in which Grant Richards, moved by conscience, offered to reconsider *Dubliners,* would end happily an eight-years' cycle of frustration, initiated by a contract to publish the volume reneged by Richards. The cycle had included another contract reneged by Maunsel & Co. (George Roberts), as well as rejections by other publishers, among them Martin Secker and—despite Joyce's offer to pay printing costs—Elkin Matthews (*James Joyce,* pp. 219, 231, 324, 328, 335, 348–49). So when he opened Pound's letter he was—as he wrote later he might have remained without Pound's efforts—"the unknown drudge that he discovered" (*Pound/Joyce,* p. 245).

The letter arrived on December 18, the day before Pound wrote to his friend "Bull" Williams, "We are getting our little gang"; a few weeks later, Joyce sent Pound a finally-revised typescript of the first chapter of the *Portrait;* promptly (January 17–19, 1914), Pound wrote a letter asserting "Your novel is damn fine stuff"—comparable to James, Hudson and some Conrad—and containing the statement, "I hope to have proofs . . . in a week"; the first installment appeared in the *Egoist* (to the omen-lover's delight) on Joyce's birthday, February 2, about six weeks after Pound's initial letter and a mere fortnight after Joyce sent him the typescript (Owen, pp. 40–41; Pound, *Letters,* p. 27; *James Joyce,* pp. 350, 353).

This event is no less exemplary of Pound's singular judgment and purposiveness, and no less significant for the history of Modernism, than his later rescuing of the harbinger of a new English poetry from Eliot's drawer, and giving to the movement the best known poem of this century, by importuning for months ("Your objection to Eliot is the climax"; "No, most emphatically I will not ask Eliot to write down to any audience whatsoever"; "*Do* get on with that Eliot") an editor who considered herself dedicated to new poetry. And—despite the small circulation of the now-renowned *Egoist*—it is an even more remarkable achievement.

Under the stimulus of serial publication, Joyce completed the *Portrait* during 1914 or early 1915.[27] The self-appointed literary director of the *Egoist* had committed himself—and secured the chief founder and then-editor Dora Marsden's agreement—to publishing the whole novel on the basis of the one finished chapter.[28] The installment in the April 1 issue was followed by five poems of Lawrence's; that and the next (April 15) issue, which concluded the first chapter of the *Portrait,* contained a full-page announcement of Lewis's Vorticist *Blast,*

---

27. Ellmann proposes Summer 1915 (*James Joyce,* p. 355); Owen, late 1914. The complicated question of the chronology of its composition is reviewed in Owen, pp. 41–60.

28. Marsden was editor of its predecessor, the *Freewoman.* Pound had been brought in by Rebecca West, assistant editor during the first four months of the *New Freewoman* (June–September, 1913), and had strongly supported Aldington for "literary editor," to succeed West. Nevertheless, and although his ways made her jealous of her authority, he sent the chapter directly to Marsden—who did not read it at the time, according to Lidderdale and Nicholson. They call its publishing the *Portrait* "the most important event in *The Egoist's* history." (*Weaver,* pp. 63–65, 77, 83, 106, 85).

promising "NO Old Pulp"; with Joyce's contribution to it, Pound's decade was well begun.

When in Feburary 1917, the Egoist Press published its first book, using sheets from the New York (Huebsch) edition of the previous December, Pound printed a promotional piece in the *Egoist* entitled "James Joyce: At Last the Novel Appears," in which he called the *Portrait* "a permanent part of English literature" (*Pound/Joyce,* p. 90). Exactly a year earlier, in a review of *Exiles,* he had informed readers that Joyce "has written a novel" and, reiterating the same key word, "that novel is permanent. It is permanent as are the works of [Eliot's model writers in the 1919 review, "Beyle and Balzac"] Stendhal and Flaubert" (p. 49). In the case of Joyce's novel, already nearly a year seeking a publisher in February 1916, apparent promotional hyperbole was sound historical judgment.

Four days before the first installment of Chapter I of the *Portrait* appeared on February 2, 1914, Joyce received a contract from Richards for *Dubliners;* but it sold only 499 copies in 1914, and 33 in 1915 (*James Joyce,* p. 400). Pound's promotion of his discovery had already begun—with "A Curious History," containing letters pertaining to the publishing history of *Dubliners* and Joyce's comments—in the previous issue of the *Egoist.* His relentless campaign, in reviews and articles—often nominally concerned with other writers and subjects—would last for more than a decade, well beyond the publication of *Ulysses.*

Pound was instrumental for Joyce's (and Eliot's) career indirectly as well as directly—chiefly by implicating John Quinn and Harriet Shaw Weaver: Joyce wrote him in 1917, while working on *Ulysses,* "I shall go on writing, thanks to the kindness of my unknown friend and also of Mr Quinn" (*Pound/Joyce,* p. 106). A founder of the *Egoist,* his then-unknown patron had become editor during its serialization of the *Portrait.* Although Yeats had long had dealings with Quinn, Pound met him independently, possibly through John Butler Yeats, in 1910;[29] early in 1915 they exchanged letters, and their modernist association began.

The remarkable Quinn was not only a benefactor of modernist artists, and shrewd collector of their work, but also an industrious and highly talented sponsor, promoter, unpaid lawyer, agent, and editor.[30] He reviewed the *Portrait* in *Vanity Fair* (May, 1917); he represented Joyce (and Eliot) in negotiations with agents, book publishers, and magazines; he bought manuscripts and proofs from Joyce, including the manuscript of *Exiles* and the Rosenbach manuscript of *Ulysses;* he defended the *Little Review* in the trial occasioned by its serialization of *Ulysses;* and he subsidized a literary section in the *Egoist* which, like that in the *Little Review,* printed chapters of *Ulysses.* Weaver "rejected a Poundian

29. See Pound, *Letters,* p. 111. Pound's outing to Coney Island with Yeats and Quinn, memorialized by the famous photograph at Luna Park, occurred in August 1910 (Stock, p. 90). Yeats later wrote his son about Pound, apparently ignorant that they knew each other (see Norman, p. 65).

30. Alfred Knopf called the contract Quinn had drawn up for Pound's *Lustra* "the clearest and best arranged . . . he had ever seen," and adopted it for general use; this is an example taken almost at random from B.L. Reid, *The Man from New York: John Quinn and His Friends* (New York: Oxford UP, 1968), p. 280.

incursion" (*Pound Era,* p. 281); but Pound had committed himself to the *Little Review* (*Weaver,* p. 137), and successfully proposed Eliot—who acted as the *Egoist's* editor for the *Ulysses* installments, with consequences that will be discussed in my next chapter.

Weaver did all that Quinn did, but with a dedicated, selfless commitment to Joyce. Her activities on his behalf and relationship with him and his family dominate the biography by Lidderdale and Nicholson. During Pound's decade, when "she dealt with Ezra Pound's letters, sometimes at the rate of two a day, about Joyce's affairs" (*Weaver,* p. 115), her most overt contribution was to print his (and Eliot's) work in the *Egoist,* and to publish the *Portrait* and *Ulysses* (and *Prufrock and Other Observations*) by the Egoist Press. But her biographers report that she secretly provided money to keep the *Egoist* going in April 1914, principally for the sake of the remaining four chapters of the *Portrait* (p. 87). Her lifelong subventions to Joyce himself, begun in 1917, had totaled 21,000 pounds in remittance and endowment—a fortune during that period—by 1923; he called her patronage, "I imagine, unique in the history of literature" (*James Joyce,* p. 556). And he probably imagined right. Ellmann deftly observes, "it made it possible for him to be poor only through determined extravagance" (p. 481). After Pound himself had made a "long and continuing fight" (Stock, p. 191) to persuade a publisher to take the *Portrait,* she created the Press specifically "in order to save a work of exceedingly high merit from oblivion" (*Weaver,* pp. 108–11, 115). And she undertook, as she would again for *Ulysses,* the frustrating and futile effort to find a willing British printer.[31] It was Pound's idea to seek an American publisher, and his contact that secured one; but her offer to buy unbound sheets for the British edition of "your wonderful book" helped persuade Huebsch to undertake it (*Weaver,* pp. 118, 122; *James Joyce,* pp. 405, 401). As Eliot gave the *Waste Land* drafts to Quinn in gratitude, so Joyce gave the manuscript of the *Portrait* to Weaver.

Pound's role in Weaver's financial support of Joyce was indirect; but he raised sums of money for him directly. For example, it was he who sold Joyce's manuscripts to, and solicited an occasional subvention from, Quinn.[32] And in 1916, he enlisted the help of Yeats—who, after reading the *Portrait* half a year later, was to write "My dear Ezra . . . I think it a very great book" (*Pound/Joyce,* p. 93)—in getting Joyce a Civil List pension, which he supplemented himself, anonymously; that same year, he also secured an allowance from the Society of Authors, and smaller sums (Hyde, p. 232; *James Joyce,* pp. 405–6).

Pound and Joyce did not meet until 1920. Five years later, Joyce wrote to

---

31. Woolf's refusal to publish *Ulysses* was mentioned in the introduction (p. xii). Weaver had approached the Woolfs on Eliot's suggestion; *The Diary of Virginia Woolf,* ed. Anne Olivier Bell (New York: Harcourt, 1977), records Virginia's vacillation. The entry after she had received Weaver's letter comments, "we can hardly tackle a book" (Wednesday, 10 April 1918); Weaver visited the following Sunday; the entry for Thursday, 18 April includes "Why does [Joyce's] filth seek exit from [Weaver's] mouth?"; on September 20, 1920 she wrote, after recording Eliot's praise, "Perhaps we shall try to publish it" (*Diary* I:136 and n.15, 140; II: 68).

32. As Quinn's biographer puts it, "One way both to assist Joyce and to lay hands on a bit of genius was to buy manuscripts"; and, "he determined to do everything he could for him short of outright charity, which was rarely Quinn's way" (Reid, pp. 274, 279).

Ernest Walsh, editor of *This Quarter* (Paris), in a letter about Pound published in the Spring number, "He helped me in every possible way in the face of very great difficulties for seven years before I met him. . . ." (*Letters* III: 117).

During the summer after his December 1913 letter, "Dear Sir: Mr Yeats has been speaking to me of your writing," Pound met Eliot; and on September 30 he made his announcement to Monroe that "He has actually trained himself *and* modernized himself *on his own,*" and "has sent in the best poem I have yet had or seen from an American" (Pound, *Letters,* p. 40). Many details of his instrumental role in Eliot's career during the remainder of "my decade" have been mentioned. A practical instance that has not is cited by Eliot as part of his "greatest personal debt" at the beginning of his 1946 *Poetry* essay, "Ezra Pound." Before describing with fond amusement the young Pound's assiduous artistic and personal attention to modernists he valued, "as art or literature machines to be carefully tended and oiled, for the sake of their potential output," Eliot declares it prudent:

> in writing at the present moment about Pound, to acknowledge one's greatest personal debt at once. I had kept my early poems . . . in my desk from 1911 to 1915 [sic] . . . . In 1915 (and through Aiken) I met Pound. The result was that *Prufrock* appeared in *Poetry* in the summer of that year; and through Pound's efforts, my first volume was published by the Egoist Press in 1917. (Sutton, pp. 17–18)

For, as Weaver had helped persuade Huebsch to publish the *Portrait* by offering to take part of the edition, Pound had helped persuade Weaver to publish *Prufrock and Other Observations* by offering (secretly) to provide—along with part of Eliot's salary—part of the printing costs (Stock, pp. 204–5; *Weaver,* p. 138).

When all three were young Pound was instrumental in Joyce's career only, but in Eliot's development as well. Both were American intellectuals—diverted from academic careers—and committed modernist poets. During the movement that established itself as the original phase of Modernism, their contrasting personalities apparently enabled them to be mentor and pupil, as well as senior and junior collaborator. In 1925 Eliot added the dedication to *The Waste Land,* his famous homage to Pound. The fact of Pound's influence on the final form of the poem was long known from the letters he exchanged with Eliot. And that that influence was as extensive as many said has been confirmed by the facsimile of the Quinn drafts. It resulted in not just dramatic cuts and verbal refinements, but the constant breaking of predominantly regular verse—the getting, as Pound declared his aim for English poetry in general to be, of Milton off Eliot's back. In a reaction against loose current *vers libre* the two poets shared, Eliot had resorted to a traditional alternative;[33] Pound led him to a new one. And as a

---

33. Both had recently written rhymed quatrains, Pound in "Hugh Selwyn Mauberly," Eliot in a number of poems. Pound wrote in 1932, "at a particular date in a particular room, two authors . . . decided that the dilution of *vers libre* . . . had gone too far and that some counter-current must be set going" (quoted in Stock, p. 206). An accidental enrichment resulted when the rhyming lines for the first two in the last quatrain of the typist's seduction were dropped: a Shakespearean sonnet, of which the seduction climax is the octave, and Tiresias's comment the sestet, with the final "couplet" appropriately discordant (III, 235–48).

consequence, among Eliot's poems *The Waste Land* is most like Pound's own mature poetry. Yeats had set Synge to work as a writer in order to effect his larger purpose; Pound did Yeats one better with *The Waste Land.*

I have drawn from the public record to document Pound's instrumental historical action in establishing the original phase of Modernism. His field of English literary activity alone was a web of vocational and personal relationships: James, Yeats, Conrad, and Stein; influential figures like Weaver, Quinn, Orage, Flint, Mencken, Amy Lowell, Hulme, Herbert Read, and Roger Fry; such now-celebrated contemporaries as Eliot, Woolf, Ford, Lewis, Lawrence, Joyce, Forster, Hemingway, Frost, Cummings, Moore, and Williams; and many lesser editors, critics, and writers. That web, centered in Paris and London and reaching across the Atlantic, was the fabric of the modernist movement in English literature. And it was he who had woven into its center both Joyce and Eliot.

Pound's embarrassing Joyce by giving him used shoes, and Eliot by soliciting money to free him from being willingly employed at Lloyd's Bank, are familiar stories. As did almost everyone else, they too no doubt found him "that difficult individual" at times. But on the evidence, even to say that he discovered both central writers in the movement that established Modernism in English literature, and that he was dramatically instrumental in both their careers, fails to do him justice. For their work had not been merely unknown before he discovered, published, and promoted it. In both cases—and the fact is historically significant, in view of their fame and central place in Modernism less than a decade later—their work had been widely and dispiritingly rejected.

V. *Ulysses, The Waste Land* and Company

The title of the present chapter is from a reference to *The Waste Land* in a long letter Pound wrote about his own poetry to a sympathetic former teacher, Felix E. Schelling. In July 1922, midway between its coming publication, and that of *Ulysses,* on Joyce's previous birthday, he declared to Schelling, "Eliot's *Waste Land* is I think the justification of the 'movement,' of our modern experiment, since 1900" (Pound, *Letters,* p. 180). Despite its facetiousness, his occasionally using "p.s.U." (for *post scriptum Ulixi*), and dating from the publication of the novel, expresses a similar appraisal. And Pound's brace of testimonials specifies the role in Modernism of both works—in the judgment of its prime mover, and the agent of that role for both. Whether they truly were the paired central achievements of "our little gang," or not, his so designating *Ulysses* and *The Waste Land* was no more idle hyperbole than were his previous appraisals of the *Portrait* and "Prufrock." Some agreed even then (Woolf has been quoted on *Ulysses*); many more soon did so.

During that time—the early twenties—Pound's "decade" was culminating in the ascendancy of the original phase of Modernism in English literature.[34] My

34. Levenson shrewdly notes (p. 213) the difference between the titles of *Blast* (1914) and the *Criterion* (1922); the latter was more confident—if not presumptuous—than complacent, since *The Waste Land* appeared in the first number of the *Criterion.*

historical sketch proposed that the original phase ended during the next few years, with the separate departure of Eliot in one direction, and of Joyce and Pound in another, from a hegemony most other writers persisted in. The appearance of, and response to, *Ulysses* and *The Waste Land* are central in that culmination. In his posthumously published *The Awakening Twenties: A Memoir-History of a Literary Period* (Baton Rouge: Louisiana State UP, 1985), Gorham Munson declares:

> Two books published in 1922 had, I felt, formed the Twenties into a definite period. They were *The Waste Land* by T. S. Eliot and *Ulysses* by James Joyce.

And he quotes MacLeish "many years later":

> "There was something about the Twenties. . . . *The Waste Land* provided the vocabulary of our understanding; *Ulysses* formed the sense of history in which we lived. (p. 291)

The novel's and poem's relations with each other are the subject of the next chapter. Two are historically significant, and relevant here. One derives from the special regard accorded that particular pair of works, beginning in 1922 with Pound and other contemporaries. It is that from the beginning they *were* paired. The other is that both evolved radically in process, and for much the same reason. Prompted by "emotion," Joyce moved toward his "third manner" of *Finnegans Wake;* and Eliot began his "feeling toward a new form and style" in the "symbolist incantation [that] welled up powerfully as he wrote the fifth section of *The Waste Land*" (Bush, *T. S. Eliot*, p. 99). Pound and Eliot both called *Ulysses* the terminal development of the novel (Lewis called it "a terminal moraine"). It and *The Waste Land* mark the point where the dynamic of change asserted itself in both writers, almost simultaneously.

That point also is the approximate apex of the unified revolutionary movement. R. P. Blackmur entitled hs 1956 Library of Congress lectures "Anni Mirabiles, 1921–1925"; and in "Lord Tennyson's Scissors" he declared, "1922 seems the great year of our time." In that year alone, which began with the appearance of *Ulysses* and ended with that of *The Waste Land,* books by Forster, Middleton Murry, Huxley, Sandburg, Graves, Aiken, Wells, Ellis, Masters, Sinclair, Glasgow, Lowell, Stein, and Conrad appeared. It was the year of Hardy's *Late Lyrics and Earlier,* Mansfield's *Garden Party and Other Stories,* Cummings's *Enormous Room,* Sitwell's *Facade,* and Woolf's *Jacob's Room.* There were two books by Fitzgerald that year, three by Lawrence, four by Yeats. "That explosion of talent . . . crystallizing between 1922 and 1925 in *Ulysses, The Waste Land* . . . and a great deal more," in Blackmur's words (*A Primer of Ignorance,* ed. Joseph Frank [New York: Harcourt, 1967], p. 16), breached the walls of the "Victorian" citadel. The movement occupied it—established the modernist period—by sheer weight of new and talented art.

Stephen Spender, who was 13 in 1922, has written thoughtfully about Modernism and his modernist predecessors for half a century. In "Remembering Eliot" (1966), he describes the three groups into which he and other literary Oxford undergraduates in the late nineteen twenties put current writers: "the book-society-chosen," who "did not seem to touch our lives at any point"; the "experimental, concerned with being new at all costs," including "James Joyce's Work in Progress, and puzzling cantos of Ezra Pound"; and the valued group, writers "concerned with our own problem of living in a history which . . . was extremely difficult to apprehend." He then provides a catalogue strikingly similar to Bush's for the original phase of Modernism (in "Modern/Postmodern"):

> The third group included the James Joyce of *Ulysses,* D. H. Lawrence, E. M. Forster, W. B. Yeats (when *The Tower* appeared) and T. S. Eliot. So *The Waste Land* was exciting in the first place because it was concerned with the modern world which we felt to be real. (*The Thirties And After* [New York: Random, 1978], p. 197.)

His catalogue begins and ends with the works that were then being distinguished in their illustrious company as the supreme exempla of the modernist novel and poem in the language, through special attacks by the detractors of Modernism, no less than the special regard of its writers and readers. This distinction accorded them by the first two generations of modernists persisted through the period, and is shared by most of us, who study it.

Respecting the singular attraction that the poem of the pair had for young poets a half-dozen years later, Spender's testimony mentions, in addition to its concern with the modern world, its "achieving a new synthesis [of intellect and emotion]"; "rhythmically the language was so exciting"; and "*The Waste Land* . . . makes [its] poetry become a passion to the reader" (pp. 198–99). His memorial essay on Eliot does not deal with his contemporaries' attitude toward *Ulysses* as well; but his autobiographical *World Within World* (New York: Harcourt, 1951) discloses that when a freshman writer, "I covered reams of paper with ungrammatical incoherent sentences which I imagined to resemble the style of James Joyce in *Ulysses*" (p. 35).

The testimony of this credible witness substantiates a fact of modernist literary culture: that in the "explosion of talent," these two works were paired as central and exemplary. In "*Ulysses* and the Age of Modernism" (in *Fifty Years: Ulysses,* ed. Thomas F. Staley [Bloomington: Indiana UP, 1974], pp. 172–88), the late Maurice Beebe effectively elicits characteristics of Modernism from "perhaps the single most inclusive and important text of literary Modernism as an independent and autonomous movement" (p. 186). He declares, "Joyce's book has taken on the stature of *the* modern myth" (p. 184); and C. B. Cox and Arnold P. Hinchliffe, editors of *T. S. Eliot:* The Waste Land, *A Casebook* (Nashville: Aurora, 1970), write of "the transformation of the poem into a myth" (p. 14).

Objecting, in a review of *T. S. Eliot* (*Southern Review* 21 [1985], 178–82), to Bush's similar treatment of "our definitive example of modernist poetry," Denis Donoghue points out that modernist poetry "is not definitively given by *The Waste Land* or indeed by any single poem" (182). He is right in principle, of course; and his objection extends to the status accorded *Ulysses* as well. But, as with the suitableness of the name *Modernism,* conceptual validity must be distinguished from actual value. Statements like those quoted are their own evidence that the novel and poem are historically—simply because they have functioned through history as—the most central, and so closest to the definitive, works of English literary Modernism. Mythic status does not inhere in the object, but in the subject's attitude toward it.

The status accorded them by their authors' contemporaries, and Spender's, and those of subsequent writers and critics for decades (including me), cannot be explained by their being truly exemplary. Although the sheer range of modernist characteristics in both, especially in *Ulysses,* is exceptional if not unique, neither is even exemplary of its own author's earlier or later writings (as "Prufrock" is not). And their status cannot be a matter of unique excellence. Even someone foolhardy enough to negotiate the quicksand of value judgment among canonical modernist works would not place those two alone together on a pinnacle above all others.

The explanation of their status readiest to mind would attribute it to their influence. At the time he was writing essays about *Ulysses* and literary antecedents back through those "monks of fiction" James and Flaubert, to Homer, Pound recast his early *Cantos* to focus on Homer and Odysseus.[35] The subtitle of *Afterjoyce* is *Studies in Fiction After* Ulysses; and in its first paragraph, Adams writes:

> The positive influence of Joyce has proved wide, deep, and enduring. Only one novelist of his day, Franz Kafka, has exercised an influence in any way comparable to Joyce's. Lawrence, Proust, Mann, Gide, Faulkner, Hemingway, and the scattering of their lesser contemporaries are simply not in the comparison. (p. 3)

Unlike the book that attempts to trace "the influence of *The Waste Land* on British novels" cited in the first chapter (pp. 4–5), Adams's study demonstrates a subtle understanding of the problem of influence:

> . . . what looks most like influence may be simply coincidence. Every novelist who lived after Joyce is no doubt a post-Joyce novelist, but none is simply that. Our subject thus consists of a relatively firm center . . . [and] a much larger and gassier band of shifting and overlapping energies . . . . (p. 4)

Hence, with *Between the Acts,* Woolf "went not farther away from Joyce but deeper into him," though "influence in the demonstrable sense isn't even alleged" (p. 78). Adams's book gives cogent evidence of the influence of *Ulysses* on a number of novelists, chief among them Woolf, Faulkner, and Nabokov.[36]

In "Remembering Eliot," Spender wrote, "to our generation, Eliot was the poet of poets, closer to us than Yeats, though Yeats might be 'greater'" (p. 208); and marks of the influence of *The Waste Land* on his circle, and on other poets such as MacLeish and Hart Crane, seem apparent. A mark of its more general

35. "The following year [1922], *Ulysses* at last read as a whole, Pound finally determined what he was doing in the *Cantos*" (*Pound Era,* p. 381). See also *Pound/Joyce,* pp. 193–94.

36. Its influence also is treated in Vivian Mercier, *Reader's Guide to the New Novel* (New York: Farrar, 1971); and Craig Hansen Werner, *Paradoxical Resolutions: American Fiction Since James Joyce* (Urbana: U of Illinois P, 1982).

influence is that its title became an "eponym" for "the cultural infirmity of Europe after the Great War" (Andrew Ross, "*The Waste Land* and the Fantasy of Interpretation," *Representations* 8 [Fall 1984], p. 134).

But if Adams is right that the influence of *Ulysses* is unrivalled by that of the work of other modernist English novelists; and if *The Waste Land* enjoyed a comparable influence, their influence was great only relative to that of their contemporaries' work. For it was not extensive enough to make either one truly exemplary—or (therefore), definitive. Yet they remain central.

Perhaps the key to understanding their central status inheres in the best historical evidence of the fact itself. Not only is neither work excluded from any list of English modernist writings, however short; but the tendency of writers and critics has been to do as Munson and MacLeish did: cite them together, and just them. It is perhaps not significant that Pound should do so, frequently, when discussing his early *Cantos*. But when in *World Within World* Spender devotes a paragraph to "What excited me [when an undergraduate] about the modern movement," he cites those two works as having "showed me that modern life could be material for art" (p. 86); and when, in his memorial essay on Eliot, the aging poet complains of critics who "read Eliot's conversion . . . into *The Waste Land*" (p. 193), the work by another writer he cites to exemplify his point is *Ulysses*. Conversely, the last sentence of Adams's book about the influence of *Ulysses* alludes to a new period that "will no doubt announce itself as decisively as *The Waste Land* and *Ulysses* announced the advent . . ." (p. 201). Three years before Spender's memorial essay, Northrop Frye, writing about "Literary Criticism" in a volume of even more general scope, makes a point by invoking "the new literature that appeared around 1922": he cites "the writers of this period whom we now take most seriously, such as Eliot and Joyce," and then specifies "the traditions of literature that made *Ulysses* and *The Waste Land* possible."[37] A decade after Spender's essay and the year before Adams's book (1976), an essay in *Modernism* by one of its editors, Malcolm Bradbury's "London 1890–1920" (pp. 172–90), describes "the 1920s . . . when some of the greatest classics of English-language Modernism, including *The Waste Land* and *Ulysses,* appeared" (p. 184). And in the present decade, confirming inadvertently the tendency to cite that novel and poem together as exemplary of Modernism, and just them, Levenson writes, "If we look for a mark of modernism's coming of age, the founding of the *Criterion* in 1922 may prove a better instance than *The Waste Land,* better even than *Ulysses*" (p. 213); a few pages later, again emphasizing the role of its "constituent ideas" in the "Genealogy of Modernism," he writes that it "achieved its decisive formulation . . . not only because of legitimizing masterworks such as *Ulysses* or *The Waste Land* but because . . . " (pp. 218–19).

Pound may have promoted Modernism in other arts and languages; but not so instrumentally as in English literature. And it evolved in many places with

37. "Literary Criticism," *The Aims and Methods of Scholarship in Modern Languages and Literatures,* ed. James Thorpe (1963; 2nd ed., New York: Modern Language Association, 1973), pp. 69–81, p. 74.

no help from him. Yet one can propose that without him, some writers who helped to establish and characterize Modernism in English literature would have remained obscure, or even unpublished. And one can propose that without his other activities as well, it may not have come to dominate English literature. Neither of these statements can be made about Joyce, or even about Eliot. It is their writing that affected history. "Prufrock," Eliot's remarkable harbinger poem, and other works by both, played their part in the movement that established the original phase of Modernism. But *Ulysses* and *The Waste Land* share special status. Hence, Levenson's recent book, concerned with "concepts . . . constituent ideas," has a final chapter on *The Waste Land;* and Stead's more recent one, concerned with Pound's role in modernist poetry, has both a chapter and an appendix on it.

Ironically, while their creators turned away from them, they were taken to be exemplary by contemporaries and younger writers. And since they are not so, that perception of them is significant. Both influenced the writing of others, in specific and in general ways. In the beginning, they were distinguished as the central achievements of English literary Modernism. For decades, they have been paired habitually by writers and critics. Furthermore, each is cited as the modernist novel or poem in English that first comes to mind, the way *Hamlet* and *The Rape of the Lock, Faust* and *War and Peace,* are cited.

These signs of their special status indicate that they began their joint career in history as marks for other writers to aim at—as high and inspiring achievements of the powerful new movement—and continued, when Modernism was no longer new, as supreme embodiments of it. When, in the time of the first "What Was Modernism?," Imamu Baraka (then Leroi Jones) portrayed a black American writer-intellectual in his play *A Recent Killing,* it was natural that the pair be primary formative influences on him, and the Leopold Bloom of his imagination a character. They became established in the literary consciousness to the extent that no one of my generation, at least, can fail to have a culturally conditioned response to the naming of either one.

In our historical myth of a movement become period in the first quarter of the century, this pair of works that marked and helped establish Modernism in English literature, by their role in realizing and defining the culmination of its original phase, are its central archetypes.

6

Ulysses and *The Waste Land*

I hold this book to be the most important expression which the present age
has found. It is a book to which we are all indebted, and from which none of
us can escape.

T. S. Eliot, "Ulysses, Order, and Myth"

Literary influence can work in strange ways. Herbert Howarth points out that
the English text of the famous lecture introducing *Ulysses,* given by the presti-
gious French critic and editor Valery Larbaud, appeared in the inaugural issue
of Eliot's magazine *Criterion* (October 1922) in company with the editor's new
poem *The Waste Land;* that the issue also contained an essay by Yeats's friend
T. Sturge Moore complaining of the neglect of the (Celtic) legend of Tristram
and Iseult; and that the next spring Joyce drafted the Tristram fragment of his
new work which was to be *Finnegans Wake* (p. 245). At the very least, the flick
of a trout's tail has disturbed the milk.

Eliot himself, however, seems to have had no discernible influence on Joyce,
unless the poet's coincidental brief use in *The Waste Land* of Wagner's version
of the Tristram legend reinforced Moore. Always a shrewd publicist, Joyce wel-
comed Eliot's arranging to print a translation of Larbaud; and he recruited Eliot
to write about his use of myth, as he recruited Larbaud to write about his formal
devices and Pound to write about the range of his vision. He apparently did not
like Eliot's work until *The Waste Land,* and is reported to have said after reading
it, "I had never realized Eliot was a poet" (*James Joyce,* p. 495). He undoubtedly
"realized" a great deal more about the poem, which I shall get to.

The reverse was not the case. From the time its literary editor whetted read-
ers' appetites for *Ulysses* in the *Egoist* of June-July 1918 and praised "the later
work of Mr. James Joyce" in the *Atheneum* of July 4, 1919, to his designating
Ulysses "the most considerable work of imagination in English in our time" in
his eloquent response ("A Message to the Fish") to the mean and stupid obituary
of Joyce printed by the London *Times* (a response they did not publish), Eliot

was—despite gradually increasing reservations—an outspoken admirer of Joyce's art, and of that work especially.[1]

That the author of the second central work in the original phase of Modernism wrote his famous 1923 benedictory essay about the first soon after their publication, makes it a document of historical significance. However, as the last clause of this chapter's epigraph from "Ulysses, Order, and Myth" suggests, the admired colleague may actually have been a dominating master.

Joyce made certain that the chapters of *Ulysses* were read in typescript by his patron Harriet Weaver, his good friend in Zurich, Frank Budgen, his two eager publicists, Valery Larbaud and Ezra Pound—and finally, by Pound's close associate and other chief beneficiary, T. S. Eliot.[2] When Joyce died, Woolf recollected "Tom" commenting on *Ulysses,* apparently just after writing the "Notes" of *The Waste Land:* "How could anyone write again after achieving the immense prodigy of the last chapter? He was, for the first time in my knowledge, rapt, enthusiastic."[3] Echoing "from which none of us can escape," Eliot wrote to Joyce of *Ulysses* on May 21, 1921, when he had begun work in earnest on his poem, "I wish, for my own sake, that I had not read it."[4] And his declaration to Quinn, "the latter part of *Ulysses,* which I have been reading in manuscript, is truly magnificent," was made twelve days earlier, in a letter that then announced "a long poem [apparently his customary way of referring to *The Waste Land* before its completion] in mind and partly on paper which I am wishful to finish." The problematic history of its composition will be discussed below; but he declared he wrote most of it half a year later, "when I was at Lausanne for treatment."[5]

No doubt the burden of all this is apparent; furthermore, some of the dozens of allusions in *Finnegans Wake* to *The Waste Land,* Eliot, and Eliot's other poetry, represent Eliot as having derived *The Waste Land* from *Ulysses.* Joyce makes him a Shaun type and rival. He seems to have regarded the two of them as competitors with their pair of central works, and Eliot as guilty of filching some of his thunder, in two respects: appropriating fame that was rightly his;

1. See Matthiessen, p. 135, and Marvin Magalaner and Richard M. Kain, *Joyce: The Man, the Work, the Reputation* (New York: Collier, 1962), pp. 275–76. Eliot's letter to the *Times,* and the one he "might have written," were published under that title in *Horizon* 3 (March, 1941) and reprinted in *James Joyce: Two Decades of Criticism,* ed. Seon Givens (New York: Vanguard, 1948), pp. 468–71; the quoted passage appears on p. 468.

2. See *James Joyce,* p. 508. A detailed account of Eliot's involvement with *Ulysses* is given in Robert Adams Day, "Joyce's Waste Land and Eliot's Unknown God," in *Literary Monographs,* vol. 4, ed. Eric Rothstein (Madison: U of Wisconsin P, 1971), pp. 137–210, on pp. 179–88.

3. *Diary* V, 353. The recollection in 1941 was of a conversation that presumably occurred before September 8, 1922, since her entry for September 7 mentions "Tom's praises" (II: 200). See II: 199–200 and 202–3, for some of her own first reactions to *Ulysses* as a whole, and afterthoughts, and for negative and additional positive comments by Eliot.

4. *James Joyce,* p. 528. The specific context of Eliot's comment is the nighttown chapter, and it may actually apply only to that; the letter is printed in "Joyce's Waste Land," p. 183.

5. Also to Quinn; dated June 25, 1922. See *Facsimile,* pp. xx–xxii. These and many other passages in the correspondence of Eliot and Quinn that concern *The Waste Land* are reproduced in Reid, pp. 489, 534–40.

and plagiarizing freely, with inferior results, details like his novel's protrayal of thunder as, in his Bunyan's phrase, "the voice of the god Bringforth" (395).[6]

Joyce's representation is not only ungenerous but also unfair, in my opinion, especially since Eliot did not appropriate more—in their common modernist practice—and no one was lionized more, than the author of *Ulysses*. Yet, on the other side of the scale, in *Finnegans Wake* Joyce treats everyone, above all himself, with hyperbolic disrespect; and his feelings probably are equally well represented by a genial parody of *The Waste Land* he sent to Weaver in 1925 (*Letters* I: 231–32), by a notebook entry (*James Joyce*, p. 495), and by the respect for Eliot that Power reports him expressing (pp. 75, 100–1).

Eliot wrote about the significance of "the way in which a poet borrows" to argue the inferiority of Philip Massinger the year before he began the actual writing of *The Waste Land,* and while he was reading chapters of the "book to which we are all indebted." In the first chapter I proposed that a writer's relation with an antecedent whose work is not the writer's subject involves two kinds of indebtedness, which some literary historians conflate. One kind is appropriation, which can be for allusion or explicit reference to its source, or can be the "higher plagiary" of "borrowing" (whether—as "Philip Massinger" specifies—the writer does so "immaturely," or makes "his theft . . . utterly different"). The other kind of indebtedness is the radical and complex one of influence.

One who coolly steals is not threatened by that which he plunders. Some historians conflate borrowing with subjection to influence because sometimes the borrowing is not cool plagiary, but a symptom of that subjection; and certain similarities between Eliot's poem and Joyce's novel document the sheer inability of the reacting man in the artist to escape from the spell of *Ulysses*. In those instances, influence was neither "congenial," nor Eliot's "deliberate choice of a model." The instances also are unimportant. The important influence of *Ulysses* was both congenial and deliberately chosen: Eliot suddenly realized that Joyce's novel was "capable of pointing the way" to the acting artist in the man.

I shall try to show this in Section I. In the three sections that follow, I shall discuss similarities between *Ulysses* and *The Waste Land* that are more important than influence. Deeper than the threatening or congenial impress of one artist's work on that of another, these similarities may be the manifestation of fundamental conditions of life and art two-thirds of a century ago. In a letter to Eliot dating from the second phase of Modernism (December 23, 1931), Joyce wrote of "what we are all trying in our different ways to do" (*Letters* I: 310). His reference to "all" reflects what has already been said about their movement and period; the deep similarities between the pair of works he and Eliot created before the modernists' "ways" became different may illuminate "what" it was they were "all trying to do."

6. See William York Tindall, *A Reader's Guide to Finnegans Wake* (New York: Farrar, 1969), pp. 33, 60, 78, 102, 142, 181–82, for citation and discussion of relevant passages of *Finnegans Wake.* Tindall declares that Joyce "always insisted that Eliot stole *The Waste Land* from *Ulysses*" (p. 60). And for a highly ingenious account of references to *The Waste Land* in *Finnegans Wake,* and of Joyce's resentment, see Nathan Halper, "Joyce and Eliot: A Tale of Shem and Shaun," *Nation* 200 (1965), 590–95. See also "Joyce's Waste Land," p. 224 n.106.

At least one fundamental difference between the works should be noted at the outset. It is not the dramatic difference that *Ulysses* underwent radical expansion in process, and *The Waste Land* extensive cutting. For this difference is less significant than it first appears: that Joyce's expansions had the practical function of integrating the novel's "First Part" with his later innovations, has been mentioned (p. 86); as the drafts reveal, most of Eliot's cuts were urged by, and some actually made by, Pound. Many years ago, in *The Art of T. S. Eliot* (1950; New York: Dutton, 1959), Helen Gardner astutely directed attention to a number of similarities of concern and method less apparent than the use of a "myth" for "order" in each (pp. 84–85); but she emphasized the "profound" "difference between the two works," that "They display fundamentally different attitudes to life" (pp. 85-88).

That *Ulysses* is not "without God" (p. 86) has been shown. Yet the novel and poem do differ fundamentally. It may be relevant that one introverted and stiff artist was reared a Catholic, the other a Puritan. *Ulysses* is a voluptuous artwork, *The Waste Land* an austere one. And the visions they embody correspond: an embracing of created life; and revulsion at a debased world generating a desire to transcend it through the spirit. That Dame Helen, percipient and sympathetic critic of Eliot's art, refers to the chapter of *Ulysses* before Molly's robust soliloquy as "the last chapter," is relevant in this context.

It also should be noted at the outset that I do not intend to contribute to the debate about the quality of *The Waste Land* as a poem, or even to that about whether or not Eliot did fully achieve its integrity. (I know that, among his poems and plays, "Prufrock," *Ash Wednesday,* and *Murder in the Cathedral* are more important to me.) My general concern is its historical relations; and my specific concern here is its relation with the other archetype of modernist literature in English.

But exploring that relation can illuminate aspects of *The Waste Land.* The three sections of this chapter devoted to a similarity between novel and poem not attributable to influence, are intended to do so. Without venturing onto the quicksand of evaluation, I hope to show that three different charges levelled against the poem are unwarranted. I propose, respectively, that the Notes are not a meretricious excrescence, but integral; the poem's development is not discontinuous, but coherent; the narrative point of view is not chaotic or even fragmented, but consistent.

I. The Influence of Mr. Joyce's Book

Of course, the influence which Mr. Joyce's book may have is from my point of view an irrelevance.

Eliot's general observation expresses no gratitude, and may be the braving out of anxiety. *Afterjoyce* declares (possibly overlooking Pound), "The first real shock-waves of Joycean influence . . . struck first, not novelists, but a poet, T. S. Eliot" (p. 37). Although by now "It is one of the commonplaces of modernism to note *The Waste Land*'s debt to *Ulysses*" (Gordon, p. 147), students of Joyce understandably have shown little interest.[7] Most interested students of Eliot, and of modernist literature generally, have concentrated on the use of myth in the two works and mentioned incidental specific details of *The Waste Land* that seem to be taken from *Ulysses.*[8] The major source adduced for these appropriations is the third chapter of the novel—which in fact, as one of the chapters published in the *Egoist,* would have been read with special care by its literary editor.

In it, Stephen wrestles with his thought through its many changes, on analogy with Menelaus, who in the *Odyssey* tells Telemachus how he wrestled with Proteus in order to learn how to escape from an island on which he had become becalmed (see *Argument,* pp. 51-62). Stephen's reflections grow out of and circle about the central question of eschatology: he ponders whether all of his dead mother is "beastly" (as Mulligan says) and so is buried, or if instead she has a resurrected soul—and he himself has a soul. Eventually they cause him to confront his past life, and the impasse to which that life has brought him.

At least two specific elements of the chapter are similar to elements of *The Waste Land:* the drowned man and drowned dog ("Death by Water"); and the gypsy's dog's digging, which Stephen likens to the "fox burying his grandmother" of the riddle he had told his pupils in a compulsive way in the preceding chapter. (Both are developments of the "ghoststory" [25] pattern of that chapter: "Lycidas"-Christ-the riddle.) The fox-dog of Stephen's thoughts is not burying but attempting to dig up, to see if indeed his (grand)mother has gone, as the riddle says, "to heaven." Even including its spiritual concern, the element seems a direct source for or influence on the end of "The Burial of the Dead":

> That corpse you planted in your garden,
> Has it begun to sprout? Will it bloom this year?
> Or has the sudden frost disturbed its bed?
> Oh keep the Dog far hence, that's friend to men,
> Or with his nails he'll dig it up again! (lines 71-75)

Melchiori's study, the first devoted to establishing and exploring the influence of *Ulysses* on *The Waste Land,* "centres . . . mainly on the third" chapter (p. 57); in it, he traces the dog imagery in Eliot's work and concludes that for

7. Stuart Gilbert (and Ernst Robert Curtius) noted that both works employ the motif of a drowned man; see Gilbert, *James Joyce's* Ulysses, 2nd ed. (New York: Knopf, 1952), pp. 122–24.

8. The most recent treatment is in Grover Smith, *The Waste Land* (London: Allen, 1983), pp. 30–31, 50, 55–64, 101, 105, 111–13. "Joyce's Waste Land" is the most extensive and sophisticated study of details; and its principal antecedent is Giorgio Melchiori, *"The Waste Land* and *Ulysses,"* *English Studies* 35 (April, 1954), 56–68, summarized in Magalaner and Kain, p. 221. Other essays more or less devoted to the subject are Halper; Thomas M. Lorch, "The Relationship between *Ulysses* and *The Waste Land,"* in *Texas Studies in Literature and Language* 6 (1964), 123–33; and an account of similarities without attributions of influence, Claude Edmonde Magny, "A Double Note on T. S. Eliot and James Joyce," in *Symposium,* pp. 208–17. A more complete bibliography includes "Appendix III: *A Note on* The Waste Land *and* Ulysses," Gordon, pp. 147–48; "The Waste Land and Joyce," Howarth, pp. 242–46, esp. pp. 243–45; Matthiessen, pp. 39, 44–45; George W. Nitchie, "A Note on Eliot's Borrowings," *Massachusetts Review* 6 (1965), 403–6; *Eliot's Poetry and Plays,* pp. 60, 79, 84–85, 313 n.17; and Spears, pp. 78–79. I am indebted to most of these for some ideas.

Eliot a dog is "the busy enquirer who founds his search on areligious, or rather on purely animal bases" (p. 61). Interestingly, he fails to note what first struck me about Eliot's apparent appropriation from Joyce: that "Dog" is capitalized, and therefore is presented in an orthographic pun as the opposite of "God"; it seems to be a significantly narrowed derivation from Joyce's portrayal of an "Adonai" who (in Stephen's fantasy of a black mass in nighttown), responds to "the voice of all the damned" strictly according to their conception of Him ("Dooooooooooog!"), before responding to "the voice of all the blessed" with the "g" before and the "d" after the eleven "o"s (600).

Melchiori's essay mentions additional similarities of motif or image, then turns to verbal correspondences. He believes Eliot deliberately appropriated these; later critics, such as Lorch (p. 134) and Nitchie (p. 405), consider them unconscious—symptoms of manifest influence. But studies of Eliot's indebtedness have concentrated on them, and proper consideration of the influence of *Ulysses* cannot ignore them.

Although in these studies the locutions "brings to mind" and "like" occur often, indebtedness (whether plagiary or influence) usually is claimed more positively. Some allegations have the grotesque lineaments of imaginary toads. For example, attributing "The rattle of bones" to Bloom's "Rattle his bones," and "picked his bones in whispers" to Bloom's observing that a graveyard rat would "Pick the bones clean," ignores that bones, like skeletons, conventionally *rattle* (Bloom is quoting from a ballad), that flesh conventionally is *picked* from bones. And in the passage in "What the Thunder Said" about "mountains of rock" (330-45): can Stephen's (not Bloom's—or Gerty MacDowell's) walking on the sand at Sandymount really have inspired "Sweat is dry and feet are in the sand"?; or his "My teeth are very bad," Eliot's apparent metaphor for the mountain range, "Dead mountain mouth of carious teeth that cannot spit"?[9] On a more general level, Howarth proposes that Eliot was "moved" by the "great achievement" of Molly's soliloquy to write the passage of the cockneys in the pub that concludes "A Game of Chess": "He must have wanted to write a comparable dramatization of the popular mind" (p. 243). Judging from Woolf's report, Eliot was more inhibited than inspired by "the immense prodigy of the last chapter"; but in any case, we now have his private assertion that the passage was "stolen" from the Eliots' maid (*Facsimile*, p. 127). Apparently, he had the genius to incorporate a maid's anecdote in his poem, and to transmute it into fine dramatic verse.

Instances of indebtness to *Ulysses* there are, nevertheless. And the problem of what to make of them is a nagging one, despite Eliot's method of incorporating lines and phrases from other works. The drafts of *The Waste Land* bear two comments by Pound to the effect that passages recalled *Ulysses*. In the first case (p. 8 [9]), Pound's inference is more evidence of the effect the novel had had on him than of the effect it had had on Eliot. But Eliot's sensitivity about the matter

---

9. Gordon, p. 147; Melchiori, p. 66. In discussing Joyce's criticism in *Finnegans Wake* of Eliot's appropriations, Halper repeats this attribution for Eliot's "mouth of carious teeth" (p. 593, col. 1), and Day infers from him that Joyce "seems to have believed" it as well (p. 188). Joyce "was a man not without malice" and "envy," as Halper says (p. 594, cols. 2 and 3); but he was not silly.

can be illustrated by the fact that in response to Pound's other comment, "Penelope J. J.," beside "Those are pearls that were his eyes, yes!," Eliot removed the "yes" (p. 12 [13]). Was that "yes," in the words of his Massinger essay, "an echo, rather than an imitation or a plagiarism—the basest, because least conscious form of borrowing"? Eliot's attitude to borrowing coincides with his doctrine of conscious adoption ("deliberate choice") of an influence. But, concerning his possible awareness of any specific words or other elements from *Ulysses* when writing his poem, unless an appropriation refers or alludes to its source in the novel (in which case it is not "an imitation or a plagiarism"), although one critic's opinion cannot be as good as another's, there is no way of knowing. And more important is the question whether such an element is truly stolen in Eliot's terms, or merely derivative, consciously or not.

In many instances, even indebtedness itself cannot be determined, because both works are so extensively allusive. An excellent example is the popular attribution of the "Burial of the Dead" passage. Although Joyce has fox and dog disinterring, and later punningly employs the literal obverse of "God," Eliot attaches to line 74, where he uses "Dog," a note: "Cf. the dirge in Webster's *White Devil.*" To one of Vittoria Corombona's brothers over the corpse of the other, their mother recites a dirge (V. iv, 92–101, 104–5) calling on birds to bury a "friendless" body with leaves and flowers, and on small boring animals:

> To rear him hillocks that shall keep him warm,
> And (when gay tombs are robbed) sustain no harm:
> But keep the wolf far thence that's foe to men,
> For with his nails he'll dig them up again.

An unmarked grave of flowers and hillocks in Webster, and a corpse buried in a garden in Eliot. Surely, the poem is indebted to the dirge exploited allusively in the close paraphrase of its final couplet and referred to in the identifying note. However, does it owe a more direct debt to *Ulysses?* That is, did *Ulysses* function as a catalyst—move Eliot to incorporate a couplet and invoke other elements from an already familiar dramatic sequence, by recalling the sequence to him? Perhaps. But Eliot's unpublished poem "The Death of the Duchess," which contributed to *The Waste Land* and accompanies the drafts, clearly is based on an incident in *The Duchess of Malfi,* and incorporates lines from that play and lines about "the dead" from *The White Devil;* and one remembers that the first two stanzas of a poem in his 1920 volume *Poems* (*Ara Vos Prec* in England), "Whispers of Immortality," are devoted to the subject stated in its opening line: "Webster was much possessed by death." His memory would not seem to have needed much prodding.

The question is complicated by the possibility that the scene in *The White Devil* also is behind the fox-dog material in the second and third chapters of *Ulysses.* For the fox "burying" his "grandmother" listens for and hears "bells in heaven"; and the bereaved mother introduces the dirge with, "I'll give you a saying which my grandmother was wont, when she heard the bell toll, to sing o'er unto her lute" (V.iv, 88–90). Joyce was less interested in Webster than Eliot, and the bell in *The White Devil* is a funeral bell. Nevertheless, Joyce may have appropriated Eliot's possible source from the play, either consciously or unconsciously, and/or been construed by Eliot as having done so.

In the light of all this, how fix Eliot's indebtedness in the passage to *Ulysses* itself? His most likely debt is the punning device of the capitalized "Dog"—which comes from near the end, not the beginning, of the novel. But how determine whether that one (inferred) element was plagiarized, or was instead "least consciously[ly]" echoed as a symptom of influence?

Even where a third work is not involved, attributions of indebtedness to *Ulysses* can be treacherous. To illustrate, I offer a characteristic case of apparent appropriation, chosen, for the sake of consistency, from the third chapter. (Strangely, it has been disregarded, although negative evidence was not available to most of the influence studies.) At a crucial point, *The Waste Land* reads:

> At the violet hour . . .
> . . . .
> I Tiresias, though blind, throbbing between two lives,
> Old man with wrinkled female breasts, can see
> At the violet hour, the evening hour . . . (218–20)

And in *Ulysses:*

> Me sits there with his augur's rod of ash, in borrowed sandals, by day beside a livid sea, unbeheld, in violet night walking . . . (48)

Stephen is speaking, and he says he has an augur's rod and his shoes are sandals; that could hardly be much closer to "I Tiresias." But is Joyce's passage invoked in the poem? Certainly not to any purpose. (Odysseus's meeting with Tiresias seems to have been ignored in *Ulysses.*) The similarity could be coincidental (an "analogue"), but seems less so than rattled or picked bones, decayed teeth, or walking on sand. The striking conjunction of Joyce's "violet night" and Eliot's "the violet hour, the evening hour" seems to settle the issue: from the third chapter of *Ulysses,* which he published, the literary editor of the *Egoist* stole, in his sense, the vehicle of a good metaphor—truly stole it—and in the process "basely" caused his poem to "echo" the context in which he found "violet."

Once again, the plot thickens; for the apparently stolen vehicle can be shown to have been owned by Eliot all along. The four poems that begin *Prufrock and Other Observations,* the first poems published since his student years, all appeared initially in 1915. And the situation of an evening or night walker in the city which dominates the fourth, "Rhapsody on A Windy Night," comes up in the other three as well. An untitled holograph poem or fragment accompanying the *Waste Land* drafts also is dominated by that situation so pervasive in Eliot's early poems (and metamorphosed in *The Waste Land*). It is strongly reminiscent of "Rhapsody on A Windy Night," and may even be the source for the beginning and ending of "Prufrock." Not surprisingly, Valerie Eliot dates this "first draft," as she calls it, to "about 1914 or even earlier" from the handwriting, and cites Conrad Aiken for confirmation (*Facsimile,* pp. 112 [113], 114 [115], 130).

The weight of evidence is that the poem or fragment antedates Joyce's completion of the first chapters of *Ulysses* by at least two years (*James Joyce,* pp. 441–42). And, in both cases using "violet" as a metaphor precisely for evening, not for night, it begins: "So through the evening, through the violet air . . ." and has for its tenth line: "Oh, through the violet sky, through the evening air."

As with the digging canine, it is possible that *Ulysses* served catalytically as an immediate source. Perhaps the "augur's rod" passage in the third chapter invoked for *The Waste Land* (consciously or unconsciously) the violet/evening metaphor Eliot had used earlier—by recalling to him his "first draft." If so, in recalling this earlier manuscript to him, *Ulysses* also was the immediate cause of his deriving from it a stanza in the last section of his new poem (lines 378–85). And if so, other similarities between Stephen on the beach and Tiresias may well be unconscious and gratuitous echo—symptoms of influence. Once again: perhaps. For it seems no more likely that Eliot needed to be reminded of his own poetry, than that he needed to be reminded of a poem for the dead in Webster.

My purpose in tracing at such length the kind of ambiguous and tenuous grounds for influence that often are adduced, is to suggest both that usually such inferred influence—and/or appropriation—is dubious, and that even when it happens to be more likely, usually it is not important. The exceptions are a few similar details to which students of influence have drawn attention, such as the digging "Dog." Eliot seems to have stolen the pun; and it is a significant appropriation because of the freight of meaning it carried from *Ulysses.* I believe that—again in his sense—he also stole Joyce's thunder. In the fourteenth chapter of *Ulysses* ("Oxen of the Sun"), Joyce contrives to assert that Bloom can achieve his salvation only by emulating the one true father in the novel, Theodore Purefoy—pure of faith; and that Stephen can do so only by submitting his will to God—as Odysseus's companions would have been saved had they shown reverence for the god of the sacred cattle of fertility. Joyce's assertion about his protagonists' ways to salvation is punctuated by "voice of the god Bringforth" thunder, and rain.[10] As always, the evidence for inferred indebtedness is circumstantial: in "What the Thunder Said," much the same thing happens.

The evidence can resemble a trout in milk. There seems little doubt that Eliot plagiarized from and imitated the novel in progress he so admired, as he mined other sources; and perhaps he did echo Joyce in places. But any such indebtedness is of minor importance, since the relations between *Ulysses* and *The Waste Land* have historical significance because they are relations of homology more than of filiation. The grander, the truly significant similarities between them seem to me not appropriations, or symptoms of influence, but rather, with one exception, elements of confluence in these paired central modernist works.

10. *Argument,* pp. 277–301. "Joyce's Waste Land" ingeniously links together thunder; rain; the "man in the macintosh" of *Ulysses* and Eliot's "hooded figure"; the drowned man and dog; and the digging dogs.

The exception is that a pattern of allusion informs *The Waste Land,* having for referent an ancient myth. The significant influence of *Ulysses* is that it "was capable of pointing the way." Not until all manuscripts of and notebooks for *The Waste Land* are available—if then—can there be certainty about the history of its composition. But the extant materials—the drafts and related poems and fragments a grateful Eliot insisted Quinn accept as a gift and Valerie Eliot published in facsimile in 1971—indicate the poet's "deliberate choice of a model" he "found most congenial." They also record, I believe, the historical circumstances of his deliberate adoption of the way of *Ulysses.*

In eliciting that history from them, I have, when possible, relegated to footnotes the complications attendant on the drafts and related materials. Employing them in an empirically sound way is difficult, not least because the evidence is equivocal in some respects, and incomplete. But in the past dozen years, a number of critics have used them to enlighten us about both poem and poet, discussing biographical elements in *The Waste Land* more explicit in the drafts, interpreting the poem in the context of the drafts, and tracing its evolution from the drafts. This account of the relation of *Ulysses* to its evolution is a revision and elaboration of one written at the beginning of that period; it benefits from subsequent Eliot criticism, as well as from second thoughts. Its five parts are concerned respectively with the general chronology of composition; the original "Fire Sermon"; Eliot's evolution of "a long poem"; his crucial inspiration; and my conclusions.

Chronology

Critics debate two related questions about the first three sections of Eliot's poem-in-progress. The only drafts of all three are typed: were sections I and II composed and/or typed up before or after the unnumbered "Fire Sermon"? And where were sections I and II typed? My concern is the relation of *Ulysses* to *The Waste Land;* but the two questions are implicated in that relation.

Some elements of the poem antedate the novel by as much as their origins in the earliest related poems and fragments included with the drafts, such as the "first draft" of 1914 "or even earlier," and "The Death of Saint Narcissus," which seems to be very early.[11] But even had he been acquainted with Joyce's use of the *Odyssey* before he put down a line, Eliot would not have followed suit, to judge from his general title for the drafts of the first two sections, "He Do the Police in Different Voices" (Betty Higden's praise, in Dickens's *Our Mutual Friend,* of Sloppy's mimicry as he reads aloud from the *People's Police Gazette*). After he had drafted those two sections of the "long poem" he was writing—at the time his (presumably) no longer extant original drafts were typed up—his conception of it apparently did not (yet) warrant its being called "The Waste Land."

Hugh Kenner proposes convincingly that the poem Eliot actually began to

11. John Hayward dates it "slightly later" than the spring of 1910 in his introduction to *Poems Written in Early Youth by T. S. Eliot* (New York: Farrar, 1967), p. ix. Spender suggests 1911 in *Eliot* (n.p.: Fontana/Collins, 1975), p. 91.

create was a neo-Augustan urban satire.[12] The drafts reveal enough of what was excised, and what was added late, to confirm that in any case it was not *The Waste Land*. Wasteland and Grail references were appropriate for direct and ironic treatment of Eliot's "unreal city" from the start; and some do appear in the early stages of composition. However, although the references he marshalled served his ultimate conception once he evolved it, initially he employed them for other purposes: for example, to contrast false with true spiritual wisdom (Madame Sosostris and Tiresias), or to suggest the quest for salvation (the "fishing" prince Ferdinand from *The Tempest*). Even such an apparently pointed wasteland element as the drought passage in "The Burial of the Dead" (lines 19–30) derives in part from "The Death of Saint Narcissus," is related explicitly (by the note to "Son of man") to *Ezekiel*, and has echoes of *Isaiah* (32.2, 13, 15, 18–20).

The Waste Land proper (less the Notes) was written during the period between Eliot's informing Quinn "a long poem" was "partly on paper," and his correspondence with Pound that records its completion; the inclusive dates are May 1921, and the weeks in January 1922 when Joyce was making final revisions to *Ulysses* (Pound, *Letters*, pp. 169–72; *James Joyce*, p. 523). "On 12 October, Eliot was given three months' sick-leave from the bank" (Gordon, p. 104). He spent the first month at Margate, the week of November 12 to 18 at home in London, and about a month at Lausanne, ending in the latter part of December; he travelled east through Paris, where his wife stayed on with the Pounds, and after Lausanne spent some days with them himself, before returning to London, his job, and completion of *The Waste Land*, less the Notes. On June 25, 1922, he wrote to Quinn of "notes I am adding."

It was in that letter that he informed Quinn the poem was "written, mostly when I was at Lausanne" (Facsimile, p. xxii). Testimony must be distinguished from evidence. Pound's testimony, that the snatches of conversation in the opening paragraph were adapted from the talk of Eliot's fellow patients at Lausanne (Stead, p. 361), would mean at least part of the first two sections were composed there. No substantive purpose would have been served by Eliot's lying; and he had a strong moral imperative not to lie to Quinn. Yet what "mostly" means remains difficult to determine.

The Original "Fire Sermon"

The original version of "The Fire Sermon"—which has a long opening passage not in *The Waste Land*, and ends abruptly a few lines after the typist sequence—almost certainly was not written at Lausanne. Only it was typed on one of the three machines used for the drafts of the poem. The first two sections were typed on a different machine; and the last two were done on Pound's machine. The

---

12. Hugh Kenner, "The Urban Apocalypse," *Eliot in His Time*, ed. A. Walton Litz (Princeton: Princeton UP, 1973), pp. 23–49. (In another essay in the volume, Helen Gardner sets out a different "theory of the composition of *The Waste Land*.") *The Invisible Poet* proposed a quarter-century ago, it should be noted, that the final form of *The Waste Land* was not in fact "foreseen by the author" (pp. 148–50).

machine used to type "The Fire Sermon" also typed the title page and, the following October (1922), the shipping label that directed the draft material from Eliot's home address in London to Quinn.[13] This apparently was a (standard?) machine Eliot used when in London, from the evidence not only of the label, but also of the draft title page. He appears to have typed that page after his return from Lausanne and Paris with the drafts of the poem in his luggage: in their exchange of letters, Pound mentions the (temporary) epigraph from Conrad's "Heart of Darkness" below the title as though it is new to him (Pound, *Letters*, p. 169). And this chronology for the title page is confirmed internally by the fact that there had been a provisional title heading the first two sections, which was abandoned before the fourth section was written out in a fair copy—that is, was abandoned some time before Eliot returned home.

We must conclude that "The Fire Sermon" was typed before the drafts of the last two sections, because these were typed on Pound's machine in Paris during Eliot's visit, and because we know from the drafts of the poem that Pound and Eliot worked over "The Fire Sermon" more than any other section, a number of times, and in typed form.[14] And, because it was typed on the machine Eliot used later in London for the title page and the shipping label, it apparently was typed in London.

I propose that it also was composed and typed up before the first two sections. All five sections were seen by Pound in Paris (*Facsimile*, p. xxii). If the first two also were typed (on a different machine) in London before Eliot's departure for the continent, how much of the poem was in fact "written . . . at Lausanne"?[15] Even if versions were composed at Margate or before Margate, it appears that the extant typescripts, at least, originated either during Eliot's week in London between Margate and his departure for Lausanne, or at Lausanne.[16]

13. The label has been preserved with the drafts in the Berg Collection of the New York Public Library, and is reproduced in Harvey Simmonds, *John Quinn: An Exhibition to Mark the Gift of the John Quinn Memorial Collection* (New York: New York Public Library, 1968), facing p. 11. Smith suggests the machine may have been at Eliot's bank office, since some of "his correspondence done on this appears" dictated (*The Waste Land*, p. 64).

14. The ribbon and carbon copies were passed back and forth between them. For example, changes in Eliot's hand to the ribbon copy, such as the revision to "demotic (French)" in line 98, are in Pound's hand on the carbon copy; yet on the ribbon copy, Pound refers to his alterations and comments on the carbon copy.

15. I concur with Hugh Kenner's proposal that the machine used was a portable typewriter belonging to the Eliots. Smith writes that Eliot had had it at Harvard (*The Waste Land*, p. 67). Some of the early poems included among the drafts were typed on it.

16. On the back of the third (last) sheet of the second section, Vivien Eliot asked her husband to "Send me back this copy" (*Facsimile*, p. 15n). Yet she stayed with him for a time, and visited him frequently, at Margate; and they were together during the week in London: unless it was extant the previous May, only when she was in Paris and he in Lausanne should it have had to be *sent* back and forth. Furthermore, the likely derivation of Madame Sosostris from Huxley's *Crome Yellow* indicates a date after early November (Smith, *The Waste Land*, p. 67), although Stead proposes (citing a letter from Gardner) that Eliot had heard the name from Huxley earlier (p. 363). Evidence against Lausanne as the origin of the typescripts is Valerie Eliot's information—in correspondence with Stead (p. 360) and me (November 26, 1985)—that Eliot's letters from there were not typed. Smith's most recent hypothesis is that the first two sections were composed at Margate and typed during the week in London (*The Waste Land*, pp. 67–70).

It may have been some state of "The Fire Sermon" that was "on paper" when he wrote to Quinn on May 9. He may merely have been referring to the earlier poems and "fragments . . . ultimately embodied in the poem" (as he described those of "Prufrock" he took abroad in 1910) he was, for that reason, to include in the drafts when he sent them to Quinn. Or, finally, he may have been referring to some state of the two sections of "He Do the Police in Different Voices."[17] Testimony and evidence exist indicating he may have composed "The Fire Sermon" at "Margate Sands" (though the reference is not in the typed draft), then typed it up on his standard machine during his week in London. When Pound visited him in London just before his month at Margate, "There was evidently no discussion of Eliot's poem"; and, "Eliot ironically attached his [Margate] hotel bill to the manuscript."[18] However, one of the important indications of its initial composition—Pound's multiple readings of both the ribbon and carbon copies—also makes it unlikely that they did not exist until the middle of November. And if the (numbered) first two sections were typed not at Lausanne, but during Eliot's week in London between Margate and Lausanne, *they* would have been composed at Margate.

In any case, the evidence indicates not only that he left for Lausanne with the typed draft of "The Fire Sermon," but also that it was the first section drafted: not only composed and typed up before the last two sections, but in existence before "Part I" and "Part II" of "He Do the Police in Different Voices" had developed enough to warrant typing—if indeed they were "on paper" at all.[19] Its priority explains why the draft "Fire Sermon" not only does not bear

17. The most ingenious as well as recent argument that the two were in some state before Eliot's May letter—and that the five sections were composed in sequence—is Stead's, in his chapter on the poem and his "Appendix: A Note on the Dating of the Drafts of *The Waste Land*." He proposes that the two were "already typed . . . by the beginning of May," and that "during 1921 [Eliot] acquired a new machine," then typed, in sequence, the draft of "The Fire Sermon"—in effect that an editor (of the *Egoist*) who was a bank officer, and who wrote poetry, criticism, and reviews at home, lacked simultaneous access to two typewriters (pp. 92, 359). Of the first line of the poem he proposes, "The April, it may be, is April 1921, and dates the composition" (p. 93).

18. Gordon, p. 105. In "Appendix II: *Dating* The Waste Land *Fragments*" (pp. 143–46), Gordon proposes that "The Fire Sermon" was composed on an "office typewriter" at Margate (pp. 96, 145); and she gives evidence for the composition of the first two sections both early, and at Lausanne. Problems with the evidence of the typed drafts discredit her inferences. Her conclusion that the last two sections were typed on different machines (p. 146), is caused by her acknowledged (p. 143) reliance on the facsimile edition, which magnifies the typed drafts of "Death By Water"; and the standard office machine that typed "The Fire Sermon" ostensibly in Margate, also typed in London the title page and, even later, the shipping label. The almost total absence of strikeouts—the one exception is caused by an omitted word (*Facsimile*, p. 32 [33])—makes doubtful her proposal that the typed drafts of the first three sections are original composition; and the fact that Eliot used pencil for almost all revisions to the typescript, as well as—not surprisingly—for all clearly rough draft (designated "first draft" in the facsimile edition), confutes it.

19. Both Kenner, in "The Urban Apocalypse" (*Eliot in His Time*, pp. 24–25), and Smith, in *The Waste Land* (p. 67; orig. in "The Making of *The Waste Land*," *Mosaic* 6 [1972–73], 127–41, 132–33), conclude that "The Fire Sermon" was written first. It is possible that the first two sections were written before it, as Gardner, Gordon, and Stead propose, and only typed up later in London or at Lausanne; but that typing sequence is unlikely, even setting aside Eliot's "written, mostly when I was at Lausanne." The evidence of the four kinds of paper used for the drafts of the poem proper (Smith, *The Waste Land*, pp. 64–65; Gordon, pp. 144–45; Stead, p. 362) is compatible with this chronology.

that general title, but is not numbered, although the holograph fair copy in Eliot's hand of "Death by Water" also is headed "Part IV" (of a poem by then between titles).[20]

The absence of even the temporary title affixed to the first two sections and a "part" number; the multiple editing by Pound and revising and cutting by Eliot; and, above all, Eliot's eventual extensive additions to it alone of the five draft sections, not only constitute compelling evidence of the original "Fire Sermon"'s probable initial composition, but also combine with that probable chronology to indicate how far removed it was from its ultimate role in Eliot's ultimate poem.

Evolution

So late in the genesis of that poem that no typed or even fair holograph copy of the passage is included in the drafts, so late that it bears no evidence of having been seen by Pound, Eliot wrote in pencil, on the back of the mock-Augustan opening of "The Fire Sermon" portraying Fresca at her morning toilet, a rough draft of nine lines and a phrase: "By the waters." It corresponds to the first part of a fourteen-line passage in *The Waste Land.* Unless for some reason the remainder of the tenth line (182) and the four that follow it (the second refrain line of Spenser's "Prothalamian" repeated, a line drawing on the variant first one, and two drawing on "To His Coy Mistress") were on a separate sheet, and for some reason it was excluded from the drafts, they belonged to a firm formulation in his mind. That the passage was composed late is further confirmed by the fact that the omitted portion of the tenth line—"of Leman I sat down and wept"—refers to Lausanne in the past tense. The most likely reason for the prior truncation—"(Sweet Thames etc)."—of the Spenserian fourth line (176), would seem to be his desire to avoid impeding a creative flow.

After the substitution of "silk handkerchiefs" for "newspapers" at the beginning of the sixth, the elimination of "and" and parentheses in two places, and the filling out of the two part-lines, those ten rough pencilled lines,

> The rivers [sic] tent is broken and [sic] the last fingers of leaf
> Clutch and sink into the wet bank. The wind
> Crosses the brown land, unheard . . . ,

and the four not even pencilled replaced the 70 original lines of heroic couplets to begin (173-86) "III. the Fire Sermon" of *The Waste Land.* Correspondingly, rough pencilled drafts provided the last 46 lines of the section (266-311), beginning:

> The river sweats
> Oil and tar
> . . . .

Corrupted water, *Götterdämmerung, Inferno,* the pilgrim Saint Augustine: and again the rough passage is almost word for word what was published. It is pre-

---

20. For some reason, neither of the last two sections is numbered on the typed drafts.

ceded in *The Waste Land* by seven rough pencilled lines written early, but bearing no comment by Pound.[21]

Those seven lines are early; Pound commented on part of what follows; and the very last lines of "The Fire Sermon" are implied in its title: some of Eliot's new last third and more was only newly used, some possibly in mind. But neither can be the case with the nine lines and shorthand phrases, for whose clear suggestion of drought and a waste land he decisively employed the back of the ribbon copy of his original opening lines. And the pencilled rough drafts he incorporated—almost word for word—at its beginning and end provide nearly half the lines (67 of 139) in "III. The Fire Sermon" of *The Waste Land.*

Although he was not moved to make additions implementing the wasteland theme to the draft of either "The Burial of the Dead" or "In the Cage"/"A Game of Chess," "The Fire Sermon" of Eliot's original poem was drastically altered to function in a new one, and altered with a sure hand.

Furthermore, that new poem seems to have evolved late. Both the first two sections antedate most if not all of the pencilled passages in "The Fire Sermon," as their typed state and the extensive revisions made to them attest. And this clear evidence of a late conceptualization of what he was about, or wished to be about, in his poem is confirmed and further clarified by the last two sections, the eventual title, and the Notes.

Of the draft of the fourth section only a small fraction, the last tenth (lines 84–93), was published as "IV. Death by Water" of *The Waste Land.* And the excision of the major part of the draft version was done neither on Eliot's holograph copy nor on the typed copy edited (extensively) by Pound. In other words, the final 10-line state of the section came into being at least as late as the unique wasteland additions to the "The Fire Sermon," for it was not done in the drafts at all; probably, it was first recorded in the lost 19-page copy of the poem mentioned by Pound in his letter to Eliot commenting on the new title page.[22]

In dramatic contrast to that of "IV. Death by Water," the final state of "V. What the Thunder Said" is almost word for word as Eliot wrote the whole section in pencil in rough draft—the case is precisely like that of the rough pencilled additions to the draft of "The Fire Sermon." And that fact about "What the Thunder Said" confirms further what had happened in the genesis of the poem. But it does considerably more. It combines with the very different history of the drastically abbreviated section just before "What the Thunder Said" to fix the point at which Eliot conceived what he was about—the point at which he contracted his debt to *Ulysses*—and *The Waste Land* evolved. A drama, in which a suddenly manifest influence "point[ed] the way"—generated or catalyzed creative inspiration—is immanent in the *Waste Land* drafts. And the key to that drama is the rough pencilled draft of "What the Thunder Said."

21. *Facsimile,* pp. 24, 48, 50, 52, 36 (25, 49, 51, 53, 37). The seven lines (259–65) directly follow the portion of "III. The Fire Sermon" derived from the original typed and edited draft.

22. It may be the worked-over copy Eliot sent Quinn in July; presumably, he prepared and sent a subsequent fair copy, with the Notes. See *Facsimile,* pp. xxii–xxiii; and Smith, *The Waste Land,* pp. 76–78. The drafts cannot be arranged to result in a 19-page text, and do not fully correspond to the final poem, anyway.

Valerie Eliot's editorial notes include a passage in "The 'Pensées' of Pascal" (1931), in which Eliot attributed to "some forms of illness" the power to make "A piece of writing ... suddenly take shape and word; and in this state long passages may be produced which require little or no retouch," and her report that Eliot was describing writing the draft of "What the Thunder Said" (*Facsimile*, p. 129). Subsequent critics have cited the passage to explain "the extraordinary facility with which he wrote" that draft, as an "almost mystical" event or a "psychological" union of "illness, automatic writing, religious illumination."[23] Presumably, his equally extraordinary creation, "requir[ing] little or no retouch," of new passages with which he recast "The Fire Sermon," has the same etiology. Eliot's exposition and the elaborations it inspired are interesting, and even may be true. But these psychological speculations do not identify the origin, or explain the precise nature, of the sudden new conception of his poem that is the immediate, *and the concrete,* source of its "suddenly tak[ing] shape and word"—although they do not contradict the explanation, or conflict with the evidence.

The typed pages that precede "What the Thunder Said" in "a long poem," and were worked over by Pound, have a total of 511 lines; exactly half that draft material, 255 lines and two half-lines, was included in or adapted to *The Waste Land*. Of the rejected 255 lines, 252 came from four places. Forty-four lines and two half-lines were edited out of the Smyrna merchant and typist sequences in "The Fire Sermon," by Pound or under his direction. The other three passages were not revised and pruned, but simply excluded: the passage about a night on the town (apparently Boston) that begins "I. The Burial of the Dead," the first part of "He Do the Police in Different Voices," is 54 lines; the Fresca passage at the beginning of "The Fire Sermon" is 70 lines; the excised introduction and narrative of a fishing voyage to the Grand Banks that was the first part of "IV. Death by Water," is 83 lines. Eliot declared that Pound "induced me to destroy" the Fresca passage because of the quality of the verse, and Pound edited it more heavily than he did the excised part of "Death by Water." Even if Eliot simply responded to Pound's advice about the Fresca passage, we do not know why, or when, he excluded the night on the town passage that opens the first section; and we do know that he reduced "Death by Water" to one-tenth its size after Pound had expended a good deal of effort working over and cutting down the rejected nine-tenths.

Inspiration

By this point, it should be evident that the poem from which those three long passages were excluded, in which were printed almost word-for-word the rough pencilled parts of "The Fire Sermon" and draft of "What the Thunder Said," and which bore the title *The Waste Land* (and was to incorporate a set of pointedly allusive notes), was—as Eliot attested in two places a decade later—the

23. Gordon, pp. 114–15 and n.61; Smith, *The Waste Land*, pp. 26–27. See also, e.g., Schneider, pp. 71–72; and Bush, *T. S. Eliot*, pp. 68–69. Bush also discusses a psychiatrist's analysis of Eliot's statement; and a number of critics cite his similar statement in the second paragraph of the "Conclusion" to *The Use of Poetry and the Use of Criticism* (pp. 137–38).

product of an inspiration both late and clear. When his inspiration came, he could decide to just cut away from the fourth section of his poem in process, if before his inspiration not surely in progress, the nine-tenths which "il miglior fabbro," until his inspiration his arbiter, even co-creator, had shaped down so laboriously in typescript. Pound approved the text of the poem without that nine-tenths in his first January letter; and Eliot followed his advice about the remainder ("I do advise keeping Phlebas") in his second (Pound, *Letters,* pp. 169, 171).

That radical excision from the draft of "Death by Water," the Notes, the title, and almost all the many rough pencilled lines added to "The Fire Sermon" which were not put into typed or even fair holograph form in the drafts, are the dénouement of the drama. It begins with Eliot's composition of the fourth section of "a long poem."

If *The Waste Land* was in any sense "written, mostly . . . at Lausanne," Eliot did not likely show Pound the original long version of "Death by Water" when he stopped in Paris on his way to Lausanne; in which case, it was not typed on Pound's machine at that time and left there for Pound to "attack," as he put it beside the opening lines of the (fair) holograph copy: "Bad—but can't attack until I get typescript." It is almost beyond doubt (and generally agreed) that both the last two draft sections were typed during Eliot's visit to Pound after his Lausanne sojourn. However, that they were typed at the same time during Eliot's visit does not necessarily follow.

Pound read, for he commented briefly at the head of, the holograph draft of each of those two sections. That Eliot showed Pound the almost scribbled rough draft of "What the Thunder Said" indicates he had not had a chance to make a fair holograph copy, as he had done for "Death by Water." The logical inference is that he experienced his crucial inspiration, and created that virtually final rough draft, either during his stay with Pound, or so shortly before as to prevent recopying—not to mention typing—it before he left Lausanne for Paris.

The fulfillment of his inspiration included his fashioning "III. The Fire Sermon" of *The Waste Land* with the passages of virtually final rough draft—its new beginning on the verso of the first sheet of the old, and its new last third and more on four pages in the drafts. In tracing Eliot's inspiration, this is the place to consider in detail his creation and use of those pencilled pages (*Facsimile,* pp. 36 [37], 50–52 [51–53].

All four pages are on sheets apparently taken from the same notepad. Some may date from Margate whence, Valerie Eliot reports, Eliot wrote of having composed about fifty lines of "a part of Part III" (Stead, p. 363). The first passage in *The Waste Land* expanding the typed draft "Fire Sermon," of seven lines (259–65), comes from the revised state of seven early lines (the major alterations are two transposed lines and "Of Magnus Martyr hold/" for "Of Magnus Martyr stood, & stand, & hold/") on the upper portion of the first page.[24] The two qua-

---

24. Its early composition is established by the fact that it is *above* the rough draft of the apostrophe to London (between the Smyrna merchant paragraph and the introduction of Tiresias with "At the violet hour") excised by Pound from the original typescript of "The Fire Sermon" (pp. 30 and 42 [31 and 43]).

trains (291–99) taken from the third page in sequence are at least early enough to have been seen by Pound, for he commented "O.K." and "echt" in green crayon. And, since "Type out this *anyhow*" and "O.K." in pencil are beside a longer unrhymed version of the first of the quatrains, written above them, he saw the page twice: he had been satisfied with Eliot's initial effort; Eliot had not. These 15 lines on the first and third pages—of the new final 53—existed, excluded from the original "Fire Sermon," before Eliot contracted his debt to *Ulysses* and created *The Waste Land.*

The 12 lines on the fourth page seem not to have existed before then; the 26 on the second may not, or may have been composed at Margate. For the 41 lines on the first three pages could be all or most of the "part of Part III" he composed there. Because neither the second nor the fourth page bears even Pound's terse "O.K.," it seems reasonable to infer that he saw neither. There is other evidence that he did not see the second page. His letter about the poem commenting on the title page of the newly conceived 19-page *Waste Land* apparently is a covering letter, for it begins "Caro mio: MUCH improved"; and Eliot's response includes a reference to "D[orothy Pound]'s difficulty" with two lines originating on that page, which she must have noted on the returned typescript (Pound, *Letters,* pp. 169, 171). He almost certainly did not see the fourth, with the twelve final lines. I have referred to *pages* rather than *sheets* because the fourth page is on the verso of the sheet bearing the third page. Subsequent to the last time Pound saw in Paris the drafts of "a long poem," Eliot turned over that sheet—as though he knew it provided adequate space—and, after a cancelled four-line false start, simultaneously integrated the two quatrains on its recto into, and concluded, "III. The Fire Sermon" of *The Waste Land.* The only revision to the concluding lines was striking out "are plain"—in the draft—and writing "humble" above; even precisely four repetitions of "burning" are in the scribbled draft. It recalls the decisiveness of his writing his new beginning on the verso of the old.

Like the beginning, the long passage on the second page, describing the corrupted Thames and invoking the *Götterdämmerung,* is a central wasteland element in the poem; and a note to its first line (266) more or less proves the functional purpose of those 26 new lines. The note declares, "The Song of the (three) Thames-daughters begins here," although the first "daughter" does not "sing" until the first quatrain, taken from the next page.

Eliot either created or incorporated this long passage—the part of "III. The Fire Sermon" that follows what he retained of the original typed draft—at the time he evolved the conception of his whole poem that also motivated his new beginning for the section. It was then that he incorporated the seven early lines; wrote the corrupted-Thames passage; with it integrating them, incorporated the two "Thames-daughter" quatrains; turned over the sheet bearing them; and wrote the concluding 12 lines, six for the third daughter's song and six for the Buddha's-fire-sermon conclusion.

The title of Eliot's eventual poem was a surprise to Pound; and the evidence indicates that he did not see in draft the three pointed wasteland passages Eliot wrote for the beginning and end of its third section. Furthermore, Eliot typed up neither of the two passages definitely written earlier, though Pound had seen one of them, and had even instructed him to type up the original unrhymed version of its first quatrain. The reasonable explanation for this is that Eliot had not decided to use either extant passage in his "long poem" before the last material for it that was put into typed form—the pencilled draft of its fifth and last section—had been typed in Paris on Pound's machine. Finally, there is no definite evidence that any of the three pencilled wasteland passages not seen by Pound (the new beginning of the section and the second and fourth pages of its last part) existed before then. I repeat: the key to the drama is the rough pencilled draft of "What the Thunder Said."

The roughness of the draft makes likely not only that Eliot composed it just before or after his arrival in Paris, but also that he typed it up himself; and the state of the typescript indicates that indeed he—and not Pound—typed it. Silent stylistic changes made during typing (such as those to lines 326 and 370), and similar details (like the reversal of an earlier choice among two phrases in line 339), seem to be the work of its writer.

Furthermore, Pound not only read the rough draft, he seems to have read it twice; for he approved it twice at its head. That fact, and the state of the typescript, indicate that he did not work on the typescript when he worked on those of the first four sections of the poem, presumably together (and "The Fire Sermon" for the last time), three sections having arrived "in [Eliot's] suitcase," and "Death by Water" having been typed up to his order. He could first have seen the typescript of "What the Thunder Said" as part of the 19-page *Waste Land*. Since it is included in the drafts and was typed on his machine, it is more likely that Eliot showed it to him before leaving Paris. But the difference between his treatment of the typescript made available for him to "attack" in detail, and his previous slashing flamboyance, is eloquent. He corrected three typographical errors (and compounded a fourth); he neatly circled elements he questioned; and he suggested very minor changes in a discreet hand: the elimination of three words and two cases of plural s, and the alteration of a phrase. The three words, two instances of "the" in a line and a single adjective, "black" (cock), were excised; the plurals remained; and Eliot made his own change to the phrase. The poet had become confident, the editor newly respectful of the poet's creation and assisting in the polishing of a completed poem. (The first sentence of the final paragraph in Pound's covering letter is "Complimenti, you bitch.")

This extremely detailed review of the evidence in the drafts enables the drama of influence, made manifest in sudden creative inspiration, to be reconstructed. It occurred at that point in the history of *The Waste Land* when Eliot created the last element of the poem for which he made a typed draft. And probably he created "What the Thunder Said" before he created crucial portions of "The Fire Sermon" not seen by Pound, which appear in the drafts on rough pencilled sheets, virtually in their published state.

He created "What the Thunder Said" either just before or during the "few days" he spent with Pound. Valerie Eliot reports his saying he wrote it in Lausanne, and Pound wrote Quinn that he arrived with the poem (*Facsimile*, pp. 129, xxii). If that is the case, when he arrived he showed Pound the pair of quatrains in "The Fire Sermon," the fair holograph copy of "Death by Water," and the just-completed rough draft of "What the Thunder Said"; Pound wrote general comments on them and returned them; then, using Pound's machine, he typed up the draft of "Death by Water" (for example, in the typescript "northern seas," rejected for "eastern banks" in the holograph draft, is restored) that Pound wanted to "get" for working over; then he typed up "What the Thunder Said."

The more dramatic alternative also is likely on internal evidence; it lacks the requisite external evidence that Eliot's portable typewriter was available, and usable, to type the two sections of "He Do the Police in Different Voices" in Lausanne.[25] It is that he arrived in Paris with the fair holograph copy of "Death by Water" but did not produce his virtually final pencilled rough draft of "What the Thunder Said" until after his arrival, conceived and wrote it while Pound was working over the typescripts of the first four sections; and he showed his new work in that state to Pound. He also showed Pound, shortly after his arrival, the pair of quatrains that succeeded the unrhymed passage Pound had seen and suggested his typing up "anyway." Thus, Pound used green crayon to pronounce the quatrains "O.K." and "echt"; and he also used green crayon to write "OK" at the head of the pencilled draft of "What the Thunder Said." His confirmation, in ink ("OK from here on *I think*"), would be appropriate after he had done his work on the first four sections and could reconsider the fifth in context.

This scenario of the drama is compromised by the typewriter question, and by the testimony already mentioned—by Pound to Quinn at the time, and by Eliot to Valerie Eliot 40 years later—that Eliot arrived in Paris with "What the Thunder Said." But it deserves consideration for at least three reasons. To begin with, that Pound read the rough draft of "What the Thunder Said" instead of waiting a bit more for a legible text, suggests that Eliot typed it up later in his visit, rather than at the time he produced the typescript of "Death by Water." The second reason also concerns typing. While the first two sections of the original "long poem" may have been written and typed at Lausanne, "Death by Water" was not typed there. If those sections were, Eliot presumably wrote "Death by Water" just before his departure—too late to type it up—and made the fair holograph copy during his journey from Lausanne to Paris; and at least some of the 113 lines of "What the Thunder Said" could have been recopied then as well, if it existed when he left Lausanne. (Indeed, the journey should have afforded more than enough time to recopy all.) But no part of a fair holograph copy is in the draft material. Finally, that Eliot did not decide to eliminate from *The Waste Land* the major part of "Death by Water" during the time Pound was working on it, or at any time before his departure from Paris for London, also points to those "few days in Paris" as the period of Eliot's initial dramatic inspiration.

Probably just before but perhaps during his stay in Paris, as though in a cre-

---

25. If it typed the sections and then broke down in Lausanne, his writing letters there by hand, and less significant external evidence, like his using Pound's machine in Pound's quarters, would be explained.

ative burst, he crystallized with rapidly pencilled lines his motifs of sterility, despair, quest, and salvation, and provided the chapel perilous, the holy river, the voice of God in the thunder. Pound approved, and confirmed his approval "from here on." After completing the original versions of four sections of his poem, Eliot had found his way; and Pound the superb critic knew it.

The Waste Land

Eliot typed up "What the Thunder Said," departed for home, and there composed his modernist archetype out of the drafts of "a long poem" by the light of the new inspiration that had produced—with such remarkable certainty— "What the Thunder Said" in virtually its printed state. With the same sure hand he excised the long passage from the beginning of each of three of the first four sections of "a long poem"; wrote and adapted the four pages to make the latter part of "III. The Fire Sermon"; on the verso of the draft of its predecessor's first page wrote a pencilled passage to begin III of *The Waste Land;* and conceived the explicit mythic title itself. To the last stage belong a few connecting lines and minor revisions apparently not even in the 19-page text of the poem with title, and the Notes, with their long expository headnote citing Jessie Weston's book, Frazer, dying and resurrected gods, the Grail legend and so on.

Though Pound's ultimate mark on *The Waste Land* is a notable event in literary history, it is actually less great than his mark on the drafts of the poem. The exchange of letters records his continuing criticism and advice; but Eliot essentially had pried the poem away from him, taken full possession of it, using for lever another influence.

To quote the title of Eliot's essay, his poem, like *Ulysses,* would derive "order" from "myth," achieve its coherence and express its meaning principally by way of a pattern of allusions to a specific ancient myth. The myth scarcely could be that of Homer's Achaean father, hero, and husband. But the Weston book was a scholarly work (however brilliantly eclectic) devoted to the Grail material Eliot himself eventually exploited as a resource for his own work of art; it "suggested," as his head note says, the "title . . . the plan and . . . incidental symbolism"—but not the uses to which they could be put. And years before Joyce completed it during the very same weeks in January 1922 when he was creating *The Waste Land* out of "a long poem," Eliot had begun to be thoroughly familiar with and admire *Ulysses,* a novel which was exploiting myth to provide a new resource for art. When these facts are set beside the considerable internal evidence of the evolution of *The Waste Land,* and set beside his statements about the importance of *Ulysses* and the pioneer significance for other writers of Joyce's "using . . . the mythical method" in it, a grand and fundamental influence seems fairly certain.

II. The Play of Allusion

In using the myth, in manipulating a continuous parallel between contemporaneity and antiquity, Mr. Joyce is pursuing a method which others must pursue after him. . . . It is a method already adumbrated by Mr. Yeats . . . . It is a method for which the horoscope is auspicious. . . . Instead of narrative method, we may now use the mythical method. It is, I seriously believe, a step toward making the modern world possible for art . . . .

Yeats did not share Eliot's view of a kinship respecting "the mythical method": three years later, in the first edition of *A Vision,* he explicitly criticized *Ulysses* and *The Waste Land* for their "using the myth" and their joint allusive strategy as a whole.[26] Eliot's statement, quoted often in full by recent critics, needs more emending. Although he represents *Ulysses* as exploiting a single pervading myth, that "myth" is, strictly speaking, a literary work. And his own practice proves his awareness that in any case the new "method" is not merely a matter of choosing an object of a particular sort to allude to; nor is it even essentially a writer's exemplifying the modernist involvement with tradition, by "manipulating a continuous parallel between contemporaneity and [the chosen myth out of] antiquity," as he describes it. The method, Eliot was aware, is rather the new methodical "giving a shape and a significance" by way of allusion that Joyce gave *Ulysses* and he eventually gave *The Waste Land.* Neither Yeats, who criticized them for it, nor Pound, in the *Cantos* then published, was employing that new allusive strategy. And the extent to which Joyce and Eliot did so in their novel and poem has rarely been equalled.

In the past, the familiar literary device of making cultural, historical, or literary allusions usually had provided a decorative and illustrative—and therefore casual and overt—enrichment. But not always: the modernists' innovation is not their use of structurally intrinsic and pervasive patterns of allusion to accomplish essential exposition or thematic statement. In Dante's *Commedia,* Herbert's *The Temple,* certain "imitations" of classical poems in the Renaissance and later, Dryden's *Absalom and Achitophel, Candide,* and a number of other earlier works of literature, the relations created between the alluding works and the objects of allusion vary, and so do the functions which allusion has; but invariably it is intrinsic and/or pervasive, and it accomplishes essential tasks. *Ulysses* and *The Waste Land* extend what such earlier works had done with both the allusive relation and the task allotted to allusion, exemplifying a new modernist conception of formal and functional possibilities.

The earlier practice was to set up in a work or section of a long work a relation with a single object of allusion. This was not the case with a burlesque, which to satirize a genre effectively would implicate more than one example of it; but burlesque actually is a means of commenting on the objects of allusion, not a use of them for autonomous ends, and so is exceptional. Still, even burlesques as comprehensive as the first part of *Don Quixote* and Buckingham's *The Rehearsal* do not equal the montages of allusive bits and pieces that Joyce and Eliot created in *Ulysses* and *The Waste Land;* and the range of different types of sources in each modernist work is totally unprecedented.

More audacious than their extension of earlier practice in this respect, is the

26. Richard Ellmann quotes from and discusses Yeat's remarks in *Eminent Domain* (New York: Oxford UP, 1967), pp. 50–51.

second development in the two works: the task Joyce and Eliot allotted to allusion. In earlier literature and drama in which allusion has an intrinsic and vital function, that function is to enhance an already coherent and complete literal discourse or action. This is so even if the augmentation or enrichment of meaning provided by the allusive presence, its own signification, eclipses in importance the bare literal entity. Allusion so enhances effect and meaning in parts of *Ulysses* and *The Waste Land* as well; but it has a more fundamental task. Neither work was given a coherent complete literal discourse or action. Rather, the very proceeding in both often is by way of the allusive referents of the words, as much as by way of their lexical referents; in both works, sense and integrity depend upon various objects of allusion. The eventual means by which Eliot won his struggle to achieve an articulate and coherent poem vividly illustrates this fact; nor can one conceive of an articulate and coherent narrative of the stories of Bloom and Stephen shorn of the allusions in *Ulysses*.

More than anything else, this second special use of allusion by certain modernist writers makes it in the fullest sense a "method"—in Joyce's words, a "way of working": when asked by a French critic why he "followed the pattern of the Odyssey" in *Ulysses* he replied, "Everyone has his own way of working."[27] And although others (and Eliot after 1922) were less systematic in their use of it, Joyce was to employ the "method" almost totally in *Finnegans Wake*. For example, both portmanteau words and multilingual puns refer the reader to elements of language itself rather than to referents beyond language—that is, they allude to *other words* (in order to invoke the referents of those words).

The rest of the sentence about Yeats interrupted in the quotation from Eliot's essay at the head of this section calls him "the first contemporary to be conscious" of "the need for" the "method." The whole passage documents the importance Eliot was then attaching to the method, and his reasons. There had been a "need" for it; it was a response to the nature of the reality he and his contemporaries faced. A "way of working" that inevitably linked present human experience with the past, the method was "a way of . . . giving a shape and a significance to the immense panorama of futility and anarchy which is contemporary history," and so a means for "making the modern world possible for art." In explaining the "revolution, or sudden mutation" three decades later, he cited new "thought" and "feeling," as well as "speech." That the value of the "method" lay in its enabling the assertion of continuity in art, culture, and society at a time of acute confrontation with the very opposite, is additional evidence that the traditional orientation of the modernists was a more fundamental matter than the invoking or exploiting of their literary heritage.

No single novel or poem could be nearly exemplary of all modernist literature, even in its own genre and language. That fact bears repeating. But the

---

27. The critic is Simone Téry, and their exchange is quoted in the *James Joyce Yearbook,* ed. Maria Jolas (Paris: Transition, 1949), pp. 189–90. For discussions of his use of allusions in *Ulysses,* see *Argument,* pp. 118–22; and Weldon Thornton, "The Allusive Method in *Ulysses*," *Approaches to* Ulysses, ed. Thomas F. Staley and Bernard Benstock (Pittsburgh: U of Pittsburgh P, 1970), pp. 235–48 (Thornton uses Eliot's essay in his discussion). For Eliot's use ("Instead of narrative method") in *The Waste Land,* see Levenson, pp. 193–205.

voluptuous novel and austere poem published in 1922 operate in similar ways; furthermore, they do so to achieve a number of similar ends; and they even express similar views of the world in which they were made, similar views of art, and similar views of the relation of art not only to that world but even to the artist himself. It is through the articulation of this rich cluster of similarities, similarities of artistic practice, thematic concern, and conception of art and the artist—a matter of confluence more often than influence, and unimpeded by the difference in composition and outlook of the two works—that their joint central status can be understood and can illuminate the nature of Modernism.

In the cluster of similarities, those that are manifestations of the method at work attest to the extent of Joyce's and Eliot's reliance on it. When in the third chapter of *Ulysses* Stephen is likened to Menelaus, the allusion is invoked principally by his thinking of Mananaan MacLir, the mythical Irish Celtic equivalent to Proteus. The Grail legend and that of Tristram and Iseult also are Celtic; and as I shall try to show, the myth of Odysseus is used (*used* is the proper term) in Eliot's poem along with its other Hellenic material. Both novel and poem use the Germanic myth of the *Götterdämmerung.* And both use the Hebraic and Christian myths of salvation based on the prophets and Jesus. Correspondingly, both use works in which these myths are embodied, or have been represented: the Bible, the *Odyssey,* the *Commedia* of Dante, Wagner's Ring cycle. These striking specific coincidences are not just accident. In addition both use Shakespeare, and each uses a number of other artifacts of European high culture. For example, the novel uses the (adopted) *Arabian Nights,* a work by Bishop Fuller, Goethe's *Faust, Don Giovanni,* a whole series of English prose works such as *Pilgrim's Progress* and *A Tale of a Tub,* and poems by Irish poets ranging in time from Thomas Moore to Yeats. The poem uses Vergil, Ovid, St. Augustine, Chaucer, Kyd, Spenser, Webster, Marvell, Goldsmith, Bauderlaire, Gérard de Nerval, and Verlaine.

In both works, the allusive method also uses elements of popular culture. Though *The Waste Land* as published uses only the "Shakespeherian Rag" and a parlor version of the song of Mrs. Porter, the drafts use American popular songs of the time extensively. *Ulysses* uses a highly popular sentimental novel, a popular pornographic novel, a sentimental opera, current newspapers, and many street ballads, popular songs, and folk and art songs sung in Dublin in 1904.

Allusive invocation of myths of major branches of our civilization, and of classic artifacts of high culture and characteristic artifacts of popular culture (augmented by references to various philosophers and specific historical figures in the two works), begins to accomplish by collective action a general and thematic purpose which is additional to the specific and technical purpose of moving the work forward that is accomplished by each particular incorporated phrase, or by the particular invocation of the source or context of that phrase. The groups of myths, masterworks, and the rest conjoin to represent a civilization in its stages—Hebraic, Hellenic, medieval, renaissance, modern.

The common thematic purpose of the two modernist writers can best be indicated by way of one of their important common sources, the poet Eliot

called "the most persistent and deepest influence" on him, and who "was per-
haps Joyce's favorite author" (*James Joyce*, p. 4). Eventually, Eliot placed Dante
at the very beginning of *The Waste Land,* dedicating the poem to Pound with a
phrase Dante had used for Arnaut Daniel. The phrase is from the latter part of
the *Purgatorio,* from an earlier part of which Eliot incorporates a line at the end
of his poem, significantly a suggestion (reinforced in the Notes) of Arnaut's ulti-
mate redemption. A corresponding allusion in *Ulysses,* more important to the
novel, has been mentioned (p. 69). The psalm Stephen "inton[es] *secreto*" is
chanted at the beginning of the *Purgatorio* by the newly redeemed souls; Dante
described it in his famous letter to Can Grande as signifying man's redemption
by Christ.

But the primary relation of both works is to the first part of Dante's poem.
The role of the Odysseus myth in *The Waste Land* is the role in it of Tiresias,
whom the Achaean hero sought out in Hades and who told him his fate. The
long fishing-voyage passage that Eliot excised from "Death by Water" he said
and the evidence shows had its source not so much in Homer's epic as in the
Ulysses Canto (XXVI) of the *Inferno* (see *Facsimile,* p. 128; and *Invisible Poet,*
p. 146, also pp. xiv, 172–73). When one recalls that Pound began his own *Cantos*
with an account of the descent of the exiled hero to Hades, and that he called
the nighttown chapter of *Ulysses*—in which all that has happened to them in
Dublin is epitomized for Bloom and Stephen—"a new Inferno in full sail"
(*James Joyce,* p. 508), one aspect at least of Dante's special significance for these
(and other) modernist writers becomes clear. In "Joyce's Planetary Music,"
Mary Reynolds confirms Pound's perception by showing concisely that at the
beginning of the nighttown chapter Joyce presents a whole series of correspon-
dences to Dante's entry into Hell in Canto I of the *Inferno* (pp. 465–69); and her
Joyce and Dante: The Shaping Imagination (Princeton: Princeton UP, 1981),
documents the extent of his use of Dante in *Ulysses.*

The pattern of allusion to the *Inferno* in Eliot's poem needs no discussion: it
all but dominates the portrayal of London in "The Burial of the Dead." The
phrases "this stony rubbish" and "a heap of broken images" refer with rich effect
to the poem itself; but most immediately they refer to London, refer, like a sim-
ilar passage at the end of Part V of Pound's "Hugh Selwyn Mauberly":

> For two gross of broken statues
> For a few thousand battered books

to western civilization. Eliot's wasteland London is Joyce's center-of-paralysis
Dublin, his city of benightedness whose brothel district he renamed. And both
works present visions of a desired apocalypse destroying the central artifact of
human civilization. In *Ulysses* Stephen thinks, "I hear the ruin of all space, shat-
tered glass and toppling masonry, and time one livid final flame" (24); and when
he makes his climactic gesture in nighttown, in imitation of Siegfried's bringing
about the *Götterdämmerung,* the phrases are repeated (583). Just before a sig-
nificant change occurs in the last part of *The Waste Land* appear the lines:

> Falling towers
> Jerusalem Athens Alexandria
> Vienna London

Hebraic, Hellenic, early Christian, renaissance, modern—Eliot's sequence, with the movement it presents westward, away from salvation and the City of God, makes my point: in their works the creators of *Ulysses* and *The Waste Land* saw fit to attempt, and by means of the commitment both made to the allusive method they achieve, similar representations of their civilization. In an essay originally published as "On the Modern Element in Modern Literature" ("On the Teaching of Modern Literature," *Beyond Culture* [New York: Viking, 1968], pp. 3–30), Lionel Trilling isolated as the "characteristic element" of modernist literature ("or at least of the most highly developed modern literature"), "the bitter line of hostility to civilization which runs through it" (p. 3). As Bell blamed for the state of contemporary civilization those reporting it, so his associate Trilling called them its enemies because they judged it. But Monroe Spears has addressed the matter more precisely:

> For the moderns . . . the City is seen as falling . . . or as fallen . . . and therefore moving toward the Infernal City . . . . Dante and Baudelaire are the poets whose infernal visions haunt the modern writer . . . . (p. 71)

And in *Eliot,* Spender remarks that *The Waste Land* and other writings of the time "show how convinced he was that civilization would collapse," and reports Eliot assured him later that had been his conviction (pp. 116-17).

Just as the allusive strategy works incrementally to express a view of civilization, it works in the same way to make other kinds of thematic statement. For example, *Ulysses* and *The Waste Land* have in common patterns of allusion to three specific kinds of mythic, literary, and historical figures; and these three common patterns express additional significant similarities of thematic concern.

The Waste Land presents a series of males and females who are victims or victimizers, and whose relationships are characterized by failure, lust, cruelty, treachery. The ancient and mythic figures are generally more violent, the recent ones more tawdry: Actaeon and Diana; Dido and Aeneas; Philomela, Procne and Tereus; Tristram and Iseult; Antony and Cleopatra; La Pia and Nello della Pietra; Elizabeth and Leicester; Sweeney and Mrs. Porter (and her daughter); the typist and the young man carbuncular. The vision of love in *The Waste Land* corresponds to that of civilization generally. But in *Ulysses* the method makes a contrary assertion about the same concern, despite an unpromising beginning and the presence of a series of temptresses: Bloom finally becomes the Don Giovanni of Molly's Zerlina; there are Martha and Lionel of von Flotow's opera, Matcham who achieves his masterstroke with the lady in the story Bloom has read, and the Purefoys; and always in the background Odysseus is rejoining Penelope—all to present connubial love (despite some genial mocking) as an alternative to the spiritually destructive City.

A second series in each work is one of saviors, martyrs, and false and true prophets. Saviors and martyrs include: Christ in both; Moses, Robert Emmet, and the "croppy boy" in *Ulysses;* and in *The Waste Land* Buddha and the dead and resurrected gods listed in the headnote. For prophets, both have Isaiah and Tiresias. To these, *Ulysses* adds the Biblical figures Elijah, Elisha, and Malachi; *The Waste Land,* Ezekiel and Koheleth, the Preacher of Ecclesiastes. In addition to Biblical figures, *Ulysses* has Proteus, Mananaan MacLir, and the (historical) false modern prophet John Alexander Dowie; *The Waste Land* has St. Augustine, the sybil, and the (Huxleyan) false modern prophet, Madame Sosostris. The lists are suggestive, for they—again by an incremental pattern—assert that a certain measure of importance attaches to spiritual guides and saviors: that both novel and poem are concerned with the question of salvation from the doomed modern City.

A final group of figures express a common representation by Joyce and Eliot of what constitutes meaningful conduct for the protagonists of the two works. Up to a point (the eleventh chapter—beginning the second "Part of *Ulysses*"— and "The Fire Sermon" respectively), Bloom, Stephen and the protagonist of *The Waste Land* are walkers in the City and doomed victims of it. Their peripatetic experiences are a means by which novel and poem both close in on the condition of modern urban man. Those experiences are accompanied by the characters' efforts to survive in things as they are, combined with nostalgia for an untroubled past, and with despair.

Then in both works a similar development occurs. The saviors and true prophets begin to have an effect: the characters begin to seek rescue from their predicaments. Hugh Kenner has pointed out the ironic echo of Chaucer:

> Whan that Aprille with his shoures soote
> The droghte of March hath perced to the roote
> And bathed every veyne in swich licour
> Of which vertu engendred is the flour
> . . . .
> Thanne longen folk to goon on pilgrimages

in Eliot's own opening lines:

> April is the cruellest month, breeding
> Lilacs out of the dead land, mixing
> Memory and desire, stirring
> Dull roots with spring rain. (*Invisible Poet*, p. 157)

But the passage is fully allusive, specifically invoking the corresponding opening lines of the *Canterbury Tales;* for the most significant irony is that Eliot's protagonist ultimately goes on a pilgrimage. Precisely as the beginning of *Ulysses* announces ironically Stephen's eventual devout action ("*—Introibo ad altare Dei*"), so the beginning of *The Waste Land* does the protagonist's.

A measure of what happens in the poem is the changing relation of the "memory and desire"—active longing, in Chaucer's word—that April has mixed in the protagonist. Like his counterparts in *Ulysses,* for whom in its early chapters memory is equally prominent, he feels trapped and despairs until his desire causes him to seek rescue. In "The Burial of the Dead" his consciousness is largely occupied by memories out of the past: the Starnbergersee, the Hyacinth garden, Madame Sosostris, what he said to Stetson. In "A Game of Chess," both his mostly silent exchange with the first woman and his witness to the anecdote of the second woman bring the past into the present of his despairing consciousness; however, the emphasis on portrayal of the women—who are linked respectively to the idle and the depraved simultaneous actions in Middleton's *Women Beware Women*—still strongly suggests the urban satire out of which the poem apparently evolved. In "The Fire Sermon," the significant change occurs: alongside static memories, which merely reinforce his despair, the protagonist actively experiences in the present, generates the desire to escape from despair.

Eliot's disposition of memory and experience/desire exemplifies nicely his conversion of the original "Fire Sermon" to its ultimate role in his ultimate poem. The protagonist remembers having met Stetson in the "Unreal City, / Under the brown fog of a winter dawn," in "The Burial of the Dead"; and in the draft "Fire Sermon" the same lines, with the last word altered to "noon," are attached to his memory of Mr. Eugenides. Also, there are his memories of fishing in the polluted canal, and of the Philomela depiction in the sitting room of the first woman in "A Game of Chess." On the other hand, in the lines of Eliot's late inspiration with which "III. The Fire Sermon" begins, the protagonist gives extended (active) expression to the despair he is experiencing; and in those with which it ends, he speaks of his purgative suffering and his belief that the Lord is "plucking" him "out." In addition, both the seduced "Thamesdaughters" and Tiresias actually are in the protagonist's present experience: the women merely talk of the past, and the prophet says he foreknew what is currently happening.

"Death By Water" calls up "the drowned Phoenician sailor" ominously designated "your card" by Madame Sosostris, but not as memory. The protagonist is confronted with an object lesson ("Consider Phlebas"); said to be only "a fortnight dead," Phlebas the Phoenician nevertheless is a stranger to him, and seems to have the weight of a traditional or mythic figure. Finally, in "What the Thunder Said," except for the one memory, the protagonist keeps to the present, directly confronting throughout his reality of arid waste. He has left the familiar scenes with their familiar memories, "plucked" out, walking no longer in the city but on a "sandy road," later a "white road," until he arrives at the "empty chapel"; he is indeed on a pilgrimage, seeking what he desires, rescue from the waste land.

As in Eliot's poem, so in Joyce's novel: after the "First Part" and *"Entr' acte"* something begins to happen. The constant movement of the protagonists ceases to be the repetition of a futile diurnal round, the "walking round in a ring" that the other citizens in both works are presented as continuing to do, and becomes a quest for the way out.

For Stephen the way out would be the freedom of his spirit through the enlightened (by Grace) submission of his will; for Bloom it would be a meaningful life as husband and father through enlightened right action; for Eliot's citizen it would be spiritual transcendence by a means similar (it is significant) to Stephen's. While in the novel the quest involves actual events, in the poem the pilgrimage to the East of Buddha, the Ganges, and the *Upanishads,* to the spiritually fertile sacred land, apparently is a metaphorical one.

The third series of figures common to the two works, of course, is of questers. Both have Odysseus, Siegfried, and Dante; *Ulysses* has as well Sinbad the sailor, Daedalus and Icarus, Faust, the ghost of King Hamlet, and the ghost from medieval Irish literature whose presence is perceptible reflexively, out of *Finnegans*

Wake: the questing avenger Maelduin. *The Waste Land* has the generalized Grail quester, Parsifal, Aeneas, Nerval's "Desdichado," Arnaut, and Kyd's Hieronymo.

The quester is a familiar type in myth and art, and currently it is fashionable to find him everywhere. At least two specific qualifying points also must be made. One is that the allusive method creates fuzzy edges. For example, does the literary ghost really belong in the list of questers in *Ulysses?*; conversely, should one—on the strength of the wasteland motif, Tiresias, and the pattern of references to eyes in the poem—add Oedipus to the list for *The Waste Land?* Finally, only reinforcement by centrally relevant objects of allusion enables the works to invoke such peripheral figures as Sinbad, Hieronymo, and Arnaut.

But the centrally relevant questers are there, and they predominate. The "song" of the "Thames-daughters" in *The Waste Land* invokes Wagner's *Rheintöchter* and Siegfried, who being spiritually impure fails to return the ring to them and so save the world. Simultaneously it invokes Parsifal, who rejects lustful maidens and secures the Holy Grail. Spiritual blight can be cured only in the spirit; and in both works, the spiritual condition of the protagonists is the field on which the crucial issue—What is to become of them?—is joined. This spiritual emphasis has two corollaries. One is that those admirable and successful questers the pilgrim Dante, the good husband and father Odysseus, and the pure hero Parisifal join the true prophets and the saviors as models, guides, and encouragers, respectively, in the proper or enlightened course. The other is that if in both works what is centrally important—the protagonists' quest for the way of rescue—is spriitual, it is psychological. The third series of figures signifies both a thematic concern common to novel and poem and a common principal field (locus) of action: the characters' consciousness.

Of these, the similar thematic concern is cosmological, inevitably: for the series of figures in each work with which the series signifying the quest for rescue combines, is of prophets and saviors. And the role in *Ulysses* of the two linked series of figures both helps to explain and extends Eliot's pronouncement in *After Strange Gods* that "the most ethically orthodox of the more eminent writers of my time is Mr. Joyce." But this subject is better suited to a formal similarity between the two works other than the allusive method: the manner in which they both end. That formal similarity, like the (formal) second similarity signified by the series of questers, their common psychological locus of action, must wait upon attention to one final manifestation of the method in *The Waste Land:* the Notes.

To demonstrate the kinship of the Notes with *Ulysses* I shall have to go into some detail; and I am delighted to do so, because a great deal of nonsense has been written about them. Most critics speak of the "notes *to*" *The Waste Land,* indicating their uncertainty about the relationship; Eliot, who was capable of employing language precisely, used the totally ambiguous "on"; my endeavor here is to justify my using the preposition "of" and my capitalizing "Notes" when speaking of them as a totality.

Critical treatment of the Notes of *The Waste Land* has ranged from "for ornithologists even the passage from Chapman would have the advantage of exact description" (Mathiessen, p. 52), justifying Eliot's quotation (note to 357) from a description of the hermit-thrush in a standard *Handbook of Birds of Eastern North America,* to the succinct "we have license . . . to ignore them."[28] The supposed license derives from a paragraph about them in "The Frontiers of Criticism," in which Eliot expresses "regret" at "having sent so many enquirers off on a wild goose chase after Tarot cards and the Holy Grail":

> I had at first intended only to put down all the references for my quotations, with a view to spiking the guns of critics of my earlier poems who had accused me of plagiarism. Then, when it came to print *The Waste Land* as a little book—for the poem on its first appearance in *The Dial* and in *The Criterion* [two months and one month, respectively, before the book was published on December 15] had no notes whatever—it was discovered that the poem was inconveniently short, so I set to work to expand the notes, in order to provide a few more pages of printed matter, with the result that they became the remarkable exposition of bogus scholarship that is still on view today. . . . But . . . I cannot think of any good contemporary poet who has abused this same practice. [As for Miss Marianne Moore, her notes to poems are always pertinent, curious, conclusive, delightful and give no encouragement whatever to the researcher of origins.] [Eliot's brackets; apparently an interpolation in the published text.] No, it is not because of my bad example to other poets that I am penitent: it is because my notes stimulated the wrong kind of interest among the seekers of sources. (*On Poetry and Poets,* pp. 121–22)

I have quoted generously from the paragraph because in it Eliot himself provided critics who are so minded a detailed brief for dismissing his own creation, one from which they have quoted and requoted phrases toward that end. The Notes originally were mere documentation in the solemn spirit of the notes to *The Shephearde's Calendar* (as distinguished from the ironic spirit of those to *The Dunciad*). The periodical publication of the poem did not include even those. "Then" he tried to expand them as filler and they became, unfortunately, "bogus scholarship." He "regrets" having inspired "a wild goose chase."

But are we to take seriously his assertion that *after* periodical publication "it was [suddenly] discovered that the poem was inconveniently short"? Or the declaration by a poet (especially a modernist poet) that he created pages of sheer filler? And is his "with the result that they became" a confession that he literally could not *avoid* "bogus scholarship"? Or does his narrative of an original intention "to provide a few more pages of printed matter" resulting in a "remarkable exposition of bogus scholarship" constitute instead an ironic historical account of how a late true augmentation of *The Waste Land* actually came about? Is his assertion to the 15,000 people who had assembled in an athletic stadium to hear him that no "good contemporary poet" has "abused this same practice" coy modesty, or is it additional cool irony? Was it "just," as he says before concluding with his "regret," that he "pay my tribute to the work of Miss Jessie Wes-

---

28. *Invisible Poet,* p. 151. On the preceding page, Kenner says, "we should do well to discard the notes as much as possible." For an extreme statement of this attitude, see Anne C. Bolgan, *What the Thunder Really Said* (Montreal: McGill-Queen's UP, 1973), pp. 32–34. Stead not only rejects them, but criticizes Eliot for having incorporated them with serious intent (pp. 124, 126).

ton," especially in the light of at least one much more pressing claim to "tribute" which he ignored? Finally: the context of this paragraph about the Notes is Eliot's general criticism of "the seekers of sources," who thereby violate one frontier of criticism proper; and he refers to the Notes as a unique "occasion" on which he was "not guiltless of having led critics into temptation"; so whose fault is the regrettable "wild goose chase" of those avid "seekers" with "the wrong kind of interest"? In other words, is this The Distinguished Poet of 1956 speaking or is it Ol' Possum?

Eliot's declaring he wrote them because "the poem was inconveniently short" engenders speculation that an understandable likely preference of Liveright's—that the poem he was about to publish as a book were longer—played a part in the genesis of the Notes. Perhaps so. But it is an injustice to any serious and honest poet for critics to infer from that statement and similar ones by Eliot that an account of the genesis of the Notes is an abject apology for their existence. Furthermore: not only is it unlikely that Eliot would undertake to provide meretricious filler in order to get out another book; it is no less unlikely that even had he been willing—and Liveright wished for sheer filler—the Notes did much in that way for the first edition of *The Waste Land*. After the head note on page 53, they occupy only 10½ pages in the 64-page volume; the very few pages difference between them and "all the references for my quotations," which he "at first intended . . . to put down," could have been adjusted with the greatest ease either by typesetting or by a flyleaf or two before the back endpaper (there are now none, and small books of verse do resort to them). And an even simpler alternative solution reinforces the doubt that there was a problem. The book is composed of 16-page gatherings, so that barring Liveright's categorical unwillingness, the text proper and the "references" he "first intended" could have been printed on 48 well-filled pages. Especially in those early days the Woolfs did not weigh commercial considerations heavily; but it is still worth mentioning that the Hogarth Press chose to make the first English edition (1923) of *The Waste Land,* complete with Notes (the accompanying numbers at every tenth line were inadvertently left off), only 35 pages long.

One possibly unequivocal indication that Eliot did regret and repudiate the Notes remains: their absence from the periodicals. However, there was little reason for his failure to substitute the original "references" if in fact his withholding the full set of Notes (despite his statement, he had developed them before periodical publication) reflects any disquiet on his part. For the editors of the *Dial* were giving him their annual award and so presumably would have been agreeable; and in any case the *Criterion* was his own magazine.

That Eliot's procedure in the periodicals signifies no disquiet about the Notes can be shown beyond reasonable doubt. The contract with Liveright to publish *The Waste Land* had been signed well before the arrangement to publish it in the *Dial* was made two months in advance of its appearance there. The *Dial* arrangement resulted from elaborate negotiations (conducted largely by Quinn), since Liveright had, both contractually and morally, prior rights in a literary property. On September 7 the parties arranged for Liveright to delay book publication slightly and for the *Dial* to publish the poem without the Notes. Furthermore, a letter by Gilbert Seldes, an admirer of the poem who was then Managing Editor of the *Dial,* establishes not only that the Notes were completed in time for the magazine to publish them, but also that they were explicitly denied to it. On August 31 he wrote to its publisher:

> We must assume that Eliot O.K.'s publication in *The Dial* without the notes . . . which are exceedingly interesting and add much to the poem, but don't become interested in them because we simply cannot have them.[29]

It is not likely that Seldes would have regarded "all the references for my quotations" as "exceedingly interesting and add[ing] much to the poem."

In other words, the Notes were withheld from a prior periodical publication to protect the value of the book, not written late and added in order to make it one; an honorable man, Eliot would have followed suit in printing the poem in his *Criterion* (which he sent late to its American subscribers out of consideration for the *Dial*).

That he did not include the Notes in the draft material when he presented it to Quinn, despite the latter's reference in correspondence to "the whole thing, poetry and prose," and more specific "the MS. of The Waste Land and the Notes" (*Facsimile,* pp. xxx, xxiii, xxiv), is of no significance here. He declared to Quinn that "the manuscript of *The Waste Land* which I am sending you" was "worth preserving in its present form" because it was "the only evidence of the difference which [Pound's] criticism has made to this poem" (p. xxiv; and Reid, pp. 539–40). The strength of this explicit motive is measured by the fact that it seems to have grown in importance for him rather than abated. Thus, although in the same letter he expressed politely his "hope that the portions which I have suppressed will never appear in print," according to his widow we owe her edition precisely to this motive. In "T. S. Eliot and I," an interview in the *Observer* (London) of 20 February 1972, she said:

> We never thought it would turn up, but Tom told me that if it did I was to publish it. "It won't do me any good," he added, "but I would like people to realise the extent of my debt to Ezra." Originally he had confided to Quinn that he hoped the portions which he had suppressed would never appear in print. (p. 21, col. 2)

And Pound had nothing to do with the Notes.

To sum up: at the very worst, the external evidence presented to this point does not show conclusively that Eliot himself disdained the Notes, and so is not even the very qualified guide to how we are to regard them that conclusive evidence of such a kind would have been.

One bit of external evidence very different from his pronouncement about the Notes a third of a century later is useful, not so much because of the "seri-

---

29. See *Facsimile,* pp. xxii–xxiv; Reid, p. 538; and Daniel H. Woodward, "Notes on the Publishing History and Text of *The Waste Land,*" *Papers of the Bibliographical Society of America* 58 (1964), 252–69, 256–60. The excerpt from Seldes's letter to the publisher of the *Dial,* James S. Watson, Jr., is on p. 260, and is quoted from William Wasserstrom, *The Time of the* Dial (Syracuse: Syracuse UP, 1963), p. 104.

ousness" it avers at a time and in circumstances that encourage credence, as because of what it reveals inadvertently. To an inquiry from Arnold Bennett about them he replied that "they were serious, and not more of a skit than some things in the poem" (*Invisible Poet,* p. 181). Furthermore, the exchange of letters with Pound includes Pound's doggerel poem about its composition, "Sage Homme," and Eliot's temporary "Wish to use [it] in italics in front" (Pound, *Letters,* pp. 170–71). In other words, there is evidence that (although with rare exceptions this was not his practice in serious poems) Eliot considered a "skit" element—literary trifling or play—suitable to *The Waste Land.* Such a relaxation of the ascetic impulse and attitude behind the poem is gratifying, because its more complex aesthetic and vision are also truer to the artist who, when assistant editor of the *Egoist,* wrote and printed pseudonymous silly letters about contributions to generate correspondence, whose light verse before and after *The Waste Land* and fondness for doing imitations and playing pranks are too easily forgotten, and whose widow recalled in the *Observer* interview, "He was always making jokes" (col. 4). Need one be solemn about

> O O O O That Shakespeherian Rag—
> It's so elegant
> So intelligent

to appreciate its specific effectiveness as irony and its general effectiveness as a portrayal of cultural debasement?

To Eliot's willingness to admit an element of literary play to *The Waste Land* one must add the fact that—despite his profound and publicly acknowledged debt to it and demonstrated "theft" of details from it—the Notes fail to mention *Ulysses;* and one must add that other sources than *Ulysses* of important lines, details, and phrases are not documented. The familiar Psalm 137 begins: "By the rivers of Babylon, there we sat down, yea, we wept"; especially since the draft has only the first phrase of Eliot's adaptation ("By the waters"), he cannot have been ignorant of the origin of his line. Or of most derivations from and resemblances to *Ulysses.* Nor was he allowing for the reader's familiarity in such cases. The altered line from the psalm is no more familiar than lines he incorporated unchanged from sources he identified like *The Tempest* (line 257) and the "Prothalamion" (176); and it is much less familiar than the beginning of Enobarbus's description of Cleopatra in *Antony and Cleopatra* (with "barge" changed to "Chair"), for which a note gives act, scene, and line. His attitude toward the Notes is revealed by his response to Pound's comment in the drafts about "J. J.": he did not "put down" the (possible) source of his "yes!" but expunged the word; and there is no "reference" for the thoroughly familiar Shakespeherian line itself at either occurrence (48 and 125), although two other lines from the same play are given notes.

Yet the belief that the Notes are serious documentation (presumably not only deficient but also of remarkable stylistic ineptitude) persists stubbornly. For example, "Precisely because some echoes are and others are not acknowledged," Nitchie reaches the opposite conclusion to mine: "the allusions are . . . instinctive or habitual rather than designed" (p. 405). In his concern for the relation of Eliot's poetry to the poet's reading, Nitchie ignores a brilliant and learned historical critic's manifest refusal to cite certain sources in the Notes. As a result, he provides a cautionary example—with Eliot's own poem—of the limited scope and limiting effects of "the seek[ing] of sources" when criticizing poetry, that Eliot warned against in "The Frontiers of Criticism."

On the basis of the evidence, it seems reasonable to dismiss the simplistic concept that the Notes are documentation, as well as to conclude that any narrow and solemn view of their possible function may be inadequate. The example of *Ulysses* provides a guide beyond such a view; for the Notes are another element of *The Waste Land* similar to an equivalent element of Joyce's novel, whether or not it "point[ed] the way."

The *Ulysses* schema Joyce prepared in 1921, gave to Larbaud for his lecture introducing the novel to Paris, and sent to his first biographer, Herbert Gorman, circulated privately in copies for a decade. When Stuart Gilbert accepted solemnly its delineation of an "organ," "art," "colour," "symbol," and "technic" for each chapter of *Ulysses;* when he printed the parts of this chart Joyce permitted (or reproduced for him) in his book *James Joyce's* Ulysses (1930); and when he spent much of his time tracing down random evidence for it, he lacked judgment as well as wit. For such arbitrary patterns, as Edmund Wilson remarked about the schema in his essay on *Ulysses* in *Axel's Castle,* cannot do serious work in a novel. They were not meant to; the chapters are discrete entities in important ways, but that is the result of the serious work which is being done in each chapter by a particular set of allusions and/or a particular narrative method. And treating with solemn critical respect the bare assertion of Joyce's chart that the "organ" of the chapter in which Bloom sautés a kidney is "Kidney," and of the chapter in which the citizen throws a biscuit tin, "Muscle," is precisely analogous to saying that Eliot's quotation from Chapman's *Handbook of Birds* would gratify ornithologists.

Yet to some extent the arbitrary patterns exist, claiming sanction from those qualities of their respective chapters that do establish integrity. To ask Why are there arbitrary patterns? is to ask what Joyce actually was trying to encompass in his sequence of chapters. The question is—as is usual with *Ulysses*—complicated. Yet it must be confronted to elucidate that element in the novel similar to Eliot's Notes. Richard Ellmann addresses it in Ulysses *on the Liffey* (New York: Oxford UP, 1972); he also prints in an appendix, with its variations from the familiar 1921 schema, the other elaborate schema mentioned in an earlier chapter (p. 85), prepared by Joyce in September 1920 for his Italian translator and friend, Carlo Linati. The Linati schema has more detail than the familiar one, and is less deceptive about what Joyce actually did in the novel. For example, whereas for the third chapter the 1921 chart specified that Menelaus is the Homeric analogue to the Irish nationalist mentioned there, Kevin Egan, in the Linati chart "Menelao" appears alone, and so his true and extremely functional correspondence—to Stephen—at least is not obscured.[30]

---

30. See the complete 1921 chart published in *James Joyce Miscellany: Second Series,* ed. Marvin Magalaner (Carbondale: Southern Illinois UP, 1959), following p. 48. The copy is that Joyce sent Gorman, and accompanies the essay by H. K. Croessman on pp. 9–14, "Joyce, Gorman, and the Schema of *Ulysses:* An Exchange of Letters—Paul L. Léon, Herbert Gorman, Bennett Cerf."

However, the Linati chart cannot answer the question of what the arbitrary patterns may be for. It is only less facetious than its familiar successor. For example, the three chapters devoted to Stephen that begin *Ulysses* are roughly simultaneous with the next three, devoted to Bloom; yet Joyce designates the two groups respectively "Alba" and "Mattina." Ellmann navigates more by independent sightings than by reliance on this chart (or the other), so that his discussion of Bloom and the kidney (p. 32), for example, is persuasive where Gilbert's smacks of inept special pleading. Ellmann postulates in the sequence of chapters an ingenious pattern of accretions, "parallelism," and "contraries" which makes the novel an intricate systematic embodiment of general concepts, philosophical propositions, and more.

Joyce had a picture of the city of Cork framed in cork. He was being not just witty but metaphysical, in the sense of the term that unites cosmology and language; and a writer who sees reality so (it might have been a major reason for his increasing commitment to the allusive method in successive works), may well endeavor to achieve a kind of encyclopedism in his novel. That endeavor *would* explain what it is Joyce wished to encompass in his sequence of chapters when he provided for each an arbitrary "organ," "art," "colour," and so forth in addition to their functional patterns.

Pound drew a strong connection with Flaubert's unfinished "Encyclopedia in the form of farce," *Bouvard et Pécuchet,* in the title and text of his French essay on *Ulysses,* "James Joyce et Pécuchet." But as the description of the novel in Ulysses *on the Liffey* suggests, likening *Ulysses* to the encyclopedic satire of *Bouvard et Pécuchet* raises a problem that Pound fails to acknowledge. For Joyce does seem to some extent, despite the mischievousness of his charts, his comicality and playfulness on virtually every page, and his wide-ranging mockery of modern civilization in the manner of Flaubert, in dead earnest. To some still uncertain extent he did seriously (with limited success for me, at least) attempt to achieve in his novel, by the various series through its successive chapters of incremental patterns—some functional in the stories of Bloom and Stephen and some not—an encyclopedic inclusiveness. He declares it, in fact. A major function of the parodies of English prose styles in the fourteenth chapter is to provide masks *(personae)* through which he can make statements about the revellers in the maternity hospital, especially the two with whom he is most concerned. (He condemns contraception and adultery as Eliot does, but celebrates erotic love and procreation.) The final parody in his sequence specifies in the style of Carlyle that the good father Purefoy is the model of right action for Bloom; and the ventriloquist's Carlyle not only addresses Purefoy directly but also, appropriately, refers to the novel itself:

> By heaven, Theodore Purefoy, thou hast done a doughty deed and no botch!
> Thou art, I vow, the remarkablest progenitor barring none in this chaffering
> allincluding most farraginous chronicle. (423)

The last phrase is quoted frequently. In it Joyce characterizes his chronicle of Bloom's and Stephen's day as, to take the multisyllable epithets in reverse order: formed of various materials (the "method"), encyclopedic, and a bandying of (playing with) words. There is no reason why he should be sincere in the manifestly accurate first and third designations and not so in the second one. His informative phrase itself (like his ventriloquist's parodic strategy) also is playful, of course; simultaneously. And this fact reminds one that while the arbitrary patterns in his allincluding chronicle are Joyce's own, the solemnity about them was contributed by others. The precise combination remains open to question, but Joyce's encyclopedism combines playfulness with serious intent.

Its element of earnest enterprise distinguishes *Ulysses* strikingly from Flaubert's satiric "Encyclopedia in the form of farce," and has a broader significance as well. In addition to comparing *Ulysses* to *Bouvard et Pécuchet,* "James Joyce et Pécuchet" mentions three novels filled with literary play: *Gargantua, Don Quixote,* and *Tristram Shandy.* Justly, for like Joyce in *Ulysses,* Rabelais, Cervantes, and Sterne were playful in those novels not because they were frivolous artists but because they were serious artists—that is, were artists seriously exploiting the formal possibilities of fictional narrative. The catalogues in *Gargantua,* the parodies and burlesques (already mentioned) in *Don Quixote,* and the typographical tricks and play with conventions of the novel in *Tristram Shandy* are all in *Ulysses.* Nevertheless, the striking difference between the playful yet very serious encyclopedism of *Ulysses* and Flaubert's satiric "farce" illuminates a more important difference from Cervantes and Sterne, if not from Rabelais.

In *Anatomy of Criticism* (1957; New York: Atheneum, 1967), Northrop Frye distinguishes four "Specific Continuous [prose] Forms" of fiction: novel, romance, confession, and anatomy (Menippean satire); and he proposes reasonably that little is accomplished by regarding characteristics in a work of one of the other three forms of fiction as impurities in a novel (pp. 303–12). He describes *Tristram Shandy* as a combination of novel and anatomy (p. 312) and finds "strains of . . . novel, romance and anatomy in *Don Quixote*" (p. 313). But first he mentions the other two works cited by Pound, in a paragraph about the anatomy:

> The Menippean satirist . . . shows his exuberance in intellectual ways . . . . A . . . sub-species of the form is . . . encyclopaedic farrago . . . . The tendency to expand into encyclopaedic farrago is clearly marked in Rabelais, notably in the great catalogues . . . . Flaubert's encyclopaedic approach to the construction of *Bouvard et Pécuchet* is quite comprehensible if we explain it as marking an affinity with the Menippean tradition. (p. 311)

The conjunction of "encyclopaedic farrago" and "allincluding most farraginous" is striking; but he attends to *Ulysses* directly:

> It is the anatomy in particular that has baffled critics, and there is hardly any fiction writer deeply influenced by it who has not been accused of disorderly conduct. The reader may be reminded here of Joyce . . . .

After specifying mimetic, parodic, psychological, and intellectual traits in Joyce's novel, he concludes:

> *Ulysses,* then, is a complete prose epic with all four forms employed in it, all of practically equal importance, and all essential to one another, so that the book is a unity and not an aggregate. (pp. 313–14)

Frye's taxonomy distinguishing four genres helps in delineating the special element of modernist fiction, of course: to portray consciousness is to write a romance and/or confession, not a novel; the "Victorian" novel of "Mr. Wells, Mr. Bennett, and Mr. Galsworthy" is Frye's *novel*. But his praise of Joyce's archetypal modernist novel as a "complete prose epic," though beguiling, raises a fundamental question about *Ulysses* that my last chapter will address: What is the relative status in it of the verbal composition or telling, and the tale of happenings that the structure of words—complete with "intellectual pattern" (p. 310) and "encyclopaedic farrago"—tells?

Frye's conception of *Ulysses* not only denies that it is a novel in his nice sense, but also asserts that its Menippean element, and its narrative—as a novel in the general sense—of quasi-real people, have "practically equal importance." In my view they do not—and that is its important difference from the works by Cervantes and Sterne. Although *Don Quixote* and *Tristram Shandy* are novels as much as they are anatomies, the play in them was created for its own sake as a quality of their art; it is "the free play of intellectual fancy" in Frye's words (p. 310). My last chapter will try to demonstrate that Joyce's modernist play is not "free." The stories of the Don's experiences and the Shandy household are more means than ends: I will argue there that the story of Bloom's and Stephen's day has primacy in *Ulysses*. Even the sequential patterns that point outward to an encyclopedic intellectual construct have the serious agenda Ellmann recognizes. And almost every other element is not only serious but engaged in doing narrative work; for essentially his telling serves its tale. That is to say, Joyce's ironic subvertings and equivocations, parodies and burlesques, tricks and manipulations of novelistic conventions in *Ulysses,* are not only ludic enrichments; the play is also and primarily—like his patterns of allusion—purposeful work. Although my case cannot be made here, the priority over its elaborate telling the "emotional" writer gave its story of quasi-life told is intimated by his disquiet, expressed to Beckett, that "I may have oversystematized *Ulysses*" (*James Joyce,* p. 702).

The occasional Rabelaisian catalogues seem to exist for the sheer delight in them (of writer as well as reader, one guesses); and *Ulysses* has a few other elements of truly free play. But even those may be functional, to enable readier acceptance of the parodies and other elements of working play; certainly, critics admired most of the various virtuosities in the novel for themselves alone long before the ways in which they work were understood.

The argument in my last chapter, that the tale of Bloom's and Stephen's day essentially is the end served by Joyce's ludic virtuosities, is a tenable one because manifestly working play—functional playfulness—is everywhere in *Ulysses*. In the Notes of *The Waste Land* Eliot too used functional playfulness to help relieve solemnity and simultaneously to extend—for focus, reinforcement, enrichment—his use of that "method" whose specific utility for his "long poem" had constituted his late sudden inspiration a few months before. Long before his sudden inspiration he praised Joyce's use of allusion in terms that show that his own use in the Notes required no second inspiration. In "A Note on Ezra Pound," published in Holbrook Jackson's *To-Day* in September, 1918 (IV.19), he wrote that Pound's "use of the past" in the first three *Cantos* involves "a very different method than that of Joyce in 'Ulysses'." The major part of his introjection of *Ulysses*—when only seven chapters in their first versions were written and five published—into an essay on Pound's poetry, is the previous sentence:

> James Joyce, another very learned literary artist, uses allusions suddenly and with great speed, part of the effect being *the extent of the vista opened to the imagination* [my emphasis] by the very lightest touch. (p. 6)

The fact is that what Eliot asserts about Marianne Moore's notes to her poems in his apparently denigrating account of his own Notes actually (playfully) describes the Notes of *The Waste Land*: "pertinent, curious, conclusive, delightful and giv[ing] no encouragement whatever to the researcher of origins."

It is Eliot's modernist assumption—expressed in the very term "method"—that allusions ought to be given important work, his concern to *use* a source not celebrate it, which explains the absence of reference to *Ulysses* and Psalm 137 in the Notes: his poem had nothing to gain from citing Joyce's novel; invoking the nationalist and violent psalm would positively work against the poem. And it is the element of play which makes some notes pedantically precise,

> The currants were quoted at a price "carriage and insurance free to London"; and the Bill of Lading, etc., were to be handed to the buyer upon payment of the sight draft

some notes casually vague,

> The following lines were stimulated by the account of one of the Antarctic expeditions (I forget which, but I think one of Shackleton's) . . .

some notes pompous,

> The interior of St. Magnus Martyr is to my mind one of the finest among Wren's interiors . . .

and some chatty,

> A phenomenon which I have often noticed.

It is the element of play, also, that causes Eliot sometimes to use "V." and "Cf." indiscriminately, that in a note to line 126 refers the reader back, apparently pointlessly, to lines 37 and 48, and that cites "To His Coy Mistress" the second time it is invoked (196) but not the first time (185).

These are not errors, for in both the (independent) 1963 editions of the *Collected Poems* such errors as the failure to count a line and the mistaken line reference in a note have been corrected. Precisely like play in *Ulysses*, all this playful inconsistency in the Notes is primarily functional. Thus, in some instances Eliot really wants the reader to "see" (bring to mind) and in others to "compare" (think of the details of) the work cited. Where his purpose is instead to associate specific material with the poem, he refers to the source in order to quote what he wishes from it, whimsically using either "V." or "Cf." on those occasions since the material is there in the note itself. And where an identified source is not made to do direct work for the poem, the citation of the classic title adds it to the fabric of allusions to artifacts of civilization.

The extent of playful functionality is nicely illustrated by the apparently pointless references to earlier lines in the note to line 126. The line *before* 126 ("Those are pearls that were his eyes") is identical with line 48 except that it lacks a final word (the excised "Yes!"), so that the final word "Look!" gains attention; and given the hint by that first inaccurate line specification, one goes to *two* lines *after* 37 to read "and my eyes failed"—and so discovers the pattern of eye and blindness imagery that runs through the poem. The playful annotation of "To His Coy Mistress" at the second but not the first allusion also is primarily functional; for the next note, to the line immediately following that second instance (197), quotes from the work of a minor contemporary of Donne's a passage that invokes Actaeon and Diana, so that the scope of the allusion to Marvell's seduction poem is controlled, limited to what will enrich *The Waste Land.*

The same is no less true of the four notes quoted above, through which I shall work backwards. "A phenomen which I have often noticed" is a subtle statement of the speaker's frequent awareness of the sacrifice of Jesus (Eliot's play here is like Joyce's placing behind Stephen the three-masted schooner with "crosstrees" at the end of the third chapter of *Ulysses*); for Jesus died at the ninth hour according to the Gospels, and the note is to "Saint Mary Woolnoth kept the hours / With a dead sound on the final stroke of nine." The pompous comment on the interior of St. Magnus Martyr is followed by citation of a book (it was an actual London County Council pamphlet[31]) entitled significantly *The Proposed Demolition of Nineteen City Churches.* The vague reference to "the account" of an Antarctic expedition that "stimulated" lines 360–65 (it is probably at the end of Chapter 10 of Shackleton's *South*) introduces its substance: that the members of the expedition had, when "at the extremity of their strength," the "constant delusion" that *"one more member"* (Eliot's emphasis) was with them. Finally, the pedantic talk about currants "carriage and insurance free to London" reinforces the parent passage in "The Fire Sermon" about the homosexual "Smyrna merchant" with currants "C.i.f. London," to prepare for the contrasting "Death By Water" far in time and place from London of another Levantine trader, "Phlebas the Phoenician," who:

> Forgot the cry of gulls . . .
> And the profit and loss.
>   A current under sea

This is not the place to demonstrate—were it in my power to do so—the functionality of every single note; and it is not necessary. Eliot's strategies vary. Beyond the modest demands made by the first two notes, "the researcher of origins" has little of any importance to occupy him: they refer the reader to major prophetic books of the Old Testament, and in each of those two cases the passage of external material merely identified in the Notes is important, as I

---

31. See A. Walton Litz, *"The Waste Land* Fifty Years After," in *Eliot in His Time,* pp. 3–22, pp. 13–14.

shall try to show. Certain notes contain irrelevant material, a playful device enabling Eliot to slip in statements that do real work in his poem; for example, the ornithological note about the hermit-thrush mentioned earlier ends: "Its 'water-dripping song' is justly celebrated." Other notes just as artfully employ a playful stylistic ineptitude reminiscent of certain chapters of *Ulysses* (especially the two before the last) to hide such truly operant statements in punning and innuendo, as do the first and fourth of the examples just discussed. Some notes simply add to the fabric of cultural allusions. Some references are made at least partly for the reinforcement offered by the cited title itself, such as those to *The White Devil, Götterdämmerung, Les Fleurs du Mal,* and *Paradise Lost.* Some invoke particular sources because of the allusive enrichment to be derived from associating the work named with *The Waste Land:* for example, *The Tempest.* Some, such as those quoting the obscure John Day on Actaeon and Diana and the eminent J. A. Froude on Elizabeth and Essex, and the early ones with quotations from Baudelaire and the *Inferno* that elaborate the vision of the City, work to expand and enrich meaning by bringing specific passages of external material into direct relation with the poem. Some, like the head note and the discussions of the Tarot pack and Tiresias, seem to be clumsy exposition; but these are more valuable for what they suggest (a quest, prophecy, enlightenment, respectively) than for what they say respectively about "the Grail legend," "the Fisher King himself," or the narrative point of view in the poem. Some notes work to enrich the poem by usng a phrase in it as a pretext (such as that to "the walls / Of Magnus Martyr"). And some have the function of pointing out connections and creating emphasis and focus—typically for the Notes, by indirect and often playful means.

Six years before his ironic mischief of that paragraph in "The Frontiers of Criticism," Eliot had offered in "What Dante Means to Me" very different testimony about the Notes:

> Readers of my *Waste Land* will perhaps remember that . . . I deliberately modified a line of Dante by altering it—"sighs, short and infrequent, were exhaled." And I gave the references [i.e., quoted Dante's actual line in its context] in my notes, *in order* to make the reader who recognized the allusion, *know that I meant* him to recognize it, and know that *he would have missed the point if he did not* recognize it. (*To Criticize the Critic,* p. 128; Dante's passage concerns the unbaptized souls in Limbo; my emphasis throughout.)

And he had recently cooperated when his friend John Hayward compiled supplementary notes for the French translation (1947), and had approved the results (Smith, *The Waste Land,* p. 86).

My purpose in this long discussion of the Notes has been to suggest their nature and their function, that they are brilliantly "of" *The Waste Land.* But it is no digression: to indicate their nature and function is to address the relation between Eliot's poem and *Ulysses.* For the Notes are principally another use of the allusive method; in them the poem has, like the novel, an element of play; and as in *Ulysses* the play is subordinate to, if not exclusively an agent of, serious artistic work. Perhaps at this point—with the demonstration that novel and poem have in common (1) a "method" crucial to both, (2) certain kinds of theme and action, and (3) certain attitudes toward the range of material and artistic strategies possible for a work of literature—some of the grounds of the joint cultural role of *Ulysses* and *The Waste Land* have been established.

III. Expressions of an Age

> If it is not a novel, that is ... because the novel, instead of being a form, was simply the expression of an age which had not sufficiently lost all form to feel the need of something stricter.... The novel ended with Flaubert and with James.

The first of Eliot's Notes refers to the beginning of God's discourse to Ezekiel as the "Son of man"; the second refers to a passage in the twelfth and final chapter of the Book of the unknown prophet Koheleth, Ecclesiastes, which describes a waste land (12:5). Before ending the Book a few verses later, the chapter reads:

> And moreover, because the preacher was wise, he still taught the people knowledge ... and set in order many proverbs.
> The preacher sought to find out acceptable words ....
> The words of the wise are as goads ... which are given from one shepherd. (12.9–11)

The allusive enrichment provided by these three verses increases in the next two, which are almost the last words of the prophet-preacher. The twelfth verse is an ironic commentary on the Notes themselves, Eliot's "bogus scholarship." The thirteenth combines with and redirects the twelfth to pronounce judgment on that of which the Notes-as-play are a parody—the secular learning of modern civilized humans, who have made with it their waste land—and to instruct the citizen of the poem respecting his civilization and the right course for him, in terms consonant with what we know about the poem:

> And further, by these, my son, be admonished: of making many books there is no end; and much study is a weariness of the flesh.
> Let us hear the conclusion of the whole matter: Fear God, and keep his commandments: for this is the whole duty of man. (12:12–13)

The religious nature of *The Waste Land* was too readily accepted, on the basis of Eliot's subsequent conversion and religious activities, and of his later poetry. The opposite—and again too readily—was the case with the novel by the presumed anti-religious Joyce. And in both cases cultural bias conflates religiosity with sectarianism (if not apologetics). When Gardner contrasts *Ulysses* with *The Waste Land* as "without God," she declares explicitly that what it lacks is "the Christian view of human life" (p. 86).

However, another (compound) similarity between the two works is that both are religious (theistic), and neither is doctrinal in the sectarian sense (Christian). As both works use Hellenic and Celtic and Germanic "myths" (religious material), *The Waste Land* uses (Judeo-)Christian, Hindu and Buddhist material (myths), and *Ulysses* uses Judeo-Christian and Theosophical material. To transform the prominent Hindu and Buddhist elements in *The Waste Land* into

Christian analogues is a presumption not grounded in the poem. In "Remembering Eliot," Spender reports "I once heard him say" that at the time of the poem "he seriously considered becoming a Buddhist," and rightly observes "A Buddhist is as immanent as a Christian in *The Waste Land*" (*Thirties and After*, p. 194). Hence, in 1922 the final note called "The Peace which passeth understanding" not the Christian Eliot's "our equivalent to," but "a feeble translation of the content of" *Shantih*. And while *Ulysses* portrays the effects of Stephen's specifically (Irish-)Catholic rearing, it is the distinctly secular Bloom who is God's agent on Stephen's behalf—in a city depicted (accurately) as full of religious Catholics and priests, which is also being visited on the day of the novel by a prominent Christian evangelist. Neither work advocates, or even acknowledges the authority of, any institutional religion.

Stephen's problem had never been the attitude in what Ecclesiastes calls "the whole duty of man," for he more than feared, was terrified of, God. But Catholic catechisms say in answer to the question (variously put) about man's basic purpose in life that it is, always in the same order, to know God, love God, and serve God. In the *Portrait* Stephen had said "I will not serve"; and a little later, continuing to reverse the order in the catechisms,"—I tried to love God, he said at length. It seems now I failed" (pp. 239–40). In *Ulysses*, the fulfillment of his dream enables him finally to begin at the proper first stage in the sequence. Bloom too, who must act for himself, not submit himself, in order to escape from his predicament, ultimately—in the phrase of Ecclesiastes that is the Old Testament equivalent of "serve God," and which Joyce makes especially appropriate to him—becomes able to "keep [God's] commandments" as a husband and father. Mathiessen quotes Eliot declaring in a Harvard lecture in 1933 that Joyce was "concerned with the relation of man to God" (p. 148). He fully recognized this similarity between *Ulysses* and his poem. In his essay on the "modern element" Trilling declared, "more than with anything else, our literature is concerned with salvation" (*Beyond Culture*, p. 8).

Mutually "concerned with the relation of man to God," both writers also eschew Christian doctrine and even the Christian cosmology in their modernist archetypes. Both *Ulysses* and *The Waste Land* strictly hypostatize the salvation of their questing protagonists, which requires help from beyond the world (no more direct than fortunate coincidences in Bloom's case). And in both works the outcome of the characters' quest is suggested but not presented. Stephen is freed to make his way; Bloom becomes able and eager to change his relationship with Molly, who ultimately is moved to give him the chance. In each case Joyce has literally presented a miracle (at any rate, a specific unexplainable complex of coincidences that is salvational) to rescue the character from helpless, slow destruction, and has left him with a new opportunity. The last lines of *The Waste Land*, like the corresponding parts of the stories of Bloom and Stephen, are subtle and complex, but seem to embody much the same combination of likelihood without finality. For another similarity between the two works is that their endings are inconclusive.

The grounds for my accounts of Stephen and Bloom were presented in detail in *The Argument of* Ulysses, and Chapter 4 has considered Stephen's story. Before discussing the implications of the similarity in the ways the works end, I must present evidence that *The Waste Land* eventually portrays potential salvation; for that proposition is by no means a consensus even among critics who do not charge that the poem is discontinuous rather than coherent.

In the first place, the protagonist's gradual relinquishing of memories of the past in favor of acting in the present is consonant with a redemptive resolution. The titles of the five sections also seem to bear out the pattern of helpless predicament followed by change. In the first section the dead are burying their dead; in the second, life is static, a set of procedures without meaning or real value. Then in the third something happens, a fiery sermon supplants the games of chess, bringing a painful heightened awareness of things ("O Lord thou pluckest/ burning") very much like those experienced by Bloom in Davy Byrne's pub and Stephen in the National Library (eighth and ninth chapters of *Ulysses*). Correspondingly, the past tense, used predominantly—both for remembered events and as narrative convention—is abandoned (with the introduction of Tiresias). In the fourth, Phlebas is invoked, dead by water, not buried under ground (dust returned to dust) like Stephen's fox-dog and the unredeemed dead of "The Burial of the Dead"; and he is said to have "entered" a spiral pattern like the purgatorial stair in Dante (and in *Ash Wednesday*). The title of the fifth and last section refers to a change in the world outside the quester and a message from above.

Taken by itself, this gloss on the sequence of titles proves nothing and is tendentious; but "What the Thunder Said," which Eliot composed with such clear purpose and control, has considerable evidence of good fortune. It begins with a verse paragraph suggesting the arrest of Jesus in Gethsemane, the crucifixion, and the quester's consequent despair. There follows a long paragraph about the wasted nature of the land and "dry sterile thunder" from the sky, expressing the quester's wish for water, and ending "But there is no water." But the third paragraph suggests Jesus's apparition to the disciples on the road to Emmaus, reinforced by the note about an Antarctic expedition—an evocation of the resurrected Christ as the agent of divine mercy. Then, following an apocalyptic paragraph about the destruction of our spiritually "unreal" civilization, and another presenting what seems to be a remembered nightmare that ends with "exhausted wells," the implications for the quester are correspondingly negative: he ends his pilgrimage at "the empty chapel," apparently unsuccessful. It is the home of "only the wind"; "only a cock" is there.

The conjunction is significant. The wind ("unheard" in "the brown land" [175]), is a familiar Christian (and Judaic) emblem of the breath of God or Holy Spirit *(Ruah Hakodesh, to Pneuma/Spiritus Sancti);* and Eliot uses it so (the breath that speaks the Word) in *Ash Wednesday*. The cock is a medieval Christian emblem (with Greek and Roman ancestry) of the annunciation both of enlightenment and of God's saving advent. According to Saint Ambrose, with the crowing of the cock, "hope returns to all" and "Jesus regards the hesitant and corrects the wanderers."[32] Finally, in those (less corrupted) versions of the

32. See Don Cameron Allen, *Image and Meaning: Metaphoric Traditions in Renaissance Poetry* (Baltimore: Johns Hopkins UP, 1960), pp. 158–65. The quotation from Saint Ambrose is on p. 161. David Ward also mentions the traditional significance of the cock in *T. S. Eliot Between Two Worlds* (London: Routledge, 1973), p. 132.

Grail legend which include the perilous chapel, the quester arrives in a storm; storms normally include rain, lightning, then the thunder of that lightning; and they begin with wind.

Promptly the presumption of the quester's repeated "only" is made plain. For the cock crows an annunciation, which the poem links grammatically to light from the cosmos; and the cock's fellow, ("only") the wind, is seen to have been announcing the imminence of both that light, whose sound will follow, and rain—pure water, falling on the waste land, coming from above. The passage reads:

> Only a cock stood on the rooftree
> Co co rico co co rico
> In a flash of lightning. Then a damp gust
> Bringing rain.

Whether the momentary guest does or does not bring *a great deal* of rain is not indicated: the rain *may* be transitory; or the quester may then hear the thunder not merely after but through rain, falling continuously from heaven, with all that that signifies for a waste land and the quester of *The Waste Land*. This contributes to the effect of likelihood without finality mentioned, and created by an inconclusive ending to the poem.

The likelihood is achieved in part through a subtle but basic alteration in the poem, one that also serves to stress the importance of the depicted annunciation and advent of rain: with the mention of the cock, *The Waste Land* undergoes a transition forward in time. The quester suddenly begins speaking exclusively in the past tense, declaring that the cock "stood"; and, of the remaining specific occurrences before it ends, that the storm thunder "spoke" and then that he "sat" fishing. The changing relation the poem reveals between the quester's memories of figures and events in the past and his confrontation with the reality of his desire for rescue was discussed. In this final section nothing but the remembered nightmare has interrupted his experience of the quest, as it unfolds, caused by desire. Now suddenly—after he arrives at the chapel, and when he experiences lightning and rain—the present time of *The Waste Land* itself becomes past time: the pilgrim's hitherto unfolding quest for salvation itself becomes something remembered. His memory of the end of the quest supplants his desire that began it, reversing the development to this point in the poem. The speaker recounts what happened to him once after he arrived at an "empty chapel": "Ganga was sunken," "Then spoke the thunder," and so forth. The effect is to suggest the powerful significance for him of that experience. It brought his quest to conclusion; and it made possible his future condition in the implicit final present time of the poem, out of which he reflects back on the conclusion of his quest. The precision of Eliot's use of this grammatical shift that preserves narrative continuity is additional evidence of the poem's (eventually achieved) coherence.

Two paragraphs remain to it. The first presents the protagonist's memory of and reflections on what the thunder said on that significant occasion. The final paragraph recalls his subsequent fishing and presents "fragments" he asserts "I have shored against my ruins."

The three words from the Upanishad he remembers having heard through the thunder, and rendered "Give, sympathise, control" in the Notes, are treated in the paragraph devoted to them as though they concern respectively the capacities for commitment, for love, and for submission "To controlling hands." The Upanishad in question has this last as the first in the sequence, and it actually means "self-control."[33] Both Eliot's alterations are significant. That of the concept signifies his concern with obedience to "Another," Dante's *"altrui,"* which he rendered so and used in his essay "Dante" and in the published drafts (see *Facsimile,* pp. 68 [69] and 128, and *Selected Essays,* p. 211). That of the sequence signifies his desire to present the submission to control as *consequent to* the two accompanying spiritual achievements: after commitment and then love, "your heart would have responded / Gaily." As a result of his two alterations the passage becomes strikingly like the sequence of "know God, love God, serve God" in the catechism, which is so relevant to Stephen's situation in *Ulysses.*

His spiritual instruction completed, the quester then sat, as he says at the beginning of the last paragraph, fishing, the arid plain, he also says, being then behind him; and the poem ends in the series of lines and half-lines (most of whose allusions are identified in the Notes). These lines, though brief, are packed with meaning. For example, "O swallow swallow" makes not only a reference to escape, by way of Tennyson's "O swallow, swallow, could I but follow" and of the escape of Philomela (or, in some versions, Procne) through metamorphosis into a swallow, but also a punning suggestion of the actual way of escape: Communion. His playful paranomasia corresponds strikingly to Joyce's use of "Epps's massproduct" toward the same end at the same point in Stephen's story (see p. 68). The line from the *Purgatorio* about a refining fire is preceded there by Arnaut's talk about his remorse for the past, suffering in the present, and hope for the future. The line with two swallow "fragments" follows. The hope for escape and for metamorphosis expressed in "O swallow swallow" is made more positive by its Latin first part, whose four words from the final stanza of the *"Pervigilium Veneris"* follow directly, and repeat the form of, another question. That one specifies in what respect the "I" of the fourth-century poem should become "as the swallow" and discloses that he not merely hopes for but *expects* metamorphosis: "when is my spring coming?" *("quando ver venit meum?").* The line from Gérard de Nerval and the next two deal with the nature of *The Waste Land* itself: the "Desdichado" in Nerval's poem likens himself to different bereft people; *The Waste Land* has been composed of "fragments"—extracts and disjointed lines and passages; and Hieronymo's "Ile fit you" is his response to a request for a play (in *The Spanish Tragedy*), which he then suggests be presented with the actors all speaking different languages. But the three lines also function in the story of the quester: the speaker of Nerval's poem remembers a consoler, and contact with the supernatural; the fragments are said to be a bulwark against "ruins"; Hieronymo's son, the victim of a treacherous hanging in a garden, is

---

33. See *The Upanishads,* tr. Swami Prabhavananda and Frederick Manchester (New York: Mentor, 1957), p. 112.

analogous to Jesus and the other savior gods; and in response to the complaint that it is "mere confusion," the avenging father says of his play to be spoken in many languages, "the conclusion / Shall prove the invention and all was good" (IV.1.174–77).

Following this, only two lines remain to the poem: the character himself pronounces the three words of spiritual instruction that have been given him by the thunder—plain evidence of a beginning; and, finally, the word first feebly translated then rendered in the Notes as "The Peace which passeth understanding" is repeated three times, in the fashion of the end of an Upanishad or sacred text of spiritual guidance.

"The conclusion" at least helps to "prove" that "all" *The Waste Land* is "good" in Hieronymo's sense—as opposed to the "mere confusion" it has been called. Additional proof is the contribution of certain formal patterns to a coherent narrative development and its resolution.

Gordon writes of "the *Waste Land* pilgrim" that "before he escapes he accumulates evidence against civilization and makes his categoric judgment: 'Unreal'" (p. 109). His judgment is pronounced in the last section, following his list of "Falling towers" in sequence both westward and through history from Jerusalem to London (374–77); they have fallen or will fall and are "Unreal," he asserts, because devoid of a saving spiritual reality. But he is generalizing his prior judgment on his own city, the most western and latest in the sequence. The phrase "Unreal City" begins the last paragraph of the first section, introducing the Dantean portrayal of the crowd of dead crossing London Bridge: "Unreal City / Under the brown fog of a winter dawn, / A crowd flowed over . . . " (60–65). And the passage of time in a coherent narrative is clearly indicated when, in the third section, Mr. Eugenides is introduced by the same phrase and intervening line, with the last word changed from "dawn" to "noon" (207–9); of course, the protagonist's evolving in the last section his geographical and historical generalization of a *sequence* of "Unreal" cities also is coherent (character) development.

A second narrative pattern is that of the protagonist's pilgrimage east— against the movement of "Unreal" civilization—which begins in "The Fire Sermon," when he undertakes his quest. In that section he moves from the Thames at London to the Channel at Margate to the Mediterranean at Carthage. In "Death by Water" he is at its eastern end. In the final section he arrives at the "sunken" holy Ganges and experiences renewing rain. Northrop Frye specifies, as corollary to his well-known "mythos" of spring/birth, summer/maturity, autumn/decline and winter/death, a "water-cycle" of rains, springs, rivers, and the sea; and he observes, "We find a great number of symbols . . . from phases three and four in *The Waste Land*" (*Anatomy,* p. 160). However, Eliot provided a sequence during the protagonist's quest. And it is: from the polluted river of autumn/decline or "phase three" in "The Fire Sermon"; to the drowning (and purifying/purgatorial) sea in "Death by Water"; to the beginning of a new "water-cycle" and life-cycle with rain in "What the Thunder Said."

As Prufrock seems to do, the protagonist goes forth in his mind only. But Prufrock's "going" should have been actual, for his predicament is social, of this world; and so his final consolation seems illusory. In contrast, the quester's pilgrimage is necessarily mental/spiritual; and so his experience of redemptive grace can be a meaningful consolation. "Prufrock" describes a chiastic movement—in the full sense of a circle of hell; *The Waste Land* describes a progressive one—in the full sense a development to its resolution.

In a letter to Bertrand Russell, Eliot described the last section of *The Waste Land* as "not the best part, but the only part that justifies the whole, at all (*Facsimile*, p. 129). To attempt to present a fully satisfactory account of the whole poem in cursory fashion here would be presumptuous, and insulting to others who have discussed it with courteous expatiation. But it is in the last section that any resolution of the earlier developments in it must occur. And my hope is that, by combining attention to formal patterns with a relatively less sketchy treatment of "What the Thunder Said," I have succeeded in indicating that Eliot has "justified the whole" in the strictest artistic sense—made his narrative poem coherent, "good."

If so, then my relevant purpose has been served, which is to affirm that, as in *Ulysses*, nothing definite has happened when *The Waste Land* ends—that once again an opportunity has been provided, rescue from helpless destruction granted, but the protagonist's destiny not portrayed: the action developed to its resolution but his story not concluded.

Eliot had ended "Prufrock" and other earlier poems such as "Portrait of a Lady" in a similar way though less overtly so; and the inconclusive end of Joyce's *Portrait* was achieved through subtle undercutting of Stephen's final boast in the immediately preceding pages. The suspended or inconclusive ending was as characteristic of modernist literature as has become the extension of it, the "open" ending—indeed "open" form in general—in the poetry and fiction of our own time. That modernist quality—called by Barbara Herrnstein Smith in *Poetic Closure* (Chicago: Chicago UP, 1968) "the non-assertive conclusion" (p. 258), and, as has been pointed out (p. 54), anticipated in *Crime and Punishment*—has now received considerable attention. The poems by Yeats that are unresolved debates or that end with a question, Paul Morel's suddenly heading toward the city at the end of *Sons and Lovers*, the people of *Heartbreak House* waiting at the final curtain for the bombers to return, are examples in poetry, fiction and drama that come immediately to mind. And it is yet another similarity between *Ulysses* and *The Waste Land*. Smith's description of

> "hidden closure," where the poet will avoid the expressive qualities of strong closure while securing, in various ways, the reader's sense of the poem's integrity (p. 244)

is a nice account of the case in both works: they end, but the substantial concerns with which they deal are given no final disposition. The passage from Eliot's essay on *Ulysses* quoted at the head of this section suggests that a modernist writer's confrontation with a reality "which had . . . lost all form" might make an inconclusive resolution to the portrayal of that reality seem the only appropriate one. Indeed "something stricter," the inconclusive ending of each of this pair of central works is the "expression" of what was a new "age."

IV. Different Voices

... in creation you are responsible for what you can do with material which you
must simply accept. And in this material I include the emotions and feelings of
the writer himself. . . .

The locus of the essential action in both *Ulysses* and *The Waste Land* is psy-
chological: each protagonist's recognizing then admitting to himself certain
truths about the cosmos and himself, and eventually making a certain resolution
for the future. A corollary similarity between the two works is that the vehicle
of the psychological action in both is the consciousness of the protagonists. More
than of anything else in the poem, the ultimately suppressed epigraph from
"Heart of Darkness" about Kurtz's "supreme moment of complete knowledge"
("The horror! the horror!") would have been "somewhat elucidative," as Eliot
wrote to Pound (Pound, *Letters*, p. 171), of these two corollary facts about it.

Direct representation of a character's consciousness conceals the authorial
voice and so creates the illusion of an autonomous work; both the title of Hugh
Kenner's book on Eliot, *The Invisible Poet,* and Stephen Dedalus's depiction of
the artist "within or behind" his work, "invisible, refined out of existence . . .
paring his fingernails" relate to this. The allusive "method" is manifestly fun-
damental to *Ulysses* and *The Waste Land.* But as shaper of each it is scarcely
more so than their authors' manipulation of point of view, which effects both
the modernist endeavor of portraying consciousness itself and the modernist
practice of incorporating (in the latter part of *Ulysses,* also metamorphosing) the
narrator. In *Ulysses,* allusion and point of view shape not only Bloom's and Ste-
phen's monologues and fantasies, but also the novel's variety of narrative strat-
agems—what Kenner calls "Joyce's voices." Similarly, the sudden shifts and
juxtapositions within and between lines in *The Waste Land* are as attributable
to the manipulation of point of view as to the "method"; even the stylistically
discontinuous Notes are so because they lack an identifiable single authorial
voice.

These examples of the effect on novel and poem of the manipulation of point
of view suggest a relation between it and the no less fundamental allusive
"method." And they suggest more strongly the presence of a stylistic comple-
ment to it that also is concomitant with the creation of a montage of allusive
bits and pieces. That third fundamental determinant of each work's formal char-
acteristics is largely responsible for its texture—which is the first quality in either
to strike the reader.

The third determinant is narrative, logical and rhetorical discontinuity, the
disruption of linear progression. A prominent trait of modernist literature, it is
so obvious in both *Ulysses* and *The Waste Land* it would need no more than
brief mention as another similarity, were it simply a deliberate effect, present in
them for its own sake. Perhaps neither Joyce nor Eliot would have refrained
from creating discontinuity for its own sake; and Pound's assiduous cultivation
of it in the prosody of *The Waste Land* has been mentioned. But this disconti-
nuity is not independently present in the two works. It is symbiotic with both
the "method" and the manipulation of point of view: the reliance on allusion in

them, and their shifting narrative modes, meet and accommodate each other in the disruption of linear progression. The intricate relation of those three principal determinants of the modernist formal characteristics of each work is a fundamental similarity between *Ulysses* and *The Waste Land.*

The manipulation of point of view in them generates much of the discontinuity. The success of Joyce's manipulation eventually was acknowledged; and in the last chapter, I distinguish six distinct narrative modes in *Ulysses,* all more or less firmly under his control (pp. 276–77). Eliot has been less fortunate with critics; but his narrative point of view in *The Waste Land* is not chaotic, or even merely fragmented. The texture of discontinuity includes an apparent multiplicity of narrators and dramatic speakers who are not clearly identified; and the complication is compounded by the confusing designation of their speeches. Nevertheless, the point of view is consistent. To demonstrate that is to answer a question I have avoided by my use of "quester," "pilgrim," and "protagonist" when referring to a person or persons unknown: Who is (or are)—to frame the unasked question—the ultimate speaker(s) of what is spoken in *The Waste Land,* its controlling consciousness(es) and voice(s)?

The "different voices" Eliot stressed when he adopted Dickens's "He do the Police in Different Voices" as a temporary title have caused some to conceive the protagonist-speaker as a composite representative citizen, "Everyman" (as Bloom was so crudely called for so long), both female and male. Speakers "merge with one another, pass into one another"; for "order in *The Waste Land* depends on a plurality of consciousnesses . . . which struggle towards . . . and then . . . past [sic] . . . unity." Accordingly, Marie of the opening paragraph and the "Son of man" addressed in the next paragraph both can be that Everyperson; either of them can be the companion of the neurasthenic woman in "A Game of Chess"; and they can be joined in their role as composite speaker by the lower-class woman who holds forth in that same section.[34]

But even if this is the case, who *addresses* the "Son of man" at the beginning of the second paragraph? When the hyacinth girl, the neurasthenic woman, and the Thames maidens speak, it is within quotation marks and directed to the ultimate speaker, indicating in each instance that she is not part of him/her. Yet, why is what Madame Sosostris said to the speaker not in quotation marks although it is being related by him/her and he/she uses quotation marks when quoting him/herself? Finally, how is one to integrate Tiresias, who, according to Eliot's note, "not indeed a 'character,' is yet the most important personage in the poem, uniting all the rest"? *The Waste Land* is said to be about many individuals; and Tiresias is said to be both distinct from all of them and a "personage" who unites all of them. The note goes on to assert that "What Tiresias *sees,* in fact, is the substance of the poem." Taken simply, this note confounds the apparent confusion; and partly on the strength of it, some maintain that Tiresias is the ultimate speaker (see, e.g., Smith, *The Waste Land,* pp. 4–5, 49–50).

The Notes, of course, are not to be taken simply. Nevertheless, there is evi-

---

34. This has been argued most recently and quite elaborately by Levenson; see pp. 175–93. (The quotations are from pp. 189 and 193.) See also, e.g., George Williamson, *A Reader's Guide to T. S. Eliot* (New York: Noonday, 1953), pp. 123–24.

dence that even before the dramatic metamorphosis of his poem, Eliot had trouble controlling his complicated narrative strategy in it. On the carbon copy of the "Fire Sermon" draft, Pound took him to task for the line "Across her brain one half-formed thought may pass" (which became line 251, "Her brain allows one half-formed thought to pass"), cancelling and circling "may," and commenting in the margin, "make up/yr. mind," then beneath a drawn line, "you Tiresias/if you know/know damn well/or/else you/don't" (p. 46 [47]).

I am unable to explain the use of quotation marks around the hyacinth girl's pair of lines (and the typist's thought); but Eliot's complex modernist narrative strategy is essentially coherent. The point of view he created is one of only three possible alternatives. Either (1) the ultimate speaker of *The Waste Land* is a single anonymous peripatetic witness-protagonist, as I have represented him; or (2) she/he is a composite of the characters in the poem, as some believe; or (3) he (and she) is Tiresias, as others maintain. Before discussing the first two, I shall try to demonstrate that the last is not, strictly speaking, a distinct alternative.

That Tiresias indeed is central, as the note about him claims, is declared wittily by the poet. *The Waste Land* has 434 lines (10 lines were printed between numbers 350 and 360 in earlier texts and between 340 and 350 in *Facsimile*), so that lines 217 and 218 are its middle. And at the very midpoint, the beginning of line 218, Eliot placed "I Tiresias"; the note is to that line, of course. What is still to be determined is: In what sense is Tiresias not a "character" and yet the uniter and "most important personage" who "sees" the "substance" of the poem?

Being blind, Tiresias can only "see" (the word is italicized in the note) in the sense of the seer; and indeed only that sort of sight has value in the "Unreal" waste land. The first appearance of "a mere spectator" in the poem (as the note calls Tiresias) is at the beginning of its second paragraph, where one addresses the speaker as "Son of man." That phrase has the first line-note, "Cf. Ezekiel II, i." And there is no better evidence that the Notes are working play than Eliot's following the expansive and oblique head note with a note that contrasts not only by its irreducible terseness, but also by its directness and its eloquent significance.

Identified by the phrase "Son of man" and the note, Ezekiel is associated with Tiresias—anticipates him in fact—as the prophet who addresses the speaker. But that phrase is used about eighty times in Ezekiel, as well as elsewhere in the Old Testament (often to refer to the Messiah), and Jesus uses it as many times in the Gospels to refer to himself. Hence, the one particular passage referred to in the note is itself the reason for the reference:

> And he said unto me, Son of man, stand upon thy feet, and I will speak unto thee.
> And the spirit entered into me when he spake unto me, and set me upon my feet, that I heard him that spake unto me. (2.1–2)

The passage is rich in meaning. God tells Ezekiel, the "Son of man," to stand and hear Him, but in the act of doing so grants His grace to make it possible. The sequence invoked by the first note in the poem resembles that of the annunciation and spiritually guiding thunder at its end. Even more germane here: to understand Ezekiel as saying he heard God's words from on high as a result of a distinct spirit's having entered him "and set me upon my feet," is to call the prophet naive. It is the spirit of God that enabled him to hear the words of God. "Him that spake unto me" had "entered into me when he spake unto me," is speaking God's words within him: the speaking in question is *a state of consciousness*. And Ezekiel the prophet, whose sacred Book begins "Now it came to pass . . . as I was among the captives by the river of Chebar" (1.1), also is the "Son of man."

My point is perhaps clear: if the prophet in the note to line 20 who heard "him that spake unto me" is himself the "Son of man," then the "Son of man" addressed in line 20 himself is the addressing prophet. The prophet-"spectator" who speaks "unto" him in that second paragraph—beginning "What are the roots that clutch . . . ?" and concluding "I will show you fear in a handful of dust" (19–30)—who warns through the voice of the bartender "HURRY UP PLEASE ITS TIME," and who points to Phlebas as an object lesson, he who has "perceived," "foretold" and "foresuffered all," is *inside* the subject of the poem, whether that subject and ultimate speaker is a single protagonist or multiple, talks to him/them from within his/their mind(s). Furthermore, the prophet within the subject is the spirit of God within him/them, because, as the passage from Ezekiel stresses, it is the spirit of God that is the prophetic power, or as Ecclesiastes puts it, "The words of the wise . . . are given from one shepherd." The association of the phrase "Son of man" with the Old Testament Messiah and with Jesus augments and reinforces its more specific function. "Tiresias" the prophet indeed "unites all the rest" and is "the most important personage in the poem"; taken in this light, the Tiresias note is as playful as any.

Joyce developed his portrayal of his subject's consciousness and his manipulation of point of view when he went from the *Portrait* to *Ulysses.* Similarly, Eliot's dramatic representation of the voice within his subject's consciousness had been achieved in a simpler form (and a secular context) in "Prufrock." In *The Waste Land,* where the voice is associated with the prophet of Ecclesiastes, Ezekiel, the Old Testament Messiah and Jesus, and identified as Tiresias, who prophesied to Odysseus and tried to guide and save Oedipus, the context is spiritual. The voice transmits the three words in the thunder; and when those words are adopted as the last utterance in the poem of the questing subject, it pronounces a concluding benediction. The voice is that of one's personal prophet or "good angel," that comes through one's inspiration of the wind or breath of God; it is the Christian third Person or Hebrew *Shechinah,* the indwelling divine Presence. It is conscience and wisdom. Mistakenly considering the function of Tiresias alone, Levenson properly observes, "Tiresias provides not permanent vision but instants of lucidity during which . . . vision is raised . . . knowledge . . . widened" (p. 192). The epigraph from Petronius that Eliot finally selected for *The Waste Land* is apt not only because the sibyl's terrible circumstances correspond to the spiritual condition of the denizens of his waste land; it is apt also because she is both a human being in despair and a prophet. The epigraph announces the relation of protagonist and prophet in the poem that follows.

On the simplest level, a discrete Tiresias would be an unlikely ultimate speaker and controlling consciousness for *The Waste Land:* a pagan, able to "see" what ordinary mortals seek, and who has "foresuffered all," is a singularly inappropriate Holy Grail quester, who despairs of success, and who suffers as he does at the end of "The Fire Sermon" and in "What the Thunder Said." Yet the clearly labelled voice of Tiresias has a distinct, and in the fullest root sense an intimate, relation with that speaker, as do the voices like it. Part at least of the seemingly incoherent series of snatches of discourse in *The Waste Land* is the working of a brilliantly functional narrative strategy.

With that encouragement, one can turn to the majority of those snatches and consider whether the ultimate speaker of whom the various prophetic voices are a coherent integral part is himself coherent. The view that the ultimate speaker is a composite is an understandable inference from the apparent absence of a single coherent entity in a poem in which so many Is and wes speak so abruptly and discontinuously. The view is an admissible explanation, but hardly a justification, of what would have been a feeble procedure in a poem—a procedure that would have evinced the very opposite of a controlling strategy. But Eliot's complex modernist narrative strategy in *The Waste Land* is, as I have said, essentially coherent throughout its discontinuous texture and despite minor inconsistencies.

His 1953 lecture, "The Three Voices of Poetry," whose published version in *On Poetry and Poets* directly precedes that of the 1956 lecture which ironically derogates the Notes, never mentions *The Waste Land.* But in the same canny manner, Eliot seems to provide in "The Three Voices of Poetry" a description of the kinds of relationship precisely of *voices* that he created in his poem of three decades before.

He begins abruptly by defining his terms: "The first voice is the voice of the poet talking to himself—or to nobody. The second . . . of the poet addressing an audience . . . . The third . . . when he is saying . . . what he can say within the limits of one imaginary character addressing another imaginary character" (p. 96). He confesses that until three years before he had distinguished clearly only two kinds of discourse created by a poet: those of "his" first "voice" ("speaking for oneself"), and ("in 1938," p. 99), "his" third ("speaking for an imaginary character," p. 100). The second voice, of "the poet in non-dramatic poetry which has a dramatic element in it" (p. 102), is illustrated neatly: "In *The Tempest,* it is Caliban who speaks; in 'Caliban upon Setebos,' it is . . . Browning talking aloud through Caliban" (p. 102). This voice he identified only in 1950 is distinct both from the discourse in true drama, in which the poet must "find words for several characters differing widely from each other," and "each . . . must be given lines appropriate to himself" (p. 100), and from the poet's "talking to himself—or to nobody," which is "directly expressing the poet's own thoughts and sentiments" (p. 106).

The last clause quoted is quoted by Eliot himself from the definition of "lyric" in "the Oxford Dictionary," and that fact is especially appropriate to what he is about in "The Three Voices of Poetry." He is redefining the three fundamental genres of poetry, lyric, narrative (he uses "epic") and drama. With characteristic shrewdness, he defines them rhetorically: the genres are kinds of discourse created by a poet moved by different purposes. While his third voice is that of drama as traditionally defined, his definition of lyric includes all poetry that is primarily declaration or utterance, "*directly* expressing the poet's own thoughts and sentiments" (my emphasis), of whatever length, and whether emotional, meditative, or expository. What remains is the third fundamental genre, that which is primarily narration or report, in which the poet employs neither the first voice nor the third, but that elusive second voice.

The phrase "directly expressing" encapsulates his rhetorical approach, also represented in his comfortable alternation of the prepositions *to* and *for*. However, Eliot's poet, who talks *to* either himself ("or nobody"), a reader of "Caliban upon Setebos," or the audience of *The Tempest,* and who talks *for* either himself or Shakespeare's character, talks in the second voice not for but "through" Browning's speaker. The disparity is heuristic. Immediately after concluding his distinction of the two Calibans, Eliot declares: "It was Browning's greatest disciple, Mr. Ezra Pound, who adopted the term 'persona' to indicate the . . . characters *through* whom *he* spoke: and the term is just" (pp. 103–4; my emphasis).

Eliot's new discovery of a second "voice" three years before was his distinguishing between the poet's providing the truly spoken words of a "personage on the stage" (p. 100) in front of an audience, and the poet's "speaking through a mask" (p. 104)—providing written words for a surrogate who is not an acted personage, who instead is *no more than* words that will be read. It is precisely the distinction between characters in drama and personae in literature—speakers, whether or not identified as named characters, who are not identifiable as the poet (as they are in the voice speaking in truly lyric poetry). The second voice of poetry, the voice of epic, is of poetry with a fictional or narrative point of view.

Eliot makes the point that in all true poetry the poet has more than one purpose, with the result that "there is more than one voice to be heard" (p. 109) in the poetry of each genre. And he provides one instance of the third voice that occurs in the poetry of the second—"a dramatic element," in a phrase already quoted—dialogue:

> In Homer, for instance, there is heard also, from time to time, the dramatic voice . . . . The *Divine Comedy* is not in the exact sense an epic, but here also we hear men and women speaking to us. (p. 105)

And in the passage immediately preceding this one, he declares:

> The second voice is . . . the voice most often and most clearly heard in poetry . . . intended to amuse or to instruct, poetry that tells a story, poetry that preaches or points a moral, or satire which is a form of preaching. For what is the point of a story without an audience, or of a sermon without a congregation? (pp. 104–5)

In *The Waste Land,* a new kind of dramatic voice—the voice within, identified by the "method" with divinely inspired prophets—distinctly preaches to the subject (or subjects) of the poem, delivers a "sermon" from within that "congregation." Considered in this context, Eliot's ostensible catalogue of kinds of poetry of the second voice seems to be like the list of epithets with which he was, in three years' time, to describe the Notes while ostensibly describing Marianne Moore's. Poetry of the second voice, he says, is poetry intended to amuse or instruct, tell a story, preach or point a moral, satirize. He does not make the ostensibly different kinds of poem each of which "implies the presence of an audience" (p. 104) grammatically distinct except in the case of "or satire"; and he promptly identifies the satire meant as "a form of preaching" ("The preacher sought to find out acceptable words"). An adequate description of *The Waste Land* would include all the terms in Eliot's list ostensibly cataloguing different kinds of poem: comic, didactic, narrative, homiletic, religious, satiric.

If Eliot's catalogue of poetry of the second voice also is slyly intended to describe his own poem of three decades before, is he engaging in wishful thinking? Or is it coherent: do his words really have so consistent a voice? In its opening lines, someone says "we stopped in the colonnade, / And went on in sunlight, into the Hofgarten, / And drank coffee, and talked for an hour." The line "And we shall play a game of chess," in the section with that name, contains a second use of *we*. And a third occurs in the opening lines of "What the Thunder Said": "We who were living are now dying." Even one who can hear an inner voice is only one. In these instances, is one individual—a distinct character—speaking of a lot she or he shares with others? Or does the *we* indicate that the poet has created a multiple speaker?

In all three instances, the speaker explicitly has companions: one in the latter two instances ("Who is the third who walks always beside you," 360); one or more in the first. If more than one, then the following lines—that in German spoken by the "echt deutsch" silly Lithuanian woman, the four by the aristocratic Marie, and the two final ones before the paragraph break that introduces the first occasion on which his inner voice addresses the "Son of man"—are samples of the hour's "talk" of the company. If instead he had only one companion on the occasion he is telling about, then those voices were at other tables, and overheard. The situation is unclear (although the fact that one speaker uses German suggests that the voices were overheard); but the distinction is immaterial. Other distinctions are both clear and material: of the last two lines, both the English syntax and the personality of the speaker of "In the mountains, there you feel free" are different from those of "I read, much of the night, and go south in the winter."

As in "The *Divine Comedy* . . . here also we hear men and women speaking to us." And their speech is no more a symptom of chaotic or fragmented narrative than in Dante: it is the "dramatic element," dialogue. In *The Waste Land,* Eliot is "talking aloud through" his own Caliban in the way of such fiction as the work of Conrad's that supplied his temporary epigraph—by creating a character-speaker who, like Marlow, tells of a crucial spiritual experience. And that speaker is giving "also, from time to time, the dramatic voice." But Eliot's speaker is not, like Marlow, a narrator speaking to *others*. All three quoted instances involving "we" are silent: respectively, a memory, an anticipation, and a reflection. In his book *The Waste Land,* Smith observes that "The great concealment was, to make the narrative an introspection" (p. 149). Eliot's innovative narrative strategy modifies both the "overhead" (in the sense first specified by John Stuart Mill) first "voice" of poetry and the second voice, and is more complex than either Marlow's testimony within Conrad's frame or the inner discourse of Prufrock's consciousness. It presents a combination of the speaker's consciousness and two impositions on it: a discrete inner voice and experienced (heard) other voices.

This is the suitable place to return to the use of quotation marks in the poem. One directly quoted speech is by the speaker himself; the others are by five women. And all but that of the hyacinth girl (and the typist's thought) are reported (registered on his consciousness) as they actually occur in the present time of *The Waste Land*. The speaker addresses "Stetson," is with the neurasthenic woman, and is addressed by or overhears the three Thames maidens. The speeches of Marie and the others in the Hofgarten, of Madame Sosostris, of the Cockney woman and her friends in the pub—all speeches in the poem not in quotation marks—are being recalled by the speaker: experienced (heard) as memory in his consciousness. The remaining directly quoted line in the poem, "This music crept by me upon the waters" (257) follows immediately in a speech by Ferdinand in Act I of *The Tempest* a line drawn on for an earlier line (191). The narrative logic of the poem indicates that the quoted line is being heard in a performance; otherwise, it is a third apparently inconsistent use of quotation marks.

Eliot's recording of *The Waste Land* (Caedmon) enables the outer ear to come to the assistance of the inner. For example: his pauses between the remembered snatches of conversation in the Hofgarten are slightly longer than line pauses; all his prophets speak in a slightly oracular voice; and when the quatrain of the "Thames-daughter" seduced in a canoe is succeeded by that of her sister, he stresses the first word: "*My* feet are at Moorgate." But as with the conversation in the Hofgarten, this assistance is required, if at all, by the reader, not by the poem. For example, the first "daughter," associated by the note with Dante's La Pia, uses Dante's word to say that she has been *undone;* the second is distinguished not only by geography, but by her contrasting attitude: "What should I resent?" The next stanza, which is not a quatrain, is spoken by a half-sister; this third speaker is identified by her line about "dirty hands," by the echo of "Moorgate" of the second quatrain in "On Margate Sands," and by the vestige of the song of the *Rheintöchter* which follows it, as much as by Eliot's note precisely specifying "(three) Thames-daughters."

But the individual to or near whom she speaks had to move east from the Thames to the Channel at Margate to hear her. The next line, "To Carthage then I came," which a note quotes in its context in Saint Augustine's *Confessions* ("to Carthage then I came, where a cauldron of unholy loves sang all about mine ears"), relates to the unholy loves that have just sung about the ears of the auditor, who has reported the songs in "the dramatic voice" of each "daughter" in turn; but the line also invokes both the confession of a sinner who redeemed himself, and a place further east. After only the repeated "burning," and Saint Augustine's "O Lord Thou pluckest me out," "Death by Water" begins, with the drowned Levantine sailor held up to the speaker-quester-protagonist as an object lesson by his inner voice, while he continues to move east in his metaphorical journey, toward the sacred river.

In *The Waste Land,* then, there are three classes of speaker: the enlightened silent voice of an inner consciousness; quoted *dramatis personae* heard in the poem and remembered; and an ultimate speaker-protagonist, who experiences the first within himself and the second within himself and in the world, and registers as "dramatic" dialogue his experience of both. One place where all three are juxtaposed in that order is at the end of the second (the recalled) experience in, and conclusion of, "A Game of Chess":

> HURRY UP PLEASE ITS TIME
> HURRY UP PLEASE ITS TIME
> Goonight Bill. Goonight Lou. Goonight May. Goonight.
> Ta ta. Goonight. Goonight.
> Good night, ladies, good night, sweet ladies, good night, good night.

The capital letters and portentous words of the bartender's warning, which had interrupted the Cockney woman's sordid account, identify its significance for the protagonist, whose conscience has heard in it "words . . . from one shepherd" addressed to him. In the next two lines, the woman and her friends take leave of each other. The final line is an exact quotation from Ophelia in Hamlet IV.v; so it is simultaneously too learned for the company, and appropriate to the character of the erudite protagonist. Its speaker is distinguished from them further because the line (complementing what is implicit in the portentous repeated line) allusively invokes a doomed woman, comments on the account by the woman that the protagonist had just overheard, and is couched in an ironic reiteration of the leavetaking by the members of the group. On the simplest level, it distinguishes the protagonist from them by the difference between their slurred "goonight" and his precise "good night" (a distinction not neglected by Eliot in his reading). The three types of speaker are quite distinct, and two types are rendered dramatically—as they were experienced—in the introspection that is the third.

The protagonist who recounts dramatically the voices he hears within himself and heard and hears in the world, also reflects ("April is the cruellest month"); quotes himself ("I . . . stopped him, crying: 'Stetson!'"); recalls his responses to characters whom he has quoted ("—Yet when we came back, late, from the Hyacinth garden, / . . . I could not / Speak . . ."); rounds out his memories with exposition, like a narrator ("Madame Sosostris, famous clairvoyante, / Had a bad cold"); quotes from poems and popular songs; recalls snatches of poems and songs he has been moved to repeat to himself; meditates; and so on. He thinks of his fortune-telling session with Madame Sosostris and (understandably) recalls only her words. He is the companion of the neurasthenic woman, and his responses to her are mostly the sort one does not speak aloud in any case.

They also are almost as desperate as her importunings. Like Stephen and Bloom at similar points in *Ulysses,* he is reaching a crisis of despair. Then, at the end of "A Game of Chess," having been told "ITS TIME" and said "good night" to the ladies, he ceases his "walking round in a ring," as has been said.

He begins, with "The Fire Sermon," the process that will separate him from those lost souls around him in the benighted city, just as Stephen and Bloom, after a time, begin to act. Thus, it is in the opening lines of "The Fire Sermon" that the erudite, reflective, suffering young male protagonist simultaneously makes explicit the implication of his identity as the controlling voice of *The Waste Land*—that he is a poet as well (the poem which is his introspection is thereby his own poem)—and indicates that in a poet's way he is about to move from memory to desire, will give expression to the despair he is feeling. In its opening lines he alludes to two prototypes for "The Fire Sermon," one painfully different and the other painfully similar. The former is the "Prothalamion," which celebrates a progress on the "sweet Thames" of noble sisters and daughters before the (in the words of Spenser's dedication) "double mariage of the two honorable and vertuous ladies"; the other is the psalmist's lament over his exile "by the rivers of Babylon."

All the quester's subsequent experiences, memories and thoughts: of the creeping rat, Mr. Eugenides, the river sweating oil and tar, Elizabeth and Essex on it in the time of Spenser, the drowned Phlebas with whom the prophet confronts him in his metaphorical-spiritual pilgrimage east, and the tortuous way to "the empty chapel" (where he heard—and reports in that tense, looking back on his waste land—what the thunder said), like all the voices without and within him, take their natural place in "his" apparently autonomous or dramatic poem, the coherent achievement created by Eliot's complex modernist narrative strategy in *The Waste Land.* That Eliot cut so brilliant and multifaceted a gem out of the crude material preserved in the drafts makes his achievement even more impressive.

Eliot's achieved poem of *his* second voice tells a story and occasionally amuses. But above all it seems to instruct and preach, in the utterances of its inner prophet, the experiences of its introspective speaker, even its satire. In *Per Amica Silentia Lunae* (1917), Yeats wrote (as he may have admonished his "Dear Ezra"), "We make out of the quarrel with others, rhetoric, but of the quarrel with ourselves, poetry." Eliot's quester employs all three voices of poetry in his introspection; but in his own poem of the second (quester's) voice, especially in his character's reflections and meditations and in the prophetic lines, Eliot also "talks" to and for "himself." If he were not personally involved in the spiritual plight of his protagonist, his account of a quest for salvation would be the preaching of the self-righteous, which is to say, the spiritually smug. The stench of sanctimony usually reaches the nostrils very soon, and there is no more trace of it in *The Waste Land* than in *Ulysses.* The last similarity I find between these two central works of English modernism I mention last because it is different from all the others—a matter neither of theme nor of way of working—and because the discussion of narrative method in them leads inevitably to it. The last similarity concerns the nature of the artist's *invisibility:* not absence but unseen presence. Despite what Stephen says in the *Portrait,* the successful artist is not always the remote God of his completed "handiwork," because he is not always "refined out of existence."

Once again, reference to the *Portrait* and "Prufrock" is enlightening. The autobiographical elements in "Prufrock" were mentioned in the second chapter

(p. 32). Stephen makes his declaration in his aesthetic discourse during the last chapter. The passage, which has its modernist counterpart in Eliot's almost exactly contemporary distinction between "the man who suffers and the mind which creates," concludes Stephen's description (for which he employs the terms Eliot uses more appropriately to distinguish the voices of poetry) of "three forms progressing" in the composition of a work of art out of its creator's experience, that process by which the fully realized or truly autonomous work, he says, is ultimately achieved. Joyce's self-glorifying Paterian autobiographical essay, "A Portrait of the Artist," written before *Stephen Hero,* the novel that portrays reality but in which the author is identified fully with the "hero," reveals that Joyce's own portrait of the young artist evolved precisely from "lyric" through "epic" (the mediate state) to the eventual "dramatic" *Portrait,* and is subtly confessing that fact of autobiography through Stephen's mouth in the very end product of the process Stephen describes.

In *Ulysses,* the action of the novel itself requires that it take place on June 16, 1904; and yet Joyce subtly made it autobiographical. He first spent an appointed evening with his wife during the time Stephen was with Bloom; the next month he wrote "The Sisters," for the first time making successful art out of his reality, then promptly wrote two more stories for *Dubliners,* and soon left Ireland. In the novel he presents Bloom as making possible for Stephen during those hours what she had made possible for him.

Eliot's poem, about a young poet among the spiritually "dead" in London, written at the time of his emotional trouble, also is more than it is. Although the words are not even the protagonist's own, but those of the third woman in the last part of "The Fire Sermon," what he heard or overheard her say, after she named the place of her seduction, seems more appropriate to the author of *The Waste Land* than to a character likened to the two daughters of the Thames: "On Margate Sands. / I can connect / Nothing with nothing." And Eliot's alteration of the line from Psalm 137 to "By the waters of Leman I sat down and wept" made it not only a lament over spiritual exile, but also a covert depiction of his emotional state while at Lausanne. After mentioning in *Eliot* the "many voices which say 'I' in *The Waste Land,*" Spender observes: "There is one other voice—the voice of the poet in the poem, who suffers" (pp. 95–96); and a dozen pages later, he asserts about "the man" in the first part of "A Game of Chess" that his series of responses to the woman "projects a character which can only be Eliot himself" (p. 108). "That the poem is autobiographical is now a truism, and I cannot remember a time when it did not seem so," Smith declares in the preface to his recent book on the poem (p. xii).[35]

---

35. Two recent studies of Eliot emphasize its personal dimension, as their relevant chapter titles suggest. Bush's emphasis on Eliot's psychological state at the time was mentioned in the previous chapter (p. 107); his chapter is entitled "'Unknown terror and mystery': *The Waste Land*" (pp. 53–78). In "The Waste Land Traversed" (pp. 86–119), Gordon directs attention to the religious aspiration Eliot expressed overtly in poems and passages in the drafts Pound successfully advised his eliminating from the poem, such as "Song (For the Opherion)." James E. Miller's psychosexual study is entitled *T. S. Eliot's Personal Waste Land: Exorcism of the Demons* (University Park: Pennsylvania State UP, 1977), and focusses almost exclusively on *The Waste Land.* Stead astutely discredits recent exaggeration of its autobiographical dimension (pp. 101–3).

In a different key, two letters to Ford Madox Ford declare: "There are, *I* think[,] about 30 *good* lines in *The Waste Land*"; and "As for the lines . . . . They are the 29 lines of the water-dripping song in the last part" (*Facsimile*, p. 129; the lines are 331–59). "Justly celebrated" the song of the hermit-thrush may be, as Eliot's note declares; but it is celebrated by him.

More than the finished poem, the draft version is personal in specific substance, with its material derived from American settings, its references to "Tom's place," "brother," and "my friend," and a line incorporated from "The Death of the Duchess" that Eliot removed from the poem at his wife's request, "The ivory men make company between us."[36] Perhaps partly for that reason, Valerie Eliot's publication of the Facsimile edition of the drafts and related material in 1971 precipitated discussion of autobiographical elements in *The Waste Land* in reviews and consequent correspondence, including the now fully aired lurid speculations.[37] In addition, a statement Eliot made a decade after he wrote the poem is placed before the facsimile pages of the volume:

> Various critics have done me the honour to interpret the poem in terms of criticism of the contemporary world, have considered it, indeed, as an important bit of social criticism. To me it was only the relief of a personal and wholly insignificant grouse against life; it is just a piece of rhythmical grumbling.[38]

The Waste Land is a great deal more than that, of course. The reviewer of the facsimile volume for the *Times Literary Supplement* declared, after objecting to Eliot's statement, that the poem does not have to be "grumbling" or confession to have an autobiographical element, that the external subject with which it deals (echoing its poet's "Prufrock") is "a screen on which is projected the meshed design of the poet's sensibility" (p. 1551). And two decades after his announcement that a poem considered "criticism of the contemporary world" "is just . . . rhythmical grumbling," Eliot said in "Virgil and the Christian World":

> A poet may believe thet he is expressing only his private experience; *his lines may be for him only a means of talking about himself without giving himself away* [my emphasis]; yet for his readers what he has written may come to be the

36. See, e.g., *Facsimile*, pp. 4 (5), 12 (13), 62 (63), 64 (65), 76 (77), 78 (79). The line followed "And we shall play a game of chess" (137), and he included it in a manuscript he wrote out for an auction sale in 1960 in support of the London Library (p. 126).

37. See, e.g., the review by Richard Ellmann in the *New York Review of Books* (18 Nov. 1971), pp. 10–16; the review in the *Times Literary Supplement* (10 Dec. 1971), pp. 1551–52; and letters in the same periodical: 17 Dec. 1971, from Peter du Sautoy; 31 Dec., from the reviewer and John Chiari; 14 Jan. 1972, from I. A. Richards and G. Wilson Knight; 28 Jan., from G. Wilson Knight; 11 Feb., from David B. Rebmann and Peter Dunn; 18 Feb., from Anne Ridler, G. Wilson Knight and H. Z. Maccoby; 25 Feb., from J. Chiari. Davies's *Bibliography* includes a section, "Autobiography and Libel: The Controversy over *The Waste Land*" that lists the works speculating about Jean Verdenal and Eliot's psychosexuality (pp. 220–22).

38. *Facsimile*, p. 1. Mrs. Eliot also has declared, "The years of 'The Waste Land' were a terrible nightmare to him . . .: if he had seen these drafts, they might have brought back all the horror"; and, "It's sheer concentrated hell, there's no other word for it, and it was the sheer hell of being with her that forced him to write it" (*Observer* interview, cols. 2 and 3).

expression both of their own secret feelings and of the exultation or despair of a generation.[39]

It is in this context that we must understand, and emphasize the first two words of, "To me it was only the relief of a personal ... grouse ... it is ... grumbling"; in the present decade, Bush has called *The Waste Land* "one of the most terrifying poems of a terrifying century" (*T. S. Eliot,* p. 71). Yet Eliot's later statement merely relates the personal and the public in a poet's work more satisfactorily than does the one placed at the head of the facsimile volume; it does not deny what the work is "for him" ("to me"). And in "The Three Voices of Poetry" he articulates his conception of precisely that relation. As Joyce cannot be dissociated from Stephen Dedalus in *Ulysses,* so the creator of *The Waste Land* is in some essential sense "himself" the poet and spiritual pilgrim in his poem.

Both *Ulysses* and *The Waste Land* have full integrity as works of art without the imposition in either of finality on its story. And as the facile open form in some of our current literature compares to this modernist achievement, so precisely does the current autobiographical intimacy compare to the achievement in them of a special invisibility: each writer places his work fully in the world and yet inhabits it. Joyce succeeds in making his invisible presence an elegant triumph of his art; but these two supremely modernist writers have in common the full commitment to the artist's psychic reality that is an important modernist inheritance from Romanticism.

In the preceding chapter, literary periods were said to be precisely myths, persuasive generalizations about literature during some portion of past time, and neither demonstrable fact nor demonstrable fiction; and *Ulysses* and *The Waste Land* were identified as the paired central archetypes of Modernism in English literature. In exploring the relations between them, this chapter has shown some intrinsic reasons for the mythogenesis of them—almost immediately on their appearance in 1922—as the supreme exempla of the modernist novel and poem in the language, through the attacks of the detractors of Modernism no less than by its devotees.

One reason is the influence Joyce's novel had on Eliot, attested to as much by the threat Eliot saw to his integrity as an artist as by actual marks of *Ulysses* on *The Waste Land.* But the major reason for their joint role in the culture of a half-century ago must be the great number and range of similarities between them whose nature indicates confluence rather than influence, similarities that are made more significant by the fundamental differences between a voluptuous and joyous work of art and a mostly austere and ascetic one.

There are the similar thematic assertions about civilization, a meaningful life

---

39. *On Poetry and Poets,* p. 137. Precisely this passage is quoted by Moody in "To fill all the desert with inviolable voice," in *The Waste Land in Different Voices,* ed. A. D. Moody (New York: St. Martin's, 1974), pp. 47–66. It is followed by an ingenious reading of the poem as not only personal but also secular: "the waste land is ... the landscape of an inward desolation .... The struggle is to recover feeling through lyrical expression"; and Eliot's "at last finding his own voice in song is the token of the reintegration of the self that had been alienated" (pp. 48–51).

for humankind, and the cosmos. There are the even greater similarities of artistic practice: the extensive use of the "method" of allusion; the common body of things alluded to; the element of working play; the pattern of action whereby the (similar) predicaments of the protagonists are presented in a diurnal situation which is then succeeded by a quest; the ending without finality; the disruption of linear progression; narrative strategies of possibly unprecedented complexity; the subject's consciousness as the locus of action in both. And there is the fact that in each work its creator is invisible but present. Finally—perhaps most significant in explaining their eventual shared historical role—each evolved from exemplary new writing into an art work of transcendent originality, its writer Mak[ing] It New while each was in process: the sudden inspiration by which Eliot conceived and fashioned *The Waste Land* recalls Joyce's second and more dramatic sudden conceptual departure while fashioning *Ulysses*.

These similarities constitute a list of singular—almost remarkable—extent and scope. It is a catalogue of concerns and ways of working which, although it does not comprise all the elements of modernist literature by any means, encompasses enough of them, and characteristic enough ones, for the appearance of two such commanding works in 1922 as *Ulysses* and *The Waste Land,* with this catalogue in addition to the external things mentioned in common between them, to be a crux of cultural history.

7

Joyce and Mann, Citizen Artists

The realm of personal attitude and belief lies beyond one frontier of criticism; but Joyce's informal concerns and formal convictions are indigenous to his art—and to literary history as well. That Joyce and Eliot—especially in "Prufrock," *Ulysses,* and *The Waste Land*—were significantly related to English literary Modernism, and even that the two works of 1922 were related to each other, has long been more or less evident. But like the relations propounded in Part I between Joyce's novel and two antecedent works not in English, his significant relation to a German contemporary has not: with one exception, in Anglo-American criticism only minor connections have been made. His attack on anti-Semitism in *Ulysses* was one aspect of a profound difference in concerns and convictions from the other members of Pound's modernist triumvirate— and of a corresponding affinity with Thomas Mann—manifested in Joyce's art.

If the particular kind of concerns and convictions Joyce and Mann share makes this chapter seem (at best) ancillary to the general enterprise of the book, the cause may lie less in the chapter itself than in expectations based on Anglo-American critical practice in our century. Critics have attended not only to a writer's representation of social reality, but also to expressions of public morality in a writer's work (such as its treatment of anti-Semitism), and even to public ideas (political ideology) adumbrated in it. But modernist and recent critics alike have tended to ignore the foundation of both morality and ideology: public values, which is to say social/political concerns and convictions. Even critics whose own perspective on literature is political pass over those values in a writer's work as unseemly if not subversive—or at least Gallic. But at the center of the critically significant relation of Joyce and Mann is their shared system of public values.

My subject is the author of *Ulysses;* I hope to show, granted forbearance when exploring the political context of his affinity with Mann and corollary distinctness from all the other major modernist English writers, how their affinity illuminates his art. His having elected to make the protagonist of perhaps the most ambitious novel ever written not a crusading newspaper publisher, intellectual columnist, principled editor, intrepid war correspondent (as Lawrence,

Woolf, Pound, Hemingway might have done), but a seller of advertising—on commission—is relevant to criticism of *Ulysses*. It also is one instance of the public values embodied in his art, shared with Mann alone among major modernist writers.

Probably everyone who has taught or written about literature has been troubled, at least occasionally, by awareness that accepting apparent evidence can help create it. This is true nowhere more than in the cumulative—consensual—selection of, and ranking within, the canon of writers and works taught about and studied: the evolved canon *could* be merely a perpetual self-fulfilling prophecy. Among writers of fiction of Joyce's generation, two in each of the three major Western languages soon were placed alone together in the first rank. Accordingly, courses began to be taught on Joyce and Lawrence, on Proust and Gide, on Mann and Kafka.

The troubling thought recurs that these now-traditional arranged couplings are as arbitrary and grotesque as the dynastic marriages of pharaohs with their only peers, their sisters. Yet, however abiding or not the canonical value judgment may prove to be, the pairings themselves are good pedagogy; for the scope of modernist fiction is nicely exemplified in the confrontation of Mann with Kafka, of Proust with Gide, of Joyce with Lawrence.

No such pedagogical justification exists for the long familiar *comparatiste* course grouping of Mann, Proust, and Joyce. The implied ranking of each as supreme in his language, and superior in the languages of the others to any but his designated associate, very well may carry exclusion to an even more foolish extreme. For example, in the reality the latter part of this century has come to know, Kafka's accomplishment seems (to us, that is) greater than Mann's; and he has been supplanting Mann in the *comparatiste* course. The traditional triad of Mann, Proust, and Joyce represents the range and the accomplishments of modernist fiction, of course; but that could be done as well by different figures among the six, or all six, or others. Perhaps its chief virtue has been to signal the affinities between two of the three which are my subject. The essence of affinity is their shared social and political values. It is because they share them that, as different as were their ways of working, and as different as are many formal characteristics of their art, of the six writers Joyce and Mann seem to me to have the most in common. And their relation adds a dimension to our understanding of Modernism as well as of Joyce's work.

If Mann seems closest to Joyce, the other English writer seems farthest from him. Eliot's shrewd contrasting in *After Strange Gods* (New York: Harcourt, 1934) of Lawrence and "the most ethically orthodox of the more eminent writers of my time" (p. 41) concerned the "cruelty" of characters "unfurnished with" any "moral or social sense" (p. 39) and the compassion of Joyce's characters; but this contrast is part of the larger one between Lawrence and Joyce. Lawrence's glorification of power, "natural" hierarchy and imposed social order (he seemed to be moving away from it when he died), in passages in *Women in Love,* prominently in *The Plumed Serpent* and *Kangaroo,* and explicitly in essays like "The Death of a Porcupine," illustrates his contrast with Joyce—and his ideological affinity with Pound, Lewis, and to an extent Eliot himself.

Pound/Joyce prints comments on Joyce and *Ulysses* from two Rome broadcasts Pound made about Cummings in 1941 and, in full, his memorial tribute, "James Joyce: To His Memory." He complained that Joyce "had no philosophy, not so you would notice it. Nothing much alive and bustin the old partitions": "some ruck end of theology and a VERY conventional outlook." He then declared, "NO; Joyce was ... not a bohemian, a small bourgeois, to the UTMOST" (p. 268). *Bourgeois* is a highly charged word; in part, this is because today its descriptive or polemical use in political economics is not kept distinct from the older use by which aristocrats, philosophical radicals, social non-conformists, and—for the chief antagonist of their martial advance—the artistic *avant-garde* expressed contempt: for example, how much is the recently popular locution "bourgeois democracy" (to signify a country with free labor unions) political philosophy, and how much is it privileged chic? But this confusion is recent; furthermore, from feudal times the term of contempt has had an objective signification, which Pound seems to be invoking. Both his known admiration and the context confirm that he combines, with his disappointment over Joyce's failure to be either philosophically radical or bohemian, high regard for *Ulysses* and its author. Because he sees no incompatibility between his disappointment and his regard, his "small bourgeois" is more a descriptive epithet than a pejorative one. Recent admirers have described Joyce so (see e.g., *James Joyce*, p. 5, and Quinones, p. 228).

That Pound translated the French *petit-bourgeois* illustrates the point with which Raymond Williams begins his discussion of *bourgeois* in *Keywords: A Vocabulary of Culture and Society* (New York: Oxford UP, 1976). Williams calls it "a very difficult word to use in English," for two reasons: the second is its association "with Marxist argument, which can attract hostility or dismissal"; but his first reason is that "although quite widely used it is still evidently a French word" (p. 37). *Burgess* is not equivalent to *bourgeois* (as a noun), because the French noun designates not the inhabitant of a borough but a *citizen:* its English equivalent as a term of abuse is the archaic slang *cit*, that denizen of London's "City" ridiculed by and for "the town" in centuries of English comedy.

The etymologies of English *city* from Latin *civitas,* body of citizens, and of *civilization (civilize)* from *civilis,* of or belonging to citizens, converge in a root word: *civis,* citizen. And the relation of *civilization, city,* and *citizen* is of three dimensions of *civil* society. Historically, the French and German equivalents of that adjective have been *bourgeois* and *bürgerlich.* Williams points out that both Hegel and Marx used *bürgerlich* in that sense; by it, Marx designated not only the dominant social class during the historical period characterized by the "capitalist mode of production," but also "bourgeois political theory (the theory of *civil society*) ... [with] what [Marx] saw as its falsely universal concepts and institutions" (pp. 38–39), and other values and beliefs of a distinct culture ("ideology").

The benign equivalent of the adjective in English-speaking countries has been *middle-class.* Defining that broad spectrum of citizenry in industrial societies—west and east—has proven much more difficult than Marx anticipated. Under the circumstances, Pound's use of *bourgeois* to signify Joyce's attitude

and values is adequately descriptive. *A Primer of Heresy,* the arrogant subtitle
of *After Strange Gods,* designates Eliot's contrast of Lawrence and Joyce in a
special way; for he explicitly excludes "the authors' *beliefs*" from consideration:
"We are . . . concerned . . . with orthodoxy of sensibility and with the sense of
tradition . . . " (p. 40). This gloss on his phrases "moral or social sense" and
"ethically orthodox" indicates that in praising Joyce so extravagantly for insist-
ing on people's proper treatment of other people, Eliot—although engaged in
contemning its public dimension respecting free thinking Jews and other here-
tics—was praising Joyce for the private dimension of the chief virtue of civil
society.

In feudal France, Williams writes, "The essential definition [of the noun
bourgeois] was that of the solid citizen whose mode of life was at once stable
and solvent" (p. 38). From the beginning, that citizen/*bourgeois*/*Bürger* inevit-
ably attracted the contempt of those who have exempted themselves from ordi-
nary status in civil society—aristocrat, radical, bohemian, and artist. Joyce's
mode of life was neither stable nor solvent; but Bloom is undeniable evidence
that his attitude toward such a mode of life differentiates him from Lawrence,
Proust, Gide, and Kafka. And from the major English modernist writers. The
letter registering Pound's negative comment on "a new style per chapter," when
the "small bourgeois" Joyce made his first major departure in *Ulysses,* goes on
to complain, "Bloom has been disproportionately on/ ???/ or hasn't he. Where
in hell is Stephen Tellemachus?" (*Pound/Joyce,* p. 158). The grounds of prof-
fered contempt for the likes of Leopold Bloom are the grounds of the relation
between Joyce and Mann. Pound's description of a "small bourgeois" who cre-
ated the revolutionary masterpiece *Ulysses* is precisely of a citizen artist.

I

Joyce and Proust were brought together at a salon in Paris in 1922, when both
had achieved recognition. According to Padraic Colum's account:

> Here is what was said:
>
>> Proust: Ah, Monsieur Joyce . . . You know the Princess . . .
>> Joyce: No, Monsieur.
>> Proust: Ah. You know the Countess . . .
>> Joyce: No, Monsieur.
>> Proust: Then you know Madame . . .
>> Joyce: No, Monsieur. (*Colum,* pp. 151–52)

Arthur Power reports Joyce saying he and Proust had a short exchange about
truffles (p. 79); "truffles" may have been a private metaphor or pun. *James Joyce*
describes three other accounts (pp. 508–9); in one, he said that Proust "would
only talk about duchesses, while I was more concerned with their chamber-
maids." Whether as artist, citizen, or merely mock-*boulevardier,* his concern is
relevant.

Joyce and Mann never met. *Finnegans Wake* acknowledges Mann's existence in a few places. In one passage Latin and German puns allude slightingly to *The Magic Mountain:* "the cocklyhearted dreamerish for that magic moning . . . bringing beckerbrose, the brew with the foochoor in it"; less slighting (and certain) are "for he's the mann to rhyme the rann," and "cstorrap" (pp. 608, 44, 310). A passage in which Oisin is said to be contending against the Sidhe, "osion buck fared agen fairioes" (p. 326), invokes Aschenbach's inner struggle in "Death in Venice." Earlier, in a catalogue of gifts, there is "a collera morbous for Mann in the Cloack" (p. 211); presumably, "collera," "morbous" and the allusions to cloaca and an author-surrogate again invoke "Death in Venice." (Mann's gift is followed almost immediately by "for Will-of-the-Wisp and Barney-the-Bark two mangolds noble to sweeden their bitters": Mann, Yeats and Shaw had received the Nobel Prize, and he had not.)

Mann was characteristically more generous to Joyce. On March 1, 1945, in a well-known letter to Bruno Walter discussing *Doctor Faustus,* he wrote of "Joyce . . . to whom I am closer in some ways than might appear."[1] And a slightly ambivalent tribute to the creator of the last chapter of *Ulysses* is rendered in Chapter XXI of *Doctor Faustus* when Serenus Zeitblom says, "Far be it from me to deny the seriousness of art; but . . . I, if I had my way, would write down the whole in one burst and one breath, without any division, yes . . . ."[2]

Mann endorses my claim that despite appearances he is close to Joyce, at least "in some ways." However, an impressive champion of his work asserted precisely the opposite. For George Lukács, Mann was exemplary in the present century of the great realistic tradition of Balzac and Tolstoy; in contrast, Joyce admitted to being—and was—the arch representative of the antithetical tradition of Flaubert, the tradition of " 'modernist' antirealism," often polemically characterized as decadent bourgeois aestheticism.[3] Any claim of a meaningful relation between the two writers whom the eminent Marxist philosopher and critic considers exemplars of fundamentally opposed traditions is compelled to deal respectfully, and therefore in some detail, with the unbridgeable gap— "between an aesthetically appealing but decadent modernism [*Avantgardeismus*] and a fruitful critical realism"—he perceives separating the "bourgeois-modernist" Joyce and Mann, the exponent of "a critical and realistic bourgeois

1. He did go on to declare, "Incidentally, I can't read Joyce either," but gave as his reason that "one has to be born into English[-language?] culture to do so." *Letters of Thomas Mann: 1889–1955,* tr. Richard and Clara Winston (New York: Knopf, 1971), p. 465. For the original text, see Thomas Mann, *Briefe 1937–1947,* ed. Erika Mann (Frankfurt: Fischer, 1963), p. 416.

2. Tr. H. T. Lowe-Porter (New York: Knopf, 1948), p. 176. For the original text, see *Doktor Faustus* (Munich: Fischer, 1960), pp. 189–90.

3. Lukács cites many other contemporaneous writers; but Joyce, and especially Mann, seem to be central. For example, the much-reprinted "The Ideology of Modernism" *(Die Weltanschaulichen Grundlagen des Avantgardeismus)* fully "compare[s] the two main trends in contemporary bourgeois literature"; and it begins with an exemplary contrast between Joyce's and Mann's use of inner monologue, in which Lukács observes, "it is not easy to think of any two novels more basically dissimilar than *Ulysses* and *Lotte in Weimar,*" and "between Joyce's intentions and those of Thomas Mann there is a total opposition." Quoted from Lukács, *Marxism and Human Liberation,* ed. E. San Juan, Jr. (New York: Dell [Delta], 1973), pp. 277–79; orig. in *The Meaning of Contemporary Realism,* tr. John and Necke Mander (London: Merlin, 1963), U.S. title *Realism in Our Time: Literature and the Class Struggle* (New York: Harper, 1964).

literature."[4] I shall do so by examining the ground of his perception: move to a different vantage point from his and the gap may narrow or disappear.

His familiar dichotomization of European fiction since the late nineteenth century, into a vital and significant art rooted in the profound ample creation of Balzac, and a sterile and meretricious art whose archetype was Flaubert's slender corpus of self-conscious craftsmanship, also is a judgment—largely dismissed or ridiculed in Anglo-American criticism—on two ostensibly opposed attitudes toward the relations of art and human reality. It is an attractive judgment, for it appears at least morally more wholesome for an artist to regard his or her art as an illumination of life, than to regard life as material for that art. Furthermore, it seems to be fair respecting at least the *attitudes* of the artists Balzac and Flaubert, whatever may be said of such broad characterizations of their own and subsequent work. And despite the familiar deplorable semi-redundant style, "decadent bourgeois aestheticism" is substantive polemic, designating (in reverse order): a commitment to art as the end served by all else, including life; the social class identity of the writer who turns from the reality created by, and/ or from the decline of, her or his class, to the aesthetic commitment; and both the ostensible immorality of that commitment, and the atrophy it is said to cause in one's art.

Lukács's ethical case is, as I say, attractive. But his history of the novel can be challenged; and the hierarchy of values on which he bases his literary judgments can be confronted with an alternative set of literary values.

His evaluation helps illuminate a familiar element of literary history relevant enough to warrant mention: the antipathy to modernist art, especially poetry and fiction, of many of its contemporaries on the political left. At the time *Ulysses* was burned in Germany it was condemned in the Soviet Union, by which time Formalism, that promising and exciting Soviet movement in art and criticism, had been ended the horribly uncivil way all proscribed works and ideas are eliminated in societies controlled by orthodoxy. In the final pages of the *Portrait*, Stephen records an exchange with a Jesuit teacher about Giordano Bruno of Nola that Joyce apparently took from life (*James Joyce*, pp. 59–60): "He said Bruno was a terrible heretic. I said he was terribly burned. He agreed to this with some sorrow" (p. 249). However, the relevant perspective for this issue is not the horrors of Stalinism, but a much longer one.

Lukács rejected Maxim Gorky's shameful formulation, "Socialist Realism is Revolutionary Romanticism," so useful to Commissar Zhdanov and so contrary to Engels's eloquent comparison (in his famous April 1888 letter to Margaret Harkness) of the truth of the royalist Balzac and the propaganda of the socialist Zola. Like Engels and Marx, and even before his Communist period, Lukács postulated the primacy for the writer of representing the essential truth beneath the particulars of reality, the Marxist's *realism*. And as it is for Marx and Engels, for Lukács the value of literature is in its enlightening effect on people, which in Marxist terms is people-in-their-society.

---

4. "Franz Kafka or Thomas Mann?" Quoted from *Marxists on Literature: An Anthology* (Hammondsworth: Penguin, 1975), p. 394. Orig. in *The Meaning of Contemporary Realism*.

This classical Marxist view that literature should represent the essential truth beneath the particulars of reality, and that its value is the truth it imparts, seems to me classical in the fullest sense. It is in the tradition of Aristotle's response (according to our derived and flawed text) to Plato's attack on poetry in Book X of the *Republic*. When he adopted Plato's metaphor in the *Poetics*, it was to argue that *mimesis* does not correspond to an insubstantial and imperfect mirror-image of a (necessarily falsified) natural reality, but is itself *poiesis*, a making-with-words (to the radical extent that a play inheres in its written words, not in its production—*Poetics* 14, 26); and the thing made uses the particulars of reality to reveal—as philosophy does—what is universally true beneath those particulars. Furthermore, this creation does not emotionally arouse and corrupt people, as his teacher charged, but prepares them to reflect tranquilly on, and by its truth gives them wisdom about, the nature of the human condition. Hence, the emotions he claimed are purged in tragedy are those generated by precisely the audience's apprehension of that human condition.

The relation drawn between Aristotle's *mimesis* (of *praxeōs kai biou*— "doings and life") and Samuel Johnson's *nature,* a critical truism, embraces Lukács's *realism.* Correspondingly, Aristotle's *universal* is Johnson's *general* is Lukács's *typical.* And all three similarly perceive and justify literature as heuristic—moving to wisdom in Aristotle, virtue in Johnson, right thinking in Lukács, "the social development of the humanization of man" as he put it in *Solzhenitsyn* (tr. William David Graf [Cambridge: M.I.T. P, 1971], p. 79), near the end of his long life.

The central concepts and values of the Hungarian Marxist's literary criticism are those of the principal tradition through most of Western history. And its limitation for appreciating the modernists' art of Making New was anticipated in Aristotle's objections to Euripides and Johnson's to the metaphysical poets (by way of Abraham Cowley). Being the classical tradition, it distrusts eccentricity, in the literal sense of the word: deviation from the center or standard. It also has no sympathy with the modernists' (in Ronald Bush's locution) "fidelity to the subtlest expressions of the innermost self." Both innovation and psychic expression it considers manifestations of egoism; its recent (Marxist) adherents usually attribute that to bourgeois writers' turning inward, because their declining civilization is unattractive or incomprehensible to them. (However, among modernist works Fredric Jameson exempts *Ulysses* from this charge, in an essay whose title is "'Ulysses' in history."[5]) Above all, it regards innovation and expression as actual impediments to rendering reality in art, not the instruments the modernists made them for rendering an unprecedented reality. Lukács grants Joyce (misguided) seriousness as well as genius. But his adherence to the classical tradition dictates that he consider Joyce's art to be both exhibitionistic

5. In *James Joyce and Modern Literature,* ed. W. J. McCormack and Alistair Stead (London: Routledge, 1982), pp. 126–41. He writes that the novel achieves a "dereification" "whereby the text itself is unsettled and undermined"; his point is not deconstructionist, but that "the whole dead grid of the object world of greater Dublin" is "disalienated and . . . traced back . . . [sic] less to its origins in Nature, than to the transformation of Nature by human and collective praxis deconcealed" (pp. 133, 132, 140).

and deficient in realism (the truth of typicality)—and so to be frivolous. Ironically—but understandably, in the context I am proposing—in attacking literature and criticism of the modernist period, Lukács and like-minded critics have perpetuated a practice that began in the most conservative bourgeois critical circles (such as Irving Babbitt's Humanists) in the early years of the century: the use of "aesthetic" and "aestheticism" not only in moral and social contexts, but as pejorative epithets for describing art.

That Lukács's "Marxist" contrasting of Joyce and Mann derives from the limiting bias of the classical tradition, is made clear by the opposed view of the younger contemporary of all three who was both anti-Aristotelian Communist and Modernist. Of course, Bertolt Brecht rejected an idealist metaphysics, according to which literature was both insubstantial and at the third remove "from the king and from the truth." But he agreed with Plato's values: it should generate thought rather than emotion; and it is justified only by its social utility. The relevance here of Brecht's systematic opposition to Lukács's critical stance concerns his express attitude toward the "valuable and highly developed technical elements" of the innovative modernist writers. Walter Benjamin reports Brecht the Marxist's critique of the hostility to eccentric or new writing of Lukács's conservative school ("Lukács, Gabor, Kurella"):

> They are simply enemies of production. Production is not safe for them, it cannot be trusted. It is the unforeseeable. You never know what the product will be.[6]

And of Joyce himself, Brecht wrote:

> The techniques of Joyce and Döblin are not merely products of decadence; if one banishes their influence instead of modifying it, the result will merely be the influence of the epigones, namely the Hemingways.[7]

Lukács's bias against Modernism and Joyce is not inherently and inevitably Marxist; instead it merely has been conventional among Marxists—quite another, and lesser, matter. And recently, Marxist critics have challenged it.[8] Furthermore, Brecht was far from alone among Marxist critics, even during the modernist period. For example, in *Literature and Dialectical Materialism* (1934; New York: Haskell, 1974), John Strachey wrote:

> What we mean when we say that these writers are decadent is that such work could only be done . . . in the closing stages of a culture. . . . [W]e certainly do not mean that Proust and Joyce, for example, were not, or are not, great artists. For decadence may have positive qualities of its own. It produces degrees of

---

6. "Conversations with Brecht," Walter Benjamin, *Reflections: Essays, Aphorisms, Autobiographical Writings*, tr. Edmund Jephcott (New York: Harcourt, 1978), p. 216. Lukács's fellow writers are Andor Gabor and Alfred Kurella, another Hungarian and a German; all three lived in the Soviet Union during the Nazi period.

7. Quoted from "Brecht v Lukács," *Times Literary Supplement* (29 Sept. 1972), pp. 1169–70, 1169.

8. For recent critiques, and a discussion of "The Brecht-Lukács Debate," see Davies, pp. 59–60.

analytic intelligence and sensitiveness which are hardly paralleled in other epochs. . . . The sunset colours of a civilisation are sometimes among its most lovely. (pp. 18–19)

With Lukács's opposition of Balzac and Flaubert, the English modernists he decried seemed to agree. It has been pointed out (p. 105) that, in "Beyle and Balzac," Eliot invoked specifically Flaubert as the salutary model for fiction against the model of Balzac. In praising Joyce and *Ulysses,* Pound singled out Flaubert. Joyce himself not only paid homage to Flaubert, but characterized the ten Balzac novels he had read as "lumps of putty"—although he drew on them (*James Joyce,* p. 354 and n). The contrary relative estimations of the same two (exemplary) French writers crystallize the antipathy separating the company of Eliot and that of Lukacs.

But the historical formulation Lukács based on his opposition of Balzac and Flaubert does not necessarily follow from the dichotomy between them. Some subsequent novelists wrote "Victorian" fiction. But the modernists not only emphasized craft, as did Flaubert: they were committed to rendering their new reality, including previously neglected dimensions of it. Lukács's formulation of two opposed traditions that persisted in the twentieth century itself created the unbridgeable gap between Joyce and Mann he thought it identified. In "The Irish Writer," his contribution to *Davis, Mangan, Ferguson?: Tradition and the Irish Writer* (Dublin: Dufour [Dolmen], 1970), the distinguished contemporary Irish poet Thomas Kinsella wrote of Joyce:

Although he rejects ["Home, Fatherland and Church"] and escapes from them, he cannot forget them. His stomach, unlike Yeats's, is not turned by what he sees shaping the new Ireland . . . . He is the first major Irish voice to speak for Irish reality since the death of the Irish language. (pp. 64–65)

Joyce wrote most of his volume of stories portraying with "scrupulous meanness" the conditions of life of ordinary people in Dublin, and the effect of their conditions on them, while writing *Stephen Hero;* and in making the *Portrait* of that, he carefully delineated the process by which the conditions of Stephen's life generated his tendency to distort reality. Finally, as my last chapter will argue, the quasi-life Joyce created is primary in *Ulysses.* When Lukács charges in "The Ideology of Modernism" that the novel's inner monologue "is itself the formative principle governing the narrative pattern and the presentation of character. Technique here is something absolute" (*Marxism and Liberation,* p. 278), and when on the next page he characterizes it as "*static,*" he actually is in agreement with much sympathetic criticism of *Ulysses.* But he and it alike fail to appreciate the great resources for embodying the reality of then-developing technological urban civilization Joyce originated—and Mann increasingly adopted.

A modification of Lukács's classical opposition of Joyce and Mann, by a modern Hungarian critic who wrote under his "personal guidance" and in his "stimulating spirit," affirms its inadequacy. Peter Egri's monograph *Avantgardism and Modernity: A Comparison of James Joyce's* Ulysses *with Thomas Mann's* Der Zauberberg *and* Lotte in Weimar, discusses differences and similarities between Joyce's novel and the two by Mann.[9] It is extracted from a book in Hungarian whose title is translated as *James Joyce and Thomas Mann: Decadence and Modernity*. Egri's conclusion expounds the relation between the two ostensible kinds of art the writers exemplify:

> The great historical merit of avantgarde art [such as *Ulysses*] is to have called attention to a social, historical crisis by disrupting the objective, plastic, dynamic and synthesizing view of the world of the realistic tradition. But avantgardism did not create a new *organic* unity out of the new phenomena of an essentially new reality. . . . It was left to modern realism [works of "modernity" such as the two by Mann] to give an accurate picture of modern man in his full individual and social polyphony.
>
> The relationship, therefore, between realistic tradition, avantgardism, and modernity can be characterized in the frame of thesis, antithesis, and synthesis. (p. 116)

Although in the first quoted sentence, Egri echoes Eliot's analysis of the ultimate source of Modernism, the virtues he grants it are negative; and the dialectical historiography—by which Mann's "modernity" improves on Joyce's Modernism—is patronizing. But Manichean dichotomy has been supplanted by process. And the process is a relation between Joyceness and Manness of sequence, influence, similitude. Furthermore, Egri's respect, even admiration, for individual works of modernist art is implied throughout the determined macrocriticism of his historical sweep, and often made explicit in his very comparison of Joyce's great novel with the two by Mann.

In his *Paris Review* interview, reprinted in *Writers at Work* (ed. Malcolm Cowley [New York: Viking, 1959]), Faulkner declared, "The two great men in my time were Mann and Joyce. You should approach Joyce's *Ulysses* as the illiterate Baptist preacher approaches the Old Testament: with faith" (p. 135). Moments later, the modernist creator of the "intact world" of Yoknapatawpha County named what he read as, "the Old Testament, Dickens, Conrad, Cervantes," and then, "Flaubert, Balzac—he created an intact world of his own, a bloodstream running through twenty books—Dostoevsky, Tolstoi, Shakespeare" (p. 136). As Faulkner's contemporary, Brecht, appreciated, accomplished artists cannot be marched lockstep in alternative left and right columns; thus, even Lukács's own pupil assumed a slightly different vantage from his own, had there a different perception, described a narrower gap.

No significant gap exists. James Joyce never wrote a word of fiction that was not about one city and the life of its citizens. To erect on the classicist dichotomy of Lukács a Manichean system for judging the fiction of the past century is to ignore that Joyce made complex, innovative, difficult works that not only are

9. Tr. Paul Aston (Budapest: Akadémiai Kiadó and Tulsa: U of Tulsa, 1972). The quoted phrases are on p. 15. For specific differences and similarities, see esp. ch. 3 and 4; for a bibliography of "passing references" to "the Joyce-Mann relationship." see nn. 3–5 of ch. 1, pp. 16–18. I was unable to determine how Egri's "A Survey of Criticism on the Relation of James Joyce and Thomas Mann," *Hungarian Studies in English* (Debrecen: L. Kossuth U), II (1965), 105–20, relates to this bibliography.

valuable art, but even have the qualities Lukács both requires, and finds in the writer he characterizes as the antithesis of Joyce: works that like Mann's embody a full concern for and rendering of the deep truths of "typical" human and social experience.

This shared concern in their writing is the basis of the special relation between Joyce and Mann—their difference from other major modernist writers. It underpins their values and attitudes: as citizens of their time and of their respective places of birth; as parents and husbands; as artists; and as civil members of human society.

II

In a letter to Agnes E. Meyer dated February 18, 1942, Mann himself cited the Anglo-American critical study that recognizes significant affinities between his work and Joyce's. (*Briefe 1937–1947*, pp. 237–40, p. 239). Harry Levin's pioneer book, *James Joyce: A Critical Introduction* (1941; rev. ed., Norfolk: New Directions, 1960) reflects his course on Proust, Mann, and Joyce in its references to both the other writers. Of the dozen to Mann, two are pertinent. One of them, delineating similarities in Joyce's and Mann's development, warrants quoting at length:

> The most significant example of all [symbolic novelists], and—since Joyce's death—the unchallenged master of living novelists, is Thomas Mann. . . .
>
> Mann's itinerary conforms so closely to Joyce's progression from naturalism to symbolism that it brings home to us the historical necessities that have molded their widely separated careers. The first stage, *Bürgertum,* is commemorated by Mann's *Buddenbrooks,* while Joyce's early impressions of his city are sketched in *Dubliners.* Significantly, Joyce's first major effort was the *Portrait of the Artist,* while Mann's stage of *Künstlertum* produced mainly sketches and *Novellen* in which the wandering artist, *ein verirrter Bürger,* from Schiller to Gustav von Aschenbach, deplores his inability to enjoy the delights of the commonplace. The post-war years conferred *Weltbürgertum* upon Mann, and saw the completion of his synthesis of the European mind, *Der Zauberberg.* . . . brought down, like *Ulysses,* from the neutral Alps . . . . His work in progress [the Joseph series], in a very different way from *Finnegans Wake,* descends through the deep well of the past to the same timeless and timely theme. . . . :
>
> > For it *is,* always *is,* however much we say It was. Thus speaks the myth . . . . Feast of story-telling . . . thou conjurest up timelessness in the mind of the folk, and invokest the myth that it may be relived in the actual present. (pp. 212–13)

The congruence drawn between the careers of Joyce and Mann may be a bit too neat, although Levin does not claim that Stephen is, like Mann's "wandering artists," a wandering/strayed citizen. Yet even after discounting, a good deal of similarity remains: certainly, like Ibsen and Strindberg before them, both moved from an almost naturalistic mode to, at the time of Joyce's death, an essentially mythic one. It can be added that, as in the work of Joyce, the element of play increased progressively in that of Mann. For example, play with names: Serenus Zeitblom, son of Wohlgemut, could be out of *Ulysses.*

The significant similarity in their artistic careers extends well beyond the sequences of their works. Levin mentions that both were exiles. Their lives also have in common a set of circumstances more singular, and at least as important for their art. Both were born into comfortable bourgeois families—not merely typical but distinctly rich families—and each experienced his father's bankruptcy, a decline to real poverty, and the consequent aura of embarrassment in humiliated, formerly rich households, during his adolescent years. This seems to have been beneficial for both of them, and in similar ways. The creation of Felix Krull, Tonio Kröger, and Stephen Dedalus comes to mind. But more important is a shared civil *(bourgeois)* trait, Joyce's and Mann's compassion for the lot of ordinary people. Its literary significance is profound; but like their common exile, it is involved in their similar politics, which must be delineated first.

In 1918, in the title of a notorious book *(Betrachtungen eines Unpolitischen)*, the youngish Mann called himself a nonpolitical person; almost echoing him, the older Joyce spoke of himself as "not political." Nevertheless, politics is an element in the works of both. Andrew White's *Thomas Mann* (New York: Grove, 1965) observes:

> The phrase "non-political" signified for Mann ... politically thoughtful ....
> Politics was for Mann an affair of conscience. The deepest concerns of his polit-
> ical conscience were the political character, destiny and actions of the German
> nation .... (p. 82)

And Joyce's case was much the same: they were not political activitists or amateurs of politics, but responsible citizens. Like the older Mann, the younger Joyce gave lectures and wrote tracts on politics out of a central consciousness of his nationality, and usually about his own country and people. During his years in Trieste, a Catholic city under foreign domination, he found a ready audience. The combination of devotion and disappointment he expressed is manifest even in some of the translated titles: "Ireland, Island of Saints and Sages"; "Home Rule Comes of Age"; "Ireland at the Bar"; "The Home Rule Comet." It corresponds precisely to Mann's attitude in his broadcasts to Germany in the last months of World War II. And in "Gas from a Burner," written in his thirtieth year (1912), the same combination occurs:

> But I owe a duty to Ireland:
> I hold her honour in my hand,
> This lovely land that always sent
> Her writers and artists to banishment
> And in a spirit of Irish fun
> Betrayed her own leaders, one by one.
> 'Twas Irish humour, wet and dry,
> Flung quicklime into Parnell's eye (lines 13–20)

although his tone feigns levity:

> O Ireland my first and only love
> Where Christ and Caesar are hand and glove! (25–26)

Joyce seems to have made politics much more prominent in his fiction than did Mann, whose strictly political books and essays occupy the last two volumes of his *Gesammelte Werke in zwölf Bänden* (Frankfurt: Fischer, 1960). In *Dubliners*, Ireland's political situation is alluded to in details (such as the harp and street-player in "Two Gallants"); figures prominently in "The Dead"; and is the subject of "Ivy Day in the Committee Room." The *Portrait* has the Christmas dinner scene; the campaign for Irish athletics; the agitation against Yeats's *The Countess Cathleen;* and Stephen's debate with Davin and discussion with Cranly. In *Finnegans Wake*, written when Ireland's colonial status had become history, that history is, like so much else, a source of comedy—for example the confrontation of Mutt and Jute. But before independence, in *Ulysses*, Ireland's political situation is not merely recurrent, but pervasive: the patronizing Hibernophile Haines, sycophant Mulligan, quisling Deasy, jingoist Citizen, English soldiers and their Irish whore, all belong to it; it recurs in Stephen's memory and thoughts, Bloom's fantasies, interpolations, the conversation of the other characters; it is the essential subject of the tenth chapter, in which the Irish are portrayed as being ground between England and the Church; and it is the eventual subject of the seventh, in which Stephen's "Parable of the Plums" combines with the end to make the whole chapter Joyce's indictment of his people for submitting to English domination. Even the anti-semitic incident in the twelfth chapter has a political dimension, made possible by hindsight and expressing Joyce's civil values: the interpolated execution of the martyr-victim following the citizen's first verbal abuse of Bloom is a scathing attack on the Easter Rising leader Padraic Pearse's doctrine of Irish blood-sacrifice. (A participant in the Rising, O'Casey, soon mounted a more extensive attack in the second act of *The Plough and the Stars*.)

Joyce and Mann shared an intense national identity and a distressed preoccupation with their nations' politics. This combination—as distinct from Pound's (or Shaw's) indignant impatience—was not characteristic of major modernist writers, Yeats excepted. And unlike Yeats, they experienced vilification in their homelands for their outspoken, critical devotion. The British Minister to Bern spoke at Joyce's funeral, but Ireland was not represented (*James Joyce*, pp. 742–43).

Both were also poor political prognosticators. According to the English text in *The Critical Writings of James Joyce* (ed. [and tr.?] Ellsworth Mason and Richard Ellmann [London: Faber, 1959]), the peroration of Joyce's Trieste lecture of April 27, 1907, "Ireland, Island of Saints and Sages," asserted:

> though the Irish are eloquent, a revolution is not made of human breath and compromises. . . . If [Ireland] wants to put on the play that we have waited for so long, this time let it be whole, and complete, and definitive. . . . I am sure that I, at least, will never see that curtain go up, because I will have already gone home on the last train. (p. 174)

The Easter Rising initiated Ireland's successful campaign for independence three days less than nine years later. Mann, in a letter to Walter Opitz, wrote:

> Germany is big, and the instinct for freedom and reason fundamentally more widely disseminated, and more powerful, than the bawling of the ruffians and blackguards would lead one to believe .... [T]hings look bad in Germany, but ... are certainly not so bad as they seem.[10]

It is dated January 20, 1933. Adolf Hitler became Chancellor ten days later, and within weeks Mann joined Joyce in exile.

Both Hitler, and Joyce's fallible political judgment, relate to Joyce's well-known grievance against Sir Horace Rumbold, British Minister to Bern during his Zurich years, the only "human being" Joyce "loathed," Pound claimed in his memorial broadcast (*Pound/Joyce,* p. 270). Joyce derided Rumbold not only in the boorish letter of the hangman "H. Rumbold, Master Barber" in *Ulysses* (303), but also in a poem alleging Rumbold's incompetence when he was appointed Ambassador to the newly restored Poland (*James Joyce,* p. 458). Rumbold became Ambassador to Germany in 1928 and remained through the first months after the Nazi *machtergreifung.* In 1931, he wrote to Sir John Simon, the Foreign Secretary, "I won't see Hitler, and I won't let any member of my staff see Hitler." And on April 26, 1933, he sent a 5,000-word dispatch insisting that *Mein Kampf* was serious, describing accurately Hitler's program for Germany and international intentions, and warning against appeasement; the whole Cabinet (including Chamberlain) read it.[11]

On the other hand, citizen Joyce probably would have appreciated Rumbold's prescience more than the British government did. For years thereafter he "referred to Germany derisively as 'Hitlerland'" (*James Joyce,* p. 708). Timothy Materer may have had especially in mind Joyce's letter to Harriet Weaver the year after Hitler's accession—"I am afraid poor Mr. Hitler-Missler will soon have few admirers in Europe apart from your nieces and my nephews, Masters W. Lewis and E. Pound" (*Letters* III: 311)—when he observed in *Vortex:*

> Although Joyce is often characterized as an apolitical writer, he had profound political intuitions that served him better than Pound's and Lewis's passionate convictions served them. (p. 179)

It has been shown that despite what is "often" said, Joyce the writer was apolitical no more than Mann was, at least through *Ulysses.* Not only the special variety of nationalist politics they shared, but also their shared general political position, contrasted with the neo-feudalist to archaeo-fascist positions most modernist writers took. For much of his life Joyce espoused, and Mann who began as a conservative seems to have adopted, variants of democratic socialism. Not surprisingly, both were internationalists and humanitarians as well.

That Mann became a socialist cannot be proven but is a reasonable inference. Among other things, he prepared a speech that was to be delivered to the

10. Tr. Andrew White; in White, p. 95. For the original text, see Thomas Mann, *Briefe 1889–1936,* ed. Erika Mann (Frankfurt: Fischer, 1961), p. 327.

11. Martin Gilbert, *Sir Horace Rumbold: Portrait of a Diplomat, 1869–1941* (London: Heinemann, 1973), pp. 351, 377–79. The Joyce affair is mentioned on pp. 178–79.

Socialist League of Culture in Berlin on February 19, 1933, "in which he pro-claimed his sympathy with the ideals of socialism."[12] He insisted in 1949 on celebrating Goethe's bicentennial in Weimar as well as Frankfurt, as he was to celebrate Schiller's six years later in Stuttgart and Weimar. There were other causes for this even-handedness; but it was to some extent a statement about the polarization (to which the northern hemisphere remains hostage) engineered by Churchill and being implemented by Truman and Stalin. And he supported Henry A. Wallace in 1948. That may have been quixotic—all protest votes can be regarded so; but Wallace's non-Communist supporters were principally dem-ocratic socialists.

The evidence for much of Joyce's life is unequivocal. While in Dublin, he went to meetings of a socialist group (*James Joyce,* p. 142). The final paragraph of his essay "A Portrait of the Artist," which he wrote in January 1904, pro-claims, "the competitive order is employed against itself, the aristocracies are supplanted," and opposes to them "the generous idea" (*Yale Review,* XLIX [1960], 360–67, 367). As the young Mann did with Heinrich Mann, he had polit-ical differences with his brother—from the opposite direction. After emigrating, he wrote letters articulating his politics to Stanislaus Joyce. In 1905, during his first stay in Trieste, he declared "my political opinions . . . are those of a socialist artist" (*James Joyce,* p. 197). From Rome, in 1906, when Stanislaus character-ized his socialism as thin, he responded "It is so and unsteady and ill-informed" (p. 239); but he continued to argue it vigorously. In a letter written a few months before, he expostulated:

> You have often shown opposition to my socialistic tendencies. But can you
> not see plainly that a deferment of the emancipation of the proletariat, a reaction
> to clericalism or aristocracy or bourgeoisism would mean a revulsion to tyran-
> nies of all kinds[?] (p. 197)

This is not nearly as impressive an example of Joyce's thinking about politics and economics as his letters contain; I quote it principally for the word "bour-geoisism." That deplorable ideological jargon to denote capitalist political con-trol, from the pen of a master of the English language, who had already created most of the stories of *Dubliners,* is an earnest of his political commitment. It also shows his narrowly socialist sense of the naturalized French word. "Bour-geois" control (logically) signifies repressed workers and other "tyrannies": from the beginning, he was committed to the individual liberty so crucial to the pol-itics of civil society (to, in a later usage, "bourgeois" democracy). In *Joyce's Pol-itics* (London: Routledge, 1980), in the process of pointing out echoes of Marx in the final paragraph of the "Portrait" essay (p. 70) and tracing political ele-ments in *Stephen Hero* and *Dubliners* (pp. 72–98), Dominic Manganiello dis-cusses the reading in liberals and anarchists that contributed to Joyce's anti-Jacobin socialism.

The civil nature of his socialism is attested by his seeking permission in 1909, when he was already at work on the *Portrait,* to translate into Italian one work by his fellow Irishman, Oscar Wilde: "The Soul of Man under Socialism"

---

12. "Introduction," Mann, *Letters,* p. xxv. In the letter to Opitz he declared that he would not deliver the speech because of the state of his health; of course, the meeting never was held.

(*James Joyce*, p. 274). And his socialist conviction persisted, though with diminishing engagement or increasing scepticism. Six years later, when at work on *Ulysses*, he declared his "political faith" to his friend Alessandro Francini Bruni:

> Monarchies . . . disgust me. . . . Republics are slippers for everyone's feet. . . .
> What else is left? . . . Do you believe in the Sun of the Future? (p. 383)

His last phrase, as Francini Bruni well knew, is from the Italian Socialist anthem. His equivocation in asking rather than stating portends his eventual abandonment of politics.

In *Ulysses* itself, he withholds from Bloom as well as Stephen his articulated socialist doctrine. Even were his political commitment not becoming attenuated, it would have been irrelevant to Stephen's situation and have made Bloom more seriously intellectual and political than Bloom's character permitted. However, he does give his ordinary citizen one by one the civil values he shared with Mann. Bloom advocates decency and compassion in public affairs, respect for human life, the rejection of war as a diplomatic policy, liberation for colonized nations, the guarantee of intellectual freedom in all its aspects—the organization of society to nourish people's life, respect their liberty, and promote their pursuit of happiness. As a young man Bloom had helped Sinn Fein; and in the course of the novel he comments on the many examples of cruelty he witnesses, on various bigotries, on social policies that cause suffering or harm for the sake of the privileged or because of stupidity, and so on.

One instance of Bloom's true civility is his response to the bibulous jingoist braggadocio of some of his fellow "small bourgeois" Dubliners in Kiernan's pub, who are denouncing the British Navy for caning sailors:

> —But, says Bloom, isn't discipline the same everywhere? I mean wouldn't
> it be the same here if you put force against force? (329)

Joyce carefully makes Bloom's combination of social innocence and humanitarian good sense contribute to the anti-Semitism of the group—and the eventual violence of the citizen. He also causes Bloom to use, at the climax of the first anti-semitic exchange, the "word known to all men," which Stephen identifies in his inner monologue in the library, in a missing passage (195) now restored to the novel (*Critical Edition* I: 419), and invokes during his climactic scene in nighttown (581). The exchange develops until Bloom says that "This very instant" Jews are being persecuted in Morocco, and is told pointedly to "Stand up to it then with force like men." Bloom's Morocco fiction ignored, the malevolent narrator reports:

> And then he collapses all of a sudden, twisting around all the opposite, as limp
> as a wet rag.
> —But it's no use, says he. Force, hatred, history, all that. That's not life for
> men and women, insult and hatred. And everybody knows that it's the very
> opposite of that that is really life.
> —What? says Alf.
> —Love, says Bloom. I mean the opposite of hatred. I must go now, says he
> to John Wyse. (332–33)

And that naked expression of Bloom's politics of compassion is given dignity as well as sincerity by his immediate embarrassment. "Off he pops" on his mission of charitable service to Dignam's widow; and immediately, "—A new apostle to the gentiles, says the citizen. Universal love." Joyce leaves little opportunity for doubt about the author's attitude.

At the beginning of this chapter, I cited the treatment of anti-Semitism in a writer's work as expressive of public morality, grounded in public values; Joyce's denunciation of it in *Ulysses* proceeds from the values of civil society. In the fourth chapter, I proposed that to express his attitude he used comic mockery of Bloom's equivocal Jewishness. In this first anti-semitic exchange in Kiernan's, his attitude—his public values—asserted through Bloom's civil opposition to "force" and "hatred," even while being victimized by them, places in its context in the novel Joyce's comically asserted indignation and contempt for anti-Semitism. Jeremy Hawthorn's "'Ulysses,' modernism, and Marxist criticism" (McCormack and Stead, pp. 112–25) identifies that context, in the course of rebutting the familiar Marxist attack on *Ulysses* as "inner thoughts and sensations" (p. 114) stripped of their relation to social reality. Hawthorn quotes the passage in which Gerty MacDowell calls the busily masturbating Bloom "a man of inflexible honour to his fingertips" (365), concedes Gerty's "comic misperception" of the "dirty old man," but uses that to advance his argument, declaring, "what Gerty feels is 'real'; the pulp-novel style . . . represents Gerty's way of perceiving sexuality" (p. 122). Then he addresses Joyce's comic irony in *Ulysses* directly:

> the deliberate reference to fingers on Joyce's part . . . clearly reveals the presence of an organising intelligence behind the passage. The humour here reveals . . . a humorist who . . . gets his laughs by building up his audience's knowledge of his assumed values. It is the construction of this 'value-centre' that allows Joyce to make the novel such an affirmation of human values. (p. 123)

Joyce mocks Bloom's social innocence before the bibulous jingoist braggadocio in Kiernan's, just as he does Bloom's equivocal Jewishness; but "knowledge of his assumed values" is provided "his audience" by the Jew-baiting and imminent erroneous accusation that precipitate the climactic anti-semitic act in the novel. That "knowledge" is provided as well by Bloom's humanitarian good sense: I discussed in the third chapter the ghostly presence in *Ulysses* of an ancient Irish poem, striking for its pacifist resolution; and while writing his novel the humanitarian Joyce was moving away from socialism probably in large part because Europe's Socialist Parties had failed to reject participation in the brutal and stupid "Great War," as his 1916 poem "Dooleysprudence" suggests.[13] A major component of the human values—often asserted by comic indi-

13. His tribute to the prudential rectitude of Peter Finley Dunn's character begins, "Who is the man when all the gallant nations run to war / Goes home to have his dinner by the very first cablecar"; and its last stanza runs, "Who is the tranquil gentleman who won't salute the State / Or serve Nabuchodonesor or proletariat / But thinks that every son of man has quite enough to do / To paddle down the stream of life his personal canoe? / It's Mr Dooley, / Mr Dooley, / The wisest wight our country ever knew / 'Poor Europe ambles / Like sheep to shambles' / Sighs Mr Dooley-ooley-ooley-oo" (*Critical Writings*, pp. 246–48).

rection—Hawthorn justly says inform *Ulysses* comprises specifically civil values.

Both Joyce's exile and Mann's were linked to their civil values. Joyce made his decisive departure from England's Catholic colony very early in his life; Mann's almost accidental necessity imposed by Nazi Germany occurred quite late. The time of exile for each may relate to the fact that Joyce's commitment to politics gradually diminished whereas Mann's gradually increased—and here, of course, they can be contrasted.

Shortly after the First War, Mann wrote in a postcard to Heinrich that politics was foaming *around* him: "*Politik umschäumt mich*" (*Briefe 1889–1936*, p. 200). But during the period between the wars, he became "fully committed to politics as a matter of humanity" (White, p. 91)—and Joyce abandoned politics. Frank Budgen reports in "James Joyce," his contribution to *James Joyce: Two Decades of Criticism* (ed. Seon Givens [New York: Vanguard, 1948], pp. 19–26), "Joyce took no part in politics and but rarely, and unwillingly, in political discussion" (p. 22). Joyce had never engaged in political activity more direct than his early essays and lectures; but after *Ulysses*, his work became nonpolitical. He put his antimilitarism in *Finnegans Wake*, for example in his treatment of the Waterloo antagonists Lipoleums and Willingdone. But in that work the outstanding Irish political figure of his generation, Eamon de Valera, is one of the elements in the sanctimonious Shaun the Post. And by the last year before the Second War, by which time the German and Italian translations of Anna Livia Plurabelle had failed to materialize because of "influential pressure," and his later work remained unloved in the Soviet Union (*James Joyce*, p. 708), he seems to have avoided all political involvement in order not to hinder the dissemination of his last and most ambitious book. Nevertheless, he helped Hermann Broch and about fifteen other refugees with his money and influence.

Finally, though in a mediated and ironic way, his and Mann's politics touched: a friend, Jacques Mercanton, asked him to contribute something to the review *Mass und Werk:*

> Joyce at first agreed, then remembered that Thomas Mann had stated his anti-Nazi position there in 1937, and said, "No, the review is politically oriented."
> (p. 709)

Finally, ironically, Mann became Joyce's index for his own avoidance of politics.

III

Yet the decent citizen's attempt to confront the social and political forces preying on people—that Joyce continued to share with Mann, as his efforts for refugees suggest. At the early age of nineteen he already understood, and wrote in his diary, "cruelty is weakness." And his compassion for Bloom extends to all the characters in his fiction made to suffer by circumstances.[14] Ethical orthodoxy, in Eliot's phrase, is expressed by both writers as much in the appealing foolishness of two characters whose names, interestingly, repeat each other—Bloom and Zeitblom—as in less ironic ways. The *bürgertum* that Lawrence attacked, Proust disdained, Kafka lamented, and Gide tried to deny in himself, Mann and Joyce not only acknowledged but treated sympathetically. Jeffrey M. Perl quotes Eliot's reference in "Ulysses, Order, and Myth" to "the immense panorama of futility and anarchy which is contemporary history," and remarks:

> Eliot believed, then, that Joyce's technique implied a negative judgment on modernity. It is more likely that the opposite is the case, for that method dignifies a modernity that Joyce, at any rate, saw as affirmable . . . .
> From this angle, modernism would appear to come in two basic kinds: one that contemns bourgeois modernity and one that (by and large) affirms it . . . .
> (Perl, p. 142)

Joyce and Mann derived from the urban middle class; so do most of their heroes. Since the first Romantics, the bohemian way of life has been available to all successful artists. Both firmly rejected bohemianism for participation in civil society. And the values, circumstances, and experiences of the citizen's way of life are prominent subjects in the work of both. Jameson approves *Ulysses* and its modernist author partly for that reason.[15] The title character of Mann's "Tonio Kröger" affirms his "*faiblesse* for the simple and good, the comfortably normal, the average unendowed respectable human being"; and any doubt that he is describing the *Bürger* is dispelled by the outcome of the story, especially Tonio's concluding letter to his artist friend Lisabeta Ivanovna, the source of his words above and in the following paragraphs.[16]

"Average unendowed respectable human being[s]" are precisely not artists. But the work of Joyce and Mann attests that both writers share Tonio's "*bourgeois* love of the human, the living and usual," even though "the *bourgeois* try to arrest me" and "are stupid." The translator's italics indicate his unease with our naturalized French adjective to render *bürgerlich*. Joyce remarked to Budgen of Stephen, "I haven't let this young man off very lightly, have I?" (Budgen, p. 52). He had not. But he gave Stephen bravery, integrity, potentiality; and he made Stephen, unlike most other Dubliners in *Ulysses,* free of snobbery

14. In *Irish Identity and the Literary Revival: Synge, Yeats, Joyce and O'Casey* (London: Croom, 1979), G. J. Watson discusses Joyce's "identity" with and compassion for his characters in *Dubliners* (see esp. pp. 166–67) and for Stephen in the *Portrait* (see esp. pp. 184–86, 197), as well as for the characters in *Ulysses* (see esp. pp. 240–42).

15. He contrasts "a certain conservative thought" and "that heroic fascism of the 1920s for which the so-called 'masses' and their standardised city life had become the symbol of everything degraded about modern life" to Joyce, who "was at least a populist and a plebeian. 'I don't know why the Communists don't like me,' he complained once, 'I've never written about anything but common people.' . . . Joyce's characters are all resolutely petty-bourgeois" (McCormack and Stead, p. 134; the quoted complaint probably is an inaccurate version of Joyce's comment to Eugene Jolas: see *James Joyce*, p. 5).

16. Quotations are from the translation of H. T. Lowe-Porter, in Thomas Mann, *Stories of Three Decades* (New York: Knopf, 1938). The letter is on pp. 131–32.

and bigotry toward the "simple and good, the comfortably normal, the average unendowed respectable" Leopold Bloom. Were Stephen not so, Bloom could not serve as the unwitting agent of Stephen's salvation; and—I believe Joyce would have said—Stephen would show himself unworthy of it.

Both Mann and Joyce embraced the life of family man and held fast to it; Joyce combined with it a libertarian-socialist's refusal to submit to the marriage procedures of a state and a Church he rejected. His letters and the accounts of friends document his devotion to his parents, his delight in his wife and children, and his suffering over his daughter Lucia's illness. The same—even to the illness of his son Klaus—is true of Mann, who wrote in 1920: "I am the son of a family and the father of a family by instinct and conviction. I love my children . . . [to the extent that] a Frenchman would talk of idolatry. There you have the 'bourgeois'": "da haben Sie den '*Bürger*'."[17]

Joyce's creation of Bloom can be fully understood only in this context. Like Odysseus, Bloom wants to be once again a true husband and the father of a son; and *Ulysses,* like the *Odyssey,* records the experience and trials of his wandering and his attempt to return home. Budgen is an important source of information about Joyce's conception of his character. For example, Joyce once remarked to him about Jews, "They are better husbands than we are, better fathers, and better sons" (Givens, p. 23). Of course the statement, and the concern behind it, are those of a good husband, father, and son. The intensity of his *bürgertum* is reflected in his reason for considering Jesus a less-than-perfect man:

> He was a bachelor, and never lived with a woman. Surely living with a woman is one of the most difficult things a man has to do, and he never did it. (Budgen, p. 191)

By no means "Everyman," as some critics once said, for Joyce Bloom is more "complete" (his word) a man than Jesus. And Humphrey Chimpden Earwicker, the father and husband who dreams *Finnegans Wake,* is also "Here Comes Everybody" and "Haveth Childers Everywhere."

Shortly after he and Budgen first met, Joyce announced that he was "writing a book based on the wanderings of Ulysses"; he asked if Budgen knew of "any complete all-round character presented by any writer"; and after rejecting Budgen's candidates, he gave his reasons for so regarding Odysseus. Budgen argued against Joyce's view and Joyce concluded the discussion by shifting suddenly from Homer's hero to his own: "I see him from all sides, and therefore he is all-round in the sense of your [example of a] sculptor's figure. But he is a complete man as well—a good man. At any rate, that is what I intend that he shall be" (pp. 15–18). Bloom the voyeur, masturbator, victim and fool has his other "sides"; and being a husband, a father, and a man of decent values and attitudes regarding his fellow humans, he is—quite simply—"good." Furthermore, he is distinct from "king" Odysseus in being—the point was made earlier—neither publisher, nor editor, nor star reporter, but a humble functionary. He and the

---

17. Letter of July 4, 1920 to Carl Maria Weber; *Briefe 1889–1936,* p. 178. The translation in Mann, *Letters* (pp. 104–5), lapses at one point, and I have substituted my own.

characters around him are not well-bred, not a professional or otherwise distinctive elite, not gentry in straitened circumstances, not even idealized laborers—who in real life would have been degraded by working almost all of almost every day. When likening Joyce to Mann, Levin wrote of "the commonplace," whose "delights" Mann's "wandering artist ... from Schiller to Gustav von Aschenbach, deplores his inability to enjoy"; in his "Introduction" to *James Joyce,* Ellmann applies Levin's key word to Joyce:

> The initial and determining act of judgment in his work is the justification of the commonplace. . . . Joyce was the first to endow an urban man of no importance with heroic consequence. For a long time his intention was misunderstood: it was assumed he must be writing satire. How else justify so passionate an interest in the lower middle class? . . . Joyce's discovery, so humanistic that he would have been embarrassed to disclose it out of context, was that the ordinary is the extraordinary. (p. 5)

Joyce asserts the values of civil society more radically than does Mann. He himself is reported to have expressed differently Pound's criticism of his "VERY conventional outlook," saying, "only my methods are difficult; my ideas are really quite simple."

Not just commitment to the values of civil society, but also the faithful portrayal of the citizen's life characterizes the work of both writers, at least in their earlier years. Mann portrayed business failure and the attendant shame in "Tonio Kröger," the 1922 portion of *Felix Krull,* and *Buddenbrooks.* Joyce treated the same theme in the *Portrait.* In addition, Joyce represents in all his fiction the tawdry and oppressive nature of urban middle-class life with little money: the louse-marked box in which the Dedalus family kept its pawn tickets; Lenehan the sponger; Hynes the borrower; Bloom's counting his money before deciding to make a purchase. Yet Stephen remains proud—nay, arrogant—and Bloom generous. And like them, Tonio Kröger and Felix Krull are more than their circumstances.

IV

The last element in the significant relation of Joyce and Mann I am proposing is their emphasizing this disparity, which they portray as a tension between individual and environment. Both Joyce and Mann deal repeatedly with the exceptional (male) individual growing up and then making his way in a society of ordinary people. Hans Castorp is as famous a twentieth-century *élève* and young *picaro* of this type as Stephen Dedalus. But the more extreme version of the theme, the only version treated by Joyce, also is the more usual one treated by Mann: the relation between the artist and society. The second highly relevant reference to Mann in Levin's *James Joyce* is much briefer than that quoted earlier. C.H. Peake begins (p. vii) *James Joyce: The Citizen and the Artist* (Stanford: Stanford UP, 1977) with it: "All of Joyce's books, like Thomas Mann's, fit into the broadening dialectical pattern of *Künstler* versus *Bürger*" (p. 66).

That both writers would present a true tension, and not simply an opposition, is suggested by what has been said about their similar choice and advocacy of the citizen's way of life as against the bohemian's. In his letter to Lisabeta, Tonio says:

> For if anything is capable of making a poet of a literary man, it is my bourgeois love of the human, the living and usual. It is the source of all warmth, goodness, and humour; I even almost think it is itself that love of which it stands written that one may speak with the tongues of men and of angels and yet having it not is as sounding brass and tinkling cymbals.

One need not agree with Tonio's extreme assertion that *Bürgertum* is a necessity for any writer who desires to excel, to detect in its intensity a measure of agreement by his creator.

The autobiographical elements in his creature further indicate his agreement with Tonio's civil values ("the source of all warmth, goodness, and humour"). Tonio the writer is thirteen years beyond his boyhood, and Mann was twenty-eight when the story was published; like Mann, Tonio is the son of a Latin mother and of a north-German grain-merchant father who becomes bankrupt and then dies while his son is still a boy; Mann even passed on his own "rather oblique [eye]brows": "*etwas schräg stehende Brauen.*"

Like the protagonist of Joyce's *Künstlerroman* the *Portrait,* that of Mann's *Künstlernovelle* "Tonio Kröger" has a special relationship with his creator. But there are other examples of the two authors' similar concern with the artist and his usually uncongenial society. In Mann, if one excludes minor characters and excludes as well special quasi-artist figures like Joseph and Felix Krull (even in the early story, Krull describes his career as "based on imagination and self-discipline"), Goethe, Aschenbach, and Adrian Leverkühn come readily to mind. In Joyce, there are the artist *manqué* Mr. Duffy of "A Painful Case," Gabriel Conroy of "The Dead," Richard Rowan of *Exiles,* and of course Shem the Penman of *Finnegans Wake.* While not the protagonist, as Stephen is not of *Ulysses,* he is very prominently the writer in that world. All the aritsts, in fact, are writers; and Joyce published no book—his poems excepted, of course—without one.

The similarities between "Tonio Kröger" and the *Portrait* are striking ones. In both, the subject is a boy growing up to his calling of writer, first in and then deprived of prosperous middle-class security and comfort. But even more, it is the story of that emerging writer's *experience of* himself and of the tension between him and the world that produced him. Eventually, the subject becomes the emerging writer's awareness that he must come to some accommodation with his world. Stephen's refusal—deep inability—to do so in the *Portrait,* which ends not with a wise letter but with a grandiloquent diary entry, results in his predicament at the beginning of *Ulysses,* so moving to any reader able to get beyond his dazzling cleverness. Eventually, like Tonio, he comes to accept the world and his relation to it. And like Tonio Kröger, Stephen Dedalus eventually recognizes that both the city he can only walk through—the ordinary world that belongs to the others—and those citizens to whom it belongs, living, in Tonio's words, "in blessed mediocrity," are the blood of his life and of his art.

In neither character's attitudes and judgments does his creator necessarily have his own say: both Stephen and Tonio are represented experiencing and discovering themselves and their worlds with extreme, almost dramatic autonomy. And yet the eventual realization of each young writer points back unmistakably to the creator who—despite the radically different temperament and habits Joyce gave Stephen—made his character so categorically like himself. It cannot be immaterial for the two real writers that each has his fictional writer eventually embrace his own relationship—as artist—to the mundane normal other. Each, like his creature, knows the mundane other to be totally alien because a writer is what he is; yearns for it in vain; and each (as Stephen and Tonio plan to do) celebrates and glorifies it in his work.

V

My concern has been to examine Joyce's commitment to portraying social reality, the nature of the reality he chose to portray, his attitude toward it, and the social and political values subsuming these central characteristics of his art. In the process, I have made much of Joyce's and Mann's similar social conscience and sense of citizenship, their humaneness, the decency and homely virtue of their chosen way of life. Consistent with these quiet and highly civilized excellences, both writers equated wisdom in the artist not with rejection of life as it is for a vision of what was or one day can be; nor with flamboyance or egotism; nor with (apologetic) eulogizing of a violent racist subculture; nor with fear of civil society or disdain for it—as did various of the major modernist writers mentioned. Both equated wisdom in the artist with a stoic and loving symbiosis with other people, the "comfortably normal."

For the fundamental concern of both Joyce and Mann as writers was that most serious of subjects, the nature of the life given to humankind in our civilization. Both were progressively less solemn in their treatment of it as the years passed—more comic in the limited sense of that term; and both were progressively less mordant in their view of it—more comic in the transcendent sense. Perhaps that is their fundamental relation. It certainly is the ultimate demonstration of the high degree of—I can think of no better word—civilization that, in common, these two citizens embodied in their art.

THE
INHERITANCE

8

To Criticize the Critics

These last thirty years have been, I think, a brilliant period in literary criticism in both Britain and America. It may even come to seem, in retrospect, too brilliant. Who knows?

So Eliot concluded "The Frontiers of Criticism" in 1956 before his large Minneapolis audience. Each in a different way, the next and final chapters will explore the relations of "Prufrock" and *Ulysses* to "literary criticism in both Britain and America." This chapter directly prepares for my attempt to demonstrate the function of "Prufrock" for criticism in the next; and it constitutes the general formulation behind the discussion of *Ulysses* in our world that follows.

Remarkably, in 1911 a graduate student barely into his twenties, and working in virtual isolation, created the principal harbinger/archetype of the English poetry of Modernism. In the movement that was evolving and soon prevailed, Eliot's youthful poem acquired special canonical status that persisted through most of the next half-century. In part, this was because "Prufrock" seemed perfectly suited to the objective literary criticism—and the related teaching method—that became dominant during Modernism. The title of M.H. Abrams's study of romantic criticism, *The Mirror and The Lamp* (New York: Norton, 1953), derives from the introduction to the 1936 *Oxford Book of Modern Verse*—which was edited by Yeats. He, Eliot, Joyce, and almost all the other major modernist writers had just about completed their work at mid-century, when Abrams's book was published. But not only had their artistic achievement become established in history: in addition, the criticism that developed during Modernism almost seemed, like modernist literature itself, the last word. After presenting his famous conceptual model of the four "Co-ordinates of Art Criticism"—Universe, Audience, Artist, Work—in the first chapter, Abrams described the changing emphasis in criticism from one to another of the four in turn throughout history, to a culminating stage of development in the middle of the present century:

> The evolution is complete, from the mimetic poet ... through the pragmatic poet ... to Carlyle's Poet as Hero ....

. . . But there is also a fourth procedure, the "objective orientation". . . . (p. 26)

In America, at least, some form of the objective point of view has already gone far to displace its rivals as the reigning mode of literary criticism. (p. 28)

By the time Harry Levin proposed that Modernism "Was," at the end of the decade, the reign had been established.

Although "Prufrock" seemed suited to the criticism that displaced its rivals during the modernist period, I believe it actually contravenes some of its important assumptions. The poem's function for criticism today consists in its simultaneously contravening those assumptions and vindicating the most basic assumption, against the radically opposed basic assumption of much criticism that has evolved since Levin's essay of a quarter-century ago. At issue is the assumed nature of a literary (to beg the basic question) work: is it an artifact that embodies meaning, as the modernists assumed?; or is it a sign-sequence that stimulates meaning(s), as many assume today?

Both decades of commentary on "Prufrock," and recent emphasis on the apposition of any particular reader to attributed evidence in a verbal composition, increasingly disclose cryptic elements in the poem. As a result, once confident and seemingly unassailable assertions have been transformed into questions. One has practical priority. "Prufrock" is in Eliot's second "voice" of poetry, "a tale told" by the poet "speaking through a mask." But what precisely is told through the mask as happening—what are the actual occurrences—in it? (Does Prufrock attend the party?; does he set out for it and change his mind *en route*—and if so, where?; does he set out?)

The specific question leads to a series of three general ones which have been asked, more or less consecutively, during the course of the past quarter-century, and all readily answered in the negative. Most immediate (and earliest in time): must what is happening be determinable? More abstracted and theoretical: is something definite happening in "Prufrock"—is the meaning in the words that constitute a poem determin*ate*? Finally, the ultimate and fundamental question: is meaning in it at all? Does this or any poem *have* (immanent) meaning? "Work" begs this fundamental question about literature so familiar today, because the term usually is understood to signify an entity made of language— a meaningful quasi-object.

Much of what I will be saying about the two opposed critical persuasions in the next dozen pages already has been said; but the summary conspectus of relevant criticism of the past half-century has a purpose. It makes explicit my own formulation of both the grounds of *opposition* between objective criticism and current views, and the historical *relation* between them. My historical sketch neglects prominent critics for the sake of brevity and ignores, as outside the relation, important developments in criticism concurrent with the two rich alternative theories, such as myth criticism, the "criticism of consciousness" of Georges Poulet's "Geneva School," and two that also are increasingly valuable perspectives on criticism itself, Marxist and feminist criticism.

A number of distinguished recent studies of the criticism of the past half-century accomplish aspects of the formidable historical enterprise I am not attempting. Of the many shorter ones concerned with North America's principal modernist criticism, René Wellek's "The New Criticism: Pro and Contra," in *The Attack on Literature* (Chapel Hill: U of North Carolina P, 1982) is commended by his authority—both knowledge and familiarity—on the subject. The essay succinctly relates New Criticism to both its antecedents and its successors, while providing a respectful but probing brief appraisal of it.[1] Abrams's "Literary Criticism in America: Some New Directions," in M.H. Abrams and James Ackerman, *Theories of Criticism: Essays in Literature and Art* (Washington: Library of Congress, 1984) complements it neatly with a succinct history and appraisal of more recent criticism, especially Deconstruction. These two complementary studies emphasize the substance of the opposed critical persuasions; the following two emphasize my other concern, their historical relation. In her introduction to the collection *Reader-Response Criticism: From Formalism to Post-Structuralism* (Baltimore: Johns Hopkins UP, 1980), its editor, Jane P. Tompkins, traces the evolution out of modernist criticism of that general emphasis in the newer criticism. The major part of Frank Lentricchia's *After the New Criticism* (Chicago: U of Chicago P, 1980), "A Critical Thematics: 1957–77," is a historical study of "the past two decades of critical theory in the United States" (p. xii).

I

From Aristotle's challenge to Plato twenty-two-hundred years ago, until the waning of Modernism the day before yesterday, critics' conception of a literary composition remained constant in a major respect. Implicit in the *Poetics* is the assumption that a philosopher can talk about plays and epics as Aristotle does because they are artifacts as verbal compositions can be artifacts. Like any other substance, the composition of words has an essence or entelechy, part of which is its meaning. In different phases of Western culture critics characterized the language of poetry differently, considering it mainly either propositional, or evocative—even to the extent of being, in Dante's phrase, "beyond sense"—or idiolectic (and its creator respectively sage, or mystic, or magician). But the critics agreed implicitly with Aristotle that the meaning of that language, though it may be elusive, even ineffable, is both there—immanent in the structure of words—and, *because it is immanent,* determinate.

Eventually, the romantic conception of organic form precluded a separable content/meaning. Then in the present century, "the meaning of meaning" was scrutinized, and the difference between an abstracted account of meaning and

1. Most studies of the New Criticism seem to be essentially polemical. Among exceptions, Murray Krieger's *The New Apologists for Poetry* (1956; Bloomington: Midland-Indiana UP, 1963) probably deserves pride of place. Gerald Graff's *Poetic Statement and Critical Dogma* (Evanston: Northwestern UP, 1970) is less broad-ranging and sympathetic. Wellek and Graff debate the former's essay in *Critical Inquiry* 5 (1979), 569–79. The last chapter of Frank Kermode's *Romantic Image* (New York: Macmillan, 1957) warrants mention for its relevant historical account of "the Symbolist conception of the work of art as aesthetic monad" (p. 157) in modernist criticism.

its embodied reality emphasized. But even through earlier phases of the culture, critics more-or-less shared Aristotle's assumption. And by 1953, "in America," the then "reigning mode of literary criticism" had articulated—as the second of what seem to me its two fundamental doctrines—a theoretical foundation for the previously implicit assumption that meaning is immanent in literature.

American New Criticism was in no sense a monolith; indeed, antagonists delighted in pointing out differences among its principal exponents. And while the imputations of political and religious tendentiousness in the criticism of its exponents were exaggerated, the New Critics' concerns about literature extended not only to its social value as a corrective to a technology-ridden culture, but even to its epistemological relation to science. Nevertheless, the theoretical emphasis of New Criticism was on the intrinsic nature of a literary *work*. And I am proposing that two particular related doctrines about that nature are common to the critics, and that they are fundamental as well; in any case, they are most relevant here. Both address traditional implicit assumptions, one of which has been mentioned.

The more prominent pillar of the then "new," carefully "ontological," American criticism (John Crowe Ransom's terms, though the first was misapplied), was the general modernist one that—although undeniably an "act," a "telic thing" both made and read—"a poem is analogously an object" (W. K. Wimsatt's). Like the assumption that meaning is both immanent in a work and determinate, the implicit assumption that, although both made and read, a literary work has autonomous integrity as a quasi-object, is as Aristotelian as it is modernist; this is so even though neither Aristotle, nor any critics from the time the effective influence of the *Poetics* began in the Renaissance to the early twentieth century, had bothered to declare that the autonomy of the poem or story "must be hypostatized."[2] What is new is the hypostasis as a concept and fundamental doctrine. The other pillar of the dyad I am proposing, the fundamental doctrine in modernist objective criticism which had been newly articulated by the American New Critics (drawing on I.A. Richards and others), was their *theoretical foundation for* the traditional assumption that meaning in "poetry" (a term usually signifying more than verse composition: for example, Wimsatt defines "poetry" as "literature in its most intensive instances" [*Verbal Icon*, p. xv]) is both immanent and determinate.

First, they distinguished the literary work, as an object made of words, from both real objects on one hand and the conventional functioning of language on the other: a poem or story is not Plato's bed, and it is not an instruction sheet— or a critical essay—but a unique artifact, a quasi-object. Then, they seem to have grounded their insistence on the particular objective status of literature very largely, though seldom explicitly, on a theory of language. Their interest is literary, not linguistic; and the theory concerns language not generally, but in lit-

---

2. "The poem conceived as a thing in between the poet and the audience is of course an abstraction. The poem is an act. . . . But if we are to lay hold of the poetic act to comprehend and evaluate it, and if it is to pass current as a critical object, it must be hypostatized." W. K. Wimsatt, *The Verbal Icon* (Louisville: U of Kentucky P, 1954), p. xvii. The Chicago "Neo-Aristotelian" critics' emphasis on "wholes" expresses the connection between Aristotle and the modernist critics; see n.7.

erature. It might be expressed briefly as follows. In a literary work, the arrangement of words is not a stimulus to (vehicle of) one's cognition of its meaning. The meaning in the language is the *manifestation* of one's cognition of it: it is right there in the arranged sounds or the printed, and silently sounded, shapes; it is there solely because apprehended—but when it is apprehended in them the meaning is there, immanent, much as energy is immanent in matter (potential) though manifest only when it becomes operative (kinetic).[3]

Of course, the two pillars reinforce each other. Their meaning once apprehended, the meaningful arranged sounds or shapes therefore constitute a formal entity. Conversely, the autonomous object actually is an articulate structure of words—an artifact whose mode of existence is meaning. The appellation "New Criticism" was inept (more so than "Modernism" for the genus) even before it was anachronistic; "Formalist-Cognitive Criticism" may be cumbersome, but it designates what seem to me to be the linked fundamental doctrines of that criticism. And the broad modernist consensus about this bi-parous conception of literature is suggested by the opening and closing lines of MacLeish's familiar poetical *ars poetica* of that title: "palpable and mute / As a globed fruit," a poem should neither say nor merely "mean / But [cognitively] be."

A poem is an autonomous structure of words existing in the cognition of that meaningful structure. An object not physically but cognitively, an apprehended formal entity, a system, the poem is a functioning "heterocosm" or "verbal icon" whose lineaments and adornments properly monopolize the critic's attention. And since it not merely imparts but is (among other things it is) meaning, meaning in it undoubtedly is both immanent and (ideally) determinate. This conception of literature, articulated in formalist-cognitive criticism, became the prevailing one during the period "Prufrock" helped to inaugurate. As will be shown, "Prufrock" does not fully confirm it.

Aristotle's mimetic *poiesis* (Work about the Universe in Abrams's terms) effectively displaced Plato's poem as expression/evocation of the appearance of an illusion. Throughout literary history thereafter, critics generally emphasized Audience and then Artist, until with Modernism those two of Abrams's "coordinates" were jointly challenged and shortly after mid-century eclipsed by the objective one. But now, as the century wanes, most major varieties of critical theory constitute their parabolic joint reinstatement.

This historical evolution simultaneously is a radical change. The full development of objective criticism in France and North America prepared the ground, dialectically, for a revolution. Those pragmatic and expressive (rhetor-

---

3. For example, in his 1941 essay, "Literature as Knowledge," Allen Tate builds on Coleridge, Richards, and Charles Morris the argument that poetry does not impart but embodies—is—knowledge:

> It is neither the world of verifiable science nor a projection of ourselves; yet it is *complete*. . . . it is complete knowledge . . . . It's "interest" value is a cognitive one; it is sufficient that here, in the poem, we get knowledge of a whole object . . . . I have been concerned . . . with . . . a formed realm of our experience, the distinction of which is its complete knowledge . . . .

The poem can "be" knowledge only if meaning is immanent in the language. Quoted from *The Man of Letters in the Modern World: Selected Essays: 1928–1955* (New York: Meridian, 1955), pp. 62–63.

ical) theories again ascendant after half a century also in effect propose—after two millennia—to restore Plato's insubstantial image.

Abstractly, the change from the habitual modernist reference to a "work," to current use of the French/linguistic word "text," is the substitution of a neutral term for a question-begging one. In fact (that is to say, historically), that substitution has proved the vehicle for the revolutionary challenge to the traditional Aristotelian myth that meaning in literature has objective (real) status, by the regenerated Platonic myth that it is subjective (ideal). Alternative myths they are—either one fully believed by most critics, neither one apparently provable. The issue seems part of our *Zeitgeist:* it invokes the general, epistemological question of the relation of knower to what is known, and has analogues not only in the alternative "God's truth" and "hocus-pocus" views of the structure of language, but also in the alternative conceptions of mathematics as "discovered" ("God-given mathematics") and "invented."[4] Although neither Aristotle nor Plato often is mentioned in these current debates, opposed reference to "realism" and either "conceptualism" or "idealism" usually occurs.

My purpose is not to participate in the current debate about criticism, but to prepare the ground for an attempt to show how "Prufrock" arbitrates the alternative conceptions of meaning and literature that are at its center. The historical relation between those conceptions is dialectical because, although opposed to each other, they are a linked sequence.[5] Considered retrospectively, the revolution had a smooth passage; for there was more than one serpent in the modernist heterocosm.

Perhaps the most important culprit is illustrated by the 1949 Bollingen Prize for Poetry. It was awarded to Pound's *Pisan Cantos* (over Williams's *Paterson*), even as civilized imaginations still were boggled by that unique technology by which the Thousand-year Reich implemented its policy toward Jewish, Gypsy, homosexual, Red Army and other populations (the cogent reports of which engineering achievement had been disbelieved in high places until confirmed by the advancing Allied armies). To some opponents of the award it seemed to express the social and political biasses of many modernist writers and critics. Defenders of it maintained that poetry does not mean, but is—works of literature are articulate heterocosms, autonomous ("aesthetic") artifacts, as *literature* not significant beyond themselves. The anti-Semites and reactionaries in a developing political albatross-cult that adopted Pound may have had other reasons; but the distinguished (and humane) poets who made the award, one of them Pound's

4. See, e.g., review by Fred W. Householder, Jr., of Zellig S. Harris, *Methods in Structural Linguistics* (Chicago: U of Chicago P, 1951), *International Journal of American Linguistics,* 18 (1952), 260–68, 260; André Martinet, "Structure and Language," *Structuralism,* ed. Jacques Ehrmann (New York: Anchor, 1970), pp. 1–9, p. 7; and Allan Calder, "Constructive Mathematics," *Scientific American,* 241 (October, 1979), pp. 146–71 (the quoted phases are on p. 146).

5. The relation between them has been argued effectively by a number of critics, including Lentricchia. One instance exemplifies the value of Marxism as a perspective on other criticism. In "From New Criticism to Deconstruction: The Example of Charles Feidelson's *Symbolism and American Literature,*" *American Quarterly* 36 (1984), 44–64, Barbara Foley shows an "affinity between the two critical schools" (p. 45) in their common denial of a work's (referential) *mimesis* of reality, and of its (external) connections in history.

friend and the creator of "Prufrock," needed none.[6] In the words of their citation of *The Pisan Cantos,* they were simply eschewing "other considerations than that of poetic achievement" in the "objective perception of value." Almost four decades later, in "The Golden Albatross" (*American Scholar* 55 [1985/86], 77–96), Karl Shapiro commented on the doctrine as well as the award he alone dissented from, by ironically echoing his fellow committee member Auden on an even more distinguished poet with objectionable politics, Pound's older friend. The others were "giving the Prize to an Ezra Pound . . . because . . . it was all right for poets to favor gassing Jews because they said that poetry makes nothing happen" (94). But in 1949 most of the opponents of the decision, over whom their modernist doctrine prevailed, normally shared the doctrine.

Of course, the modernist critics did not originate emphasizing the idiolectic dimension of literature at the expense of its mimetic dimension. The formalist-cognitive critics' own account of its history back through the aesthetes and the *symbolistes'* "aesthetic monad" to Coleridge and Kant is familiar. Coleridge's "willing suspension of disbelief" can be seen as a suppression of its own mimetic dimension that the reader is prepared to be cajoled into by the work; and Kant's no less famous phrase from the *Critique of Judgment, "zwecklichkeit ohne zweck,"* asserts a legitimating principle for the hermetic conception of literature.

Nevertheless, it was a fundamental doctrine among modernist critics, though a few—such as Trilling and Leavis—modified it. And the general insistence of those objective critics that the meaning in a literary work is hermetically isolated from its referential and propositional significance smoothed the passage to current critics' more radical modifications of its status.

Certain specific formalist-cognitive doctrines did so as well. An obvious one (which again designates a unique status for meaning in works of literature) is "the heresy of paraphrase." The categorical principle that a poem ultimately is untranslatable follows from its status as a distinct entity; however, a doctrine specifying that accounts of meaning in a work inevitably are inadequate to the unique meaningful artifact itself, provided a bridge to two sequent denials: first, that meaning ever is determinable; and then, that meaning resides in language at all.

Two other implicated formalist-cognitive doctrines concern not the unparaphraseable nature of the words of the hypostatized objective Work, or its relation with the Universe the words mention, but its relation with each of Abrams's remaining "co-ordinates" respectively: the doctrine that denies relevance to authorial intention; and the one that postulates an "ideal" reader. Their sensitive and thoughtful proponents never claimed that the concept of an Intentional Fallacy and that of an Ideal Reader were True in the absolute sense, but offered them as procedurally useful for criticism. The challenges to which both manifestly were vulnerable, are part of the history.

In the former case, formalist-cognitive critics distinguished "the designing

---

6. The other members of the award committee were Conrad Aiken, W. H. Auden, Louise Bogan, Robert Lowell, Karl Shapiro, Allen Tate, and Robert Penn Warren. Only Shapiro voted against the award, but Tate implicitly challenged William Barrett to a duel on the grounds that Barrett had accused him (the committee) of anti-Semitism. Eliot's pre-war anti-Semitism was a complication.

intellect as a *cause* of a poem" from "the design or intention as a *standard*," in the words and emphasis of "The Intentional Fallacy." Promptly, the no-less-objective Chicago "Neo-Aristotelians" pointed out the relevance to the nature of a work of its genre—and the consequent connection between the "causal" intention of its author, and the generic affinity of her or his product.[7] To be strictly consistent in regarding a writer's conception of genre as antecedent and external, fully disposed of by the essay's initial "axiom" that a poem "come[s] out of a head, not out of a hat," is to neglect the particular sonnetness, for example, of a sonnet, which was not made so as an undifferentiated poem.

Thereafter, the useful critical procedure of ignoring that "the poem is an act" (Wimsatt) was challenged frequently. In *Validity in Interpretation* (New Haven: Yale UP, 1967), E.D. Hirsch, Jr. offered a direct refutation; he designated—literally—authority over "*Meaning* . . . which . . . is what the author meant" (p. 8): "For once the author had been ruthlessly banished as the determiner of his text's meaning . . . the study of 'what a text says' became the study of what it says to an individual critic . . . . What had not been noticed . . . was that the text had to represent *somebody's* meaning—if not the author's, then the critic's" (p. 3).

Hirsch's concern, like that of the advocates of what he called "authorial irrelevance," was to guard the integrity of meaning in a literary "text" against critical (hermeneutic) relativism. But ironically, the concurrent advocacy of critical *pluralism*—by Roland Barthes, Susan Sontag, and others—on the grounds that an objective explication of meaning is impossible (meaning is not determinable) in any case, was reinforced by his charge that the formalist-cognitive "theory of semantic autonomy" from the author's intention provided "no adequate principle . . . for judging the validity of an interpretation" (p. 3).[8]

The historical effect of the challenge to the formalist-cognitive concept of an Ideal Reader, by critics who accepted that meaning in a poem or story is not only immanent and determinate, but also (ideally) determinable, was similarly ironic. Arguing that the doctrine was untenable because contrary to reality, in one case advocating purposeful ("creative") misreading, they promoted the very critical relativism against which the Ideal Reader concept was, in Cleanth Brooks's phrase, "a defensible strategy."[9]

---

7. For example, R. S. Crane describes criticism as "an inquiry into the specific characters . . . and . . . elements, of possible kinds of poetic wholes, leading to an appreciation, in individual works, of how well their writers have accomplished the . . . tasks which the natures of the wholes . . . imposed on them." "Introduction," *Critics and Criticism, Ancient and Modern* (Chicago: U of Chicago P, 1952), p. 13. Frye writes, "One may pursue the centripetal intention as far as genre, as a poet intends to produce, not simply a poem, but a certain kind of poem" (*Anatomy*, pp. 86–87).

8. Another critic who attacked the concept of an Intentional Fallacy for the purpose of promoting values (then) shared with the Formalist-Cognitive critics, was Paul de Man. In "Form and Intent in the American New Criticism," the second chapter of *Blindness and Insight,* he claimed that "suppression of its intentional character" distorts the nature of a literary "text," because while intention may be irrelevant as a psychological fact, it has crucial relevance as a structuring power (see esp. pp. 24–27).

9. See Cleanth Brooks, "The Formalist Critics," *Kenyon Review* 13 (1951), 72–81, 75. That Harold Bloom does not deny determinate meaning to poetry is indicated by the prefix of "misreading."

Addressing himself to "the exact place in history where we find ourselves" a decade after Abrams published his descriptive diagram of co-ordinates, Wimsatt proposed a "tensional" theory as a corrective to inadequacies in formalist-cognitive criticism. The tensional conception of a work would resolve the centrifugal claims of the four co-ordinates by integrating them; Wimsatt's prescriptive diagram has his tensional theory at the center of two perpendicular axes, with the four co-ordinates at their extreme ends. The vertical axis is "Genetic"-"Affective"; the horizontal and principal axis is mimetic-objective (for one end his terms are "Contentual" and "Didactic," for the other, "Formal" and "Stylistic").[10] But "a new turn in poetic taste" had occurred, in the words of Wellek's essay, and "attempts to dismiss T. S. Eliot both as poet and critic and to reduce the role of all modernism imply a rejection of the New Criticism also" (p. 101). Critics were beginning to move from Wimsatt's horizontal axis to his vertical one, and a critical consensus to become more remote than ever.

II

By the time Wimsatt published his corrective to formalist-cognitive theory, some critics in France and North America had not just denied that the meaning in literature is positively determinable, but rejected the belief that any "sign-sequence" has determinate meaning. Their doctrine derived, of course, from the attitude toward language and meaning propounded in the newly revived structural linguistics of the Swiss pioneer, Ferdinand de Saussure.

From the Structuralist principle that social phenomena are understood not by the specific content of their elements or instances, but in their relations, it follows that "language is a form and not a substance." (Barthes and others argued against determinable meaning partly on this basis.) And Saussure specified the relations constituting that "form" in his doctrine that every verbal structure is a sequence of signs having two components, the signifying set of (sounds or) shapes and the mental events they signify—*signifiant* and *signifié*—and having only those two. The reading of the "sign sequence" involves no immediate connection beyond the shapes and the mind experiencing them: nothing outside the reader's mind is implicated in reading. Although the *user* of language normally is being referential, the *experience* of it is only a response-thought, a *signifié* generated in the mind—evoked—by the *signifiant* read. The thesis is neatly expressed in the hermetic autonomy—root *sign* with two conjunctive suffixes—of this "lexicon of signification" (Barthes).

Since the two-part signs are autonomous structures—rely on no (necessarily external) referent, literary "texts" are hermetically sealed off from referential meaning not because of any claimed special status as "aesthetic" artifacts, but *a priori:* language may embody referential meaning, but *as apprehended* it does not refer; it stimulates mental events (based on prior experience). Simultane-

10. In "Horses of Wrath: Recent Critical Lessons," which is based on three essays, published in 1956, 1958, and 1962. It is printed in *Hateful Contraries* (Lexington: U of Kentucky P, 1966), pp. 3–48. See esp. pp. 33–48. The quotation is on p. 48.

ously, Saussure's doctrine raises the experiencing mind to correlative status with the experienced language in a stimulus-response model. And therefore it makes the free-floating, subjectively apprehended, meaning indeterminate.

However, only a short step has been required to negotiate the recent passage from the structuralist doctrine that a totally autonomous and indeterminate meaning is signified in language, to the doctrines called—with historical appropriateness—post-structuralist. Jacques Derrida's doctrine of *différance* (deferment as well as distinction of meaning) displaces the structuralist concept that all discourse (Saussure's *parole,* Chomsky's *performance*) is an instance of a controlling language-structure *(langue, competence),* with a concept of writing as itself productive of its meaning, each text a *"monde de signes sans faute, sans vérité, sans origine"* (*"il n' y a rien hors du texte"*). Still, for Derrida and the deconstructionist critics, as for Saussure and the structuralists, the meaning of language may be undetermined (by reference or even by language-structure), but it inheres in the stimulating sign-sequence itself. Hence, while for them paradoxes/ironies cannot be ultimately resolved by a critic's emulation of the Ideal Reader, because contending significations are simply not assimilable to a unitary Reading, the careful teasing out of meanings *in* the text—made familiar by modernist critical practice—abides in much (especially American) deconstructionist criticism.

This is not the case with a second post-structuralist doctrine: that response, the mental event, itself *composes* meaning. Quarantined against external implication in the "globed fruit" of the literary *work* by the modernist critics—hence the case of the *Pisan Cantos*—that wholly immanent meaning was first called indeterminable by critical pluralists, then totally isolated in literary—because in all—*texts* from any determining external referentiality by the French structural linguists, then made inexhaustible by certain post-structuralists, and finally eliminated by other post-structuralists.

III

Post-structuralist conceptions of the relation of language and meaning in literature developed out of the structuralist one, which was founded on Saussure's doctrine that language is apprehended as a structure of hermetic two-part signs. Setting aside that all reality is known as the mental experience of it, the mental act (Saussure's signifié) must be conceptual—"idea"—since it is not referential. But poems and stories are neither round nor tree-borne nor edible: "globed fruit" is both an image and the instrumental part (Richards's "vehicle") of a trope. And with their affection for imagery and tropes, modernists might object that Saussure's doctrine is refuted by the way imagery actually works: it does not work conceptually. That I would share their objection is relevant, in part because the structuralist misrepresentation of the way imagery works corresponds to the modernist misrepresentation of the way allusion works; and with the eloquent example of "Prufrock," I shall object to that in the next chapter.

Most discussion of imagery involves its role in metaphor. The extensive attention of philosophers, linguists, literary critics, and psychologists has emphasized the creation of metaphor (Aristotle first addressed this); the process of understanding it; and its truth-value. My concern is limited to a different question: What makes metaphor *effective?* The basis for my objection to the structuralist view of language (and the analogous modernist view of allusion) is the way imagery seems to work to make metaphor so.

A recent contribution by Paul Ricoeur to "the somewhat boundless field of metaphor theory" characterizes the image as accomplishing "the *picturing function* of metaphorical meaning" in "a pictorial or iconic moment." The moment is not strictly cognitive but more broadly psychological, as his title suggests: "The Metaphorical Process as Cognition, Imagination and Feeling." And by the last word he does not mean an emotional reaction, but something akin to what Eliot meant by it: "Feelings . . . are interiorized thoughts" which "accompany and complete the work of imagination as schematizing a synthetic operation . . . ."[11] Ricoeur is concerned with making and understanding metaphors, not with the source of their effectiveness. But he insists that their images are apprehended in a "synthetic operation" of "cognition, imagination and feeling." I shall not presume to make an equally authoritative assertion, but attest instead that, for me (in me), an image is effective, and so endows a metaphor employing it with its effectiveness, because my apprehension of the image is just such an inclusive—"synthetic"—activity.

When I apprehend an image, it does not simply signify. Instead, it functions in me precisely imagistically: it transcends the hermetic complex of signifier-signified to invoke—as experience, immediately and directly—the vicarious equivalent of the bit of experienced reality it names. Not just "cognition" occurs, but also something like "imagination and feeling." This seems to be so for other readers, too. Hence, the *power to function as image* of any image in literature is coextensive with the experience—in fact or imagination—of the bit of reality the image names. An image that is universally effective is so not because its words are universally understood, but because they invoke a community of experience.

On the first page of a classic work of modernist criticism, which also influenced greatly the later development being recapitulated here, *Seven Types of Ambiguity* (1930; rev. ed. London: Chatto, 1947), William Empson discusses his slight elaboration of a common specimen sentence, "The brown cat sat on the red mat." Are one's experienced instances of brownness-and-catness/redness-and-matness merely coalesced in mental acts? How can an image function effectively in a metaphor (for example: "as it set, the sun laid a red mat on the lawn"), if the reality-as-object-of-sensory-experience that the image names is not *invoked?* It is *actual* (the reality of) red-matness that transforms the equation *in* language into an experience *of* language. Indeed, when Othello says, without imagery, "But yet the pity of it, Iago! O Iago, the pity of it, Iago!," is the effective

11. In *Critical Inquiry,* 5 (1978), 143–59; the quotations are on pp. 143, 144, 145, and 156, respectively. It is reprinted in *On Metaphor,* ed. Sheldon Sacks (Chicago: U of Chicago P [Phoenix], 1979), pp. 141–57. Ricoeur's distinguished book *La métaphore vive* is translated as *The Rule of Metaphor* (Toronto: U of Toronto P, 1977).

meaning of the repeated phrase merely what the words signify? Or is, instead, the human experience relevant to the represented life of the play invoked to supply what mental act would never discover in the simple phrase of four words and five syllables?

Whatever the merits of my testimony, to resist the hermetic view of language marks one as decidely *ancien régime.* The objective criticism of literary Modernism dialectically implemented a historical development that first promoted the doctrine of indeterminable meaning in a poem or story, then rejected determinate ("metaphysical" in a term of deconstruction) meaning, then denied that language has any immanent meaning at all, and so enabled (in the idiom of phenomenology) "The production of the meaning of literary texts."[12]

The revolution seems to have crested. In *Is There a Text in This Class?* (Cambridge: Harvard UP, 1980), Stanley Fish declared:

> No longer is the critic the humble servant of texts whose glories exist independently ... ; it is what he does that brings texts into being .... (p. 368)

Fish's title is a student's question to a colleague, elucidated, "I mean in this class do we believe in poems and things, or is it just us?" (p. 305). The information is characteristic: his discussion of one's "beliefs" about a text ("I spend most of my time ... fielding questions that sound disconcertingly like objections from my former self") constitutes a witty, humane, and intelligent endeavor to justify "a persuasion model" in which "critical activity is constitutive of its object"— an endeavor to justify the contemporary myth that meaning is not immanent in the *text*—against its venerable contrary myth, which maintains that "critical activity is controlled" by the *work* (pp. 364–65).

Although by no means uniquely, "Prufrock" nevertheless tangibly discredits the contemporary denial of immanent meaning to poem or novel, as I hope to show in the next chapter. In the last chapter, I hope to show that this doctrine is the latest form of the dominant tradition of *Ulysses* criticism, and that the alternative tradition is more faithful to what Joyce wrought.

---

12. Quoted from Wolfgang Iser, "The Reading Process: A Phenomenological Approach," in Tompkins, pp. 50–69, p. 68. It is reprinted from his *The Implied Reader: Patterns of Communication in Prose Fiction from Bunyan to Beckett* (Baltimore: Johns Hopkins UP, 1974). The evolution in "reader-response" criticism Tompkins traces, in the course of introducing the selections in her volume, corresponds to the more general history given here. For example: "Michael Riffaterre shares with [Walker] Gibson and [Gerald] Prince the assumption that literary meaning resides in the language of the text, but he attacks the idea that meaning exists independently of the reader's relation to it" (p. xiii); "What Wolfgang Iser sees when he examines the same process is ... a reader actively participating in the production of textual meaning .... But he does not grant the reader autonomy ... from textual constraints" (p. xv); "The next event in the drama ... is that ... the reader's activity is declared to be *identical with* the text .... Stanley Fish [is] the first critic to propose this theory of reading .... Meaning, according to Fish, is ... an experience one has in the course of reading" (p. xvi).

9

The Function of "Prufrock" for Criticism

I. Is There a Work in This Text?

It was pointed out in the second chapter (pp. 39–40) that only one of Eliot's early poems is a direct verbal enactment of the process itself of consciousness, and that the poem rendering J. Alfred Prufrock's uninterrupted thought anticipated the most sensational, and famous, instance of the use of a special narrative method to represent the events of psychological reality. In both "Prufrock" and Molly's soliloquy, the verbal "stream" portrays an inner conflict, and in both cases, the conflict is crucial—because its issue is fundamental to the character's destiny. Finally, as in most persuasive attempts to represent consciousness, in both cases the process of the character's consciousness is associational.

Hence, "I" says "Let us go . . . when," then "Let us go, through," then "Let us go and make our visit" to "the room," with "the women" inside, and "the yellow fog" outside. Committed to the character's associational process by the method, an author can endow his or her portrayal with coherence and teleology only by digging, discreetly, a channel for the character's stream—only by employing controlling devices not *relinquished in* the method.

Some controlling devices are compatible with the character's process of consciousness because their function is indistinguishable from it. The two paragraph breaks between his proposing the visit and describing the fog also are hiatuses in Prufrock's thought; the satiric, soon repeated, jingly, *go/Michelangelo* couplet also is Prufrock's mental play. But other devices remain compatible with the character's process although distinctly the author's product.

The difference can be illustrated in Joyce's chapter. The eight typographical units in which he disposed Molly's soliloquy, whose relations to each other impose form and direction on her paratactic reflections, also act as naturally occurring shifts in her thought and so are an indistinguishable controlling device. But the point in her reflections at which the chapter begins and the point at which it ends are clearly the author's *selection from* his character's ostensibly longer stream of thought, and *imposition of* significant form, that makes a portion of Molly's stream function as the final component of Joyce's novel. She is unaware of her creator's selection, so one's distinguishing *his* product from *her* process is not a naive attempt to separate the form of her soliloquy from its content; it is recognizing that a telic design informs a character's discourse *totally innocent of such design.*

The young Eliot was resourceful in informing Prufrock's process with controlling devices both indistinguishable and clearly distinct from it. And the telic design that makes the poem (his product) out of its discourse (his character's thought process as a composition of language) also illuminates the critical dispute about language and meaning in literature. I believe that it shows "Prufrock" to be no mere sign-sequence stimulating mental acts that create different meanings in different readers or at different times, but a quasi-object constituted by its immanent meaning.

Two theoretical challenges to this assertion about any literary work can be anticipated. Like the separation of form from content, the pure Cartesian separation of apprehending-subject from the object apprehended is naive: as Georges Poulet observed, every thought is a thought about something. But it does not follow that the subject *creates* the object: so long as no one has successfully disproven that a community of discourse to some extent constrains, and directs, the apprehension of language, the subject-object relation does not signify that nothing definite can be said about meaning associated with a literary work. Put simply: even if some combinations of words can mean (or be taken to mean) many things, there are countless more things that any combination of words cannot mean (or be taken to mean). The issue is, strictly, whether Eliot's composition of words is a stimulating sign-sequence or a meaningful quasi-object—the precise *nature* of the subject-object relation when a poem is read.

The second challenge is the charge of circularity: of assuming "Prufrock" to be "out there" as more than a stimulus of black marks on white paper, even while drawing evidence from it to make that case against the currently popular denial that any more substantial entity *can* exist. But no such a priori assumption has been relied on. Instead, the modernist doctrine will be shown to provide a more adequate account of Eliot's poem—to accommodate more of its characteristics, whether the marks on paper be stimulus or cognitive entity—than the current alternative doctrine. And the phrase "its characteristics" will be shown to refer, in some cases, to elements as substantial as the margins on this page.

The initial controlling device with which Eliot informs Prufrock's process of thought is distinct from it simply because that process has not yet begun. Whether they embody their meaning or merely stimulate it, the words "The Love Song of J. Alfred Prufrock" introduce Eliot's poem. Like the title Joyce gave his novel, the title Eliot gave "Prufrock" is a key to significant relations in it. Two equal-length strikingly incongruous phrases mediated by a brief genitive preposition, the title announces Prufrock's immobilizing predicament; in addition, it indicates the three principal forms of the (indistinguishable) controlling device Eliot used to emphasize Prufrock's inability (like a patient etherized) to overcome his predicament. The title embodies frustrated expectation, binary opposition, and chiasmus. And these are the principal forms of Eliot's indistinguishable controlling device: the first two are stylistic tropes of vacillation and equivocation, the third, of return or inertia.

Instances of their use in the poem come readily to mind (the two lines beginning "In a minute" combine all three); but it is the ubiquity of this stylistic complex that identifies it as a controlling device, Eliot's product. For example, in the first verse paragraph: "Let us go"—not now but "when"; you—and (the opposition is yet to emerge) I; the conventional romantic reference to the evening sky—and the unexpected completing simile; the streets which do not invite going—but repel it; half-deserted—those streets mutter; they do not lead—they follow; like an argument tedious—but insidious; (chiastically, "a tedious argument" ends the line before "Of insidious intent); following—they lead; not "us"—but "you"; and the question that "you" is told not to ask—is put.

The stylistic pattern does not demonstrate the deconstructionist proposition that all sign-sequences subvert their meaning. It is Eliot's telic design for making his poem express *formally* the crucial meaning the poem portrays—that the process of Prufrock's consciousness is a doomed psychomachia. Hence, an important binary opposition is not semantic but spatial. Carrying forward both the literal meaning of *fondo* in the epigraph and its figurative tenor of "hell," the street, "here on the floor," the "floors" of seas (and "drown"), all associated with Prufrock, are opposed to the room with "one" upstairs and to the mermaids "riding . . . on the waves." The action of his ascending and descending the stairs is related, and so by extension is the "lift[ing] and drop[ping]" of a question.

Two other major controlling devices enabling Eliot to shape his product in Prufrock's process are prosody in the poem and, most important for the question of the relation of language and meaning in literature, his formal arrangement of his character's stream of consciousness.

Couplet rhyme and variants of it—triplets, one couplet or two in an envelope rhyme—ends the great majority of the lines. People do not think—or normally even speak aloud—in rhymed couplets; but the mere presence of a prosodic pattern in a poem could be no more than convention. The first three paragraphs of "Prufrock" assert that its prosody is not conventional, but functions positively: as the index of a controlling presence.

In the first paragraph, "an overwhelming question" is followed by three dots, a conventional mark for interruption that Eliot uses elsewhere in "Prufrock" and in other early poems. All the other lines form couplets except the third, which presents the unexpected and shocking simile. The second paragraph is the jingly couplet. The third breaks the poem's pattern of couplet rhyme temporarily, but substitutes a metrical pattern for it. The arch proto-imagist cleverness of its fog-cat (presumably Eliot's earliest cat poetry) can be attributed to Prufrock; but Eliot informs Prufrock's extended metaphor with a pattern of iambic lines. The first two lines accentuate the established tight regularity of couplets by repeating the five final syllables "(-on) the windowpanes," but combine with the accentuated regularity, in opposition, iambic heptameter—which is inherently *un*stable. The latter five lines alternate iambic pentameter and hexameter. And to reinforce his controlling presence, again the poet made the third line irregular.

Prosodic pattern functions as a controlling device most emphatically at the single place in "Prufrock" where Eliot temporarily suspends it; and there, as will be shown, it functions in combination with his ordering of the parts of the poem.

His most overt means of ordering the parts is refrain. Refrain in the poem is indistinguishable from his character's natural thought process, as when Prufrock repeats "Let us go" three times in the first paragraph; yet Eliot makes it a controlling device. When the couplet second paragraph recurs as the fifth, the paragraphs bracketing it have the repeated phrase "there will be time" and numerous other repetitions of the word "time." This verbal refrain emphasizes the common subject of the fourth and sixth paragraphs, and links them. The refrain couplet between them, which also occupies the central position in the first three paragraphs, thereby functions in a symmetrical grouping of paragraphs four through six and creates another (retroactively) of one through three; once registered, it is reinforced by the symmetrical pattern in which paragraphs describing a respectively anaesthetized, and foggy, crepuscular exterior bracket a couplet tersely specifying a contrasting interior. The controlling device remains indistinguishable. Even the refrain couplet central to both sets of three paragraphs is precipitated by Prufrock's thought first of making "our visit," then of taking "a toast and tea."

Not individual verses, but verse paragraphs, are the significant formal elements of "Prufrock." The next three paragraphs are unified by the phrases "I have known" and "how should I" (and by "know" and "should"). And the last nine paragraphs in the poem are grouped like the first nine in three sets of three, although this is achieved less by refrain than by other means. (Refrain phrases are used only in the latter two paragraphs of the fourth set, and not at all in the fifth and last sets.) The last set of three concerns the mermaids, and is introduced by the line "I have heard the mermaids singing, each to each." The fifth set, which concludes with that line, is Prufrock's appraisal of his present condition and future prospects.

That fifth set is all, appropriately, in the indicative mood (mode). The verb forms that record the process of Prufrock's "love song" evolve in a pattern conforming to and so reinforcing Eliot's disposition of most of the poem into two clusters, each with three sets of three paragraphs.

The ambiguous "Let us go *then*" aside, the verbs in the first three paragraphs all are present indicative. Those in the second set of three are future indicative, with general statements and the question "Do I dare?" in the historical present. The third set combines the present perfect indicative—in which Prufrock reviews his chronic situation—with the more malleable subjunctive mood, in which he poses the question "should I?" The fourth set—first of the second cluster—repeats the combination of the third, except that the subjunctive is no longer used as possibility, but as conditional contrary-to-fact ("would it have been worth . . . /If one . . . /Should"). The fifth set perpetuates the chiastic symmetry in two ways: like the second, it is future indicative, with general statements in the historical present; and its final paragraph devolves significantly the question repeated in the corresponding final paragraph of the second set—"*Do I dare* to eat a peach?" Following the denial of a better prospect ("I do not think that they will sing to me"), the last set completes the chiastic pattern by reasserting in the present *perfect* indicative the constancy of Prufrock's unaltered predicament.[1]

That its paragraphs are the significant formal elements of the poem, and are disposed in sets of three, is confirmed by the pattern of paragraph lengths: a number are, in effect, stanzas. The mode is announced in the first paragraph, which is 12 lines. Thereafter: the second set of three is a couplet bracketed by two 12-line paragraphs; the third set is a sequence of 6-, 7-, and 8-line paragraphs; and the fourth set consists of 12-line paragraphs. That this quasi-stanza pattern is functional is suggested by its absence—in conjunction with the absence of refrain—in the two concluding sets of paragraphs.

If Eliot's strict ordering by mutually reinforcing patterns of prosody, paragraphing, refrain, and verb form were obtrusive, his poem would be as pedantic and dull as this recapitulation. He made the ordering devices indistinguishable, assimilated their working into Prufrock's process. His reasons for the whole enterprise are indicated by the bit of the poem he excluded from the pair of clusters of three subsets of three paragraphs: the tenth and eleventh paragraphs, set between the two nine-paragraph clusters. It is in those two central short paragraphs of different lengths that he makes prosodic pattern function most by suspending it (he avoids refrain as well).

That they embody a definitive development in Prufrock's story, in two stages having a familiar pattern, is indicated by the respective tenses of the two paragraphs. The first follows the set of three paragraphs reiterating the subjunctive "should I"; and it comprises a single future *indicative* question: "Shall I say . . . ?" The second returns to the subjunctive. And here "should" expresses neither the possibility expressed in the set of three paragraphs preceding it, nor the conditional contrariness to fact of the set following it, but the psychological bridge from aspiration to rationalization: complaint. It specifies a preferable alternative the desolate nature of which, conveyed at the center of the poem as much by "scuttling" and "silent" as by the crab image itself, eliminates doubt either about the futility of his "love song" or about his destiny.

The third and fourth sets of paragraphs are grammatically alike, and so are the second and second-from-last sets; even the functional difference of simple and perfect, in the present indicative of the first and last sets, is slight. This minor symmetry, and the major symmetry that disposes the 20 paragraphs in two clusters of three sets of three with one plus one between them at the center,

1. Elisabeth Schneider discusses the relation between "the changing moods and tenses of verbs" and "The rise and fall of the merest possibility of action" (Schneider, pp. 25–26). And in "Concentric Structure and 'The Love Song of J. Alfred Prufrock'," *T. S. Eliot Review* 3 (1976), 25–28, R. G. Peterson adduces Eliot's "roots in old traditions of number and symmetry" (p. 28), and proposes "the repetition in reverse order of nine thematic groupings of obviously related images" (p. 26), around the couplet concerning perfume from a dress "at the exact numerical center of the poem (ll. 65–66)" (p. 25). Although some of Peterson's formulations seem Procrustean to me, enough of the images and themes in the poem are symmetrically disposed to augment its other chiastic patterns. In "Critical Calculations: Measure and Symmetry in Literature," *PLMA* 91 (1976), 367–75, Peterson discusses "numerological and symmetrical patterns" throughout Western literature, and recent critical attention to them.

reinforce the repeated instances of verbal and phonetic chiasmus in the poem to express stasis, inertia, futility. The chiastic pattern even extends to certain themes, such as evening in the first set and aging in the last; his physical appearance in the second, and in the fifth.

But the important point for the controversy about language and meaning in literature is Eliot's undeniable ordering of Prufrock's process; and his most explicit ordering device is most significant.

A series of five dots appears at three points in the poem: after the first cluster of nine paragraphs; before the second cluster (bracketing the tenth and eleventh paragraphs); and after the first set of three paragraphs in the second cluster.[2] The crucial (in more than one sense) two bracketed paragraphs present the decisive development in Prufrock's process and portend his destiny. The third series of dots separates his contrary-to-fact conditional rationalizing of inertia from "No! I am not Prince Hamlet," which initiates the set of paragraphs that project his future life and end with the line introducing the mermaids. In other words, two series of five dots mark off the climax or crisis of the action of Prufrock's psychomachia, which rises in the first part of the poem and falls in the symmetrical second part: frustrated expectation, binary opposition, chiasmus. And the third series of five dots designates the conclusion of the poem, comprising the last two sets of paragraphs—which, like the two central paragraphs, lack patterns of refrain and paragraph length.

The three series of dots are distinct poet's product, not inside but *between* the units of language: they do not simultaneously belong to Prufrock's thought-discourse. And they not only shape the discourse, but shape it meaningfully. Especially the two series of dots at the center enact a meaning for the poem containing Prufrock's thought-discourse which is *independent of* the meaning in (or those meanings signified by) that discourse. Furthermore, the meaningful shaping *is not itself verbal:* Prufrock's discourse has been subsumed in a *physical* composition. Overtly enacted by the three series of dots, Eliot's physical composition incorporates his elaborate arrangement of 20 verse paragraphs.

There is an analogy with picture poems; but those do not clarify the question whether meaning is immanent in a *work* or just stimulated by a *text,* because they employ visual mimesis of an actual shape, achieve a kind of pictorial paranomasia. (The case with concrete poems is more involved.) The meaningful shape of "Prufrock" is geometrical, not pictorial: it conveys the poem's own anatomy, rather than an external object's morphology. Therefore, the shape of the poem enacts—articulates in both senses—meaning *for* the language of the poem.

Lyndall Gordon points out that when Eliot copied "Prufrock" into "the Notebook, in his spiky hand, in July-August 1911," four pages in the middle were left blank, and that subsequently he copied onto those blank pages "Pruf-

---

2. He used this typographical device of five dots again between certain stanzas in three of the quatrain poems in *Poems,* (1920): "A Cooking Egg," "Whispers of Immortality," and "Mr. Eliot's Sunday Morning Service."

rock's Pervigilium," an unpublished set-piece that "recounts a night-long vigil which climaxes in a terrifying vision of the end of the world" (pp. 45–46). The meaning articulated by Eliot's central placement and typographical bracketing in "Prufrock" of two sets of paragraphs is illustrated by what the consequence would have been had he not excised the vigil passage. For it occurred at the end of the first cluster of nine verse paragraphs—before the central set of two—and would have destroyed both their centrality and the symmetrical form of the poem.

The basic critical views about form in a work of literature correspond to those about the relation of language and meaning. That the form in a work is conceptual, an abstraction from the composition of words, is agreed. But the currently popular view is that this abstraction is a model *created* by each reader, each model of the work's form an instance of the "process by which men give meaning to things"; and the modernist (objective) retort to this idealist view is that a reader's "model is not [*itself*] the structure, for the structure is always in the object, latent as it were but only if latent is not opposed to real."[3]

In "Prufrock," the form is not wholly latent but partly manifest; and that part of it could scarcely be more real. Its reality is attested to by patterns of physical arrangement too complex to be accidental, any more than justified margins are accidental. *Within* his character's stream of consciousness, which constitutes the language of the poem—and so indistinguishable from that language totally innocent of its presence—Eliot created the geometrical configuration of paragraphs described. (As though to assert this creation, in one instance he made a paragraph of a single verse.) He *added to* his indistinguishable articulation of the parts of his poem, the distinct demarcations created by the three series of dots. The form of three threes as nine, one and one as two, and three threes as nine, with the final two sets of paragraphs the conclusion, must be conceptualized, is "latent as it were"—"but only if latent is not opposed to real." (The paragraphs can be counted, for example.) In the same way, the "silently sounded" (Roman Jakobson) prosody—as well as its absence at the center of the poem—is real sounds; so also are the instances of phonetic chiasmus: an oscilloscope could record them.

These agencies of formal articulation are "in the object"—immanent in "Prufrock": where else can they be? And they do not convey *Prufrock's* quasi-spoken meaning; for he cannot be the source of some, and is unaware of most. They enact fundamental components of the meaning of *Eliot's poem*. In other words, the meaning in "Prufrock" is not a matter of the language of the poem alone, but partly the product of physical properties creating a geometrical context for that language. In the "sign-sequence" of "Prufrock," "The production of the meaning of literary texts" is built-in: Prufrock's thought-discourse cannot

---

3. Roland Barthes, "The Structuralist Activity" (from *Essais Critiques*), quoted from *European Literary Theory and Practice: From Existential Phenomenology to Structuralism*, ed. Vernon W. Gras (New York: Dell, 1973), p. 161; Martinet, p. 4. An instance of Kenneth Burke's attraction for recent critics is his modulating these opposed views by defining form in literature, in the aptly named "Psychology and Form," as "the fulfilment of expectation."

be *given* meaning by a reader's processing it, because Eliot has processed it already in his poem embodying it. Eliot's poem comprises Prufrock's thought-discourse and his own processing of, *giving* meaning to, it.

This augmentation of the meaning of the "sign-sequence" or "text" of Prufrock's language itself—which is partly outside that language, to which Prufrock the quasi-speaker of that thought-discourse is not privy—seems to me the crucial evidence that a literary composition is a *work embodying* meaning. For although Eliot's physical augmentation of verbal meaning could be taken to effect merely the ordering of a reader's mental acts, it is more likely that the meaning in the speaker's "text" shares the *ontological status* of the elements of the poem which have the power to augment the meaning: that meaning is not less immanent in the language than in the physical context Eliot created for it. Certainly, there is no experience of cognitive disjunction: meaning in the text of Prufrock's thought-discourse contributes directly to meaning in the formal context Eliot created in making his poem out of his character's text.

One can never *prove* that the meaning originating in Prufrock's language is not solely the product of a reader's mental act, for the alternative myths about meaning and language abide because they are impervious to final proof. But the relation between Prufrock's text and the partly physical context it manifestly does have indicates—and the physical elements of Eliot's meaningful context prove with respect to themselves—that the Aristotelian myth more adequately accounts for the reality of this *work* of literature.

One result of the conception central to Modernism of artworks as—and of the pressure modernist artists felt to create—quasi-objects, is that Eliot's canonical modernist poem discredits the current doctrine that denies immanent meaning to language. Instead, "Prufrock" comports with the objective modernist doctrine implicit in the previously cited metaphor for a poem a prominent formalist-cognitive critic took from Donne's "Canonization," and made famous among later modernist critics: it indicates that, in literature at least, language embodies meaning.

II. A Well Wrought Urn?

It is a historical irony as well as a tribute to the potter's artistry that formalist-cognitive and other modernist critics overlooked some of Eliot's prodigious formal working in "Prufrock." But the irony is much less important than the doubt "Prufrock" raises about two related implications of Donne's metaphor (or W. K. Wimsatt's own "verbal icon") which suited those critics: the "cognitive" implication that, although unparaphraseable, and fully knowable only by the avowedly fictional Ideal Reader, meaning in a work is not only immanent but also definite; and the "formalist" implication that, when its intrinsic nature as literature is respected, meaning in a work has a hermetically *isolated* status—a poem is an "aesthetic" entity, an idiolect. This section of the chapter invokes "Prufrock" to probe the first, the remaining two sections to probe both, of these two central modernist critical doctrines.

Cleanth Brooks himself (and his collaborator, Robert Penn Warren) helped create the modernist canonical status of "Prufrock." The first two extended critical studies of the poem both appeared in 1938. One became widely known; it was in the first edition of their classic textbook—probably more famous and more influential on literary culture in America than any other since McGuffey's elementary-school *Eclectic Readers.*[4] About understanding "Prufrock" *Understanding Poetry* declares: "The poem has some complication, of course, but its primary difficulty for the reader is the apparent lack of logical transitions" (p. 595). The revised commentary of the 1950 and 1961 editions points out that "the events are not as fully indicated in Eliot's poem as in Tennyson's" dramatic monologue "Ulysses," but says a careful reading will "permit us to realize the implications of the whole poem" (pp. 433–34; p. 390). In a more recent *festschrift* for Wimsatt, Brooks wrote: "One can make out in 'The Love Song' a vague narrative . . . . "[5] And the subject of the *festschrift* had already written in 1952, the year before Abrams described objective criticism as the new "reigning mode":

> In *Prufrock* it is nearly possible, tantalizingly plausible, to suppose a basic story of a little man approaching a tea party at which there is a woman to whom he might . . . propose marriage, or to whom he stands, rather, in such a casual relation that his very thoughts of proposal are almost hallucinatory.[6]

The extent of the "uncertainties" Wimsatt labelled four sentences later is revealed in his total subverting of an initial "plausible" supposition by the alternative he introduced quietly with "or" and "rather"; the final words of his essay are "the introspectively shifty meaning of *Prufrock*."

Formalist-cognitive critics acknowledged the ineffable dimension in poetry, insisted that its meaning cannot be paraphrased adequately, and augmented our understanding of the richness of plurisignation. But "Prufrock" confronts what Abrams called "the objective point of view" with—precisely—uncertainty. The doctrines of both structuralist and post-structuralist criticism make the reader's uncertainty a consequence of the interaction of language and experience, and welcome it. To modernist criticism, uncertainty is far more disquieting, for the doctrine that meaning is definite dictates that uncertainty be attributed only to inadequate reading, or to a defective work. "Prufrock" shows that both the recent and the earlier doctrines simplify the reality of poetry, because each is partly right. The poem discloses three sources of uncertainty: reading compe-

4. All four editions (1938, 1950, 1961, 1974) were published in New York by Holt. The commentary originally emphasized irony in the poem. It was reprinted, extensively revised and expanded, in 1950, and slightly revised and cut in 1960; both poem and commentary were removed from the fourth edition. Unless otherwise specified, references are to the third (1960) edition. The other study is: Roberta Morgan and Albert Wohlstetter, "Observations on 'Prufrock'," *Harvard Advocate*, 125, no. 3 (Dec. 1938), pp. 27–30, 33–40.

5. "T. S. Eliot as a 'Modernist' Poet," *Literary Theory and Structure: Essays in Honor of W. K. Wimsatt*, ed. Frank Brady, John Palmer, and Martin Price (New Haven: Yale UP, 1973), pp. 353–77, p. 365.

6. W. K. Wimsatt, "*Prufrock* and *Maud:* From Plot to Symbol," *Yale French Studies*, no. 9 (Spring, 1952), pp. 84–92, p. 92. It is reprinted in *Hateful Contraries*, pp. 201–12.

tence, "Prufrock" itself, and the critic's 'bias" (Barthes)—the existential conditions of a particular reading. Meaning may be immanent in a poem, but even if it is so, it is not necessarily all stable, or even definite.

In his recent book on Eliot, Piers Gray asks, "What is the nature of the very opening lines . . . ?," and declares, "the poem immediately opens before us several levels of [sic] uncertainty" (Gray, p. 56). Its first four words illustrate the case. Does "Let us go" mean "[you] permit us to go," or is it imperative? In either case, who is the auditor, "you"? Does "then" relate to "When" at the beginning of the second line, signifying that evening has not yet come, which would be stylistically clumsy? Or does it mean "consequently," in which case "when" may or may not mean "now that"? In either case, do "you and I" go at evening?

Who is "you"?, and Do "you and I" go?, have been answered by many critics in many ways over the past half-century. But the questions cannot properly be separated, nor isolated from the meaning of "then" and that of "When." If it is not yet evening, the visit simply cannot take place in the poem; a later reference to "the afternoon, the evening" specifies that it can take place in the poem, and so indicates that "then" means "consequently." That being so, one is returned to the first question. For whether or not the visit takes place is more or less significant depending on whether or not *You* can compel *I*—whether I's "Let us go" is complying, petitioning, or even commanding—which depends on who You is. For example, I may be announcing his own resolve, as a consequence of consideration with You (before the poem begins), of the proposal by You to make the visit ("Let us go then"). If that is so, and yet they do not go, the poem constitutes a subversion of the apparent resolution that is its starting point.

The reader's irresolution about the meaning of the opening words mirrors Prufrock's irresolution throughout the poem, and may be a strategy of Eliot's to stimulate negative capability respecting Prufrock's predicament. The interdependence of one's alternative inferences about those first words is another warrant (if one is needed) of the poem's coherence. But the very range of critics' answers to the questions Who is You?, and Do You and I go?, documents the uncertainty.

In the "Words Set Free" section of *The Pound Era,* Hugh Kenner asks of the opening line, "what meaning do we attach to it, for instance to *you?*" He mentions the three most common alternative answers to the question: You "is possibly the reader . . . ; or is possibly some other part of . . . Prufrock; or is possibly . . . Dante or some analogue of Dante's." Then he dismisses the question as anachronistic ("Georgian"); for the modernist line "now causes no difficulty," its "words set free" to embody not meaning but "effect" (quoting from Yeats's 1900 essay "The Symbolism of Poetry") "too subtle for the intellect" (pp. 130–31). Kenner's argument bridges modernist and structuralist approaches: uncertain meaning is no problem because, since poetry is idiolectic and—citing Mallarmé (as reported by Valéry)—"made not of ideas but of words . . . the poem can convey" effects, not meanings.

Many passages of poetry and even some whole poems are accessible only in terms of effect (and so refractory against formal analysis); in those instances, concern for uncertainty about substantive meaning is frivolous. But that is not the universal case, even in *symboliste* and modernist poetry. Critics continue to try to identify You because the identity has an instrumental function in Eliot's poem.

In the same year, 1950: an extended "Reading" announced simply "Prufrock is speaking to us. We are the 'you'"; and the second edition of *Understanding Poetry* both declared You to be "the generalized reader," and proposed that the poem "in the end, is not about poor Prufrock": like Guido da Montefeltro in the epigraph, Prufrock "speaks to the 'you' of the poem—the reader—only because he takes the reader to be damned too," afflicted by "a general disease" in modern Western society.[7] These two studies may have been the first to identify You in print as the reader. Subsequently, Frederick W. Locke used the epigraph more elaborately than Brooks and Warren to make the same identification, in "Dante and T. S. Eliot's *Prufrock*" (*Modern Language Notes,* 78 [1963], 51–59); but he drew the opposite wider social inference from theirs. He explained "then" as a transitional word, whose function is to link Prufrock's self-revelation rhetorically to the epigraph; and as Guido is thus pointedly made to correspond to Prufrock, so Guido's auditor the poet Dante corresponds to—the reader. However, Guido's presumption about Dante is erroneous, which signifies that Prufrock's reader is not "damned too" in a poem of comment on modern society but only, like Dante, "visiting." In the present decade, the more direct and strictly logical connection has been made: the You whom Prufrock addresses, who "functions . . . to elicit confidences . . . and write the poem— bring back the story," "the Dante-figure of the poem," has now been identified as the analogous poet—as Eliot himself. In support, Eliot's statement in a letter that "the 'you' in THE LOVE SONG is merely some friend or companion" is quoted, and this instance of the usual evasive politeness of Ol' Possum interpreted as signifying that You is himself.[8]

Of course, the conclusion of most critics of Eliot's poetry, beginning with F. O. Mathiessen in his book published in 1935, is the least ingenious one—that You is neither the reader nor the poet, but a constant *inner* "companion" of Prufrock's, one able to "hear" his consciousness.[9] The logic of the poem's narrative method indicates this, and a wealth of supporting detail makes uncer-

7. Morris Weitz, "A 'Reading' of Eliot's 'The Love Song of J. Alfred Prufrock'," *The Philosophy of the Arts* (Cambridge: Harvard UP, 1950), pp. 93–107, p. 95; *Understanding Poetry,* 2nd ed., pp. 434, 440. For the persistence of this view, see Burton Raffel, *T. S. Eliot* (New York: Ungar, 1982), p. 26. In "Narrative 'You'," *Novel and Film: Essays in Two Genres* (Chicago: U of Chicago P, 1985), pp. 108–40, Bruce Morrissette examines "a family of cases in which 'you' invites the reader to place himself in the position of the writer" (p. 109) or otherwise implicates the reader directly. His broad survey includes some of Browning's poems, but not "Prufrock."

8. Philip R. Headings, *T. S. Eliot, Revised Edition* (Boston: Twayne, 1982), pp. 24–25. The interpretation is not in the original (1964) edition.

9. Mathiessen, p. 53. See also, e.g., Elizabeth Drew, *T. S. Eliot: The Design of His Poetry* (New York: Scribner, 1949), p. 34; George Williamson, *A Reader's Guide to T. S. Eliot: A Poem-By-Poem Analysis* (1953; New York: Noonday, 1957), pp. 59–60; *Eliot's Poetry and Plays,* p. 16; Robert Langbaum, *The Poetry of Experience: The Dramatic Monologue in Modern Literary Tradition* (1957; New York: Norton, 1963), p. 190; and Kenner's earlier *Invisible Poet,* p. 6.

tainty about it derive from the first of the three sources mentioned, reader competence. For example, the reader neither can be "here," beside Prufrock on that particular evening, nor preparing a face, and receiving a plate, at the tea. As for Eliot's being Prufrock's Dante, although "then" can be seen as stylistically sequential to the epigraph, the meaning "Because you cannot repeat what I *say, then* let us *go*" (and go where, if forever in hell?) is not a logical sequence. Indeed, if Prufrock were addressing Eliot in the mistaken belief that the poet could not reveal what he confided, and the poet betrayed his confidence, it would be a cruel joke on a pathetic figure—and a morbid joke as well; for after all, Prufrock is the product of Eliot's own words.

Eliot does not have to be addressed by Prufrock for the analogy he made with Dante's portrayal of a character in hell revealing himself to operate. Prufrock's auditor *shall* never repeat what he "says," for it is his silent thoughts. A symptom of his problem is that he does not—would not, cannot—say to another person what he is thinking. Like Guido he is in a hell and assumes that his confidences will be kept because they are imparted there; but his assumption is more sound than Guido's, because in his private hell he speaks only to a You who perforce cannot but keep his confidences. The critical consensus that, in Mathiessen's phrase, Prufrock is engaged in a "debate with himself," is the reasonable inference about a thought process which is a response.

It is the inference I made in the second chapter, citing Eliot's reference to *"dédoublement"* in Laforgue's poetry and the then current literary motif of doubleness (pp. 40–41). Bush quotes Eliot referring, in his Milton Academy address, to his youthful self, who "does not like me any better than I do him" (*T. S. Eliot*, p. 4). And Gordon (p. 31), Jay (p. 97), and he (p. x) all, in their recent books, describe the young Eliot's portraying in "Prufrock" and other early poems contrary impulses in himself. In the first "Satyre" of Eliot's beloved Donne, the reprehensible "humorist," to accompany whom the speaker has "sinned against my conscience" ("come lets goe," he says), seems literally inseparable from the speaker; and Eliot used doubleness to express "debate with [one]self" in *Murder in the Cathedral*, although Thomas's Tempters raise no question because of the allegorical mode of the play. Gray writes:

> If one speaks to oneself . . . you has been given a role, in a sense, independent from I. And one is therefore . . . both subject and object. The French for this statement is *dédoublement* . . . .
>
> Eliot himself uses the term in describing Laforgue's irony as the instrument "to express a *dédoublement* of the personality against which the subject struggles."[10]

In the poem I—its manifest aspect of Prufrock—presents his response to You about a possible action involving also (perforce) You; presumably You desires it, or it would not have been at issue ("Let us *go then*"). When "they" do "go" (if they do), only You meets faces—and a single face is prepared (for You: one says "How do I look?" but thinks "How does me look?") on those

10. Gray, p. 68; on pp. 67–74, Eliot's conception of "double selves" is related specifically to the thought of Bergson and of the contemporaneous French psychologist, Pierre Janet.

occasions; You and I both may be talked about; I speaks of his physical attributes, of daring to eat a peach, of determining—and of the satisfaction he takes in—his dress; both "have lingered" by the "sea-girls," but only I has seen them—one's I monitors the optic nerve. Affixing to I and You names from Cartesian philosophy, or Freudian or Ego psychology, is unnecessary—and would itself engender uncertainty. The poem discloses who I and You are, and we all know both from personal experience, though the I in most of us is less timorous and forlorn. In "'O Where Are You Going?' Said Reader to Rider," Auden presents both sides of an anti-Prufrock's *dédoublement;* it is not a debate, for the I is resolute; and in contrast to Prufrock, "he" (rider, farer, and hearer) frees himself from "them" (reader, fearer, and horror, I's paralyzing inhibitions), to precisely "go." The identity of neither antagonist, in neither poem, need be uncertain.

Do Prufrock's You and I also go? The answers of critics who have addressed the question directly are a mirror of uncertainty. Prufrock goes to the party and then to the beach; attends then leaves the party; attends the party; "has mounted" but then descends the stairs; goes to the outside of the house; and is walking to the party but "is not there yet as we hear him speaking."[11] Three decades ago, Grover Smith boldly proposed the significant alternative to all these various inferences, that "the action [is] limited to the interplay of impressions, including memories, in Prufrock's mind" (*Eliot's Poetry and Plays,* p. 16). Subsequently, others treated the question diplomatically: "it is impossible to say which . . . elements are externally 'there' and which are the *disjecta membra* of a disordered consciousness" (Bernard Bergonzi, *T. S. Eliot* [New York: Macmillan-Collier, 1972], p. 16); "As he enters the room, or as it enters his consciousness" (Moody, p. 33). Or they acquiesced in Smith's view, with diffidence: "the streets and fog to be traversed (or, more likely, contemplated)" (Headings, p. 21); "One of the puzzles of the poem is . . . whether Prufrock ever leaves his room. It appears that he does not . . . " (Miller, p. 139). But in recent years, Bush implicitly (*T. S. Eliot,* p. 11) and Gordon have concurred that Prufrock "never, in fact, leaves his room" (p. 45).

Most of the various inferences of the first group of critics occurred earlier than the proposals that Prufrock never stirs. As this fact suggests, while the poem cannot be absolved of all responsibility for the prevailing uncertainty, it is more definite than the multifarious criticism indicates.

The most purposeful (richest) alternative is that Prufrock does not stir: the poem begins when I expresses to You a willingness to "go then," and then subverts the apparent resolution that is its starting point. This alternative is most consonant with its narrative strategy, and with the elaborate patterns indicating equivocation, vacillation, and inertia. It also seems to be promoted by a careful use (again) of verbs. For example, when the coming and going of the talking

11. See, respectively, *Understanding Poetry,* pp. 392, 395 (2nd ed., pp. 436, 439), and Eric Thompson, *T. S. Eliot: The Metaphysical Perspective* (1963; Carbondale: Southern Illinois UP, 1969), p. 10; Langbaum, p. 190; Morgan and Wohlstetter, p. 27, and Williamson, p. 63; *Moments and Patterns,* p. 164 (but see p. 19); Alwyn Berland, "Some Techniques of Fiction in Poetry," *Essays in Criticism* 4 (1954), 380–85, 381–84; and *Invisible Poet,* p. 24.

women is first mentioned, the account is made a general one by the description that immediately follows in the past tense of the fog "curled" about the locale of the party: what is described is not being witnessed, but remembered. Almost every detail of experience in the poem—involving the streets, the party, the beach, etc.—is carefully made general, proleptic, or conditional: "streets that," "there will be," "They will say," "I have known," "I have seen," "when I am," "would it have," "I shall wear," etc.; hence, most are in the future, the present perfect, and the subjunctive.

There seem to be three exceptions to this pattern of general, proleptic, and conditional reference, in addition to the initial "Let us go"—three instances in the poem in which specific present circumstances are mentioned. The first is the couplet, "Is it perfume from a dress / That makes me so digress?"; the second is the passage in which "the afternoon, the evening, sleeps . . . / . . . / . . . or it malingers / Stretched on the floor, here beside you and me"; and the third is the passage in which Eliot deftly characterizes his poem by way of Prufrock's simile: exasperated by sunsets, dooryards, streets, other details made familiar by the poem, and "this" itself, Prufrock exclaims: "It is impossible to say just what I mean! / But as if a magic lantern threw the nerves in patterns on a screen: / Would it have been worth while / . . . ."

Perhaps anachronistically for a poem written in 1911, some critics see a "cinematic-type structure" in "Prufrock," the magic lantern "presenting fragmentary shots" in place of Prufrock's saying just what he means.[12] But while the nerves are his, the "lantern" making the elegant patterns of them and the "screen" on which they are focussed have been shown to be the poet's. Prufrock's simile cannot warrant characterizing Eliot's poem as indefinite. However, the passage does not contradict, and even suggests, that Prufrock is still at home.

The second of the three passages in which Prufrock mentions specific present circumstances provides additional evidence that he never stirs. It follows directly upon the determination, in the poem's two central paragraphs, of the outcome of his whole deliberation. The afternoon-evening is personified as either tired or malingering "here beside you and me." To characterize evening— an inevitable and constantly changing natural phenomenon—as tired or malingering, is nonsense unless the epithets express I's perception and so apply as well to "you and me," who are "here beside" the evening that is "Stretched on the floor" of the room You and I have not yet left (although the party has already largely been described). The afternoon has begun to be evening—time to go— Prufrock acknowledges. So he is not tired, precisely malingers. His decision having just been made in the two central paragraphs, he can be expected to continue to—as he himself puts it—malinger.

The first of the three passages is the one element in the poem not wholly consonant with a reasonably certain answer to the question "Do You and I go?" The couplet is an instance of uncertainty whose source is "Prufrock" itself—as distinct from reader competence, and from what I have called the existential conditions of a particular reading.

12. Gertrude Patterson, T. S. Eliot: Poems in the Making (Manchester: Manchester UP, 1971), p. 110; Morgan and Wohlstetter, p. 27. See also, e.g., Moments and Patterns, pp. 19–20.

It is not perfume that causes Prufrock's digression. The poem gives the cause—arms. But to explain the question in his thought is difficult unless he is in the vicinity of dresses and perfume. Possibly, the perfume too is recollected from a familiar experience; but the words say something else.

This couplet is not the only element in the poem that engenders gratuitous uncertainty. For example, considering "all" those bare arms that actually have hair, is the "one" Prufrock mentions a specific person he wishes to court or—in Gordon's apt phrase (p. 46)—"establish rapport with"? Presumably, but by no means certainly. However, that uncertainty is a pointless minor ambiguity, not a significant inconsistency in the portrayed situation. The inconsistency of "Is it perfume from a dress" is a positive flaw in a supposed "heterocosm" which otherwise has no evidence that Prufrock stirs from his room. It makes uncertain Eliot's otherwise coherent and powerful portrayal of Prufrock as epitomizing his predicament by his immobility—as totally subverting the ostensible resolution with which he begins.

However often uncertainty about a work of literature may derive from inadequate reading, a second potential source is the work itself; Eliot's apparent inconsistent use of quotation marks in *The Waste Land* is an instance mentioned in the sixth chapter (p. 183). The third kind of uncertainty can be attributed to no failing, either in the reader or of the poem; I call it existential because its source seems to be the human condition. This third kind of uncertainty contravenes the formalist-cognitive doctrine, and general modernist assumption, that unless a poem is flawed, meaning in it is definite: that—at least ideally—there can be an Ideal Reader. The locus of uncertainty is the mimetic dimension of Eliot's poem—specifically, attitudes Prufrock is expressing.

This apparently endemic human uncertainty must be distinguished not only from a failing in the reader or the poem, but also from gratuitous uncertainty—pointless ambiguity in the poem—about Prufrock's attitudes. An example of such ambiguity is his asking if he dares to eat a peach. Is he intentionally citing something trivial to mock himself by its contrast with the symmetrically opposed portentous question, "Do I dare?"? Or is his speaking of precisely a peach positively functional—perhaps metaphorically, or symbolically? His question may even originate in some current health fad; for it is bracketed by his references to current youthful fashions of hair and trousers bottoms. Hence, although self-mockery is not unusual for Prufrock, or inappropriate at this point, the context does not indicate whether or not his question is ironic—and it ought to do so: the poem is gratuitously ambiguous about Prufrock's attitude.

A good example of the kind of uncertainty in "Prufrock" that is not gratuitous, nor attributable to a failing either of reader or of poem, is Prufrock's proto-imagist extended metaphor of the fog as a cat. At one extreme of a range of interpretations, A. D. Moody says of it, "the nightmarish and the seductive become confused. The cat is familiar, yet vaguely terrifying . . ." (p. 33). Hugh Kenner's *Invisible Poet* describes the "inimical clouds of yellow fog" as part of Eliot's "incantation" of "a hell" (p. 10). Grover Smith's chapter on Eliot's pessimistic early poems is entitled "The Yellow Fog"; and he believes that an opposition between the house of the tea party, and the fog around it, helps convey "Prufrock's sense of impotent inferiority or isolation" (*Eliot's Poetry and Plays,*

p. 18). Elizabeth Drew selects Smith's first alternative: "mingled self-pity and self-disgust, are ... brought home to us through the images of the tortuous streets and the fog-cat" (p. 35). Brooks and Warren specify Smith's other suggestion, isolation—but it is "of the drawing room"; they find the passage signifying the "relaxed, aimless quality of Prufrock's world" as well (p. 391). J. Hillis Miller sees the fog as "express[ing] Prufrock's wish that he too could curl once about the house and fall asleep" (p. 139). Morgan and Wohlstetter take the cat to be a "a sexual symbol," with the fog expressing Prufrock's "desire" as well as his "indecision" (p. 33). George Williamson's similar interpretation is slightly more positive; the "mental state" it "reflect[s]" is unalloyed "desire which ends in inertia. If the cat image suggests sex, it also suggests the greater desire of inactivity" (p. 60). And a note about the fog-cat by Arthur E. Waterman in the *Explicator* (XVII [June, 1959], no. 67 [n. pag.]), calls "this beautiful image" Prufrock's first "allusion to" the idyll he contrasts to his situation: "it [the fog] is capable of natural freedom within the filth of the city . . . ."

What is Prufrock's attitude toward the fog he likens to a cat? Whatever his uncertain attitude may be, his extended metaphor expressing it functions strictly to develop the portrayal of him; and *all* the quoted interpretations of his attitude toward the fog are consistent with the character portrayed elsewhere in the poem. Hence, there is neither a problem of gratuitous uncertainty in the poem, as with the references to perfume, "one," and a peach, nor a problem of inadequate reading.

Precisely because none of the proposed answers to the question misread or ignore elements in the poem, and yet they differ so widely, they must derive from sources within the respective readers quoted that are not strictly readerly—must be, in the most precise sense, subjective. Hence, I have called the third kind of uncertainty existential. It indicates how far from real reading is the Ideal Reader, belies the modernist assumption that unless flawed, meaning in a poem is definite. Not all instances of this kind of uncertainty are so congenial as Prufrock's fog-cat.

It has been observed often that "Prufrock" is filled with references to parts of the body. Actually, with the exception of the back of the fog-cat, they are all to the two most expressive parts: the head (muzzle, tongue, hair, chin, face, eyes, head) and—in one instance "arms and legs"—the arms (hands, claws, fingers, arms). Recognizing the exquisite interplay of related images of head and arms is one of the rewards the poem offers. The scant hair on Prufrock's head, the hair on the woman's arms, and the metaphorical hair of the waves combed by Prufrock's mermaids connect, and together augment Eliot's portrait. Even more elaborately: "restless nights in . . . hotels" relates to the "lonely men . . . leaning out of windows" on their arms, which Prufrock thinks of invoking to support a pathetically inept suit: an appeal for rescue from loneliness. He contemplates making the inept appeal at the climax of the poem, in the one single instant he contemplates doing anything; the leaning-men image of that instant relates by way of their unmentioned forearms to the impetus for and reaction to the instant—respectively the female arms in the room above, and the crustacean claws he "should have been," claws purposefully "Scuttling across" their floor, in contrast to his irresolute inertia. Finally, all relate to the fingers that "smooth" his malingering immediately after the climactic middle section in which the instant occurs. Considering the centrality in the poem of this complex of images, and the spatial binary opposition in it already discussed, the question "hands" "lift and drop" "on your plate" may well be the "overwhelming" question.

But is it? Are the two complexes of images actually brought together at the end, when Prufrock—not crab but "human"—"drowns"? Does he drown because he lingers by the mermaids of his imagination, who are combing the *hair* of the waves? Is the secondary meaning of *overwhelm*—to submerge, engulf—invoked? Respecting these subordinate but tangible and coherent potentialities of meaning, is there a definite text in this class?

The issue is focussed by

> Arms that are braceleted and white and bare
> (But in the lamplight, downed with light brown hair!)

The exclamation mark, the persistence in his consciousness of the arms through the intervening perfume-from-a-dress couplet, and the immediate occurrence of the climax:

> Arms that lie along a table, or wrap about a shawl.
>   And should I then presume?
>   And how should I begin?
>
>   . . . . .
>   Shall I say . . .

indicate two things. The first is that his "digression" is not caused by the perfume of the terse couplet between these two passages, but by that which is in parentheses: his image of real human female arms. And the second is that his image directly precedes and so precipitates his feeble and momentary resolution to act and save himself.

The resolution seems to me salutary in "The Love Song of J. Alfred Prufrock." And Prufrock's "digression" (characteristically) into what should be his proper state of mind, is prompted by the impulses of his You, responding to the image of the real arms—the healthy impulses which have compelled I to engage in his whole psychomachia that is the poem. I read "downed with light brown hair" and the exclamation mark as indicating a favorable response to the physical reality Prufrock's image embodies. (It may not be irrelevant that I consider such a response understandable and healthy.) Consequently, I read the prompt frustration of his inclination to act as an index of the hopelessness of his predicament.

However, my account of the climax of the poem and its motivation depends on my inference that Prufrock is *attracted* by the real woman's human arms. Perhaps, instead, they repel him, and his repulsion is what causes his prompt abandonment of any attempt to save himself. Uncertainty about Prufrock's attitude toward those arms is far more critical than the similar situation with his fog-cat. Does the image motivate, or does it in fact defeat, Prufrock's brief inclination to act? The difference is fundamental to our understanding of him, and so significant for our understanding of the poem.

Moody's ambiguous remark, "And what a complex of feeling there is in 'But

in the lamplight, downed with light brown hair!'" (p. 34), may be his acknowl-
edgement both of the problem and of the contrast between my reading and the
exactly contrary one. That one is put succinctly by Brooks and Warren, who
quote the line, then ask:

> Is this a mere observation, or does it indicate something about Prufrock?
> The fact that the observation of the "real" arms is put in contrast with the
> "romantic" arms, modifies the attraction: against the attraction there is a hint
> of revulsion, a hint of neurotic repudiation of the real, the physical. (p. 392)

Of course, the "something" his image of real arms indicates "about Prufrock"
can be "the attraction," not "revulsion." The dimensions of the problem are
revealed in the context in which J. Hillis Miller quotes the line and the one
preceding:

> Eliot's early poetry is dominated by disgust for the body. The protagonists . . .
> recall James's heroes in their fastidious distaste for "Arms . . . . " (p. 184)

Theories about Eliot's "emotive imagery" are no help here. Does one gen-
eralize about his early poetry to learn how, at the age of twenty-two, he would
have regarded not a moral issue, but a natural and fairly common fact of human
anatomy? Alternatively, ought the poem to have specified—more than by the
conjunction of elements it presents, and the familiarity with its subject's mind
it allows—what response Prufrock would have had to that particular image? (Is
the passage gratuitously ambiguous?) Perhaps the answer is Yes in both cases.
But both the nature of the particular image at issue, and the weakness of either
a complaint of ambiguity or a resort to speculation about young Eliot, suggest
that the contrary inferences about Prufrock's response—about this aspect of
Eliot's mimesis of a human—derive not from uncertainty in the poem, but from
a source closer to home in each reader. And if that is so, is *one's own* possibly
unformulated "aesthetic" (in the most radical sense) response to down on wom-
en's arms not relevant to one's inference about Prufrock's response to arms
"Downed with . . . hair!"?

This last question is partly answered by the fact that a reader unaware of the
contrary inference from the parenthetical line draws his or her own inference
with certainty, rather than apprehending ambiguity in the passage. Each of us is
existentially—endemically—bound by her or his own attitude to hair on wom-
en's arms. This procedure is very different from the reader's in analogous cases
not involving an image that, in a sense, reads the reader. For example, although
we know Prufrock, we do not know how sound his suspicion is that the "voices
[he recalls] dying with a dying fall" would be doing so because they had been
talking about him. But we are aware we do not know—and aware one's own
attitude toward such voices might differ from his; furthermore, his suspicion is
more relevant than the fact, and even it is not vital.

Meaning may be immanent in the work of literature, but the act of cognition
is a particular human's act; and "Prufrock" provides evidence that in *certain*
instances the existential human particularity and not the structure of words is—
as many recent critics say of *all* instances—definitive.

III. Ghostlier Demarcations

The point has been made (pp. 154–56) that when in "Ulysses, Order, and Myth" Eliot praised *Ulysses* for pioneering "the mythical method," he was referring to its reliance on systematic allusion to the *Odyssey* as, in Joyce's phrase, a "way of working": for Eliot, the efficacious "method" ("a step toward making the modern world possible for art") consisted not in employing mythic material, but in "manipulating a continuous parallel between contemporaneity and antiquity." Enabling felicities the modernists valued, such as historical juxtaposition, tonal enrichment, and parsimony, allusions understandably were used to do work of fundamental thematic and structural kinds in a great deal of modernist literature. Correspondingly, modernist critical practice was alert to the functioning of allusions in literature of all periods.

But the literary device was given little theoretical attention: the autonomous status of a work was not considered compromised by the allusions in it. For example, formalist-cognitive critics likened allusions to direct references, such as proper nouns and cited book titles; and all such special references were taken to be simply analogous to the references to their lexical meanings made by conventional words and phrases. The general view was that a literary work employs a fact of a particular culture, its language, some of which is lexical, and some of which is referential to persons, places, concepts, myths, and works of literature in the culture. Readers "need to understand the language of the poem including the ideas and the allusions."[13] And the special information readers require to "understand" references in a work compromises the intrinsic status of those references—the autonomy of the work—no more than the special information required to understand obsolete meanings or dialect words.

However, although the term *allusion* can be used loosely to designate any reference, its strict meaning of tacit, *as distinct from* explicit, reference not only is more useful, but also reveals the fallacy in ignoring the distinction. To treat as language a ghostly quasi-reference, an inferred presence whose very existence *by definition* is uncertain, is to simplify its relation to other elements of the work; and no less than the uncertainties in "Prufrock" attributable to readers' human subjectivity, some of its allusions controvert the doctrine of definite meaning. But there is a more important consequence. To treat allusions as language is to obscure what an allusion does, when the manifest presence of the ghost in a work—for example, the presence in Ralegh's "The Nymphs Reply to the Sheepheard," Donne's "The Baite" and C. Day Lewis's "Come, Live with Me and Be My Love," of Marlowe's "The Passionate Sheepheard to his Love"—overcomes the uncertainty that the apparition is real. To treat the allusions in "Prufrock" as language-in-an-autonomous-artifact is to obscure the way the literary device actually operates in the poem.

13. Cleanth Brooks, "The Problem of Belief and the Problem of Cognition," Appendix 2 (pp. 226–38) in *The Well Wrought Urn: Studies in the Structure of Poetry* (London: Dobson, 1949), p. 227. See also, e.g., the comment on "our habitual knowledge of the language," in "The Intentional Fallacy," *Verbal Icon*, p. 10.

In other words, "Prufrock" exemplifies that the formalist-cognitive conception of allusion—as a species of referential "language" in an autonomous artifact—obscures two significant characteristics of the device. Allusions in the poem controvert both the "cognitive" doctrine that meaning in a literary work is definite, and the "formalist" doctrine that a literary work is an autonomous artifact. For the two significant characteristics are that allusions are not explicit, but *tacit,* and not integral, but *conjunctive.*

Formalist-cognitive critics did identify a problem of some other critics with allusion: their failure to distinguish relevant special information from that which is irrelevant. An aspect of Intentionalism addressed in "The Intentional Fallacy" is "to suppose that we do not know what a poet means unless we have traced him in his reading"; for "There is a difference between internal and external evidence for the meaning of a poem" (*Verbal Icon,* pp. 14, 10). In contrast to external "author psychology," however, "allusiveness" in a poem is cited as an instance of internal evidence for meaning, a kind of language that functions as part of the poem, and so does not violate its integrity (pp. 14–15).

The last two pages of the revised and expanded commentary on "Prufrock," in the second (1950) edition of *Understanding Poetry,* are devoted to the "question . . . raised by [its] literary allusions": "has the poet a right to expect this knowledge . . . ?" (p. 442). The answer given is that the allusions in it are precisely both language and functional: "the reading of any poetry requires some preparation" (p. 444); and "the critics and scholars are there to help us. Then we can try to see if the allusions . . . are really functional . . . " (p. 443). Although in the next edition and its final form (1960), the commentary was shortened by a number of excisions, an addition was made to the end of its last paragraph, the whole of which concerns literary allusions generally. Its new conclusion comprises a pair of sentences with two subjects. One is the then still-current calumny that formalist-cognitive critics—who worked to recast the history and revise the canon of English poetry—were antihistorical; the other is the status of allusion as "language of the poem." "A poem does not exist in isolation. It exists in history," Brooks and Warren declare; and, to "understand and appreciate" it, one must know about both "the world that brought it to being and the world to which it refers" (p. 399).

The conception of reference (including allusion) in literature as a kind of language—both definite and integral—seems more or less adequate for *explicit* references. For example, no important distortion of "Prufrock" occurs when "Michelangelo" or "the eternal Footman" is conceived of as language, merely requiring identifying information analogous to the lexical information required by archaic words. This is true as well of explicit references that are literary, such as "Prince Hamlet" and the dual reference in "I am Lazarus, come from the dead" (to the brother of Martha and Mary in John 11 and the beggar of the parable in Luke 16). It can be argued perhaps that since there are two, one of the Lazarus references *must* be tacit (allusion) rather than explicit—or be irrelevant; but characters in specific works are designated, explicitly, distinct from historical Jews or Danes, or even from the Amlothi of the *Prose Edda* or Saxo's Amleth: the language is definite, so to speak.

But tacit literary references are a different matter. The allusion in "Prufrock" to another character originating in the Gospels reveals the inadequacy of the formalist-cognitive conception of allusion as definite (language):

> Though I have seen my head (grown slightly bald)
> brought in upon a platter,
> I am no prophet. . . .

The readiest "meaning" to be given this "language" would be the account of the death of John the Baptist in Matthew 14 and Mark 6. However, an alternative meaning proposed for the ostensible language designates "the hero of Wilde's *Salomé* ("Jokanaan"); and a third proposed identification is "Laforgue's John the Baptist" (in *Salomé*, one of the *Moralités légendaires*).[14] Unlike the two accounts of different characters "come from the dead" named Lazarus, the natures of the three very different works portraying John's death are such that all cannot be "meant" by the "language" of the passage in "Prufrock."

According to the eminently practical criterion invoked by both "The Intentional Fallacy" and *Understanding Poetry,* the narrative in the Gospels can be set aside as irrelevant (not functional). Comparing himself to the prophet, Prufrock speaks of his head as brought *in* on a platter—that is, into the room with "tea and cakes and ices" in which "one" sits. In the Gospels, Salomé is a young girl who has no relationship with or attitude toward the prophet, and asks Herod for his head at her mother's bidding. Wilde's "tragedy in one act," in contrast, is an erotic action of heroic stoicism, unrequited love, and revenge. Also, much is make of Jokanaan's thick black hair; and the seductive and implacable agent of his beheading laughs at his head when it is brought 'in' to Herod's party. The analogies and contrasts with the situation of the balding, self-conscious Prufrock, afraid to invoke, at a party, the banal power and mockery of his own temptress, are both apparent and richly functional.

In fact, both of the then-recent works about the death of John the Baptist are suitable ("functional") objects of literary allusion in "Prufrock." Laforgue's *Salomé* is relevant to Prufrock's situation and sense of himself. Furthermore, the general affinities Eliot's poem has with the characteristic tone, diction, and versification of Laforgue's poetry constitute "internal evidence" of the relevance of the French poet's *oeuvre,* whose influence Eliot declared. However, Laforgue's *Salomé* is totally incompatible with Wilde's *Salomé,* its decadence the very opposite of sensual—enervated and nihilistic, with both principals rejecting life as trivial ("*nous desséchons de fringales supraterrestres*").

The problem with the conception of allusion as language is a variant of the problem some have raised about the true language in the poem: indeterminacy. There is absolutely no basis on which either Laforgue's *Salomé* or Wilde's *Salomé,* or both, can be positively identified as the work being alluded to. The criterion of functionality weighs against the simultaneous allusion to both, and seems to indicate Wilde's play; but the process of determination is in the realm

---

14. The phrases are quoted from Williamson, p. 64, and Moody, p. 35. See also, e.g., Morgan and Wohlstetter, pp. 27, 36–37, and *Understanding Poetry,* p. 393, for the Wilde identification.

of degree, not kind. Identification originates in nothing more positive than a subjective assessment. Allusion being by definition tacit, the evidence for a suspected allusion always is circumstantial. And the weight of evidence assessed in reaching a judgment (the degree of likelihood determining attribution) is the cumulative testimony of such things as similarity of details in the two works, and the number of similar details which *all* have relevance/value for the alluding work. A suspected allusion exists because, like Thoreau's trout in milk, it is present; and it is present because it functions. But how many of the three—and which—apparent allusions to works about the death of John the Baptist are (is) real? Whether or not a suspected allusion is functioning can itself be a difficult question.

The conclusion of "The Intentional Fallacy" raises the question of indeterminate allusion in precisely "Prufrock":

> ... the line: "I have heard the mermaids singing, each to each," ... bears a certain resemblance to a line in a Song by John Donne, "Teach me to heare Mermaides singing," so that ... the critical question arises: Is Eliot's line an allusion to Donne's? (*Verbal Icon*, pp. 17–18)

The concern of Wimsatt and Beardsley is to distinguish the procedure of intentionalist "seekers of sources" in coping with the question—whereby "the critic writes to Eliot and asks ... if he had Donne in mind"—from "the true and objective way of criticism": "the way of poetic analysis and exegesis, which inquires whether it makes any sense .... " They ignore the *cognitive* implications if their ostensible (allusive) "language" itself actually is indeterminate; but they are fully aware of the determinancy problem:

> This method of inquiry may lead to the conclusion that the given resemblance between Eliot and Donne is without significance and is better not thought of, or the method may have the disadvantage of providing no certain conclusion. (p. 18)

The circumstantial evidence inclines Wimsatt and Beardsley to the not-certain verdict that "the given resemblance" to Donne's "Song" fails to function in Eliot's poem—"makes [no] sense"—so "Prufrock" does not allude to it.

However, Piers Gray renders the opposite verdict. He cites the "winde" that "Serves to advance an honest minde" in Donne's poem, associates it with the wind blowing the waters in the "Prufrock" passage, and eloquently makes an unusual case about the conclusion of Eliot's poem: that it is positive, portraying "the transcendence of the lyric over the ironic," on the grounds that Prufrock precisely *has* heard mermaids singing, signifying that his "honest" mind, his imagination, will comfort him (pp. 74–79).

Wimsatt and Beardsley mention "a line of a sonnet of Gérard de Nerval" as evidence against Donne's "Song" (p. 18). Presumably the line is one in "El Desdichado": *"J'ai rêvé dans la grotte où nage la sirène."* (It is quoted in the book that led the undergraduate Eliot to the French poets, Symons's *Symbolist Movement in Literature*.) Gray invokes the same line, declares "We have lingered in the chambers of the sea" to be "a rendition of" it, and uses the Nerval to *reinforce* his contrary interpretation *based on* the Donne (p. 79).

What "Prufrock" exemplifies in this case is that even the arbitrary but practical modernist criterion of functionality ("makes sense," is "really functional") can be not merely simply but doubly unreliable. It always involves a judgment incapable of proof; in addition, it can be logically and hermeneutically faulty.

For in this case, two totally different putative allusions are invoked as paired elements in alternative explications of the ending of "Prufrock"—each of which views of the ending, by circular reasoning, *then* is used to demonstrate either that only one of the putative allusions functions and hence exists, or that both do so, together. Whether the apprehension of either putative allusion helped generate the corresponding view of the ending, or instead was stimulated by it, explication itself has been determined by a prior, and so premature, higher-order act of interpretation. Furthermore, the irreconcilable possible significations of the putative allusions make this logically and hermeneutically faulty procedure unavoidable.

A putative allusion whose signification—if it exists—is plain, is the one called problematic in the second chapter (p. 33). Arguing the more familiar alternative view that the end of "Prufrock" is negative, A. D. Moody finds a persuasive allusion to Arnold's poem in which a merman at the shore calls without success to his mortal wife to leave civilization and rejoin him in the sea, and which has a song, a reference to combing, and other similarities. However, Moody's bald assertion, "The allusion to Arnold's 'The Forsaken Merman' is obvious," actually emphasizes the indeterminate status of his proposal (pp. 34–36). Allusion to Arnold's poem, direct or ironic, certainly would be incongruous with the positive ending Piers Gray describes, in which Prufrock has achieved "an imaginative triumph," his mermaids either "an image of happiness" (Gray, p. 79) or "an antecedent type of the female figure who is later to represent spiritual guidance" (*Moments and Patterns,* p. 33). It even would be incongruous with a less totally positive ending, in which Prufrock's imagination "negates negation" (Spender, *Eliot,* p. 39), or the "drowned" Prufrock has been made to "enter into real life" (Weitz, p. 102), much as baptism is "the first stage of true life or salvation" (p. 106). Alternatively, allusion to Arnold's poem would be congruous with and enrich the negative ending Moody and most critics find, in which Prufrock's lingering in the sea by mermaids is terminated by human voices (perhaps his own two voices) waking "Us," causing something like death.

But do the voices drown him, or do the mermaids? Mermaids traditionally drown humans; however, his mermaids ignore him, so that he can be undersea with them safely until wakened. In fact, does he (metaphorically) die—"drown"—at all? Mermaids do not really exist, so "waking" is accepting reality; is that as onerous as Prufrock himself believes? The many difficulties presented by the ending of the poem are relevant here because of its possible allusions. The Nerval line could be alluded to in either case. But a positive ending to the poem is major circumstantial evidence that the ending also is alluding to the Donne poem; and a negative one is major circumstantial evidence that, instead, it is alluding to the Arnold as well as the Nerval. Simultaneously, the contrary potential allusions reciprocally help to effect the contrary potential endings.

Even when the circumstantial evidence by which an allusion is identified does not include a controversial interpretation (to which it reciprocally contributes), the identification remains—by definition—indeterminate. The fact is that, while indeterminate *meaning* is only an exceptional circumstance in the case of lexical language, and even in the case of explicit reference, indeterminate *status* is the lot of all presumptively identified allusions in a work. This fact alone creates a fundamental doubt about the formalist-cognitive conception of allusion as language.

That conception, expressive of the objective critics' insistence on the autonomy of a work of literature, paradoxically withholds objective status from another literary work that is the *object* of an allusion. And if the indeterminacy of allusion illuminates the cognitive flaw in their conception of it as language, this paradox illuminates the formalist flaw. Allusions not only are tacit; they also are conjunctive. If indeed the work alluded to were merely language to be "understood," it would constitute relevant literary history *absorbed into* the autonomous alluding work. As the object of an allusion, the work alluded to is a discrete entity with *a relation to* the alluding work.

The denial of separate status to the object of allusive "language" is one manifestation of a general inadequacy in the formalist-cognitive hypostatizing of the autonomy of a work. The inadequacy was identified early by the neo-Aristotelian critics, who argued that formalist-cognitive critics are not objective with sufficient rigor, consider poetry "one of many modes of discourse" rather than "a special class of made objects," and so fail to make generic distinctions between "kinds of wholes"; hence—as was mentioned in the preceding chapter (p. 228)—the concept of "the intentional fallacy" fails to accommodate some implications of the artist's sense of genre.[15]

By definition, the ineluctable context of any individual work that is not literally *sui generis* includes "kinds of wholes," whether they are part of its creator's former experience and operative awareness, or not; that context includes as well conventions, motifs, types of character and action, persistent imagery, all the elements of the entity literature that are exemplified in the work. The neo-Aristotelian *Critics and Criticism, Ancient and Modern* was published the year before *The Mirror and the Lamp;* and four years before that, in 1948, Northrop Frye published "The Function of Criticism at the Present Time," which he transformed into the "Polemical Introduction" of *The Anatomy of Criticism.* A principal subject of polemic in both essay and introduction was the failure of criticism to evolve a "conceptual framework." The "organizing or containing forms" of that framework would derive from "the assumption of total coherence" in literature enabled by the axiom that "literature is not a piled aggregate of 'works,' but an order of words" (*Anatomy*, pp. 16–17).

The four "Co-ordinates of Art Criticism" in *The Mirror and The Lamp* are restricted to one plane. A complete or three-dimensional conceptual model would situate *behind* Work—that is, in a different *order* of relation to it than

15. See p. 228, n.7 and Crane, pp. 13–17; the quoted phrases are on p. 13. Crane's thesis is that Aristotle was supplanted by a "Hellenistic-Roman Romantic tradition," to which the formalist-cognitive critics belong; hence, they lack "sufficient theoretical bases for" considering "the peculiar natures of the artistic wholes" writers "were engaged in constructing" out of their artistic "commitment to certain kinds of poetic structures and effects rather than others" (p. 15).

Universe, Artist and Audience—if not the whole "verbal universe" of literature as Frye maintains, certainly those Works that form the more limited context within literature of its genre, its imagery, and other characteristics (such as apparent allusions).[16]

Although in practice they appreciated the function for a particular work of its context within literature, the formalist-cognitive critics denied *theoretically* the importance to literary works of their external, and so contextual, relations. They accommodated relevant literary history by absorbing its manifestations *into* the work. Hence, a sense in which they indeed were anti-historical is that they suppressed the relations that are the data of a true history of literature. The first chapter pointed out (p. 9) how radically their doctrine of the autonomy of the work contrasts with the view of the relation of a "new work" (and Talent) to the "monuments" of Tradition articulated in his first theoretical essay by the creator of "Prufrock." Their inadequate conception of allusion is part of this radical difference between them and Eliot.

The title of Frye's essay alludes to that of Eliot's 1923 essay, and (presumably) to that of the 1864 essay by Arnold (presumably) allusively truncated by Eliot to create his more sweeping one. In the revised version of his essay, Frye wrote:

> Mr. Eliot's essay *The Function of Criticism* begins by laying down the principle that the existing monuments of literature form an ideal order among themselves, and are not simply collections of the writings of individuals. (*Anatomy,* p. 18)

Eliot placed it second in *Selected Essays,* directly after "Tradition and the Individual Talent," in whose third paragraph he made his famous statement that:

> the historical sense compels a man to write . . . with a feeling that the whole of the literature of Europe from Homer and within it the whole of the literature of his own country has a simultaneous existence and composes a simultaneous order. (p. 4)

The next paragraph is the one that has been seminal for critics discussing literary influence in this century; and he chose to quote much of it verbatim six years later, to begin the essay cited by Frye:

> No poet, no artist of any art, has his complete meaning alone. His significance, his appreciation is the appreciation of his relation to the dead poets and artists . . . . The existing monuments form an ideal order among themselves . . . . (pp. 4–5; quoted from, p. 12)

After his brief paraphrase, Frye declared of his *magnum opus,* "Much of this book attempts to annotate" the seminal passage Eliot had written then quoted (*Anatomy,* p. 18).

---

16. It may be possible to extend the concept of mimesis to include existing literature. The relation of a work either to antecedents in a genre, or to an object of its allusion, would then be a mimetic one, and in the province of the Universe co-ordinate. But even to me, this seems more ingenious than helpful.

A distinction must be made between Frye's postulation of a significant literary context for every literary work (or the structuralist concept of "utterances" in literary works as "permutation of texts" that Julia Kristeva named *intertextualité*) on one hand, and on the other, the neo-Aristotelian concern for a writer's awareness of literary provenance. The former relation of the individual work is to the "verbal universe" of literature, and is inevitable; the latter is to a *specific* literary context, and is the writer's own doing. It is to this telic relation that a writer's use of allusion is analogous. Eliot's "ideal order" of "existing monuments" anticipates Frye in postulating the former relation. But at the same time, Eliot is concerned with how "the historical sense compels a man to write," and with the telic relation of a writer to Tradition that is literary influence. Moreover, the conclusion of "Ulysses, Order, and Myth," published the same year as "The Function of Criticism," declares that the value for modernist writers of "the mythical method" of fundamental reliance on allusion, derives from those writers' own strong sense of the relation between their contemporary culture and the past. It seems plain that, for the creator of "Prufrock," the formalist-cognitive conception of allusion as language, with the object of each of its allusions absorbed into "Prufrock" itself, denies "the relation" between his poem and its context in the "order" of literature.

Since allusion is tacit, its indeterminacy is unavoidable, with the potential consequences already shown to be exemplified in "Prufrock." But that is the minor significance of the inadequate formalist-cognitive concept that allusion is language contained in an autonomous work. Its major significance is that in denying the conjunctive nature of allusion, the concept obscures the way all allusions function.

Being tacit, the allusion in "Prufrock" to the circumstance of the prophet's death in the sensual *Salomé* of Wilde (or—*in my judgment* less likely—in the nihilistic one of Laforgue) exists only because it functions. But in functioning, it does more than only exist. The allusion makes into a context for "Prufrock" the work it alludes to; the result is that *the nature of that work* determines the attributes and the quality—supplies the value—of the functioning allusion to it. In other words, aspects of Wilde's *Salomé* itself are *invoked* by the allusion to it; and so, if the allusion to *Salomé* in "Prufrock" is to accomplish its full effect, Wilde's play *must have been experienced by the reader.* Even the simple and explicit reference, "No! I am not Prince Hamlet," functions more eloquently for one who has experienced the play than for one given the relevant information (having the "language" explained).

An allusion (be it even a pun) is a kind of analogical trope. It is like the instrumental part (Richards's "vehicle") of a metaphor in that both are tacit, and both rely on relevance (functionality) to assert presence. And as the irrelevant qualities in the instrumental part of a metaphor are excluded from the analogy (such as the soft texture of red mats in the metaphor for a setting sun), so are irrelevant writings about the death of the prophet John the Baptist (such as the Gospel accounts) "better not thought of," as "The Intentional Fallacy" says of Donne's "Song."

The currently popular doctrine that the apprehension of language is a nonreferential "mental act," it was pointed out in the preceding chapter (pp. 230–231), denies the apprehender's invoked real or imaginative experience on which an image such as "red mat" depends, when those two words are functioning effectively as the instrumental part of a metaphor. Correspondingly, the formalist-cognitive view of allusion as language "internal" to an autonomous work denies the apprehender's invoked experience (of Oscar Wilde's play) on which an allusion to *Salomé* depends, when that allusion is functioning effectively in "Prufrock": the modernist critics misrepresent how allusion functions, and the post-modernists imagery, identically. Whether it be mimetic of the climax of Wilde's play, or strictly referential to it, the alluding passage in "Prufrock" creates a relation with that discrete other work.

It is probably with one particular compound allusion whose circumstantial evidence generally is considered incontrovertible, that "Prufrock" demonstrates most eloquently that literary allusion functions, as I propose, by invoking the literary object alluded to—by making that work a context in literature for the alluding work. Even the title of his poem is implicated in the ironic relation Eliot seems to have created between it and the most famous courtship poem in English.

Two elements in Prufrock's "Love Song" effect the allusion to "To His Coy Mistress" most overtly. One is his question "would it have been worthwhile" to have ended "some talk of you and me" in order "To have squeezed the universe into a ball / To roll it toward some overwhelming question." The other is his repeated insistence that "we," in contrast to Marvell's couple, have "enough" time. The two elements are linked when the first paragraph associates making "our visit" with confronting the "overwhelming question," and "Do I dare / Disturb the universe" occurs in the context of "there will be time." Prufrock does not dare disturb his ordinary universe of "tea," "porcelain," and "talk of you and me," by squeezing all of it into the ball Marvell's lover proposes for breaking "Through the iron gates of life"—the ball Prufrock would (if only he dared) use on the question that overwhelms him. The analogy suggests that to put his question would be to break through the iron gates of his life; and Eliot's poem seems to indicate that. Prufrock's overwhelming question corresponds to the question the very putting of which is the confident exhortation by Marvell's lover that is Marvell's poem. Yet if he dared shape his ball, Prufrock believes, it would only roll "towards" his question. In other words, the analogical relation to "Prufrock" of the seventeenth-century poem is profound, involving Prufrock's character, predicament, and whole deliberation about his predicament; and the analogical relation cannot fully do its work for these fundamental elements of Eliot's poem unless Marvell's poem itself—the order of words that creates the lover's wit, self-assertiveness, patronization, sarcasm, erotic intensity, and triumphant confidence—is part of the reader's experience. For the compound allusion to it invokes "To His Coy Mistress" as an experienced reality.

Although Eliot belittles the "syllogistic relation" of the "three strophes" of Marvell's poem in "Andrew Marvell" (*Selected Essays,* p. 254), that "relation" enters into the ironic functioning of the allusion. For the three elements in Marvell's logical sequence of *If* ("Had we"), *But,* and *So* ("Now therefore") employ respectively the subjunctive mood, the indicative mood, and the imperative mood; and the body of "Prufrock" (to the set of dots before the six-paragraph conclusion)—which corresponds to the lover's exhortation—exactly reverses the sequence: *So* ("then"), the sham conclusion in the imperative mood with which Prufrock begins, is followed promptly by *But,* employing various forms of the indicative ("the women come and go" "there will be time," "I have known"), after which he progresses to his rationalizing *If* ("would it have been worth it") in the subjunctive. The "information" that the logical sequence in the object of Eliot's allusion is reversed in his own poem could be imparted, like nuances of meaning in an archaic word. But here too, the eloquent and devastating irony Eliot has created cannot be fully experienced by a reader of "Prufrock" unless the reader's prior experience of "To His Coy Mistress" is available for "Prufrock" to invoke.

IV. Conclusion

My purpose has not been to discredit formalist-cognitive criticism, but to point out certain limitations in its theory. My general commitment to its practice is apparent. And its chief exponents deserve what may be the greatest tribute that can be rendered to a teacher: many of those whose challenges to them I have been quoting were their students.

"Prufrock" itself is the object of allusion in "The Love Song of J. Edgar Hoover," a poem by Sean Kelly in the *National Lampoon* (August, 1972, pp. 65–66). Kelly's poem is not a parody, for "Prufrock" is its subject in no respect: it is an imitation, deliberately and systematically echoing Eliot's familiar poem, almost line-by-line. For example, corresponding to lines 41–46, with the thin/chin/pin/thin rhyme sequence and the couplet "Do I dare / Disturb the universe?," it has:

> (They all say: "Look, his arse is getting fat!")
> They criticize my shapeless suits and snappy G-man hat.
> My collars all a size too small, my simple string cravat—
> (They all say: "His neck is thick, his head is fat!")
> Do I dare
> Wiretap the universe?

According to recent reader-response criticism, the relevance of "Prufrock" to this systematic allusion—parenthetically quoting "them" complete with exclamation marks, substituting "fat" for "thin," and "simple string cravat" for "simple ["necktie"] pin"—is not manifest. An "interpretive community" no doubt will invoke "Prufrock" as a relevant context for reading "Hoover." But however numerous they may be, and however many persuaded reader-response critics the community may include, those readers have legitimated their understanding of "Hoover" only for themselves: strictly speaking, they have not demonstrated that a reading of it totally ignorant of "Prufrock" is any less valid— hence, adequate—a reading of "Hoover." The excesses attributable to the formalist-cognitive critics' zealous *opposition to* critical relativism seem (to me, I am obliged ironically but inevitably to add) benign by comparison.

The title of Paul de Man's *Blindness and Insight* designates his thesis that a critic's insights controvert her or his (inevitably partially blind) general formulations about literature. Frank Lentricchia expresses my hope as well when he invokes that sense of "blindness" in the preface to *After the New Criticism:*

> One of the lessons that I hope I've learned from reading contemporary criticism and philosophy is that no one is in a worse position to judge the blindnesses of a particular point of view than the one who subscribes to it . . . . (pp. xi–xii)

Few would deny that the sixty years from the ascendancy of the literary movement that identified "Prufrock" as one of its seminal works, to today, has been one of the richest times for literary criticism in history. One aspect of the historical significance of Eliot's poem is its relevance both for the criticism belonging to its own period, and for the challenges by critics of the past quarter-century. The insights produced by the more recent criticism augment the bountiful legacy of modernist criticism, to enrich us all; but there were inevitable blindnesses in general formulations throughout the six decades. Some fostered critical doctrines about the fundamental nature of literature that have important limitations.

Those doctrines concern the relation of the meaning in a literary work to its nature as a composition of words; the extent to which its meaning, if immanent, also is determinate; and the extent to which its status is autonomous. "Prufrock" eloquently exemplifies their limitations. That it could serve this purpose confirms more certainly its historical place; that it could do so without being diminished confirms more certainly its perpetual power.

10

The Adventures
of *Ulysses* in Our World

I

To begin the chapter, I offer a plausible historical account of the criticism of *Ulysses* to date. This plausible history designates three major phases, the first of them initiated two months before the book itself was published—by Valery Larbaud's statement, in his lecture introducing it and its author to Parisians, that it "has a key": "It is, I venture to say, in the door, or rather on the cover."[1] As has already been mentioned (p. 167), Larbaud also was the first critic to dwell on the non-Homeric aspects of the "design" of the novel that gave each "episode" its own "symbol . . . organ . . . colour" and the rest. Nearly a decade after publication, Stuart Gilbert's *James Joyce's* Ulysses (1930) elaborated, according to the same one of Joyce's variant schemata, the "design" only sketched by Larbaud.

In this history of *Ulysses* criticism, the first phase began in earnest with Gilbert's book. It extended through the next quarter-century, which coincided with the institutionalizing of modernist (objective) criticism. During that period critics analyzed the "Work," and provided accounts of manifestations in *Ulysses* of literary works other than the *Odyssey;* expositions of Irish and other local, topical, historical, musical, legendary, philosophical, theological, etc., material incorporated and invoked in it; delineations of different allusive and analogical patterns; and attributions of symbolic significance. During that quarter-century of identifying-and-explicating, Bloom—mostly as Wandering Jew, mock-epic anti-hero and symbolic Everyman—had been the Odysseus of critics' attention.

Informative work of identification and explication continued—and continues—to be published. But according to this history, about a quarter-century ago the second phase, a phase of attention to the evolution of *Ulysses* during Joyce's more than seven years of composition, was inaugurated by the major part of

1. He printed the lecture in his magazine, *La Nouvelle Revue Francaise,* XVIII (1922), 385–409. The quotation is from the translated portion dealing with *Ulysses,* printed by Eliot in *Criterion,* I (1922), 94–103, 97.

Walton Litz's *The Art of James Joyce* (1961). The result of that attention is our current awareness of the process of Joyce's movement out of what he called the "initial style" of the "First Part of *Ulysses*," which is documented for posterity in the periodical versions of the earlier chapters.

The fact that "he markedly altered many of his artistic goals while writing *Ulysses*" (Groden, p. 18) was mentioned, and his two major new creative departures were described briefly, in the fourth chapter (pp. 85–86). The first such "shift" or "radical change" in "intention"—I have proposed (pp. 85–87) it was his response to "emotional promptings"—occurred halfway through his seven-year odyssey. Whether or not indeed "the last nine of the eighteen episodes transfer concern from character to technique" (Groden, p. 37) is my principal subject in this chapter. And the place of Joyce's first major creative departure bears directly on my subject: that tenth chapter (his *"Entr'acte"*) punctuates the significant change in the action of his novel. The exact concurrence there of altered action with his alteration into a *Ulysses*-in-progress Made New (which, introducing the altered action, initially disconcerted Pound) indicates a connection in his "concern" between "character" and "technique."

Joyce's first creative initiative and his more radical departure—after four chapters—from that new departure, are responsible for the succession of new narrative modes and strategies that continued to "dismay" his "staunchest advocate, Ezra Pound" (p. 17). Taken together, the two successive "radical changes" (*Joyce's Voices*, p. 41), and the revisions and elaborations of earlier chapters that accompanied his second new departure, caused *Ulysses* to "turn into a different sort of book altogether" (Kenner, *Ulysses*, p. 71): "in the space of three or four years he travelled most of the distance from *Dubliners* to *Finnegans Wake*" (Litz, p. 35).

Beginning with his *"Entr'acte,"* Joyce "stretched and distorted," in Groden's phrase (p. 115), his "initial style," Then from the twelfth chapter, in which Bloom confronts his Cyclops, through the fourteenth, with its sequence of English prose styles, he combined different narrating voices and parodies of styles. With the nighttown chapter, he embarked on—and evolved the first form of—his second and more dramatic "shift." In each of the final three chapters he changed the narrative mode again, chapter by chapter, to the end of the novel. Presumably, it is because the nature of *Ulysses*, altered when he was moved to abandon its "initial style," was altered even more radically when he adandoned the narrative mode of the second group of chapters, that his elaboration—in its final stages so exasperating to the French printer—of the earlier chapters "occurred almost exclusively" while he was working on the last group of four strikingly dissimilar chapters.[2]

According to this plausible history, in the second phase of the criticism not his protagonist, but the writer himself in his creative adventure writing it, became the Odysseus who concerned critics of *Ulysses*.

The third major phase in this history began recently and is in full flower

---

2. Groden, p. 52. For evidence of Joyce's two major unplanned changes in "intention," see esp. pp. 13–23, 37, 52, 54–55, 60, 115, 118–22, 125–29, 170–71. See also Kenner, *Ulysses*, pp. 151, 153.

today. It is an aspect of the general current trend, discussed in the last two chapters, of abandoning objective for rhetorical methodologies: today, *ontological* inference about *Ulysses* as a postulated Work often is displaced by inferred *strategies* of Joyce composing, and *formulations* of readers experiencing, a postulated Text.[3] John Paul Riquelme's attestation (including his emphases) in *Teller and Tale in Joyce's Fiction* (Baltimore: Johns Hopkins UP, 1983) is both characteristic and thorough:

> Joyce's *Ulysses,* Joyce *as* Ulysses, is a Homeric *correspondance* from author to reader and between teller and character. When we read *Ulysses* ... we will be concerned with the multiple *relations* of the tale and the telling: the text's relatives ... the teller's acts of relating the tale, the structural relations within the telling and of telling (as style) to tale, and the relations among teller, character, and reader. (p. 134)

According to the criticism of the third and current phase, in *Ulysses* Joyce was not so much Homer's voyager as his cunning strategist—Odysseus *polytropos,* originator of verbal tropes and artistic strategems—an ingenious and intrepid hero-artist engaged in a creative adventure that cunningly arranged our hermeneutic adventure. And so the third and current phase in this plausible account of what has happened to *Ulysses* in the world of its readers involves a transposition of agent and object (recipient); today each of us readers has become an Odysseus responding to a succession of encounters with Text in his or her journey through Joyce's Book as word-World—or at least a deutero-Odysseus.[4]

The three kinds of criticism I have just sketchily described have been important, and roughly successive, emphases. But if a history consisting of these three phases is plausible, in my judgment it is not sound. It has two conceptual flaws and, complementary to the more important flaw, an egregious omission.

One conceptual flaw must have been apparent immediately: Joyce's process of composition is not a phase in the history of *Ulysses* criticism; it is a special subject that (inevitably first addressed at a specific historical point) has concerned a relatively small number of critics—after Litz, principally Phillip Herring and Groden. The second and more important flaw is that the most significant historical pattern is not this diachronic one, but a *bifurcation* from the beginning of *Ulysses* criticism to now. Consequently, most of the first and third

3. I am being reductive here, in characterizing current critical methodologies as rhetorical; for example, much deconstructionist criticism takes the form of *explication de texte.* But even in that case, since determinate meaning is denied to a "sign-sequence" such as *Ulysses,* the fundamental assumptions are rhetorical ones.

4. One recent critic who actually uses the hovering metaphor is Brook Thomas; he describes his *James Joyce's* Ulysses: *A Book of Many Happy Returns* (Baton Rouge: Louisiana State UP, 1982) as recording "my odyssey through the book" (p. 2). The general metaphor of "the reader's" or "Our voyage of discovery" (Riquelme, p. 151) occurs often in recent criticism. Joyce uses his phrase "the initial style" while likening Harriet Shaw Weaver as reader to Odysseus: "I understand that you may begin to regard the various styles of the episodes with dismay and prefer the initial style much as the wanderer did who longed for the rock of Ithaca" (*Letters* I: 129). But his analogy is both playful and limited.

kinds of criticism described are fundamentally alike. To be precise: both today's popular rhetorical hermeneutics of Joyce's strategies in his Text and our experiences of it; and most of the modernist identifying-and-explicating of elements of the Work begun in earnest by Gilbert's *James Joyce's* Ulysses, derive from a shared fundamental conception of the novel.

That a single tradition in *Ulysses* criticism has persisted through old-fashioned objective explication and new-fangled rhetorical hermeneutics can be illustrated with two quotations separated by a half-century. In 1932, Carl Jung wrote:

> *Ulysses* . . . pours along for seven hundred and thirty five pages . . . one single and senseless every day of Everyman . . . a day on which, in all truth, nothing happens. . . .
>
> . . . It not only begins and ends in nothingness, but it consists of nothing but nothingness.

And in 1982, Wolfgang Iser wrote:

> If traditional modes of interpretation are rendered helpless by *Ulysses,* this is because the novel dispenses with a basic concept that was virtually taken for granted throughout the history of interpretation: namely, that the work of art should represent reality. In spectacular fashion, *Ulysses* puts an end to representation.[5]

Although a "novel" (Iser), "*Ulysses* puts an end to representation";[6] it portrays a "senseless every day of Everyman" in which "nothing happens," for the good reason that "it consists of nothing but nothingness." Both these extreme assertions are accompanied—and belied—by their authors' perceptive observations about what the novel does represent; but both also express the persisting single conception of *Ulysses* fundamental to the dominant tradition of criticism. Two years before Jung wrote, Gilbert declared that conception, in the objective idiom of the time, in *James Joyce's* Ulysses:

> The meaning of *Ulysses* . . . is not to be sought in any analysis of the acts of the protagonist or the mental make-up of the characters; it is, rather, implicit in the technique of the various episodes, in nuances of language, in the thousand and one correspondences and allusions with which the book is studded. (pp. 8–9; 2nd ed. [New York: Knopf, 1952], p. 22)

Gilbert's formalist-cognitive concern in the time of Jung for "the meaning of *Ulysses*" conceals the fact that, as the primary sources of that *meaning* (of a

---

5. C. G. Jung, "Ulysses—A Monologue," tr. W. Stanley Dell, *Nimbus,* II (1953), 7–20, 7–8; Wolfgang Iser, "*Ulysses* and the Reader," *James Joyce Broadsheet,* no. 9 (Oct. 1982), p. 1.

6. My own use of *novel* throughout this book may seem like question-begging; but the following pages should supply the grounds of it. For the view that *Ulysses* is best not called a novel, see, e.g., A. Walton Litz, "The Genre of *Ulysses,*" in *The Theory of the Novel,* ed. John Halperin (New York: Oxford UP, 1974), pp. 109–20; and Thomas, pp. 141–42. An alternative would be to regard the term as designating, like *tragedy,* the sort of humanistic concept the late aesthetician Morris Weitz called "open": an "open concept" changes, and cannot be defined precisely; but it has the same cogency as Wittgenstein's family of different individuals.

Work), he identified precisely elements that now—in the time of Iser—are designated important *strategies/experiences* of a Text. In other words, a conception of *Ulysses* like Gilbert's, in which "the acts" and "mental make-up of the characters" are literally less meaningful than "technique . . . nuances of language . . . correspondences and allusions," is a conception in which elements of the novel that essentially refer to its quasi-reality *are subordinate to* elements of it that essentially are idiolectic ("nothing happens"; "an end to representation"). Today we are more fully conscious than were critics before the 1960s of the implications of that subordination: it readily assimilates to the currently popular doctrine of the novel as Text. But the fundamental conception of *Ulysses* shared by most critics throughout the past half-century is the subordination itself.

Hence, despite the theoretical and methodological dissimilarities between *Ulysses* criticism dating back to the thirties, and *Ulysses* criticism increasingly characteristic of the eighties, most constitutes a single *continuous* tradition that has been the dominant one. Hence, Riquelme's 1983 *Teller and Tale,* whose concern is "how we may understand our relation and the teller's to the tale" (p. xv) in Joyce's text, echoes in its first words Gilbert's general statement about the source of "the meaning" of Joyce's work:

> This study deals with the styles, techniques, structures, and conceptual implications of narration in Joyce's fiction. (p. xiv)

This dominant tradition comprises most criticism, but not all. A smaller body of criticism constitutes a tradition no less continuous, and complementary *because directly antithetical* to this dominant one; that tradition is the egregious omission in the plausible three-phase history of *Ulysses* criticism.

The year after *James Joyce's* Ulysses, Edmund Wilson published *Axel's Castle* (New York: Scribner's, 1931). Its chapter "James Joyce" declares, "with 'Ulysses' Joyce has brought into literature a new and unknown beauty," calling him "really the great poet of a new phase of the human consciousness" (pp. 220, 221). But again and again that sympathetic and acute discussion of *Ulysses* qualifies its praise with instances of sharp censure. In the course of the censure Wilson—while echoing Larbaud—reveals implicitly a basic conception of the novel directly opposed to what Larbaud had originated and Gilbert had just articulated. It is best represented in his own words:

> "Ulysses" . . . must be approached from a different point of view than as if it were merely like ["Joyce's other books"], a straight work of Naturalistic fiction.
> The key to "Ulysses" is in the title—and this key is indispensable if we are to appreciate the book's real depth and scope. (p. 192)

> But as we get further along in "Ulysses," we find the realistic setting oddly distorting itself and deliquescing . . . . (p. 206)

> "Ulysses" suffers from an excess of design rather than from a lack of it. Joyce has drawn up an outline of his novel . . . and from this outline it appears that Joyce has set himself the task of fulfilling the requirements of a most complicated scheme . . . . (p. 211)

We had been climbing over these obstacles . . . in our attempt to follow Dedalus and Bloom. The trouble was that . . . beneath the surface of the narrative . . . too many different orders of subjects were being proposed to our attention. (p. 214)

And do not the gigantic interpolations of the Cyclops episode defeat their object by making it impossible for use to follow the narrative? (p. 214)

The worst example of the capacities for failure of this too synthetic, too systematic, method seems to me the scene in the maternity hospital . . . . Now something important takes place in this episode—the meeting between Dedalus and Bloom—and an important point is being made about it. But we miss the point because it is all we can do to follow what is happening . . . . (pp. 214–15)

The night-town episode itself and Mrs. Bloom's soliloquy, which closes the book, are, of course, among the best things in it—but the relative proportions of the other three latter chapters and the jarring effect of the pastiche style sandwiched in with the straight Naturalistic seem to me artistically absolutely indefensible. . . . Joyce has here half-buried his story under the virtuosity of his technical devices. (pp. 216–17)

Wilson agrees with what I have called the dominant tradition in distinguishing (in his words) "story" from "technical devices"; and he agrees that one is fundamental in *Ulysses;* but he holds the opposite view of *which* one is so. The opposition between his conception of the novel and that of most other early critics is encapsulated in the contrast between their common unquestioning adoption of Joyce's Larbaud-Gilbert schema, and his exceptional impatience with it.

I believe our world evolved, soon after *Ulysses* came into it, the complementary antithetical traditions of criticism I have identified, a dyad that has persisted for six decades: every primarily critical study attaches itself to one or the other tradition. And both have contributed to our understanding of *Ulysses.*

The traditions are complementary because between them they accommodate the compound Joyce achieved in his novel, of idiolectic sign-sequence, and narrative about fictional humans; they are antithetical because they have opposed conceptions of its essence as being either one or the other of the two elements.

Terms already quoted for one element of Joyce's compound are his and critics' "styles," and critics' "technique(s)" and "telling"; for the other element, critics' "happenings" and "tale." To substitute less general terms used recently in pairs, precisely to specify the two elements: the critics of the dominant tradition implicitly or explicitly conceive *Ulysses* as *essentially* a "symbolic structure" employing its complementary mode of "characters" or "drama" as instrumental adjunct—hence, for example, the prevailing adoption of Homeric tag-names for the chapters; those of the alternative tradition conceive it as essentially akin to most novels in being a "human drama" employing its (strikingly original) complementary mode of "language" or "surface" as instrumental adjunct.[7]

7. The phrases "symbolic structure" and "human drama" are from Groden, p. 21; the terms "characters" and "language" are from *Joyce's Voices,* p. 41, and "drama" and "surface" from David Hayman, Ulysses: *The Mechanics of Meaning,* 2nd ed. (Madison: U of Wisconsin P, 1982), p. 88.

My subject is not *Ulysses* itself, but those two continuous opposed traditions of its criticism I conceive, and the important consequences of the contrariety for one's appreciation of *Ulysses.*

That some contributors to the canon of criticism emphasized "the tale of the telling," and others contrarily "the naturalistic [sic] tale," has been discussed in recent years; and the Wilson-like complaints of a number of the latter—especially S. L. Goldberg, in his nonetheless-praised *Classical Temper*—have been criticized.[8] Although the particular (conscious or unconscious) conception of the essential nature of *Ulysses* Wilson also articulated does not oblige the complaints, they derive from that conception. It persists today—I am among those who conceive *Ulysses* as essentially a "human drama." And so does the contrary conception shared by most *Ulysses* critics—that it is a "symbolic structure"— no matter how much those in that dominant tradition writing today may fail to recognize their kinship with their earlier predecessors during the past half-century and more, or may disagree with them on certain issues in literary theory.

The sensible escape from the dilemma would seem to be a view of *Ulysses* that transcended it by integrating the contraries; and this has been proposed and attempted by a number of cirtics.[9] However, all these critics, too, seem fundamentally committed to one conception of *Ulysses* or the other.[10] I shall try to show that the dilemma of alternative conceptions cannot be negotiated: their respective consequences for understanding important elements of the novel are so contrary, that the sounder alternative must be identified, if possible.

II

In 1912, shortly before he began work on the novel, Joyce delivered his pair of lectures on two English writers who exemplify the extremes of *"Verismo ed*

8. S. L. Goldberg, *The Classical Temper: A Study of James Joyce's* Ulysses (London: Chatto, 1961). See Groden, pp. 18–20, and Thomas, pp. 8–16. The parallel phrases recur in Thomas.

9. Among the authors of book-length studies, Marilyn French, Arnold Goldman, David Hayman, James H. Maddox, Jr., to an extent Brook Thomas as well (see e.g., p. 18).

10. The inability of these critics to integrate the alternative conceptions of the novel's essential mode can be illustrated neatly by two valuable discussions of the relation of the two modes themselves: Barbara Hardy, "Form as End and Means in 'Ulysses'," *Orbis Litterarum* 19 (1964), 194–200; and the relevant parts of Peter K. Garrett, "JAMES JOYCE: The Artifice of Reality," *Scene and Symbol from George Eliot to James Joyce* (New Haven: Yale UP, 1969), pp. 214–17, 245–71. Garrett uses "mode" as I do: his subject is Joyce's "progress from a realistic . . . toward a more symbolic mode" (p. 214) through *Ulysses.* Hardy's title refers to the three purposes served by "form" (p. 197); and two correspond to the two modes.

Garrett finds an increasing "conflict of modes" in the course of the novel; Hardy proposes instead that the two functions of "form" achieve throughout "a human complexity" eliciting "the admission of paradox" (p. 199). What is to the point here is not their contrary views of the relation of the two modes of *Ulysses,* but their own shared implicit conception of the novel. While granting due acknowledgement to the presence of gratuitous idiolectic play—"free play," "form as end rather than means" as Hardy puts it (p. 196)—both critics share a concern with, in Garrett's words, "the respective roles ["of symbolism and realism in *Ulysses*"] in the creation of meaning" (p. 256). Hence, both subvert their common intention of providing a conception of *Ulysses* that integrates the two modes, because both conceive the novel as essentially "tale"—the "meaning" created in it.

Idealismo nella letteratura inglese." Defoe (as Iser says Joyce "dispenses with" doing) "represent[s] reality" (Veri-similitude); and Blake adopts or devises intrinsic formulations (relies on intellect or imagination, *idea* in the root sense). In Walton Litz's words, these lectures "established the twin frontiers of his art and looked forward to *Ulysses*" (Hart and Hayman, p. 387).

Only a poor reader would claim that the lecturer's extreme example Defoe does not also exploit formal potentialities, or Blake also render experience, in their creations; but Homer, Dante, and Shakespeare, whom Joyce was soon to mine in making his novel (simultaneously claiming for it kinship to all three), were models for syncretizing storyness and textness. And only a poor reader would fail to recognize the ways in which the tale in *Ulysses* is compromised and qualified by unreliable narrators, and by the expressive strategies of its obtrusive author in newspaper headlines, interpolations, the "overture" of phrases, the setting and fantasies of the nighttown chapter. But its textness does not consequently displace its storyness as its informing principle.

Joyce's own syncresis succeeded in encompassing the two extremes he had exemplified in "Daniel Defoe—William Blake." *Ulysses* is, at what seems close to the limit of each, both a veristic "chaffering . . . chronicle" as its "Carlyle" calls it, and the idealistic "structure" of "a votary of the way to do a thing that shall make it undergo most doing," as Henry James said of Conrad (in his 1914 essay, "The New Novel"); it is an exquisitely realized symbiosis of fictional quasi-reality embodied, and form of embodiment. C. H. Peake eschews my temporizing "at what seems close to the limit of each," and declares simply, "No other novel had concerned itself at such length and in such detail with daily life . . . and yet no other novel had been so consciously and even ostentatiously artistic" (p. 347).

In "Ithaca," the essay whose comment on Joyce's *"Verisimo ed Idealismo"* lectures is quoted above, Litz warns against "the notion—always a reductive one—that the novelistic elements in *Ulysses* can be separated from the *schema* and claimed as the true line of the work's meaning" (Hart and Hayman, p. 405). One must avoid such a reductionist abstraction of one, and neglect of the other, of its two symbiotic elements. And this essay attempts to establish the grounds for doing so—by determining their functional relation in the novel. The practice of critics for more than half a century has documented what I shall try to show: that the relation is one of means and end. To distinguish—as a *critical* activity— quasi-reality embodied and form of embodiment, no more claims that each exists autonomously in *Ulysses* (no more claims that content and form "can be separated" in art), than to distinguish—as a *scientific* activity—sight from the optic nerve claims that they are autonomous. Therefore, critics should not be disturbed about making a distinction constantly made both in the dominant schema-tist tradition in *Ulysses* criticism and in the alternative novel-ist one.

In their dismissive generalizations to the effect that *Ulysses* does not "represent" anything "happening," Jung and Iser simply express in a hyperbolic way the dominant conception they share: that the things his novel's embodying words do represent as happening ultimately are a novelistic action Joyce devised, to serve (as its occasion or "subject") his embodying composition of words itself. An adherent of the alternative tradition, I assert the contrary: that its form of embodiment ultimately—despite his increasing innovation—serves its created life. Furthermore, my position is radical: today most critics in the dominant tradition would not claim that the "textness" of *Ulysses* is primary in its first chapters; I claim and shall try to demonstrate that its "storyness" is its essence even in its last and most stylistically innovative chapters.

III

Having made my declarations and radical assertion, I must now either deal (at least briefly) with certain issues these declarations raise, or fail to do justice to the many critics in the dominant tradition who have helped me read the novel. And to critics like myself as well; for the view of the alternative tradition, that however rich may be the tale of the telling, the telling serves what it tells, can seem simple-minded. The critic who holds this view can seem to be perverting the complex reality of *Ulysses,* seeking—or only able to see—in it a Classics Comics version of itself. (Wilson's "it is all we can do to follow what is happening" was written during the first shock wave.)

No distinction in the novel between Art and Life is implied: all is art by definition, Molly herself as much as the stream of words that embodies her. And it bears repeating that to distinguish the two symbiotic modes in the heterocosm *Ulysses,* as I have just done with its last chapter—and as all do who share the current critical concern with its textness—is not a pre-Romantic's claim that form and content are separable in art. Someone who did think these separable could not—and probably would not want to—read beyond Stephen on the strand in the third chapter. Only a reader who loves what language can achieve in literature would read a language-structure so rich that reading it and studying it are the same.

It follows that studying Joyce's Work "for the meaning" is not being opposed to the pure (phenomenal) experience of encountering the words of his Text. Furthermore, in many places the words— or other effects of idiolectic textness—are not primarily serving the quasi-life mode: they are significant in and for themselves. Those idiolectic effects support the dominant critical conception of the whole of *Ulysses* as essentially its textness (and Joycefully express the creative power of this massively egotistical great writer). But its many instances of textness do not make it *essentially* this mode described as "technique . . . correspondences and allusions" (Gilbert) yesterday, and "word-World" today. To oppose generalizing from those instances—to dispute so conceiving of *Ulysses*— no more involves ignoring them, than it does being insensitive to the working of language in the novel.

In his fine recent book in the dominant tradition, which I cite because I have learned from it, Brook Thomas charges:

> But despite Joyce's fascination with words, an entire strain of *Ulysses* criticism has chosen to ignore, minimize, or complain about the role of language in the book. (p. 8)

He also points out reasonably "that to read the book as book" is "not ruling out the possibility of reading the book as world" (p. 16); and he adduces Hugh Kenner (whose "appreciation of the human story," he says shrewdly, "seems to have sharpened over the last twenty years") in support of the proposition that we must "rid ourselves of the belief that the story exists prior to the book's language" (pp. 16–17). I concur with his positive points and plead innocence of his charge.

Unfortunately, neither plea nor concurrence will save me from the charge of naive empiricism. I adhere to the alternative critical tradition that conceives the quasi-reality it embodies to be the essence of the novel; and the alternative tradition directly confronts the prevailing current view of both the reader's relation to language, and the relation of language to reality. Currently, we who so conceive *Ulysses* are said to betray, in Thomas's phrase, our "objectivist-positivist notion of meaning" (p. 23). This local instance of today's general controversy in criticism is the last preliminary matter that must be brought up. To what has been said in this section's preceding chapters two points about the nature of narrative can be added.

The thesis originated by Saussure, that while the author may be referring with his or her written language, the reader's apprehension of meaning in the language excludes—is isolated from—what the language refers to, is directly related to the doctrine of indeterminacy in language. And *Ulysses* lends itself to the doctrine in a number of ways.

However, I propose that the narrated events in the novel—its explicit thoughts, speeches, and actions—give that doctrine no encouragement. Whatever aporias of language may or may not exist in *Ulysses,* even in the language that is necessarily the medium of its events, it embodies those events: a sequence of actions, speeches, and thoughts *is specified.* And that specified sequence in *Ulysses,* as I said in the fourth chapter (p. 53), constitutes an unequivocal language of fiction. To extend the doctrine of indeterminacy to narratives, on the grounds that all apprehended sequences are readers' constructs out of language, ignores the difference between possibly indeterminate signs *put* in a sequence by an author, and events *caused to occur* in a sequence by an author.[11] Language does designate (refer to) each event. But usually only its significance, not the event itself, is debatable. Even in the rare instance that the language saying what has happened is equivocal, the other events in the sequence provide a context for determining what has happened. Hence, the coherent sequence of events occurring in *Ulysses* is a *metalanguage;* and that distinct component of narrative is beyond the reach of the current hot debate between what seem to be alternative myths (each believed, neither provable) about the relation of language and meaning.

11. A similar flaw seems to me true of attempts, such as that by Roger Fowler, in *Linguistics and the Novel* (London: Methuen, 1977), to liken the elements of a novel to those of a linguistic structure. For example, lexical items may be paradigmatically exchangeable, but narrative "items" are not. A character is what he or she has done and been as plot since the opening paragraph; hence, to substitute a different character is not to change meaning within the (syntagmatic) action of the novel, but to subvert that action.

My second point about the nature of narrative concerns character. It is true that Bloom, for example, not only does not exist prior to the language of the novel, but also is, as Thomas vividly describes his textness, "a verbal construct . . . the result of words marching across the pages of *Ulysses*" (p. 15). But how important a true observation about the nature of narrative is that? In *Six Characters in Search of An Author,* Pirandello dramatized the paradox involved; and he discussed it in the preface. The evidence about Bloom the verbal construct is that the observation is as undeniably true as, and little more important than, one's observing that his creator was less than a dollar's worth of chemicals at 1922 prices. Recently we have had both a book extrapolating a prospective account of Bloom and Molly from the "Defoe-esque or narrative side" of the novel, and a "biography" of Bloom.[12] Every issue of the *James Joyce Broadsheet* contains illustrations from one or two new series of paintings or graphics portraying Bloom and other characters that (who) are just words. Whatever the value of any one series, all are testimony to the impress of the quasi-life in *Ulysses* called Leopold Bloom on the actual lives of the denizens of our world. Writing about Bloom in *A Colder Eye* (New York: Knopf, 1983), Hugh Kenner exemplifies Brook Thomas's observation about him—as much in the wily tribute to Joyce of "seemingly" and "seems," as in his positive statement:

> Bloom, though, grows in stature throughout the day . . . . His emergence as a man to care about and ponder is among the greatest of literary miracles, seeing that we encounter it in a book so seemingly insistent on its own indifference to . . . anything but schemes of formal consistency. By less than the halfway point the book seems wholly preoccupied for good with stylistic pastiche, yet already Leopold Bloom is so firmly established we cannot lose sight of him . . . . (pp. 195–96)

While he originates in the words marching across the pages, our Bloom is not meaningfully reducible to them. We know well that character in narrative can have such a quasi-life, unconfined (and unexplained) by the language that constitutes it/her/him. Most true paradox is mystery.

The dominant tradition in *Ulysses* criticism has made and continues to make an indispensable contribution to all our understanding. This must be emphasized in the course of proposing that the alternative tradition has the sounder conception of the novel. Of course, every writing that represents happenings is, to some extent, an idiolectic composition of words as well; and in certain such writings the idiolectic element is prominent enough to be a joint mode of reification. But one of the two modes usually is identifiable as essential, with the other its instrumental adjunct. For example, although both novels repeatedly draw attention reflexively to their own textuality, most critics would agree that the essential mode of *Moby Dick* and *The Ambassadors* is the quasi-life embodied in the book of words; and most would agree that the book of words is the essential mode in *Tristram Shandy* and *Finnegans Wake*.

Critics have been unable to agree about *Ulysses*. Three questions are

---

12. John Henry Raleigh, *The Chronicle of Leopold and Molly Bloom: Ulysses as Narrative* (Berkeley: U of California P, 1977); Peter Costello, *Leopold Bloom: A Biography* (Dublin: Gill, 1981). The quoted phrase is from Raleigh, p. 6.

involved, not one: Is one of its two modes really essential and the other instrumental?; If so, which is which?; Does which is which matter for our criticism? I have indicated my answers to all three, and shall try to defend them.

IV

Discussing in *The Odyssey of Style in* Ulysses (Princeton: Princeton UP, 1981), "the tension in the book between an emphasis on the telling of the story and an emphasis on the story itself," Karen Lawrence, one of the recent critics who express the view (alluded to above) that the "emphasis on the telling" does not occur until after the nine chapters of Joyce's "First Part," specifies that "Beginning in 'Aeolus' . . . and continuing in . . . 'Sirens,' the writing of the text begins to dominate our attention":

> The book does not abandon its interest in the characters and their stories, but one can locate a shift of attention from the dramatic action of the plot to the drama of the writing . . . . (p. 12)

And Michael Groden declares, "after 1919 Joyce was no longer writing a novel based primarily on human actions . . . ."[13] Unlike Kenner's "a book so seemingly insistent," these statements are positive answers to the first two questions: they agree with my claim that the modes are never equipoised—that a critic cannot weight them equally, for one is always essential, the other instrumental; and they propose that, after the early chapters, the essential mode is "the telling of the story"/"drama of the writing." I hope to show that even in the three chapters of III (the "nostos"), the essential mode of *Ulysses* is, in Lawrence's phrase, "the story itself."

But first the third question must be addressed. Does it matter for our criticism? Must one mode be shown to have primacy, one conception of the novel prevail, as the critical practice of both traditions suggests? I shall cite one instance of critical generalization and one of specific reading in support of my affirmative answer.

Lawrence makes the valuable point that Joyce employs *topoi* of classical rhetoric throughout the catechism chapter, and concludes:

> The performance of the catechism is really a school performance in the rhetorical classification of facts. . . . Using these topoi for comic purposes, Joyce plays with the idea of the human wish to arrive at truth. (p. 196)

This generalization about the form of the catechism chapter does not admit an equipoise of the two modes. If the form itself is the subject of the chapter—if the essential function of all the pedantic factuality about Stephen, Bloom, Bloom's house, etc., is to implement Joyce's rhetorical performance commenting on a universal human trait—Bloom and Stephen, being quasi-human, are included in that comment. But as a direct consequence, their importance in the

---

13. Groden, p. 21. He characterizes the two modes as "balanced" in the novel's "middle stage" (from the end of the "First Part" to the nighttown chapter), which "serv[es] as a bridge" (p. 4). See also, e.g., *Joyce's Voices*, pp. 41, 45; and Riquelme, p. 217.

chapter and so in the novel is diminished. They have been reduced to two particular examples of the universal humanity. And if so, the tale of their particular quasi-life, carried forward by the rhetorical performance Joyce uses to comment on humanity in general, must be merely the instrument of what the chapter is (essentially) about—the central tale is of the telling.

As with general critical propositions, so with the specific reading process, the two fundamental conceptions of the novel can be irreconcilable. An instance of the tale of the telling cited by Thomas is Stephen's mental sentence in the first chapter about the key to the tower, in which a full stop between two sentences has been ungrammatically elided to a comma: "It is mine, I paid the rent" (20). Thomas and other critics have proposed recently that Stephen is quoting Mulligan, and so Mulligan paid the rent for the tower.[14] The issue not only is important for subsequent events, but also bears directly on our understanding of Stephen. For example, the last paragraph of the chapter, after Stephen has given Mulligan the key and twopence "for a pint," is a single word, representing his thought: "Usurper" (23). Is the accusation the author has emphasized so heavily Stephen's legitimate projection of the incident onto the symbolic plane? If indeed Mulligan paid the rent, Stephen Dedalus is given a last word both inaccurate and a touch whining. Literally illegitimate, it also is symbolically pretentious. Therefore, who paid the rent has no trivial significance for this major character at the beginning of this long novel.

Either of two irreconcilable alternative meanings (Stephen paid/Mulligan paid) can be inferred from the ungrammatical sentence, by a critic in either tradition. The issue is relevant here because one's actual inference about what it says tends to be directed by whether one reads it primarily as a discrete structure of words, or primarily in its context in the action. For it must be taken *either* as its own textness (conveying the special status as Stephen's quotation that the comma then indicates), *or* as functioning essentially for the tale (disclosing ungrammatically who did pay the rent, Stephen or his "usurper"). And if no strict causal connection exists, since the comma does not require the inference that Stephen is quoting Mulligan, a manifest correlation does—between two irreconcilable meanings on one hand, and on the other, two irreconcilable conceptions of which mode of the novel is the essential one and so must prevail, the mode represented by the rhetorical possibilities in Stephen's ungrammatical sentence, or the mode represented by the place, in the story of the quasi-life it helps compose, of the thought his sentence conveys.

It also is relevant that the recent subtle reading of the language of the passage seems to be simultaneously a limited reading of the nature of human character:

> He wants that key. It is mine, I paid the rent. Now I eat his salt bread. Give him
> the key too. All. He will ask for it. That was in his eyes. (20)

I shall focus attention on three words in the two sentences following the one at issue—"Now," "Give," "too"—and on the next sentence—"All."

---

14. Thomas, p. 158; Kenner, *Ulysses,* p. 55. Thomas cites Fritz Senn, and Kenner, Arnold Goldman, as suggesting the reading to them. It should be mentioned that Kenner invokes the quasi-life in support: Stephen is too poor and profligate to have been able to pay the twelve pounds rent.

Stephen's specifying that Mulligan provides his food *now* seems to invoke a time when he supplied their or at least his own food. But if the problematic sentence that precedes *now* really is his anticipation of the words of Mulligan's legitimate demand, and so is interrupting the sequence of his thought, a question arises: What has food to do with the key (He wants that key [of his]. Now I eat his salt bread)? If Mulligan indeed "paid the rent," Stephen seems to be *connecting* receiving Mulligan's food *now* (as against the unspoken *then*), with having been receiving lodging *all along;* but if so, why does he not make explicit the otherwise incomprehensible connection with receiving lodging, specify the contrast with formerly providing his own food (Now I eat his salt bread *too*)? To me, what Stephen's *now* signifies is a rueful contrast of his present reliance on Mulligan for his very food, with a time when he had enough money to pay the rent on the tower; it is a familiar human sentiment.

Give does not seem the correct word, if Mulligan paid the rent; for then the key is, as Stephen ostensibly has him say, his. Furthermore, with the connective *too* Stephen does use, he links with taking Mulligan's food, not accepting lodging from Mulligan, but *giving* Mulligan the key. If Mulligan paid the rent, they are not corollary. If Mulligan paid the rent, the action on Stephen's part corresponding to *eating* Mulligan's food would be *retaining* Mulligan's key (I eat his food; I'll keep his key *too*). Of course, this would make nonsense of *now,* since Stephen has had the key.

The isolated word *all* not only connects the key and the food, but signifies a general resignation. If Mulligan paid the rent, Stephen is not submitting to very much by relinquishing the key to its rightful owner, who also feeds him; and so the sentence "All." joins the final paragraph "Usurper." as a grandiose pose by this major character. If, however, the key is Stephen's because *he* paid the rent; yet *now* he must submit to eating *Mulligan's* bread; and he will submit to *giving* to Mulligan *his* rightful key (and, it turns out, twopence) *too;* then indeed he is submitting in *all*—to Mulligan's usurpation. He is no shallow *poseur,* but the depressed and isolated young man we get to known better in the next two chapters and in the National Library. That young man is irreconcilable with the primacy of the textness of the passage; and as with the example of general criticism, two alternative novels begin to emerge from two irreconcilable conceptions of which is the essential mode of *Ulysses,* and which the mode instrumental to that mode.

Having demonstrated the consequences of inclining to accord greater weight either to a comma or to a quasi-live character, I should mention that the particular issue of whose words Stephen is thinking seems to have been obviated for the future. According to the *Critical Edition,* not a comma but a full stop follows "It is mine" (I: 36). ("Salt bread" replaced "food" on the second proof.)

V

In "Error and Figure in *Ulysses,*" a chapter (pp. 160–74) in his book *Inventions: Writing, Textuality, and Understanding in Literary History* (New Haven:

Yale UP, 1982), Gerald L. Bruns invokes rhetoric to describe the nighttown chapter:

> "Circe" is really nothing more than this: an episode of contrivances . . . repressions . . . and (above all) rhetoric, which is the art of making anything appear to be the case . . . . (pp. 171–72)

Bruns begins his chapter with an explanation of the phrase in its title: "error" and "figure" are alternative interpretations critics make of "misperception or misconstruction" by Stephen, Bloom, and other characters. He cites Hugh Kenner and Fritz Senn as readers of *Ulysses* whose criticism "emphasizes [respectively] Joyce's naturalism and its consequent irony" (error), and "figural transformation" (pp. 160–61). And he calls these emphases "the two most coherent and satisfying positions on *Ulysses* that Joyce criticism has given us" (n3 [p. 194]).

My reason for mentioning his instructive distinction is his own emphasis. For the concern of both his exemplary "positions" is restricted to "how things make sense in Joyce's fiction"—to the reader's process of apprehending. The product thereby apprehended, the quasi-life of a character who sometimes is self-deluding (error), sometimes self-ennobling (figure), and sometimes—true of both Stephen and Bloom—the latter by way of the former, is literally dis-regarded.

Yet the concentration of recent critics in the dominant tradition on the process of apprehending the textness of *Ulysses* has expanded all our sensitivity to, and awareness of, the complexity and variety of Joyce's telling in it. For example, when I first wrote about the novel, I believed Joyce was trying to conceal the authorial presence, and his strategies of concealment were unwittingly drawing attention to it (*Argument,* p. 144). It is this recent criticism that has taught me how mistaken I was—how precisely Joyce meant the personal implications of his simple word *styles* for the varieties of language, pattern, and narrative strategy his telling employed.

Of the six forms of telling I now distinguish, nothing needed to be taught about Joyce's three familiar ones: dialogue; a character-narrator; and the "invisible" non-participating narrator of a "dramatic" narrative—the anonymous "voice" that is self-effacing, and sometimes adopts the diction of the subject-character (a device also being used by other modernists, such as Conrad and Lawrence). I failed totally to recognize the ubiquity of a fourth: the non-participating narrator who, while remaining anonymous like the last mentioned, makes himself "visible," asserts his presence.

That fourth form of telling in *Ulysses* is Joyce's modernization of the familiar blatantly authorial voice addressing the "Dear reader," as in, "As said before he ate with relish . . ."(269) and, two pages later, "Bloom ate liv as said before." (*Who* said before? It is being "said" again and again for the sake of that word.) A fifth form is the modernist convention of arranging words to represent the largely non- or pre-verbal phenomenon, thought—inner monologue, interrupted by other forms of telling except in the last chapter, where it is an uninterrupted stream. What I realized only recently is how profoundly different inner monologue is *as a form of telling* from dialogue, which in other respects it resembles. Dialogue is a printed reproduction, in a narrative, of actual words of the language as they would be spoken by people; inner monologue is an arranged disposition of words in a narrative to represent something that is not language. And the disposition is arranged by an arranger.

But the arranger that enables its arrangings to be read through (past) itself is as old as written narrative: inner monologue is a form of telling in the novel employing the *transparent* arranger that also (for example) arranges into paragraphs the words of the novel's *self-effacing* narrator.

These five are the forms of telling used before *Ulysses*. For example, although he tells things he could not know, the character-narrator himself takes responsibility for the transparent arrangement of such things as the marbled page in *Tristram Shandy;* and although Ishmael is not clearly responsible, the arranger of the facsimile stage directions in late chapters of *Moby Dick* is transparent. *Ulysses* takes the next step. The new sixth form of telling Joyce developed in it is an arranger different from the traditional transparent one precisely as the blatant authorial "voice"—the opaque ("visible") non-participating narrator who asserts her or his presence with "Dear reader" or "As said"—differs from the self-effacing narrator of "dramatic" narrative. The sixth form is the new kind of arranger—that (*who* almost seems more appropriate) blatantly asserts its opacity.

The "non-human voice" first distinguished by Arnold Goldman in 1966 and named by David Hayman in 1970 *The Arranger,* Hayman describes as "a significant, felt absence in the text" and Kenner designates "perhaps the most radical, the most disconcerting innovation in all of *Ulysses*. It is something new in fiction," is—though "not a voice at all," as Kenner says—nevertheless "heard," "a felt absence," because it is a clamorous presence: it is this second, blatant, arranger originated by Joyce that attention to his telling in *Ulysses* has disclosed to us.[15] Responsible for the headlines in the newspaper chapter, typographical arrangements in the library and catechism chapters, extravagances in the nighttown chapter, interpolated passages, and so much else, the blatant arranger raises as well as settles questions. For example, when the unnamed narrator of the doings in Barney Kiernan's tells of urinating (335), his narrative includes his thoughts and the sounds of his spitting as happening while he speaks, although they happened in the past he is telling about. Is the blatant arranger time-warping?; our Homer nodding? There is no way to know.

The explications, in the early decades of the dominant tradition, of formal and allusive patterns, and of symbolic and tropistic meanings, built bridges to *Ulysses* over which all of us have passed. No less is the current concern with the tale of the telling doing so. Furthermore, this valuable development in *Ulysses* criticism acknowledges the symbiotic presence of the novel's mode of quasi-life, for its considers that mode the instrumental medium of the novel's essential textness. Mine is not a theoretical concern with its conception of which mode is

---

15. Goldman, p. 82; Hayman, 1st ed. (Englewood Cliffs: Prentice, 1970), p. 70 (the quotation is from the 2nd ed., p. 123); Kenner, *Ulysses,* pp. 64–65.

the essential one. I am concerned about the consequences of that conception: an unavoidable methodological bias I detect in critical *practice*.

For decades, Wilson, Goldberg, and others complained about the indifference of their contemporaries in the dominant tradition to the possible *function*, for *the quasi-life* in the novel, of elements of its textness. A general example of the bias in current practice is the persistence of that indifference. Hence, early explicators of the Homeric pattern, informed by the Larbaud schema that the third chapter is "Proteus," failed to ask what Telemachus had to do with Proteus—and to recognize the *function* for *Stephen's story* of Menelaus's wrestling with Proteus in the *Odyssey*. Hence, critics of today in the dominant tradition study Joyce's dramatically increased emphasis, after the novel's "First Part," on his telling—and neglect the *function* of that new emphasis for *the story* told by the audacious new tellings. They point out that with Bloom's confrontation with his sirens in the Ormond, the tale of the telling begins in earnest; and ignore that at precisely that point in the novel (marked by an *"entr'-acte"*) at which the changes in Joyce's "style" commence, Bloom commences to change in both attitude and conduct toward the situation which is the major subject of its action.

Whether the change in the tale or the change in the telling is primary—which is the means and which the end—is the subject under consideration. But two points are beyond debate. That the simultaneous change in its tale and its telling—that its quasi-life changes concurrently with its form—is a relevant fact about *Ulysses*, is self-evident. The other point is that the conjunction is not mentioned in any of the rhetorically oriented recent criticism I have read, although it was elucidated two decades ago. In this case, the bias that neglects the quasi-life in the novel also obscures an accomplishment of its form.

The contrary bias of the alternative to this dominant tradition occasionally expressed itself in a shortsighted impatience with stylistic and formal innovations in *Ulysses;* but I am proposing that its conception of the novel is the sounder one. My thesis is most appropriately tested against the final part, III, whose three chapters Joyce drafted last, from January through October, 1921 (*James Joyce,* p. 442)—in the most advanced stage of his evolution of its textness. In the next three sections I shall try to show that Joyce's telling in each of the three chapters of the "nostos" perpetuates to the end of *Ulysses* the primacy of the mode complementary to its textness—that of the quasi-life it embodies.

VI

Most critics in both traditions always have characterized the blatantly arranged narrative of the first chapter of III as "fatigued" or "tired."[16] And recently, some in the dominant tradition—expressing the current rhetorical emphasis of that tradition—have augmented its ostensible function: in addition to "depicting Bloom's [or both characters'] exhaustion," it embodies the author's comment

16. See, e.g., Wilson, p. 208, and Gilbert, p. 351; among recent critics, see, e.g., Groden, p. 53, and Lawrence, p. 168.

on the state of discourse, or the state of all language.[17] Declaring it "indeed the 'narrative old' that Joyce described to Gilbert," Lawrence writes:

> If the language of "Eumaeus" is enervated, it is not merely to reflect the fatigue of the characters or a narrator but to reveal that language is tired and "old," used and reused so many times that it runs in grooves. (p. 168)

I believe this more general ostensible function of the narrative style must be attributed to the concerns of current critics, not to the style itself. In the version of his schema that was embraced *ab initio* by the dominant tradition, the "technic" Joyce specified for the chapter was recorded as "Narrative (mature)"; it was changed to "(old)" in the revised (1952) edition of Gilbert's book. Neither of its (very different) parenthetical epithets makes this designation of "technic" more enlightening than is its corollary/contrary, the "technic" for the chapter that begins the novel: "Narrative (young)." In either case: Who—or What—is young or mature (or old)? Possible answers are embarrassingly silly. "Relaxed prose" (*"Prosa rilassata"*), in the schema Joyce gave Carlo Linati, at least has the virtue of being suggestive.

But setting Joyce's schemata aside, most demotic discourse always has been "formulaic," "of the tribe," as Gerald Bruns says is true of the narrative style (Hart and Hayman, p. 367), and most written language has been as well. Inferring that the style functions to make doleful general statements about the language of his time, attributes to James Joyce arrogant superficiality and a lack of historical sense; also, his not having discontinued his own novel-in-progress in despair of writing vital and original prose contradicts that sort of ostensible statement *prima facie*.

Bruns points toward a more intrinsic function for Joyce's telling than general commentary on discourse, in his remark that the "spirit of ordinary life . . . which dominates the episode" (because of the "collectivity" that is the narrator) is "the spirit of Bloom, perhaps" as well (pp. 364, 366). Other critics provide additional guidance. Goldman "assumes" that Bloom specifically is associated with the narrator's mode of discourse, "speak[ing] 'in the style' of the chapter: that is, Bloom did not really say this in this way" (p. 101). Groden makes Bloom more instrumental: Joyce "created . . . a literary equivalent of the state of Bloom's [exhausted] mind at 1:00 A.M." (p. 53). And Hayman confidently reverses Goldman's assumption by averring that although "Bloom, like his style, is tired," "the voice [of the narrator] . . . is Bloom's": "The technique is parody . . . of a Bloomish mind turned inside out" (2nd ed., pp. 102–3).

The attributions of the narrative mode to Bloom's, or "a Bloomish," mind do two things simultaneously—invoke the tale to explain the telling, and in doing so put into relief the unanswered, central question of the essential function of Joyce's rhetorical performance in the chapter. By this point in his novel, hundreds of pages of inner monologue have portrayed Bloom's mind; why did Joyce employ this singular mode of discourse to portray it here?

17. See respectively, e.g., Gerald L. Bruns, "Eumaeus," pp. 363–83 in Hart and Hayman, pp. 363–67, and Lawrence, p. 168. (The quoted phrase is Groden's.) Jameson considers it "Joyce's attempt at a parody or pastiche of . . . Henry James" (McCormack and Stead, p. 138).

The way to the answer is indicated by those few critics, again of both tradi-
tions, who characterize the narrative as the very opposite of fatigued: in the
words of the most recent of them, Thomas, "the style shows a mind gushing
forth."[18] The same critics all specify more precisely the association, noticed by
Hayman, of the narrative style with Bloom's "voice." They identify the style as
the exact correspondence *in written narrative* to Bloom's way of speaking to Ste-
phen: even cursory comparison of a narrative passage with Bloom's adjacent
dialogue indicates that were he in fact "to pen something out of the common
groove . . . *My Experiences,* let us say, *in a Cabman's Shelter*" (647) in the way
he has taken to speaking to Stephen, it would have the periphrastic and other-
wise pretentious, cliché-ridden style of the narrative.[19] Hence, when the narrator
gives Bloom's thoughts, his/its idiom is more or less indistinguishable from
Bloom's.

A (limited) function for the narrative style might be clear at this point, did
Joyce not insist that the arranged narrator is a presence in his own right, distinct
from "The irrepressible Bloom" (638) he/it tells of—as when his/its heavy jocu-
larity extends to the mistaken name in the *Evening Telegraph* report of Dig-
nam's funeral: "Boom (to give him for the nonce his new misnomer) whiled
away a few odd leisure moments in fits and starts with the account of the third
event at Ascot" (648). The subject of Bloom's "fits and starts" warrants atten-
tion, because it is central to the actual function of the narrator's egregious style;
but the contemptuous phrase itself separates narrator from character as much
as his/its prior jocularity at Bloom's expense.

Thomas describes the mind "gushing forth" in the narrative as "trying to
express sophisticated ideas": "The style of 'Eumaeus' approximates the style
Bloom would like to adopt to impress his companion in intellect." And here too,
Bruns's ingenious account of a "collective" narrator is enlightening: he/it
"speaks not to the reader—not to Joyce's audience—but to an imaginary audi-
ence of his peers" (Hart and Hayman, p. 367). These perceptions bear on the
function of the chapter's bizarre mode of telling. Their needed increment—and
corrective—is supplied by proper attention to *the tale.* For its chief character is
speaking—*literally* speaks—in a style that is the *oral equivalent* of the style of
the narrative, and is speaking so to impress his *actual* "companion"/"audience."

In other words, to explain the narrative style as strictly a model *Bloom* would
like to *adopt,* is to abstract both Bloom and it from the tale. Bloom cannot be
aware of the style, for a character cannot know an external narrator, while the
narrator must know Bloom; and his/its style is arranged prose *corresponding to*
Bloom's actual way of speaking to Stephen in the chapter. Hence, the radical
status of the style is the reverse of *Bloom's* model. For Bloom's speech is the
quasi-reality reported by the narrator; and having the elementary priority of (fic-
tional) prior existence, his speech is the informing context of the narrative style

18. Thomas, p. 134. Also *Joyce's Voices,* p. 38; and *Argument,* p. 364. The energy of the style is
a bit more apparent in the *Critical Edition,* because of the removal of about six hundred spurious
commas.

19. *Argument,* p. 364, and Thomas, p. 134; *Joyce's Voices,* pp. 35–38.

employed by that *persona:* if reported speech and reporting prose correspond, Bloom's way of speaking must be *the narrator's* model.

In addition to its (logical) radical priority as utterance reported, the style of oral discourse by way of which Bloom tries to impress Stephen has the primary significance because of the role of his endeavor—which constitutes the chapter's central action—in the novel. His endeavor and his reasons for it are important in the development of his story, and crucial to Stephen's story.

The rest of this section is devoted to presenting the grounds for my assertion, because doing so will establish for the present chapter my thesis that the quasi-life *Ulysses* embodies is primary through all three chapters of III, the "nostos," to its end. The chapter's telling does serve its tale if the style of telling, which is modelled on Bloom's way of speaking, *thereby* functions to emphasize a double crux in the plot of the novel whose locus is Bloom's pretentious table talk.

Bloom's sordid endeavor fails, of course: Stephen will not become a son/lover, replacing Rudy and supplanting Boylan. But the relationship he simultaneously—and unknowingly—establishes with Stephen results in the conclusion of Stephen's story in *Ulysses.*

Joyce made instrumental both in that story, of his Telemachus's search for the Father who would rescue him from the predicament that held the young man helpless, and in the no less but differently ironic and comic story of his Odysseus's efforts to return home, the two elaborate sets of coincidences involving Bloom that he worked into the novel. The set of coincidences originating in Stephen's dream of deliverance ("I flew") the night before, and its function for Stephen's story, was discussed in the fourth chapter (pp. 62–67). Even more elaborate is the set of coincidences originating in "the third event at Ascot," the *Evening Telegraph* "account" of which occasioned Bloom's "fits and starts": the Gold Cup race run there on June 16, 1904. The race is the single public event of that day in history made crucial to the novel; and being crucial, it is a legitimate *intrinsic* reason why that is the day of *Ulysses.* That set of coincidences is instrumental in the story of Bloom's exile and—along with the other set—in that of Stephen's predicament as well.

Following Stephen's third recollection of his dream, in the parlor of Bella Cohen's brothel, Bloom (characteristically) identifies himself unwittingly as the agent of delivery dreamed about. And Stephen (characteristically) understands the literal significance of Bloom's repeated "Look," and rejects the agent of the *dio boia:* "Break my spirit, will he?" (571–72). Immediately, he has a fantasy involving his earthly father and a race run by the Ascot horses. The "favourite," a "stumbling" and "broken-winded . . . nag" ridden by the anti-Semite Deasy, comes in last, while the winner is "A dark horse, riderless" (573). Stephen's fantasy-race contrasts significantly with Lenehan's (nevertheless inaccurate) account, in Stephen's presence at the maternity hospital, of Throwaway's close win of the Ascot race from Sceptre (415); and it reflects Lenehan's (equally inaccurate) statement, in Stephen's presence at Burke's, that the "sheeny" knowingly predicted the unexpected winner (426).

Immediately after Stephen's rejection of—and equestrian fantasy about—

God's prophetic Jewish agent, the cycle of events described in the fourth chapter occurs (pp. 65–67), beginning with the "noise in the street!" of the soldiers and girl, involving the advent of "The Mother" and his climactic blow to the chandelier, and ending in exact retribution for his blow, imposed by the "noise in the street" Who initiated the sequence (587–601). In other words, the metalanguage of linked events associates at the dramatic climax of Stephen's story his dream, Bloom, the Ascot race whose "prophet" Bloom was, and the central elements in Stephen's story.

The elaborate set of coincidences by which the Ascot race figures in Bloom's story associates him with Throwaway and with Elijah, in the complex: Bloom/ the "throwaway" announcing "Elijah" Dowie/ the "dark horse"/ the Jewish prophet-agent of deliverance.[20] In the catechism chapter, Bloom himself recapitulates the essential elements of this instrumental conceit: his "Reminiscences of coincidences, truth stranger than fiction, preindicative of the result of the Gold Cup flat handicap," stimulated by sight of the torn tickets for Boylan's bet on Sceptre, include connecting his inadvertent tip to Bantam Lyons with the "throwaway (subsequently thrown away), advertising Elijah" and with prophecy (675–76).

The association of him with Elijah and Throwaway that the novel effects, by way of the set of coincidences relating to the Ascot race, serves as a vital element in all of exiled Bloom's major relationships: not only with Stephen and with Molly, but even with his fellow Dubliners. On the very page after the set of coincidences is initiated—by his "I was just going to throw [the *Freeman's Journal*] away" and Bantam Lyons's excited response (85–86)—the sixth chapter, portraying the first overt anti-semitic treatment of Bloom, begins with "—Come on, Simon. . . . —Are we all here now? Martin Cunningham asked. Come along, Bloom" (87). Subsequent coincidences which involve his relationship with his society—and with Molly—include his passing by *while* Lyons tells companions in Davy Bryne's of the tip, and so being identified as its source (the only response is "scorn," 179); and his being seen by Lenehan and M'Coy *seconds after* Lenehan tells of meeting Lyons "going to back a bloody horse . . . that hasn't an earthly," whereupon Lenehan identifies the source of Lyons's tip, then launches into his anecdote about pawing Molly after the Glencree reformatory dinner (233–35).

These two coincidence-filled rejections of Bloom's coincidence-based unconscious prophetic act prefigure the interpolated "trial" of the bumbling messiah "ben Bloom Elijah" by an Irish "sinhedrim" (323), and the corresponding trial by the twelve Irishmen actually in Barney Kiernan's. Their verdict, executed by the citizen's attempt to "crucify" him "By Jesus" (342), is the direct consequence of Lenehan's allegation that his errand on the widow Dignam's behalf "is a blind. He had a few bob on *Throwaway* and he's gone to gather in the shekels" (335).

During this chapter, the set of coincidences figures in Bloom's relationship with Molly as well; and appropriately, Lenehan again is the agent. Although he

---

20. For details of the associative pattern, see, e.g., *Argument*, pp. 252–53, 256–57, 434–35.

is arguing with the citizen at the time, and apparently misses Lenehan's news that Throwaway won the Ascot gold cup with "the rest nowhere" and "Bass's mare" "still running," Bloom overhears Lenehan's disclosure that on his advice Boylan bet on Sceptre "for himself and a lady friend" (325). This is revealed in the maternity hospital (417), immediately after Lenehan gives his directly contrary (and less inaccurate) account of the relative performance of the two horses, again—coincidentally—in Bloom's (as well as Stephen's) presence. Between that instance and Bloom's shabbily motivated endeavor to impress Stephen in the cab shelter, Throwaway's victory, and the twenty to one "dark horse" odds he paid, are mentioned in nighttown by Joyce's renditions of Bloom's "Bello" (534), and of Corny Kelleher (604).

This review of the working in the novel of coincidences originating in the Gold Cup race at Ascot on Bloomsday is necessarily sketchy; it is intended only to help establish my thesis that the telling of the first chapter of the "nostos" functions to serve the tale. I have proposed that this set of coincidences, and the set originating in Stephen's dream of deliverance the night before intertwined with it, bear directly on a crucial development of Stephen's story in *Ulysses,* whose locus is Bloom's endeavor to impress him across the cab shelter table. The function in the novel of the two sets of coincidences actually culminates in that development.

Significantly, it commences immediately after the words pointing up the kinship between Bloom's pretentious table talk and the narrative style:

> Suppose he were to pen something out of the common groove . . . *My Experiences,* let us say, *in a Cabman's Shelter.*
> The pink edition . . . of the *Telegraph* . . . lay, as luck would have it [!], beside his elbow . . . . (647)

Before the "fits and starts" proper, Bloom has "a bit of a start" as "his eyes went aimlessly over the respective captions": but its cause "turned out to be only" the name "H. du Boyes." There are articles about: an earlier "dark horse" that "*Throwaway* recalls" and "Lovemaking . . . damages"; Deasy's letter on "Foot and mouth"; and the account of Dignam's funeral, which he reads aloud. Then, while Stephen reads Deasy's letter, he begins his "fits and starts with the account of the third event at Ascot on page three" (648).

Given what he already knows about the race and Boylan's bet, their initial cause can only be the news that Throwaway did not just barely beat out "Mr W. Bass's bay filly Sceptre," which came in third, but "Secured the verdict cleverly by a length": "so that Lenehan's version of the business was all pure buncombe . . . . Different ways of bringing off a coup. Lovemaking damages."[21] And—perhaps even more—his "fits and starts" mark a sudden understanding, recorded

---

21. Joyce seems to have copied much of the actual *Evening Telegraph* phrasing in the passage (e.g., "Throwaway/.3 won cleverly at the finish by a length"); but his inserting "bay filly" and having characters call Sceptre a mare seems to subvert the phallic significance of the name of the horse backed by Boylan and favored to defeat the "rank outsider." For the *Telegraph* article, see Don Gifford and Robert J. Seidman, *Notes For Joyce: An Annotation of James Joyce's* Ulysses (New York: Dutton, 1974), pp. 357, 451.

in the remainder of the paragraph. It is of the connection between his inadvertent tip to "that halfbaked Lyons"—who, he believes, stayed with Throwaway and had "positive gain" (676)—and his brutal treatment in Barney Kiernan's pub. He correctly infers that Lenehan misconstrued, and so misrepresented to the others in his absence (335), his "light to the gentile": "—There was every indication they would arrive at that, Mr Bloom said" aloud to Stephen, when the paragraph ends.

Bloom's "Different ways of bringing off a coup. Lovemaking damages" just before it ends, adapting one of the headlines, does little for his exile. But he has commented to Stephen on the consequence, for his relations with his fellow Dubliners, of the set of coincidences involving Throwaway and invoking Elijah. For Stephen, the consequence also is that of the set of coincidences about Stephen's dream intertwined with it. And *immediately* after Bloom's comment about what "they would arrive at," the portrayal of the consequence for Stephen begins.

Stephen understandably responds "—Who?" to Bloom's comment; the cabman (who had originally "laid aside" the *Telegraph* at Bloom's elbow, 632), says that "One morning . . . the paper" would announce *"Return of Parnell";* and Kitty O'Shea and her cuckolded husband are discussed (650). Bloom reflects that she "also was Spanish or half so," announces this to Stephen, and produces his photo of Molly with the disingenuous question, "—Do you consider, by the by . . . that a Spanish type?" (652).

Of his deliverer, Stephen had dreamed "A creamfruit melon he held to me" (217). Despite his fantasy race being won as Bloom had "prophesied," he knows nothing about the set of the coincidences associating Bloom with Throwaway and Elijah, which Joyce has intertwined with the set relating to his own dream; but he has identified Bloom as the Jewish-prophet/agent of the God he condemns and resists. Now Bloom has, as Stephen put it in his first recollection of his dream, "held against my face" Molly, "The melon he had" at home (47). And so unknowingly (of course), the compassionate and vulnerable Bloom has revealed that God's emissary is simultaneously the deliverer Stephen dreamed of.

When Bloom next speaks, it is to ask Stephen when he ate last (656); and next after that, to "propose . . . while prudently pocketing her photo," that "you just come with me and talk things over" (658). Stephen not only goes with him ("That man led me, spoke. I was not afraid. . . . said. In. Come. Red carpet spread. You will see who," 47), but begins to sing. Telemachus failed in his quest to find his father, but Odysseus returned to reunite them; and transformed in appearance by divine agency, he made himself known to his son in Eumaeus's hut. The same has happened with Stephen and his Father—appropriately, by comic inversion.

A major crux in Stephen's story, Bloom's table talk has a less significant role in his own. His shabby endeavor to end his exile by using Stephen to displace Boylan ultimately—ironically—succeeds, at least in Molly's thought: after thinking of Stephen as a potential lover, she dismisses "the ignoramus that doesnt know poetry from a cabbage" from her mind and the novel (775–76);

then she thinks of Stephen as a son instead, and decides to "just give him one more chance" and make Bloom's breakfast (778–80).

I have tried to indicate Joyce's articulation in the chapter, and in the intertwined sets of coincidences culminating in it, of a metalanguage of events so purposeful, and so elaborate, as to mock any proposal to ignore elements of it, or attempt to explain it away piecemeal. It is insisted on by coincidence compounded, insisted on by conjunction, sequence, and juxtaposition. That is the most significant tale of Joyce's telling.

A juxtaposition as gratuitous as the narrator's reference to Bloom's "penning" his experiences in a cabman's shelter just when the crucial sequence described above begins, and therefore as eloquent a declaration of the function of the narrative style of the chapter, occurs in an earlier chapter, "at commons in Manse of Mothers," where the Ascot race is mentioned (coincidentally) in both Bloom's and Stephen's presence. There, in Joyce's parody of Landor, Lenehan gives the one account of the race Bloom apparently has heard (reading the *Telegraph* story, Bloom refers to a single "version" as "buncombe"), and the company notice that Bloom is staring at a bottle of Bass's ale—brewed not by the owner of Sceptre, as Lenehan says, but by his uncle (415–16). Then a paragraph praises Bloom's "astuteness" and presents his thoughts, which concern "two or three private transactions of his own" related to "the turf" (416–17). He is "astute" enough to have become aware that Boylan lost the bet he placed for himself and Molly, and probably also that Bantam Lyons "ran off at a tangent" in the morning because he had inadvertently named the "dark horse" who won. (The "Light to the gentiles" catechism passage lists Davy Byrne's, where Lyons identified Bloom as the source of the tip when he walked past Lyons's group, as one place where "previous intimations" had "been received by him," 676.)

This paragraph placed between the Landor parody and the next parody (of Macaulay), and so made to interrupt the roughly chronological sequence that constitutes the chapter until its final pages, is in a style the first-time reader meets again after the interval of the nighttown chapter. Devoted to "The individual . . . as astute if not astuter than any man living" and his thoughts about "the turf," it begins:

> However, as a matter of fact though, the preposterous surmise about him being in some description of a doldrums or other . . . . (416–17)

Against the sequence of parodied classic English prose stylists, Joyce has juxtaposed a specimen of the egregious narrative style that will tell of Bloom's perceptions, thoughts, and table talk in the cab shelter. What his striking juxtaposition does is identify that style simultaneously with Bloom and the set of Throwaway/prophecy coincidences. The author has announced, before the cab-shelter chapter begins, the connection its narrator's stylistic ineptitude has to the two chief agents of its vital plot developments: Bloom's kindly and basely motivated conduct with Stephen; and the intertwined sets of coincidences whose function in *Ulysses* culminates there.

In the first chapter of III Bloom's endeavor to impress Stephen is the vehicle of the important plot developments; an inept pseudo-eloquence is the means he employs; and the style of the narrative corresponds to his oral style—and so emphasizes the endeavor of which his style is the instrument. Joyce's prior announcement reaffirms the abundant evidence in the chapter itself that its telling functions to serve its tale.

VII

The disrespectful narrator of the chapter derides "woolgathering" by his/its model (630). But his/its account of a vagrant thought, "Sulphate of copper poison SO_4 or something" (635), does not amend Bloom's defective knowledge by completing the formula $CuSO_4$—does not even comment on it. The reader is informed that the narrator probably cannot do so in its early pages, when Stephen meets one of the ignoble characters from *Dubliners* who appear in the novel, "Lord" John Corley of "Two Gallants." The narrator promptly demonstrates his/its omniscience by explaining Corley's nickname ("his genealogy came about in this wise," 616). However, in the next paragraph the omniscient explanation is first amended to "No, it was the daughter of the mother," then helplessly subverted with "if the whole thing wasn't a complete fabrication" (617). The narrator's unreliability is only compounded by the next paragraph, which purports to disclose truly omniscient knowledge of Corley's thoughts and condition.

Like the narrator of the first chapter of III, the catechetical respondent of the second chapter is unreliable. Although exhaustively informative, the respondent is—like that narrator—less than adequately informed; and he/it is error-prone as well.

If it were an isolated instance, the catechetical respondent's rendering of the year of *Ulysses* in the impossible Roman number MXMIV (669) might be the nodding of our Homer. (The "editorial emendation" to MCMIV in the *Critical Edition* lacks textual authority.) But, for example, he/it blithely designates Bloom "a jew" (691), despite Joyce's elaborate equivocation in the novel. And a striking instance of error occurs when Bloom boils water for cocoa. The description of "The phenomenon of ebullition" concludes "an expenditure of 72 thermal units [is] needed to raise 1 pound of water from 50° to 212° Fahrenheit" (673–74), although the correct figure is 162 British Thermal Units. The error may be a miscalculation, but the more likely cause is defective knowledge, which is to say, ignorance. The "Unit" is so called because it is specifically the amount of heat "needed to raise 1 pound of water" *one* Fahrenheit degree. All the respondent needed to do was subtract correctly the lower temperature from the higher: the point of the misinformation he/it provides is its egregiousness.

Furthermore, the defective knowledge cannot be reasonably attributed to Joyce. The repondent's phrasing insists on the precise definition of a B.T.U., which uses water, by weight, specifically one pound avoirdupois; and any dictionary would have aided Joyce's uncertain or partial memory, from elementary physics, of the equation. But he most likely thought to use it because its sensible neatness (1 unit: 1 pound/degree)—allowing easy computation, and so the display of ignorance (or bizarre error)—was fully familiar. Not the author outside the chapter, or even the blatant arranger of both the queries and the responses by which it proceeds, but its arranged quasi-narrator, the encyclopedically knowledgeable catechetical respondent, has defective knowledge, unreliable (usually exhaustive) information.

Only attention to the textness of the novel can reveal this characteristic of the second chapter of III. And it is because of recent criticism in the dominant tradition that I was prepared to perceive the respondent's misinformation about "ebullition"; for it has augmented our understanding of the chapter greatly. Writing about its form in a passage quoted from earlier, Lawrence simultaneously throws light on the ignorance and errors:

> In "Ithaca," Joyce employs the rhetorical topoi of "inventio," the first part of classical rhetoric. The narrative proceeds by ingenious "arguments" from analogy, difference, cause and effect, example.... The ... catechism is really a school performance in the rhetorical classification of facts.... Using these topoi for comic purposes, Joyce plays with the human wish to arrive at truth. (p. 196)

Furthermore, the coldly objective "aridities," in Joyce's word, of the respondent's endeavor to embody truth, are subverted not only by the instances of ignorance and error, but also by his/its ambitious tropes, romantic phrasing, and other manifestations of a totally incongruous human subjectivity. Lawrence points out that this occurs even in the relentless scientism itself:

> we try to understand the relationship among characters and encounter mathematical tangents and algebraic equations.
>
> These seems to be a mechanism of avoidance in the narrative.... [It] sometimes dovetails with Bloom's own mechanism of avoidance .... Bloom's strategy for dealing with his domestic situation merges with the narrative strategy. (pp. 182–83)

In *Joyce's* Ulysses *and the Assault upon Character* (New Brunswick: Rutgers UP, 1978), James Maddox observes the psychological trait and relates it to the respondent's errors—by extending his/its similarity to Bloom:

> the style loses sight of the human significance of the question and becomes absorbed in a purely mathematical calculation.
>
> Now this kind of thinking is not unlike Bloom's. Repeatedly throughout the day Bloom mentally approaches some thought of major emotional import but then shies away from it—frequently by substituting some mathematical or scientific speculation.... For example:
>
>> A million pounds, wait a moment.... Yes, exactly. Fifteen millions of barrels of porter.
>>
>> What am I saying Barrels? Gallons.... (79)
>
> This is Bloom's mind, sharp, active, calculating—and always tending toward errors of computation.... There is, in fact, enough error in "Ithaca" to at least suggest the use of error as a motif—as if the style itself were committing Bloomisms.
>
> The "Ithaca" style, then, partakes of certain very definite qualities of Bloom's mind. (pp. 188–89)

The egregious style of the previous chapter, resulting from attempted eloquence, was attributed to "a Bloomish mind"; in this one, egregious errors result from attempted omniscience—and are "as if the style itself were committing Bloomisms."

Hayman draws a more definite—and positive—conclusion:

> In a sense this chapter . . . is the warmest of them all. This is largely because, despite his elaborate pose, the speaker is . . . after all a projection of Bloom's scientific mentality rather than of the spirit of inquiry pure and simple. (2nd ed., p. 103)

And using a phrase from Joyce's *Letters* (I: 173), Litz makes the general statement (in his essay "Ithaca") that "the 'dry rock pages of Ithaca' are supersaturated with Bloom's humanity" (Hart and Hayman, p. 393).

"Bloom's humanity" is in the catechetical respondent's "habit of mind . . . in its displacement," as Lawrence puts it (p. 184); in his/its ambitious tropes and romantic phrasing; in response after response throughout the catechism, to the sleepy wordplay at its end. Bloom was "woolgathering" in the previous chapter "on the enormous dimensions of the water about the globe" (630). Not just the respondent's errors, but his/its defective knowledge as well, and all these "very definite qualities of Bloom's mind" so incongruous with even a flawed scientific objectivity, have the same provenance as the prose style of the previous chapter's narrator. Hence, as the *narrative* of that chapter focusses on Bloom, even when Stephen is present, so does *what is divulged* in this one.

This chapter's pedantic catechism is even more outlandish and arbitrary than that one's garrulous narrative style. And it more insistently raises the question of its reason for being. I am among those readers for whom the ugly duckling gradually grew into a swan; but the unfailing ineptitude of the cab shelter narrative is no less beguiling to me because Joyce makes it accomplish the work of the novel by way of its connection with Bloom. This chapter too functions in the novel—the striking and arbitrary telling of the catechism serves the tale—by way of its connection with him.

To begin with, the catechism is fully as revealing of Bloom's inner life as are the early inner monologues and his fantasies in nighttown. The respondent portrays the way Bloom's mind works, and expounds the things he generally treasures, aspires to, and craves. Most instrumentally for the novel, the respondent divulges Bloom's remembrances, reflections, deliberations—and conduct—in his unended exile. But as with the previous chapter, so with this, what is disclosed about Bloom does not itself explain the form of disclosure.

The explanation is the salient—indeed, dramatic—fact about the form that, in the words of D. H. Lawrence's admonition, one distinctly cannot "trust . . . the teller": that the exhaustively informative catechetical respondent not only fails to be consistently objective, but also proffers unreliable information. For example, directed to "Compile the budget for 16 June 1904" (711), the Bloomian respondent produces a minor inaccuracy—Bloom did return one pound seven (695), but Stephen had given him only one pound six and eleven (559)—and a major omission. The money Bloom gave Bella Cohen for Stephen's damage to the ceiling light had to come from his own pocket, and it is not listed. As Hugh Kenner put it in "Molly's Masterstroke" (*James Joyce Quarterly,* 10 [1972], 19–28), "This is not the budget *an sich,* but such a version as Bloom might let Molly inspect" (23).

Like his/its scientism, "shie[ing] away," and the rest, the respondent's unreliable statements of fact reflect his/its defining "Bloomism." As in the preceding chapter the narrative was formally distinct from Bloom but essentially identified with him, so is the catechism in this one. And the purpose of the singular telling is—as in that chapter—to emphasize happenings significant in the tale.

The unreliable budget, Bloom's in every sense, is unreliable as misrepresentation. It has been pointed out that other of the respondent's ostensible facts about Bloom and his story are unreliable as error and as ignorance. An example of the latter most significant for Bloom's and Molly's story, is the ostensible "preceding series" of Molly's lovers the respondent provides when Bloom joins Molly in the marriage bed (731), a list lacking the name of Boylan's most likely predecessor in that bed, of whose very existence Bloom is ignorant. In "Joyce's Unreliable Catechist: Mathematics and the Narration of 'Ithaca'" (*ELH,* 51 [1984], 605–18), Patrick A. McCarthy points out that the respondent "proceeds to contradict himself by initially stating that the series has no first term, then assuming that the first term of the series was ["someone who did not have intercourse with Molly"] Mulvey" (614–15).

The ostensible catalogue of her lovers is best discussed with the help Molly gives in the last chapter. That in proffering it the respondent—characteristically—represents Bloom's ignorance without amendment or comment, and inconsistently, is additional evidence of the nature of the telling in this chapter; that the inconsistency and shared ignorance are significant, indicates the function of the telling for the tale.

VIII

The two traditions in *Ulysses* criticism have tended to disagree about whether or not the major action of the novel has any prospect for success when it ends. A complication is that the ultimate issue of Bloom's belated effort to return home does not depend solely on his quasi-heroic conduct and Molly's willing response: his story must end in ironic failure if meaningful return is foredoomed by the nature of the deeply loved wife with whom he strives to reunite. What the proffered list of (exactly) twenty-five other occupants of her bed, almost every one during their marriage, does or does not signify about his Penelope, is crucial for the novel.

Maddox has called "Molly's sexual history" "the most hotly debated question in recent Joyce criticism" (p. 221). That in his/its "series" the catechetical respondent may be expressing not only Bloomian muddled thinking and ignorance, but—as in the budget—misrepresentation as well, is suggested *prima facie* by such unlikely lovers as two priests, an organ grinder, a bootblack. As long ago as the first edition of *James Joyce* (New York: Oxford UP, 1959), Richard Ellmann perceptively discounted the list not only because of unlikely inclusions, but for two other reasons: it is Bloom's catalogue (its source actually is ambiguous, which helps indicate the Bloomian nature of the respondent); and "the book" contradicts it:

> But on examination the list contains some extraordinary names: there are two priests, a lord mayor, an alderman, a gynecologist . . . . In the book it is clear that she has confessed to the priests, consulted the gynecologist, and coquetted with the rest. . . .
> The two lovers Molly has had since her marriage are Bartell D'Arcy and Boylan. (p. 388)

The opposing position in the debate has a much longer history. On the basis of the list, the equally reliable gossip of Bloom's fellow Dubliners, and her sensual reflections, Molly was relatively benignly called "the compliant body" with "animal placidity" in 1941, but more recently such things as "a great lust-lump," "at heart a thirty-shilling whore," and (elegantly) "a swine."[22] One critic cites Ellmann's discrediting of the list in the course of a detailed discussion of "The Twenty-five Lovers of Molly Bloom," and remarks that "a really skeptical scrutiny" by "a really determined doubter" would remove every name but Boylan's. Nevertheless, "her sexual appetites are literally insatiable"; and in a second book published four years later—in which "She is a slut, a sloven, and a voracious sexual animal"—the list is implicitly rehabilitated:

> She is mad for men, all men, indiscriminately, tramps, bootblacks, lord mayors, Boylan, Poldy, Mulvey—so that "he" and "him" come to refer[,] in the course of her soliloquy, to an almost limitless array of lovers.[23]

Acknowledging difficulty with the list, another critic nevertheless declares that "if" in fact Molly has not "been unfaithful," it is "against her will and her nature" (and on "16 June 1904 . . . she loses her title as 'faithful Penelope' after all").[24] Although today most critics are aware of extensive evidence contradicting it, the belief that *Ulysses* depicts a grossly promiscuous Penelope has continued into this decade.[25] In fact, it is a grotesque distortion of the novel's third principal character.

22. The first phrases are from Levin, p. 125. For the sources of the others, see Maddox, p. 222n.5. In the course of a functional explanation it proposes for "her most salient characteristic—marital infidelity" (p. 50), Phillip F. Herring, "The Bedsteadfastness of Molly Bloom," *Modern Fiction Studies,* XV (1969), 49–61, gives a detailed account of such appraisals of Molly's character (pp. 57–59).

23. Robert M. Adams, *Surface and Symbol: The Consistency of James Joyce's* Ulysses (New York: Oxford UP, 1962), pp. 35–43, pp. 37, 40; and *James Joyce: Common Sense and Beyond* (New York: Random, 1966), p. 166.

24. Bernard Benstock, "Ulysses Without Dublin," *"Ulysses": Fifty Years,* ed. Thomas F. Staley (Bloomington: Indiana UP, 1974), pp. 90–117, p. 112.

25. For example, Costello perpetuates it in his 1981 "biography"; and a paper read at the English Institute the same year accepted it without question. Gilbert and other critics have discussed the possible relevance to *Ulysses* of post-Homeric accounts of Penelope as adulterous—most often the lover of the god Hermes and mother of Pan, although Joyce also may have recalled Vico's statement in *La Scienza Nuova* that "In other versions Penelope prostitutes herself to the suitors." For details, see Herring, pp. 53–55.

The list itself is discredited above all by its exclusion of "Gardner Lieut Stanley G" (749:1; also 746:37, 747:17, 762:19–20), the one person in addition to Bloom, Boylan, and her girlhood lover Mulvey, with whom Molly's revery reveals a serious erotic involvement; it also is discredited by specific information Joyce provided—both in the chapter and elsewhere in the novel—about the others it catalogues. More than a dozen of the twenty-three men come up in the chapter itself; and of them she both knew and thinks of without scorn only Bartell d'Arcy, who "commenced kissing me" on the single occasion "after I sang Gounod's *Ave Maria*" (745:32–33).[26]

From her thoughts, we learn that she remained a virgin with her pre-marital lover, Mulvey (761:7–8), and (besides those of Mulvey, Bloom and Boylan) has felt the phallus of Gardner (746:37), and seen those of two "disgusting" exhibitionist Scots soldiers in kilts (753:25–30). We learn also that, despite more than a decade of erotic frustration, degradation, and neglect by her husband, she just committed adultery for the first time. When the chapter has barely begun, she thinks of Bloom's perverse physical activities with her and their mutually degrading spoken accompaniment:

> question and answer would you do this that and the other with the coalman yes with a bishop yes . . . who are you thinking of . . . the German Emperor is it yes imagine Im him think of him can you feel him trying to make a whore of me . . . simply ruination for any woman and no satisfaction in it pretending to like it till he comes and then finish it off myself anyway and it makes your lips pale anyhow its done now once and for all with all the talk of the world about it people make (740:22–37).

The unlikely partners aside, the adulterous "this that and the other" Bloom's masochistic and provoking questions propose his wife "would . . . do" constitute the obvious alternative (the only feasible one for an Irish Catholic middle class wife in 1904 Dublin) to the situation he has imposed on her for the past "10 years, 5 months and 18 days" (736). It is because only "now" she has finally "done" it, that her very long and very sensual revery lacks thoughts about actual sexual intercourse except with Bloom and Boylan: as the day of the novel is a singular one for Stephen and Bloom, so it is for Molly as well.

Critics have "hotly debated" the character of Molly with much less reason than in the strikingly similar case of Chaucer's Criseyde, because Joyce has been much less equivocal—although no less subtle—in his portrayal. That Molly was so stubbornly misrepresented—a fictional character ("words") calumniated as though living, in despite of the evidence—has interesting implications for the recent past of our culture: but its only relevance to novel or character is the support it gives her low estimation of men.

Certain recent critics, unimpeded by a negative misconception of Molly, have increased all our understanding of what Joyce wrought in her. About her

---

26. For a detailed exposition, see *Argument*, pp. 431–33. See, also: Hayman, 2nd ed., pp. 23–24, 117–18, 154 (n.5, which records an exchange in print about the list); Robert Boyle, S. J., "Penelope," Hart and Hayman, pp. 407–33, pp. 413–15; Marilyn French, *The Book as World: James's Joyce's* Ulysses (Cambridge: Harvard UP, 1976), pp. 252–56; Maddox, p. 221.

thoughts on one of her confessors, "Father [Bernard] Corrigan" (741:1–19)—
they occur just ten pages after he is listed in the "series"—Hayman writes:

> It is worth noting that Molly's yearning is more appropriate to an adolescent
> than to a hardened woman. Still, she has had no relations with a priest, and she
> will go on to disprove most of the list in detail and to show herself to be even
> less worldly than Bloom . . . . (2nd ed., p. 118)

This is quoted not for the central point, first made by Ellmann, but for the com-
ments about Molly herself at either side of it. Father Robert Boyle's essay
"Penelope" describes her attitude "toward sex" as "often naive" (p. 411), and
observes shrewdly from "Her somewhat adolescent musings on the details of
genitalia and of coition" that "Molly's actual sexual experience is indeed lim-
ited," (pp. 413–14). Marilyn French notes certain reticences (pp. 255–56). Most
recently, Maddox, whose comment on the debate about Molly was quoted at the
beginning of this section, has examined the nature of her eroticism in extensive
and persuasive detail. He demonstrates that it is not only "appropriate to an
adolescent" emotionally, "naive" in attitude, and "limited" in experience, but
also extremely conventional. His evidence shows Molly to be—behind her "rov-
ing eye" and "obscene tongue"—"actually tentative and conservative about sex-
ual acts themselves even as she is curious about variations from the sexual
norm" (p. 223). And he concludes:

> She likes to imagine herself as sexually daring and adventurous, but she is adept
> at finding excuses for refraining from anything very far from the very ordinary.
> . . . beneath Molly's image of herself as a sexual dynamo, there is reticence and
> a girlish curiosity. (p. 224)

This fuller understanding of the character Joyce has created in Molly Bloom
redirects attention to other details in the novel. Her progressive inflation of Boy-
lan's virility (and response to her)—"he must have come 3 or 4 times" (742:2–
3), "4 or 5 times" (763:7), "5 or 6 times" (780:23)—noted by McCarthy (p. 614),
is an instance of Joyce's benevolent mockery directed at her. It also belongs to
her portrait. Not only his response to her, but also the virility of the lover she
has attracted, reflects on her. Almost at the beginning of the chapter, she
"wonder[s] was he satisfied with me" (741:19–20), and later "whether he likes
me" (749:29–30), "really likes me" (758:27); rapturously recalling a climax with
him, she discloses she did not "shout out" obscenities "only not to look ugly"
(754:28–30); she "wonder[s] was I too heavy sitting on his knee" and "hope[s]
my breath was sweet after those kissing comfits" (769:42–770:4). This concern
extends well beyond Boylan. The context of the second tally of his response to
her in that series is "see if they [some "Irish homemade beauties"] can excite a
swell . . . like Boylan to do it 4 or 5 times"; her desire "to be embraced 20 times
a day almost" by "somebody if the fellow you want isnt there" is "to make ["a
woman"] look young" (777:25–27); even her not "pick[ing] every morsel of that
chicken out of my fingers" is "only for I didnt want to eat everything on my
plate" (750:9–11). Although inexperienced and conservative, Molly also
undoubtedly is robustly sensual; but the principal concern of the character Joyce
created is for approval, including a lover's response to her, rather than for erotic

gratification in the narrow sense. Hence, she wants to receive letters, especially love letters, and thinks of her first, from Mulvey (759:4), the many from Bloom when they courted (747:11–12 and 771:4), and Boylan's of the morning, which (prudently) "wasnt much" (758:31). The contrast of husband's and lover's letters is not explicit, in the manner of "Poldy has more spunk in him" (742:33); but her first thought of Bloom's letters (and flowers) occasions, "I liked the way he made love then he knew the way to take a woman," and her second, closer to the end of the chapter, the memory that his "mad crazy letters . . . had me always at myself 4 or 5 times a day sometimes" (771:4–8).

Filling out the portrait of Molly as she really is are details of her moral sensitivity. One recognizes the equivocation edging toward reluctance behind her "anyhow its done now once and for all." There is the genuine guilt about having "done" "it" in her fear (shades of Stephen) that the thunderstorm was "the heavens . . . coming down about us to punish when I blessed myself and said a Hail Mary" (736–37). Both equivocation and guilt are reinforced, when she is planning in the final pages of the novel to "just give him one more chance" (780:6), and serve Bloom breakfast in bed, by the self-conscious but indignant protest, "its all his own fault if I am an adulteress as the thing in the gallery said" (780:28–30)—especially by its key term.

And reflecting back to the pages that introduce her and her husband to the novel, one appreciates how thoroughly inexperienced is the supposed career adulteress. After bringing her the card from Milly and a letter he has guessed is from Boylan, Bloom "waited till she had laid the card aside" and then "delayed" further, before going for her breakfast; but she refrains from opening the letter (62). When he returns, the letter he delivered is—incompletely—hidden under the pillow, and she admits Boylan sent it (63). Although the evidence is against him, this Molly Bloom very well could have had Boylan move the parlor furniture in an attempt to tire him and so avoid sexual relations, as Kenner suggests in "Molly's Masterstroke."[27]

Maddox quotes Molly's wish "to be embraced 20 times a day almost . . . to be in love or loved by somebody if the fellow you want isnt there" (777:25–27), and comments:

> The combination of sexual indiscriminateness ["at a safe distance," he points out] with the phrase "if the fellow you want isnt there" brings Molly's eroticism into clear focus. Molly has a roving eye ["imagined promiscuity"] because she is unwilling to set her sights exclusively on one man beyond Bloom, the fellow she wants who isn't there. (p. 222)

Following his point about her conventional eroticism, Maddox writes,

> Molly's combination of bravado and reticence makes her in some ways the ideal partner in Bloom's sexual fantasies. (p. 224)

The ingenuous conduct toward Boylan's letter, simultaneously comic and poignant, of both distressed husband and desperate wife, shows them to be ideal

27. Richard E. Madtes, *The "Ithaca" Chapter of Joyce's* Ulysses (Ann Arbor: UMI, 1983), challenges Kenner's thesis, citing Joyce's notes to the effect that Molly herself moved the furniture (pp. 100, 23). The chapter discredits it in any case: see 769:43–770:2 and 776:24–27.

partners in a more touching way as well. That conduct occurs with their very introduction to *Ulysses;* Molly's final chapter fulfills what it portends: completes the novel's abundant documentation of their relationship with the surprising revelation of its mutuality. This wife and husband show reciprocal: doting admiration—hence, each considers collecting the other's sayings; solicitude—hers for him repeatedly punctuates expressions of her justified resentment; and most important, profound commitment. French observes, "Given the view of her held by Dublin males, it seems unlikely that it would take Molly all these years in sex-starved Dublin to find a lover," likens Molly's commitment to her husband to Penelope's as "a little unbelievable" (p. 257), and declares:

> Molly is finally faithful to Bloom: fairly faithful physically and totally so emotionally. That is, her emotional commitment is to him above any other man. (p. 260)

The final qualifying phrase is explained by her next and concluding paragraph on Molly:

> Her deepest commitment, of course, is to . . . hearing the voice of her own body and merging it with the voices of nature. . . . she embodies the life force. (pp. 260–61)

The character of Molly Bloom in *Ulysses* takes on symbolic meaning more insistently than does that of either Leopold Bloom or Stephen Dedalus. This is not only explained but also within limits warranted by her nature, by her subordinate but instrumental role in the novel, suggestive of a *dea ex machina,* and above all by Joyce's way of presenting her—first in sketchy details and indirection, then with repeated overt symbolic suggestiveness in the catechism chapter, and finally in her uninterrupted recumbent memories and reflections. The hyperbolic sensualist so presented is symbolic enough to anticipate the archetypal sleeping giant of Joyce's next book.

But Molly's eventual symbolic meaning emerges principally out of—and simplifies—specific structural relations and precise information that are functional story. Her chapter is a shaped sequence of (mental) events prepared for, and required by, the preceding action. Even more distracting from her role in the novel's story than the elevation of her undoubted symbolic suggestiveness to primary significance, is the recent preoccupation of the dominant tradition with "the tale of the telling," as when—in a currently popular idiom—Riquelme writes about her chapter solely as the last installment in that tale:

> The substance of the episode is and will remain beyond the horizon of writing and reading . . . because [*"unwritten"*] it is inaccessible to writing. (p. 228)

It is legitimate to set against this critical observation that by Ralph W. Rader in "The Logic of *Ulysses:* or, Why Molly Had to Live in Gibralter" (*Critical Inquiry* 10 [1984], 567–78):

> in Molly's soliloquy, the prominence of language as language, style as style, sharply recedes, leaving us with an overwhelming sense of the materiality . . . of

Molly's body which, though made of words, is as realistically substantial as any object in literature. (572)

But I will address Riquelme's point directly.

That thought is not written language is beyond dispute; however, neither is physical action written language; nor is situation/scene. To limit one's attention to an abstracted model of the telling itself in "this last style, which presses the mimesis of consciousness toward the nonlinguistic," is precisely to *place* "the substance of the episode"—simplistically—"beyond the horizon of writing and reading." For abstracting a single telling from the told overlooks (fails to read) *Joyce's* telling *of* Molly's telling, an eight-part composition of *writing* initiating, developing, and concluding, like "Prufrock," the action that is its subject's psychomachia.

Although our increasing understanding of her nature, based on her true testimony, shows that much of her own telling was long beyond the horizon of our reading, the chapter representing Molly's mental acts as language manifestly portrays her nature. But in addition, the chapter provides a dual revelation that is made instrumental by its final position in the novel. It reveals her patiently enduring more than a decade of neglect and perversity, and the abiding commitment to Bloom that that patience implies.

The texture of the chapter alone—the verbally rendered mental acts that are Molly's telling—reveals her decade of self-denial. But the structure by which Joyce tells her telling is the necessary vehicle of her attitude to the husband who exacted the self-denial. That attitude is the *dénouement* of narrated (mental) action, a decision she arrives at. And her thought process may continue until sleep, but only in the sense that the landscape continues beyond the margins of a landscape painting; Joyce's novel concludes with Molly's decision. Although the texture of the chapter is revery, almost totally passive stream of consciousness, its structure is auto-debate, recording the process by which she resolves her psychomachia about both her general attitude toward her husband and its specific index. Of course, the index is her husband's final action in the novel, his specific initiative to alter the routine in—and mark of—their usual relationship that normally would occur next, when they awake, and with which their story in the novel began. What both Molly and Joyce make of Bloom's initiative transforms its apparent triviality, in the last major instance in *Ulysses* of comic irony.

The eight sections, or "sentences" as Joyce repeatedly called them (*Letters* I: 168, 169, 170), present roughly symmetrical stages in the parabolic evolution of Molly's initially and ultimately favorable general attitude toward Bloom (*Argument*, pp. 422–25). That parabolic structural pattern probably is the covert meaning of Joyce's reference to "the final amplitudinously curvilinear episode Penelope" (*Letters* I: 164).

Placement in the chapter, and sequence, indicate how she will respond to the initiative that is Bloom's final action, revealed only in its plot consequence, her initial reaction, "Yes because he never did a thing like that before as ask to get his breakfast in bed since ..." (738:1–2). After her surprised reaction, she ignores Bloom's request until almost the last third of the chapter; then she thinks about it four times, in a sequence first of scorn (764:6–10), next of plaintive resentment (772:36–733:2), next of bluster (778:10–14), and finally, two pages later and at almost the end of the chapter and novel, with the decision to "give him one more chance" (780:6).

The structure is elaborately articulate when she reaches this specific conclusion. Her decision coincides with a desire to dress as Bloom had dreamed of her the night before; the key references are to "red slippers" and "Turkish"/"Turks." As with Stephen's dream of delivery, the thought/sentence "Wait." occurs when Bloom first remembers his dream (381)—which correspondingly is of return, for the mode of dress Joyce has him dream of, and her now want to wear, is said in the hospital chapter to signify "a change" (397). Her decision also promptly precipitates the complaint "its all his own fault if I am an adulteress"; an extensive and vehement expression of her resentment of him; and her plans to tempt him, "make his micky stand for him," and even "put him into me." Then on the next page she plans to "make him want me thats the only way" (781:15–16); and then begins—with the realization "and it was leapyear like now yes" (782:16)—her final rhapsodic remembrance of their idyllic first love on Howth precipitated by her initiative, which ends in her conflation of Mulvey with her husband at the time their relationship began. In *Characters of Joyce* (Totowa: Barnes, 1983), David G. Wright proposes that the issue "may be" whether or not "the Blooms [will] . . . break their 'fast' in bed" (p. 97); and Joyce is fully capable of having decided on the specific subject of Molly's auto-debate partly to play on the original meaning of the key word of "breakfast in bed."

It is impossible to recount here the details of Joyce's integration and resolution of significant elements of Bloom's story in its final chapter. It also is unnecessary for indicating the use to which he put the relatively familiar form of telling he caused to follow a sequence of strikingly innovative ones. The chapter's apparent simplicity of texture subtly portrays Molly's true nature, and is disposed in a purposive structure.

Apparently not circumstances but story explains why Joyce worked on the two last chapters simultaneously (Groden, p. 187; *Letters* I: 175, III:49). After attending Stephen's departure from his home and the novel, Bloom returns by way of the parlor—and promptly bumps his head against the sideboard. Although the narrative technique of the ostensibly objective catechism chapter contrasts strikingly with that of the ostensibly subjective stream of consciousness chapter, from that point of Bloom's abrupt confrontation with his marital situation, it is the final chapter's functional complement.

The sequence of proffering in the one, and ironic and significant discrediting in the other, of the list of lovers, is an obvious example of their complementary function. A no less significant inter-chapter *peripeteia* is the list's sequel, Bloom's tortuous rationalizing to indifference his distress over Molly's infidelity ("slaying the suitors"), and her obviating his sophistry by revealing her commitment to him; it is another instance of Joyce's benevolent mockery of him. Following his process of rationalization, four pages after the respondent proffers the list and less than two before the chapter ends, the first part of a third inter-chapter *peripeteia* occurs. The catechist asks, "What limitations of activity and inhibitions of conjugal rights were perceived by listener and narrator concerning themselves . . .?" (735–36); and using the first phrase, the respondent reveals the decade of limited "activity" suffered by the listener, and a nine-months' limitation of "mental intercourse" "perceived" by the narrator—but never addresses the second part of the question. The *peripeteia* consists in Molly's revelation that until the day of the novel the "limitations of activity" involved not just her husband, but all men.

However, the respondent's suppression of the second phrase exemplifies another use to which Joyce puts the Bloomian catechism: emphasis. Hence, the chapters also are complementary in that precisely what the catechetical respondent has suppressed in one, and Molly's "perception" emphatically articulated in the other, Bloom's "inhibition" of her "conjugal *rights*" (my emphasis), is what both motivated her resentful imperious treatment of "the fellow [she] want[s]" and justifies her response to Boylan's desire for her. After all, Bloom was not taken off to a Trojan war against his will. It is in the suppressed phrase the suitors are slain, if anywhere in the catechism chapter, for Molly really wants not lovers but her conjugal rights.

Revealing her true nature, her compatibility with and commitment to Bloom, and even her specific response to his specific final initiative to alter their relationship, Molly's chapter of mental acts is no less significant for what it reveals about Bloom himself. The author's mockery in Bloom's total ignorance of Gardner is more gentle than in Bloom's rationalizing about nonexistent lovers; it is the same tone that informs his equivocal Jewishness ("so I . . . told [the citizen] his God, I mean Christ, was a jew too . . . like me, though in reality I'm not"). Eclipsing Joyce's fun with him is Molly's confirmation of his stature. The novel does not mock his emotional commitment to her as the degrading and foolish yearning for a promiscuous featherbrain. It discloses that she both desires and deserves his cherishing her and wanting her back. The soundness of his commitment is the key to Bloom's stature, as his folly would be if Molly were as his fellow Dubliners, and the Bloomian respondent, believe her to be. Of course, if he is actually responsible—even momentarily—for the respondent's list, organ-grinder, bootblack and all, it is another example of how silly his ephemeral ideas can be, and how grand his abiding instincts; and Joyce has, once again, had it both ways.

The respondent's list of lovers received so much attention in the critical debate about Molly because its significance is far greater than as a detail in a rhetorical gambit—because it is implicated in the novel's quasi-life. The debate concerned not telling, but tale—not "words marching across a page," but the quasi-person unconsciously acknowledged by Brook Thomas in the very metaphor of his vivid phrase.

As at any point in life, so at the end of *Ulysses,* there is no closure. But the complementary tellings of its two final chapters have concluded Joyce's tale of Bloom's desire and endeavor to return to Molly: they have told her willingness to alter the destructive pattern of the marriage; and they have completed the novel's subtle revelation of the extent of both mates' commitment, and suitability, to each other. Strikingly different as the chapters are, Joyce used those two singular forms of embodiment together in the service of the quasi-life they embody.

IX

In his prelude to its publication, Larbaud initiated the attention early critics in the dominant tradition of *Ulysses* criticism gave to its Homeric pattern and other elements of "design." During the year it was published, Eliot noted its "singular" achievement of totally eliminating a recognizable style.[28] Now, after six decades—in our world—the attention critics working in that still-dominant tradition are giving to the extreme innovation and resourcefulness of Joyce's telling is increasing all our understanding of the elegant artistry of his novel. I have put and been trying to answer a three-part question about the relationship in that novel between the composition of telling words those critics conceive (or assume) to be its essential mode, and the mode of *Ulysses* conceived (or assumed) by the alternative tradition to be its essential one: the things told by its telling words. The three-part question is: do its symbiotic modes of a quasi-life embodied, and a book of words consitituting the form of embodiment, relate as end and means?; if so, which is the essential mode, and which the mode instrumental to it?; and, finally, does their relation to each other matter?

Joyce's first new creative initiative during his odyssey of composition culminated in the ultimate parody-pastiche of the hospital chapter; and he began his second and more radical initiative with the stunning *tour de force* of the nighttown chapter. Each of the three chapters of III contributes to a dramatic sequence of innovative narrative strategies. Yet all three radical forms of telling serve the quasi-life told—and the same is true of the nighttown chapter that began his final adventure in creative telling. It is no accident that the quasi-life the four chapters tell is continuous—a narrative uninterrupted by intervals of time—throughout, something not done before in the novel. For each of the four innovative narrative strategies was tailored to function in the service of the story.

This is most apparent, perhaps, in the last chapter. Instead of being some final, transcendent, *tour de force* of the previously dominant blatant arranger, Joyce made Molly's soliloquy a self-effacing, transparent arrangement, a direct verbal enactment of a character's thoughts. It is really subtle telling, of course—in both texture and structure. But its narrative strategy is only an extreme version of the inner monologue that characterizes the familiar "initial style." And Joyce's reason for an apparent regression (duly chastised by some recent critics), from his sequence of radical new blatant arrangings, cannot be unrelated to the fact that the representation of thought was required to tell what needed to be

---

28. "*Ulysse* n'est . . . que le gigantesque aboutissement d'une époque révolue. Avec ce livre Joyce atteint à un résultat . . . singulièrement distingué . . . elle ne possède aucun des signes qui permettent de diagnostiquer la présence d'un style." T. S. Eliot, "Lettre d' Angleterre: Le Style Dans La Prose Anglaise Contemporaine," *La Nouvelle Revue Française*, XIX (1922), 751–56, 754.

told: that Molly is qualified, and intends, to play her part in Bloom's endeavor to return home—achieve his "nostos."

A fact about the *Odyssey* obscured by the chapter-tags in Joyce's schemata is that its "nostos" occupies the latter *half* of its 24 books, not the final three: Books XIII–XVI, whose locale is Eumaeus the loyal swineherd's hut, are roughly invoked in Joyce's tag "Eumaeus" for the sixteenth chapter of *Ulysses;* XVII–XXII in his "Ithaca" for the seventeenth; and the *next* to last book—portraying the reunion of Odysseus and Penelope, their going to bed, and his telling her (as Bloom tells Molly) of his experiences—in Joyce's designation "Penelope" for the final chapter of the novel. But that designation is as misleading as it is obvious. Joyce's exploitation of the *Odyssey* was consistently more functional than the simple correspondences suggested to so many in the dominant tradition for so long; and despite his schemata, Book XXIII of the *Odyssey* manifestly corresponds to the latter part of his seventeenth chapter. Hence, Molly's soliloquy corresponds to the last book of the *Odyssey,* or to nothing.

Most dramatically from the point "in the middle of things" at which Homer begins his story of Odysseus himself (the mortal man's rejection of Calypso's offer of immortality, because he wishes to return home to his family), but actually from the very beginning of the poem (with Telemachus's search for his father), the primacy of domestic values is the ordering principle of the *Odyssey.* Hence Book XXIV, and Homer's poem, ends when Athene (with Zeus's help) prevents Odysseus and his men from chasing and killing the routed families of the dead suitors, so that all may return to their homes and live in civil peace. And Joyce's final chapter, which follows the (inadequate) reunion of his Dublin wanderer and waiting wife in their bed, seems to be his correspondingly civil conclusion to his corresponding story: his indication that, in the world of his characters, domestic values—which have been of prime importance from the beginning of their story—will prevail.

The requirement that the telling serve the tale explains Joyce's regression from his sequence of radical new blatant arrangings in that final chapter. It also explains something else: why both Molly's soliloquy, and the catechism chapter drafted simultaneously with it, which, Hayman writes, "as though in an after-thought, carries so much of the book's exposition" (p. 103), contain between them immense amounts of—and are such apt vehicles of—sheer information. A book of words would have been permitted by its author to disdain such extreme claims upon it—dilution of its idiolectic integrity—by information about the lives and stories of characters.

Most of the information in the two chapters is about Bloom and Molly. The role of the complementary elements of the chapters in completing Bloom's story has been discussed; but the corrective revelations about his wife's character and attitudes that complete his story are—because they do complete it—part of a pattern Joyce created in the "nostos" as a whole. It is a pattern in which, once again, telling is to tale as means to end. The narrative strategies of all three chapters are effective instruments of characterization, and they comprise a portrayal, in its last phase, of the two principal persons of Bloom's odyssey. The "Bloomian" first two chapters render, respectively, Bloom's public idiom *in extremis* (hundreds of pages have given his private idiom), and his aspirations, values, mental habits, and deliberations about those things he values and craves. Molly's soliloquy renders her private idiom and her aspirations, values and the rest.

The emphasis on characterization in the "nostos" is no more than a persistence of that emphasis in *Ulysses* to its end. The point has been made (p. 83) that only one of the eighteen chapters, that in which Bloom contends with the citizen in Barney Kiernan's, involves little psychological portrayal, and that thirteen chapters, numbering more than three-fourths of the novel's pages, primarily portray the principal characters' mental events.

Perhaps more than anything else, the consistent emphasis of Joyce the modernist on the inner lives of his characters establishes the primacy he accorded the quasi-life he was creating. *Ulysses* portrays situations crucial to the destinies of three Dubliners; and the resolution of each situation requires no more— though demonstrably no less—than a change of attitude.

The portrayal of a crucial conflict or crisis by way of a character's consciousness was not new in literature and drama in 1922. The immediate relation in this respect of James, Laforgue, and Dostoevsky to the modernists Joyce and Eliot has been discussed. But what was new with *Ulysses*—and with "Prufrock" and *The Waste Land*—is that the crucial situation is portrayed in an *action* that has, as its significant *arena,* the mind itself in which the attitude must change, and, as its significant *outcome,* the change of attitude itself—only that mental event—or in the case of "Prufrock," the thwarting of it. In *Ulysses:* the story of Stephen resolves in his own mind in nighttown and in the cab shelter; that of Bloom (and Molly) in his own mind in nighttown, in the portion of the catechism following his collision with the sideboard, and in her "indispensable [mental] countersign," as Joyce described "the last episode" to Budgen (*Letters* I: 160). In none of the three works are the consequences of the mental event functionally important; and in *Ulysses* they are not even portrayed.

In the interplay between the novel's form and its life, textness and storyness, idiolexis and mimesis, Joyce increased the idiolexis brilliantly as he worked. And there is no doubt that he encourages us to admire and vicariously reproduce his creative odyssey: one need only recall his exultant "How's that for High?," in the letter to Budgen describing the hospital chapter (*Letters* I: 139). Furthermore, the study of literature in our late twentieth-century world causes us to conspire with him by its emphasizing technique, allusive pattern, irony and/or indeterminacy, rhetorical and stylistic strategies of narration and/or equivocation. But we would be doing his grand achievement a disservice if we thereby failed to appreciate the end of those means. And because in the reality that is a work of art, means and end are dancer dancing dance, we would simultaneously be partly denigrating the means as well.

Joyce's making of *Ulysses* enlightens for our world the relation of telling and tale in it. His two dramatic creative departures rose not out of ingenuity, or colored pencils, but out of a felt necessity to change direction. Paradoxically, his increasing emphasis on the formal mode of his book was achieved by the source of its quasi-life—his capacity for experiencing, and using creatively for it, his feelings about it. Able to feel his own life as artist so well, he could feel and create for us as well as he did the life—and so the world—of his characters. Even the tale of the telling is a tale of human experience—of a seven-year lived artistic odyssey; it culminated in immortal achievement, and the bequest of an abiding treasure.

Works Cited

(Single citations are excluded.)

ABRAMS

Abrams, M. H. *The Mirror and the Lamp.* New York: Norton, 1953.

ADAMS, "WHAT WAS MODERNISM?"

Adams, Robert Martin. "What Was Modernism?" *Hudson Review,* 31 (1978), 19–33.

AFTERJOYCE

Adams, Robert Martin. *Afterjoyce: Studies in Fiction After* Ulysses. New York: Oxford UP, 1977.

ANATOMY

Frye, Northrop. *Anatomy of Criticism.* 1957. New York: Atheneum, 1967.

ARGUMENT

Sultan, Stanley, *The Argument of* Ulysses. 1964. Middletown: Wesleyan UP, 1987.

"BEYLE AND BALZAC"

Eliot, T. S. "Beyle and Balzac." *Atheneum,* May 30, 1919.

BEYOND CULTURE

Trilling, Lionel. *Beyond Culture.* New York: Viking, 1968.

"BEYOND MODERNISM"

Bell, Daniel. "Beyond Modernism, Beyond Self." *Art, Politics and Will: Essays in Honor of Lionel Trilling.* Ed. Quentin Anderson et al. New York: Basic, 1977. Pp. 213–53.

BLOOM, *YEATS*

Bloom, Harold. *Yeats.* New York: Oxford UP, 1970.

BRIEFE 1889–1936

Thomas Mann, Briefe 1889–1936. Ed. Erika Mann. Frankfurt: Fischer, 1961.

BRIEFE 1937–1947

Thomas Mann, Briefe 1937–1947. Ed. Erika Mann. Frankfurt: Fischer, 1963.

BUDGEN

Budgen, Frank. *James Joyce and the Making of* Ulysses. London: Grayson, 1934.

BUSH, *T. S. ELIOT*

Bush, Ronald. *T. S. Eliot: A Study in Character and Style.* New York: Oxford UP, 1983.

COLUM

Colum, Mary M. and Padraic. *Our Friend James Joyce.* London: Gollancz, 1959.

CONSCIOUSNESS OF JOYCE

Ellmann, Richard. *The Consciousness of Joyce.* New York: Oxford UP, 1977.

CRANE

Crane, R. S. *Critics and Criticism, Ancient and Modern.* Chicago: U of Chicago P, 1952.

CRAWFORD

Crawford, Fred D. *Mixing Memory and Desire: The Waste Land and British Novels.* University Park: Pennsylvania State UP, 1982.

CRITICAL EDITION

Joyce, James. *Ulysses.* A critical and synoptic edition. Ed. Hans Walter Gabler, Wolfgang Steppe and Claus Melchior. 3 vols. New York: Garland, 1984.

DAVIES

Davies, Alistair. *An Annotated Critical Bibliography of Modernism.* Sussex: Harvester, 1982.

"DEACON DEDALUS"

Day, Robert Adams. "Deacon Dedalus: The Text of the *Exultet* and its Implications for *Ulysses.*" *The Seventh of Joyce.* Ed. Bernard Benstock. Bloomington: Indiana UP, 1982. Pp. 157–66.

DE MAN

De Man, Paul. *Blindness and Insight: Essays in the Rhetoric of Contemporary Criticism.* New York: Oxford UP, 1971.

DREW

Drew, Elizabeth, *T. S. Eliot: The Design of His Poetry.* New York: Scribner, 1949.

DIARY

Woolf, Virginia. *The Diary of Virginia Woolf.* Ed. Anne Olivier Bell. 5 vols. New York: Harcourt, 1977.

ELIOT IN HIS TIME

Litz, Walton A., ed. *Eliot in His Time.* Princeton: Princeton UP, 1973.

ELIOT'S COMPOUND GHOST

Unger, Leonard. *Eliot's Compound Ghost: Influence and Confluence.* University Park: Pennsylvania State UP, 1981.

ELIOT'S POETRY AND PLAYS

Smith, Grover. *T. S. Eliot's Poetry and Plays.* 1956. Chicago: U of Chicago P, 1961.

FACSIMILE

Eliot, T. S. *The Waste Land: A Facsimile* . . . . Ed. Valerie Eliot. New York: Harcourt, 1971.

FOKKEMA

Fokkema, Douwe, W. *Literary History, Modernism and Postmodernism.* Amsterdam: Benjamins, 1984.

FRENCH

French, Marilyn. *The Book as World: James Joyce's* Ulysses. Cambridge: Harvard UP, 1976.

GILBERT

Gilbert, Stuart. *James Joyce's* Ulysses. 1930. 2nd ed. New York: Knopf, 1952.

GIVENS

Givens, Seon, ed. *James Joyce: Two Decades of Criticism.* New York: Vanguard, 1948.

GOLDMAN

Goldman, Arnold. *The Joyce Paradox: Form and Freedom in His Fiction.* London: Routledge, 1966.

GORDON

Gordon, Lyndall. *Eliot's Early Years.* New York: Oxford UP, 1977.

GRAY

Gray, Piers. *T. S. Eliot's Intellectual and Poetic Development: 1909–1922.* Sussex: Harvester, 1982.

GRODEN

Groden, Michael. Ulysses *in Progress.* Princeton: Princeton UP, 1977.

HALPER

Halper, Nathan. "Joyce and Eliot: A Tale of Shem and Shaun." *Nation* 200 (1965), 590–95.

HART AND HAYMAN

Hart, Clive, and David Hayman, eds. *James Joyce's* Ulysses: *Critical Essays.* Berkeley: U of California P, 1974.

HATEFUL CONTRARIES

Wimsatt, William K. *Hateful Contraries.* Lexington: U of Kentucky P, 1966.

HAYMAN

Hayman, David. Ulysses: *The Mechanics of Meaning.* 1st ed. Englewood Cliffs: Prentice, 1970. 2nd ed. Madison: U of Wisconsin P, 1982.

HEADINGS

Headings, Philip R. *T. S. Eliot.* Rev. ed. Boston: Twayne, 1982.

HOWARTH

Howarth, Herbert. *Notes On Some Figures Behind T. S. Eliot.* Boston: Houghton, 1964.

HYDE

Hyde, Lewis. *The Gift: Imagination and the Erotic Life of Property.* New York: Random House, 1983.

INVISIBLE POET

Kenner, Hugh. *The Invisible Poet: T. S. Eliot.* 1959. New York: Harbinger-Harcourt, 1969.

JAMES JOYCE

Ellmann, Richard. *James Joyce.* Rev. ed. New York: Oxford UP, 1982.

JAY

Jay, Gregory. *T. S. Eliot and the Poetics of Literary History.* Baton Rouge: Louisiana State UP, 1983.

JOHANSEN

Johansen, William A. "Toward a Redefinition of Modernism." *Boundary 2,* 2 (1974), 539–56.

JOYCE'S VOICES

Kenner, Hugh. *Joyce's Voices.* Berkeley: U of California P, 1978.

"JOYCE'S WASTE LAND"

Day, Robert Adams. "Joyce's Waste Land and Eliot's Unknown God." *Literary Monographs,* Vol. 4. Ed. Eric Rothstein. Madison: U of Wisconsin P, 1971. Pp. 137–210.

KENNER, *ULYSSES*   Kenner, Hugh. Ulysses. London: Allen, 1980.

LANGBAUM   Langbaum, Robert. *The Poetry of Experience: The Dramatic Monologue in Modern Literary Tradition.* 1957. New York: Norton, 1963.

LAWRENCE   Lawrence, Karen. *The Odyssey of Style in Ulysses.* Princeton: Princeton UP, 1981.

LENTRICCHIA   Lentricchia, Frank. *After the New Criticism.* Chicago: U of Chicago P, 1980.

LETTERS   Joyce, James. *Letters,* 3 vols. Vol. 1, ed. Stuart Gilbert. New York: Viking, 1957. Vols. 2–3, ed. Richard Ellmann, New York: Viking, 1966.

LEVENSON   Levenson, Michael H. *A Genealogy of Modernism: A study of English literary doctrine 1908–1922.* Cambridge: Cambridge UP, 1984.

LEVIN   Levin, Harry. *James Joyce: A Critical Introduction.* 1941. Rev. ed. Norfolk: New Directions, 1960.

LITZ   Litz, A. Walton. *The Art of James Joyce: Method and Design in Ulysses and Finnegans Wake.* London: Oxford UP, 1961.

MADDOX   Maddox, James H., Jr. *Joyce's Ulysses and the Assault upon Character.* New Brunswick: Rutgers UP, 1978.

MAGALANER AND KAIN   Magalaner, Marvin, and Richard M. Kain. *Joyce: The Man, the Work, the Reputation.* New York: Collier, 1962.

MANN, *LETTERS*   Mann, Thomas. *Letters of Thomas Mann: 1889–1959.* Tr. Richard and Clara Winston. New York: Knopf, 1971.

MARTINET   Martinet, André. "Structure and Language." *Structuralism.* Ed. Jacques Ehrmann. New York: Anchor, 1970.

MARXISM AND LIBERATION   Lukács, Georg. *Marxism and Human Liberation.* Ed. E. San Juan. Jr. New York: Dell [Delta], 1973.

MATERER   Materer, Timothy. *Vortex: Pound, Eliot, and Lewis.* Ithaca: Cornell UP, 1979.

MATHIESSEN   Mathiessen, F. O. *The Achievement of T. S. Eliot.* 3rd ed. 1958. New York: Galaxy-Oxford UP, 1959.

McCARTHY   McCarthy, Patrick A. "Joyce's Unreliable Catechist: Mathematics and the Narration of 'Ithaca'." *ELH,* 51 (1984), 605–18.

McCORMACK AND STEAD   McCormack, W. J., and Alistair Stead, eds. *James Joyce and Modern Literature.* London: Routledge, 1982.

MILLER

Miller, J. Hillis. *Poets of Reality: Six Twentieth-Century Writers.* 1965. New York: Atheneum, 1969.

MODERNISM

Bradbury, Malcolm, and McFarlane, James, eds. *Modernism.* 1976. Harmondsworth: Penguin, 1978.

"MODERN/POSTMODERN"

Bush, Ronald. "Modern/Postmodern: Eliot, Perse, Mallarmé, and the Future of the Barbarians." *Modernism Reconsidered.* Ed. Robert Kiely. Cambridge: Harvard UP, 1983. Pp. 191–214.

MOMENTS AND PATTERNS

Unger, Leonard. *T. S. Eliot: Moments and Patterns.* 1956. Minneapolis: U of Minnesota P, 1966.

MOODY

Moody, A. D. *Thomas Stearns Eliot: Poet.* Cambridge: Cambridge UP, 1979.

MORGAN AND WOHLSTETTER

Morgan, Roberta, and Albert Wohlstetter. "Observations on 'Prufrock.'" *Harvard Advocate* 125, no. 3 (Dec. 1938): 27–30, 33–40.

NITCHIE

Nitchie, George W. "A Note on Eliot's Borrowings." *Massachussetts Review* 6 (1965): 403–6.

ON POETRY AND POETS

Eliot, T. S. *On Poetry and Poets.* 1959. New York: Noonday-Farrar, 1961.

OWEN

Owen, R. W. *James Joyce and the Beginnings of Ulysses.* Ann Arbor: UMI Research P, 1983.

PEAKE

Peake, C. H. *James Joyce: The Citizen and the Artist.* Stanford: Stanford UP, 1977.

PERL

Perl, Jeffrey M. *The Tradition of Return: The Implicit History of Modern Literature.* Princeton: Princeton UP, 1984.

POPE

Pope, John C. "Prufrock and Raskolnikov Again: a Letter from Eliot." *American Literature* 18 (1947): 319–21.

PORTRAIT

Joyce, James. *A Portrait of the Artist as a Young Man.* (Corrected text.) New York: Viking, 1964.

POUND ERA

Kenner, Hugh. *The Pound Era.* Berkeley: U of California P, 1971.

POUND/JOYCE

Read, Forrest, ed. *Pound/Joyce: The Letters of Ezra Pound to James Joyce, with Pound's Essays on Joyce.* New York: New Directions, 1967.

POUND, LETTERS

Pound, Ezra. *The Letters of Ezra Pound: 1907–1941.* Ed. D. D. Paige. New York: Harcourt, 1950.

POUND, LITERARY ESSAYS

Pound, Ezra. *Literary Essays of Ezra*

Pound. Ed. T. S. Eliot. 1954. New York: New Directions, 1968.

POUND-PERSPECTIVES — Stock, Noel. *Ezra Pound—perspectives: essays in honor of his eightieth birthday.* Chicago: Regnery, 1965.

POUND, *SELECTED POEMS* — Eliot, T. S. Introduction. *Selected Poems.* By Ezra Pound. London: Faber & Gwyer, 1928.

POWER — Power, Arthur. *Conversations with James Joyce.* Ed. Clive Hart. London: Millington, 1974.

PRITCHARD — Pritchard, William H. *Frost: A Literary Life Reconsidered.* New York: Oxford UP, 1984.

QUINONES — Quinones, Ricardo J. *Mapping Literary Modernism: Time and Development.* Princeton: Princeton UP, 1985.

RAFFEL — Raffel, Burton. *T. S. Eliot.* New York: Ungar, 1982.

REID — Reid, B. L. *The Man from New York: John Quinn and His Friends.* New York: Oxford UP, 1968.

RIQUELME — Riquelme, John Paul. *Teller and Tale in Joyce's Fiction.* Baltimore: Johns Hopkins UP, 1983.

SCHNEIDER — Schneider, Elisabeth. *T. S. Eliot: The Pattern in the Carpet.* Berkeley: U of California P, 1975.

SELECTED ESSAYS — Eliot, T. S. *Selected Essays, 1917–1932.* New York: Harcourt, 1932.

SEVENTH OF JOYCE — Benstock, Bernard, ed. *The Seventh of Joyce.* Bloomington: Indiana UP, 1982.

SMITH, *THE WASTE LAND* — Smith, Grover. The Waste Land. London: Allen, 1983.

SPEARS — Spears, Monroe K. *Dionysus and the City.* New York: Oxford UP, 1970.

SPENDER, *ELIOT* — Spender, Stephen. *Eliot.* n.p.: Fontana/Collins, 1975.

STEAD — Stead, C. K. *Pound, Yeats, Eliot and the Modernist Movement.* New Brunswick: Rutgers UP, 1986.

STOCK — Stock, Noel. *The Life of Ezra Pound.* New York: Pantheon, 1970.

STRUGGLE OF THE MODERN — Spender, Stephen. *The Struggle of the Modern.* Berkeley: U of California P, 1963.

SUTTON — Sutton, Walter, ed. *Ezra Pound: A Collection of Critical Essays.* Englewood Cliffs: Prentice, 1963.

SYMPOSIUM — *T. S. Eliot: A Symposium . . . .* Ed. Richard March and Tambimuttu, 1948. Freeport, N.Y.: Books for Libraries P, 1968.

THIRTIES AND AFTER	Spender, Stephen. *The Thirties and After.* New York: Random House, 1978.
THOMAS	Thomas, Brook. *James Joyce's* Ulysses: *A Book of Many Happy Returns.* Baton Rouge: Louisiana State UP, 1982.
THOMPSON	Thompson, Lawrance. Robert Frost: *The Early Years: 1874–1915.* New York: Holt, 1966.
THOMPSON AND WINNICK	Thompson, Lawrance, and R. H. Winnick. *Frost: The Later Years: 1938–1963.* New York: Holt, 1976.
TO CRITICIZE THE CRITIC	Eliot, T. S. *To Criticize the Critic and Other Writings.* New York: Farrar, 1965.
ULYSSES	Joyce, James. *Ulysses.* Corrected and reset ed. New York: Random House, 1961.
USE OF POETRY	Eliot, T. S. *The Use of Poetry and The Use of Criticism.* Cambridge, MA: Harvard U P, 1933.
VERBAL ICON	Wimsatt, William K. *The Verbal Icon.* Louisville: U of Kentucky P, 1954.
WEAVER	Lidderdale, Jane, and Mary Nicholson. *Dear Miss Weaver: Harriet Shaw Weaver 1876–1961.* New York: Viking, 1970.
WEITZ	Weitz, Morris. "A 'Reading' of Eliot's 'The Love Song of J. Alfred Prufrock.'" *The Philosophy of the Arts.* Cambridge: Harvard UP, 1950. Pp. 93–107.
WELLEK	Wellek, René. "The New Criticism: Pro and Contra." *The Attack on Literature.* Chapel Hill: U of North Carolina P, 1982.
WHITE	White, Andrew. *Thomas Mann.* New York: Grove, 1965.
WILLIAMSON	Williamson, George. *A Reader's Guide to T. S. Eliot: A Poem-By-Poem Analysis.* 1953. New York: Noonday, 1957.
WORLD WITHIN WORLD	Spender, Stephen. *World Within World.* New York: Harcourt, 1951.

Index